The
Thirty Years' War

Contributors

Simon Adams	Lecturer in History University of Strathclyde
Gerhard Benecke	Lecturer in History University of Kent
Richard Bonney	Professor of History University of Leicester
John H. Elliott	Professor of History Institute for Advanced Study, Princeton
R.J.W. Evans	Fellow and University Lecturer Brasenose College, Oxford
Christopher R. Friedrichs	Associate Professor of History University of British Columbia, Vancouver
Bodo Nischan	Associate Professor of History East Carolina University
Geoffrey Parker	Professor of History University of Illinois
E. Ladewig Petersen	Professor of History University of Odense
Michael Roberts	Institute of Social and Economic Research, Rhodes University

Research assistants

André W. Carus	University of Bielefeld
Sheilagh C. Ogilvie	Trinity College, Cambridge

The
Thirty Years' War

Geoffrey Parker

MILITARY HERITAGE PRESS
New York

Section I.iii © Simon Adams 1984, 1987
Section II.ii © Geoffrey Parker and Simon Adams 1984, 1987
Section II.iii © E. Ladewig Petersen 1984, 1987
Section III.i © R.J.W. Evans 1984, 1987
Section III.iii © Gerhard Benecke 1984, 1987
Section III.iv © John H. Elliott 1984, 1987
Section IV.i © Bodo Nischan 1984, 1987
Section IV.iv © R. J. Bonney 1984, 1987
Section V.i © Michael Roberts 1984, 1987
Section VI.ii © C. R. Friedrichs 1984, 1987

First published in 1984
Revised edition published in 1987
by Routledge & Kegan Paul Ltd.

This edition published by Military Heritage Press,
a division of Marboro Books Corporation,
by arrangement with Routledge
1988 Military Heritage Press

ISBN 0-88029-296-2
(formerly ISBN 0-7100-9788-3)

Printed in the United States of America
M 9 8 7 6 5 4

Contents

Illustrations

Material for the captions was kindly provided by the following: Professor R.J. Bonney (Plate 16); Dr Paul Dukes (Plate 10); Professor C.R. Friedrichs (Plates 1, 5, 8, 9, 11, 12, 13 and 15); and Professor E. Ladewig Petersen (Plates 2 and 24).

Tables

Maps

(Note: Maps 1 and 3 were prepared with the aid of some material supplied by Professor C.R. Friedrichs and Professor R.J. Bonney respectively.)

'Well, since you aren't thinking about anything you can tell me the date of the signing of the Peace of Westphalia.'

Antoine neither moved nor answered. His father remonstrated in a shrill voice . . . 'You hear that, everyone? He doesn't know the date of the Peace of Westphalia. He ought to be ashamed of himself.' . . .

The carriage was filled with a shocked silence. For her brother's benefit Lucienne mentally recited a prayer recommended by the Desmoiselles Hermeline as an aid to recalling the Great Dates of History. Frédéric drew the figures in the air with his finger, and Mme Haudouin tried to catch her son's eye in order to comfort him with an affectionate smile. But Antoine, staring down at his boots, refused to see anything . . .

Finally, Antoine's breast heaved with a sob . . . He gulped, and muttered in a stifled voice: '1648'.

Marcel Aymé, *The Green Mare* (New York, 1963), 100–1: set in the year 1885

Acknowledgments

This book is the work of a team of ten historians. In 1977, not long after I was invited by Andrew Wheatcroft of Routledge & Kegan Paul to write a new account of the Thirty Years' War, it became clear that the volume of relevant published work, let alone the quantity and variety of the surviving documents, was greater than any individual scholar could ever cope with alone. Various experts were therefore invited to cover those aspects of the war where the tangle of unsynthesized, unfamiliar material was thickest – the Scandinavian lands, Brandenburg and Saxony, the aftermath of the war, and so on – and their contributions form an integral part of the text, narrating, analysing and explaining in their proper place the events and developments that together made up the conflict. But herein lay a serious practical difficulty. Since all the contributors wrote their sections at the same time, a substantial amount of revising and rewriting was required to ensure that their chapters fitted in with, yet did not overlap, the others. My first, and greatest, debt of gratitude must therefore be to my fellow authors, who graciously accepted more editorial interference than any scholar should be asked to suffer and provided invaluable assistance in ways too numerous to mention.

Another important debt, which it is a pleasure to record, arises from the munificence of the British Academy and the Newberry Library. In 1981 they provided me with a three-month fellowship to work in Chicago and it was there, in America's 'Second City', backed by the resources of several magnificent libraries and surrounded by many distinguished scholars, that I drafted almost all of my sections of this book. Next, Andrew Wheatcroft has offered sympathetic support and helpful advice at all times, for which I am most grateful. Suggestions, references to obscure (and not-so-obscure) works, and assistance also came from Professor Robert Bireley, SJ, Mr Bruce Lenman, Professor Konrad Repgen, Dr Hamish Scott, Dr Lesley M. Smith, Professor

Hugh Trevor-Roper, the late Dame Frances Yates (who was to have been a contributor) and, above all, Dr Simon Adams. Finally, the editor and all the authors are grateful to Nancy Wood, who expertly typed and retyped our text on a word-processor.

Addendum

In preparing this revised edition for the press, the contributors and I have taken the opportunity to correct a number of errors that crept into the text and notes. We are most grateful to Professor Dieter Albrecht and Professor Konrad Repgen for drawing them to our attention. A number of further works published on our subject are noted on page 303.

One contributor, however, was unable to revise his text, for Gerhard Benecke died in August 1985. His loss has been felt by scholars everywhere: not only in St Andrews, where he was a student and research student, and at Canterbury and Vancouver, where he taught, but by early modern historians in general. And he is especially missed by his fellow contributors.

Conventions

Currency   As far as possible all sums of money are given in Imperial thalers (*Reichsthaler*). Conversions from other currencies have been made according to the following scheme:

4.8 thalers
4.5 *escudos*
12 *livres tournois*   } equal £1 sterling
10 Dutch florins
6 Rhine florins

Dates   All 'new style' unless otherwise stated.

Place and personal names   Where a recognized English version exists, we have used it (thus Vienna, The Hague and Rome; Wallenstein, Bethlen Gabor and Gustavus Adolphus); otherwise we have used the form generally preferred by the particular place or person (thus Regensburg rather than Ratisbon, Bratislava rather than Pressburg or Posnonia, and Mazarin rather than Mazzarini).

Preface

It is often claimed that Samuel Pufendorf, the eminent seventeenth-century jurist and historian, was the first to coin the term 'The Thirty Years' War' to describe the series of conflicts which ravaged Europe between 1618 and 1648. That phrase certainly appears in his book, *The Present State of Germany*, first published in 1667; but by then it was hardly new. In May 1648, even before the fighting stopped, one of the delegates at the Westphalian Peace Congress spoke of 'the Thirty Years' War' that had ravaged his country; and in 1649 the English weekly newspaper *The Moderate Intelligencer* began to publish a series of articles entitled 'An epitome of the late Thirty Years' War in Germany'. Issue 203, dated 8 February 1649, summarized the 'Bohemian war', 1618–23; issue 204 followed with the Dutch phase of the war; issue 205 covered the Danish phase; and so on. Within three months of the signature of the peace of Westphalia, which brought the war to an end in October 1648, English readers were thus provided with a framework for interpreting the war which was recognizably modern. At the same time, a similar service was provided for German readers in a pamphlet in that language entitled 'A short chronicle of the Thirty Years' War', which not only gave the dates and places of the major military actions but also offered a rough calculation of the losses of life and property caused by the conflict.[1]

But, in the seventeenth century, historians were rarely as free from bias as their modern-day descendants claim to be. All of the publications discussed above were composed by Protestants who had an interest in emphasizing that the various wars fought in Europe during the decades following 1618 were linked together in a single struggle in defence of religious and constitutional liberty. They sought to justify retrospectively the rebellion of Bohemia in 1618–21 against Emperor Ferdinand II by reference to his subsequent behaviour. At the time, the Bohemians' cause seemed far from just to many observers – which is why so many Protestant princes refused to support it. Only afterwards, as Imperial strength increased and constitutional proprieties were forgotten, did they repent of their neutrality and oppose the Habsburgs themselves. Thus rewriting the history of the war helped to salve their consciences. When Gustavus Adolphus, king of Sweden, claimed in 1628 that 'All the wars that are on foot in Europe have been fused together and have become a single war', he was in part expressing a wish that it should be so, since it helped to justify the transfer of his armies from Poland and Livonia to Germany.[2]

Catholic Europe, however, saw matters otherwise, One of the Habsburgs' official historians, Eberhard Wassenberg, published an interim account of the war in 1639 which handled each campaign as yet another unjustified attack on the emperor: its title ran 'Commentary upon the wars between Ferdinand II and III and their enemies'. Wassenberg's account of 'the Danish War' of 1625–9 was accompanied by descriptions of 'the other Austrian war' (i.e. the 1626 Peasants' Revolt), 'the third Transylvanian war', 'the Dutch war', 'the Mantuan war' and so on. This was, perhaps, an extreme view; but even Catholics who lacked Wassenberg's neat, compartmentalized vision still perceived a grave difference between the campaigns up to 1629, in which the emperor was opposed principally by his own subjects with some foreign aid, and the struggle after 1630, in which he fought mainly against foreign powers whose German supporters were, at most times, few in number and limited in resources. Bishop Gepeckh of Freising (1618–51), in the heart of Bavaria, always distinguished in his correspondence between 'the Bohemian troubles' of the 1620s (little different in nature from the series of alarms and petty wars which had disturbed the peace of the Empire since the Augsburg Settlement of 1555), and 'this war' (which began with the Swedish invasion in 1630 and forced him to flee from his capital eight times before the peace was signed in 1648). For the bishop, the war lasted not thirty years but eighteen.[3]

These, of course, are the opinions of but half a dozen individuals. Now that all public archives for the period are open to historians, tens of thousands of opinions are available. In Czechoslovakia alone, twenty-seven repositories today possess important collections left by participants in the war; twenty folio volumes concerning just the Edict of Restitution, issued in 1629, are available in the Saxon archives alone; and so on. Admittedly, heroic efforts have been made to print some of the more important sources. No less than forty-five volumes are envisaged to publish in full the correspondence and negotiations generated by the peace of Westphalia; thirteen volumes will be needed to publish the edited correspondence of Maximilian I of Bavaria and his allies between 1618 and 1635; scores of volumes would be needed to calendar the relevant State Papers Foreign in the Public Record Office, London. And this still represents only a fragment of the available unpublished material. Everywhere, the war increased paperwork. In Protestant Bremen, the secretariat of the ruling archbishop-administrator had to be doubled in 1632 in order to cope with the exigencies of the armies in the area; and when, in the 1650s, the archives of the Catholic diocese of Würzburg were reclassified, two series were required – one 'pre-war', which stretched back into the mists of time; the other 'since the war began', which was of almost equal bulk.[4]

We live, as Lord Acton once predicted, in the 'documentary age . . . which will tend to make history independent of historians, to develop learning at the expense of writing'. Certainly, the miles of documents produced by a continent at war present a daunting challenge to stamina.[5] Yet even superhuman dedication to archival research will not be enough, for the documentary records of the Thirty Years' War are written in too many different languages. The Habsburg Monarchy included a German, Czech and Hungarian chancery; the court of Spain maintained secretaries for correspondence in French, Dutch, German, Latin, Italian, Aragonese, Portuguese and Castilian; and there are documents in each tongue which refer to the war. It is true that, on the Protestant side, the lingua franca tended to be an inexorably verbose High German liberally peppered with Latinisms; but correspondence and state papers couched in Latin, Danish, Swedish, English and Dutch are also to be found in abundance. At the distant court of Bethlen Gabor, prince of Transylvania, documents concerning the war were composed in German, Hungarian, Romanian, Latin and (when the Ottoman Porte was concerned) Court Persian.

There have been a number of homeric attempts, despite the obvious problems, to provide an acceptable synthesis of this material. In the West, two of the most celebrated were produced on the eve of the Second World War: C.V. Wedgwood (in 1938) saw the struggle as essentially a German conflict influenced from time to time by the northern and western powers, while G. Pagès (in 1939) seemed obsessed by the importance of France as the arbiter of Europe's destinies throughout the war, to the exclusion of almost all other considerations. In the East, similarly circumscribed views have been advanced by the Czech historian J.V.

Polišenský (1971), who argued that events in his native Bohemia were at all times central; while the Russian B.F. Porshnev (1976) claimed that the climax of the war in 1630–41, when the Swedish armies dominated the Empire, could only be explained in terms of Russia's policy towards Poland.[6] German historians have tended to be even more parochial: writers from Bavaria and Brandenburg, in particular, have tended to study the war in almost exclusively regional terms. There is nothing to rival the three-volume German synthesis of Moriz Ritter, *A History of Germany During the Age of Counter-Reformation and the Thirty Years' War 1555–1648*, first published in 1889 and never translated. Since then, although there have been hundreds of studies of the conflict – almost all of them entitled (like this one) *The Thirty Years' War* – the persevering student of the subject looks almost in vain for a modern survey that pays attention not only to Germany, Scandinavia, England and France, but to Spain, Italy, Transylvania, Poland and the Netherlands as well.

The sole exception was recently published by an East German historian. Herbert Langer's *The Thirty Years' War* (Poole, 1981) offers a cultural history of Germany during the war based on little-known data drawn from all over continental Europe, with text and illustrations pleasingly integrated. But it is not a history of the war. Langer's book makes it possible for this volume to pass over most of the cultural impact of the war; but his study should be seen as a complement, not an alternative, to the present work, which seeks to provide a structured analysis of the conflict itself.

Not all periods are covered here in the same detail, because some periods – particularly the 1620s – are more complex than others.[7] Moreover the text covers more than just Germany and more than just the thirty years: the war of Mantua and the Swedish campaigns in Poland are included because they were crucially important for developments in the Empire; and the narrative goes back to the 'Donauwörth incident' of 1607, which accelerated the polarization of Germany into hostile confessional camps, and stretches onwards to the final agreement in 1650, at Nuremberg, concerning the demobilization of the armies that still occupied Germany. Donauwörth to Nuremberg: on the ground barely 150 kilometres separate them, yet in history more than forty years of war and rumours of war lie between. Sometimes the conflict seemed to become so intense, and to involve so many states, that it has justly been termed 'the European Civil War'.[8] To do justice to such turmoil within the framework of a single volume, without over-simplification or distortion, is not easy.

Chronology

† = death
⚔ = victory for Habsburgs or allies
⚔ = defeat for Habsburgs or allies

All dates are New Style.

Important events are CAPITALIZED

Date	Germany	The Habsburg Lands	Spain and the Netherlands
1606		*June.* Peace of Vienna ends Hungarian revolt *Nov.* Peace of Zsitva Torok ends 'Long' Turkish war	
1607			*Mar.* Cease-fire in Dutch wars (to 1609) *Nov.* Spanish bankruptcy
1608	*17 Dec.* 'DONAUWÖRTH .INCIDENT' *Jan.* Imperial Diet at Regensburg (to 3 May) *12 May.* PROTESTANT UNION FORMED	*Feb.* Treaty of Bratislava *June.* Matthias becomes reigning archduke and king of Hungary	
1609	*Mar.* First Cleves-Jülich crisis (to Oct. 1610) *10 July.* CATHOLIC LEAGUE FORMED	*Mar.* Matthias's concessions to Protestants *9 July.* Letter of Majesty: 'defensors' appointed	*Apr.* TWELVE YEARS' TRUCE (to 1621)
1610			
1611	*Oct.* † Frederick IV of the Palatinate; Frederick V succeeds *July.* John George I Elector of Saxony (to 1656)	*Mar.* Passau troops attack Prague *May.* Matthias crowned king of Bohemia	*Mar.* Franco-Spanish marriage treaty
1612	*20 Jan.* † Rudolf II; Matthias elected Emperor (to 1619)		

France, Britain and Italy	Scandinavia, Poland and Russia	Transylvania and the Turks
		June. Peace of Vienna
		Nov. Peace of Zsitva Torok
	Sept. Poland invades Russia (to 1618)	
14 May. † Henry IV of France; minority of Louis XIII (to 1617)		
Mar. Franco-Spanish marriage treaty		
	Apr. Denmark invades Sweden (war to 1613)	
	Oct. Gustavus Adolphus king of Sweden (to 1632)	

Date	Germany	The Habsburg Lands	Spain and the Netherlands
1612			
1613			
	Feb. Marriage of Frederick V and Elizabeth Stuart		
	Apr. Elector of Brandenburg becomes a Calvinist		
	May. Dutch–Union treaty		
	July. Wolfgang William of Neuburg becomes a Catholic		
	Aug. Imperial Diet at Regensburg (to Oct.)		
1614			
	May. Second Cleves-Jülich crisis (to Sept.)		
	Aug. Aachen recatholicized; Fettmilch revolt at Frankfurt	*Aug.* General Diet at Linz	
	Nov. Treaty of Xanten		*Nov.* Treaty of Xanten
1615	Lutheran rioting in Brandenburg		Dutch fleet attacks Pacific coast of Spanish America
		Dec. Uzkok war (to Feb. 1618)	
1616			
1617	Lutheran Jubilee year; 'Military Academy' opened at Siegen		
		20 Mar. OÑATE TREATY	*20 Mar.* OÑATE TREATY

France, Britain and Italy	Scandinavia, Poland and Russia	Transylvania and the Turks
Apr. Anglo-Union Treaty of Wesel *Dec.* † Francis, duke of Mantua		
	Jan. Peace of Knäred (Denmark and Sweden)	
Apr. First war over Mantuan succession (to June 1615)	*Mar.* Michael Romanov elected Tsar (to 1645)	Bethlen Gabor prince of Transylvania (to 1629)
Jan. French civil war (to May)		
Oct. French States-General		
June. Treaty of Asti ends first Mantuan war *Aug.* French civil war (to May 1616) *Dec.* Uzkok war (to 1618) *Sept.* Second war over Mantuan succession (to 1617) *Feb.* French civil war (to Apr.)		
	Mar. Peace of Stolbova (Sweden and Russia)	

Date	Germany	The Habsburg Lands	Spain and the Netherlands
1617	*Apr.* Evangelical Union renewed (to 1621); Catholic League dissolved		
		July–Dec. Ferdinand of Styria recognized as king-designate of Bohemia and Hungary	
			Aug. Oldenbarnevelt raises waardgelder troops
1618	Brandenburg annexes Prussia	*Feb.* Peace of Wiener-Neustadt (Archduke and Venice)	
			Mar. Don Balthasar de Zúñiga becomes Spanish chief minister (to 1622)
		23 May. DEFENESTRATION OF PRAGUE	
		June. Savoy subsidies to Bohemia (to Apr. 1619)	
			Aug. Fall of Oldenbarnevelt
		Sept. Mansfeld captures Pilsen	
1619	*Jan.* Catholic League re-formed		
	20 Mar. † Matthias	*20 Mar.* † Matthias; Ferdinand of Styria succeeds	
		May. First siege of Vienna	*May.* Archdukes send aid to Ferdinand; execution of Oldenbarnevelt
		10 June. ✕ Záblatí. Moravia joins confederation	
	28 Aug. Ferdinand elected Holy Roman Emperor	*22–6 Aug.* DEPOSITION OF FERDINAND; ELECTION OF FREDERICK	
	8 Oct. Treaty of Munich (Spain–Bavaria–emperor)		

France, Britain and Italy	Scandinavia, Poland and Russia	Transylvania and the Turks
24 Apr. Personal rule of Louis XIII begins (to 1643)		
	June. Sweden invades Livonia	
9 Oct. Peace of Pavia ends second Mantuan war		
Feb. Peace of Wiener-Neustadt	Swedish truce with Poland (to 1621)	
	Jan. Peace of Deulino (Poland and Russia)	
Feb. French civil war (to Apr.)		
		Aug. Bethlen conquers Hungary (to Oct.)
	Oct. Poland attacks Turks	

Date	Germany	The Habsburg Lands	Spain and the Netherlands
1619		*Nov.* Second siege of Vienna	
1620			
	20 Mar. MÜHLHAUSEN GUARANTEE *3 July.* TREATY OF ULM *Aug.* Spínola invades Palatinate	*July.* Bavarians occupy Upper Austria (to 1628)	*Aug.* Spínola invades Palatinate
1621	*21 Jan.* Frederick outlawed *Feb.* Segeberg conference	*Oct.* Confiscations Court created (to 1623) *3 Nov.* ✗ WHITE MOUNTAIN *Jan.* Mint Consortium formed: 'Kipper- und Wipper' period (to 1623)	
	Apr. Cease-fire in Palatinate (to July) *27 Apr.* Frederick allies with Dutch Republic *14 May.* Union dissolved		*31 Mar.* † Philip III; Philip IV king of Spain (to 1665) *Apr.* WAR IN NETHERLANDS (to 1648); Frederick V. arrives in Dutch Republic *15 July.* † Archduke Albert
	Oct. Bavarians occupy Upper Palatinate; Kipper- und Wipperzeit (to 1623)		
1622		*Jan.* First peace of Nikolsburg	
			Feb. Spínola captures Jülich

France, Britain and Italy	Scandinavia, Poland and Russia	Transylvania and the Turks
		Nov. Poland invades Transylvania *20 Jan.* Bethlen concludes nine-month truce with Habsburgs
Apr. Rebellion of Marie de Medici (to Aug.) *July.* Valtelline massacre *Aug.* End of French civil wars; Louis XIII invades Béarn; Habsburgs occupy Valtelline		*Aug.* Bethlen invades Hungary again
	20 Sept. ✗ Cecora (Poles versus Turks)	*20 Sept.* ✗ Cecora (Poles versus Turks)
Feb. French Huguenot war (to Oct. 1622)	*Feb.* Segeberg Conference	
Sept. Habsburgs occupy Grey Leagues' lands	*Sept.* Sweden captures Riga *Oct.* Polish–Turkish truce	*Oct.* Polish–Turkish truce
Jan. Pope founds Congregation for the propagation of the Faith		*Jan.* First peace of Nikolsburg (emperor and Transylvania)

Date	Germany	The Habsburg Lands	Spain and the Netherlands
1622	*Mar. Spanish Chancery* published *Apr.* ✗ Wiesloch *6 May.* ✗ WIMPFEN (George of Baden defeated) *June.* Brussels conference (to Nov.) *20 June.* ✗ HÖCHST (Christian of Brunswick defeated) *13 July.* Frederick dismisses Mansfeld and Brunswick *26 Aug.* ✗ Fleurus		*June.* Brussels conference (to Nov.)
			4 Oct. Spínola abandons siege of Bergen *Oct.* † Zúñiga; OLIVARES CHIEF MINISTER (to 1643)
1623	*25 Feb.* Palatine Electorate transferred to Maximilian *Mar.* Surrender of Frankenthal		
	6 Aug. ✗ STADTLOHN		
1624	*Jan.* Mansfeld disbands army		
			June. Treaty of Compiègne (France and Dutch Republic) *July.* Spanish siege of Breda (to June 1625)
			Oct. Almirantazgo del Norte formed *Dec.* Mansfeld's army sails for Holland

France, Britain and Italy	Scandinavia, Poland and Russia	Transylvania and the Turks

Feb. League of Lyons formed; Spain agrees to evacuate Valtelline

Bethen invades Hungary; Turkish war against Persia (to 1639)

Apr. Buckingham and Prince Charles go to Madrid for Spanish match
Aug. Urban VIII elected pope (to 1644)

Apr. Richelieu enters Council of Louis XIII

May. Second peace of Nikolsburg; Persians take Baghdad

June. Treaty of Compiègne (France and Dutch Republic)

Aug. RICHELIEU CHIEF MINISTER OF FRANCE (to 1642); French occupy Valtelline

Date	Germany	The Habsburg Lands	Spain and the Netherlands
1625			
			Mar. Spain at war with England (to 1630)
	Apr. Christian IV elected Kreisoberst of Lower Saxony		*Apr.* † Maurice of Nassau; Frederick Henry becomes Captain-General of Dutch Republic (to 1647)
			June. Spanish capture of Breda (to 1637); Spanish river blockade in Westphalia (to 1629)
	July. Wallenstein raises new Imperial army; Spanish river blockade in Westphalia (to 1629)		
		Oct. Reformationskommission in Upper Austria	
			Nov. Anglo-Dutch attack on Cadiz
1626	*9 Dec.* HAGUE ALLIANCE		*9 Dec.* HAGUE ALLIANCE
			5 Mar. Treaty of Monzón (ratified in May)
	Apr. ✗ Dessau Bridge		
		May. Upper Austrian revolt (to Sept.)	
			July. Union of Arms scheme published
1627	*26 Aug.* ✗ LUTTER. Imperialists advance northwards		
	Feb. Mecklenburg given to Wallenstein as pledge; Imperialists conquer Mecklenburg, Pomerania, Holstein		*Feb.* Spanish decree of bankruptcy
	Mar. Hesse partition favours Darmstadt; Maurice of Hesse-Kassel abdicates		
	May. Treaty of Königsberg (Emperor–Brandenburg)		

France, Britain and Italy	Scandinavia, Poland and Russia	Transylvania and the Turks
Jan. New Huguenot revolt in France (to 1629)		
Mar. War with Spain (to 1630); Savoy invades Genoa		
Apr. † James VI and I; Charles I king of England (to 1649)	*Apr.* Christian IV elected Kreisoberst of Lower Saxony	
	June. Swedes invade Prussia	
Nov. Anglo-Dutch attack on Cadiz		
9 Dec. HAGUE ALLIANCE	*9 Dec.* HAGUE ALLIANCE	
	Jan. ✗ Wallhof (Swedes defeat Poles)	Bethlen invades Moravia; Turks fail to retake Baghdad
5 Mar. Treaty of Monzón (ratified in May)		
	May. Gustavus campaigns in Prussia (to 1629)	
	26 Aug. ✗ LUTTER	
		Dec. Peace of Bratislava
Mar. Franco-Spanish alliance against Britain		
June. War between France and Britain (to 1629)		

Date	Germany	The Habsburg Lands	Spain and the Netherlands
1627	*Oct.* Mühlhausen Electoral meeting (to Nov.) *10 Nov.* Capitulation of Fransburg (Pomerania)	*Sept.* New constitution for Bohemia and Moravia	
1628	*Jan.* Wallenstein becomes duke of Mecklenburg; Imperialists overrun Jutland *May.* Bavaria annexes Upper Palatinate *May.* UNSUCCESSFUL SIEGE OF STRALSUND (to July) *Sept.* ⚔ Wolgast (Wallenstein defeats Danes)	*May.* Upper Austria returned to Habsburg rule	*Sept.* Dutch capture Spanish silver fleet
1629	*6/28 Mar.* EDICT OF RESTITUTION *7 July.* PEACE OF LÜBECK; Imperialists send aid to Poland		*Apr.* Dutch besiege 's Hertogenbosch (to Sept.) *Aug.* Spaniards take Amersfoort; Dutch take Wesel *14 Sept.* Dutch take 's Hertogenbosch
1630			*Feb.* Dutch occupy Pernambuco (Brazil) to 1654

France, Britain and Italy	Scandinavia, Poland and Russia	Transylvania and the Turks

Dec. Third Mantuan War (to June 1631)

June. Sweden relieves Stralsund
Sept. ✗ Wolgast (Wallenstein defeats Danes)

28 *Oct.* SURRENDER OF LA ROCHELLE
Mar. French under Louis XIII invade Italy

14 Mar. Ulfsbäck meeting (Christian and Gustavus)

Apr. Peace of Susa between France and Britain
May. Imperialist army invades Italy
28 *June.* 'Grace of Alais' ends Huguenot revolt

17 June. ✗ Honigfelde (Stuhm)
7 July. Peace of Lübeck

26 Sept. Polish–Swedish truce of Altmark (to 1635)

Nov. † Bethlen Gabor; George Rákóczi succeeds (to 1648)

French occupy Savoy; plague ravages Italy (to 1631)

Date	Germany	The Habsburg Lands	Spain and the Netherlands
1630	*Apr.* Annaburg meeting (Saxony and Brandenburg)		
			17 *June.* Franco-Dutch subsidy treaty
	6 *July.* Gustavus invades Germany *July.* REGENSBURG ELECTORAL MEETING (to Nov.) *Aug.* Magdeburg defies emperor (to May 1631) 13 *Aug.* Wallenstein dismissed *Sept.* Zabeltitz conference (Saxony and Brandenburg) 13 *Oct.* PEACE OF REGENSBURG		
			15 *Nov.* Peace of Madrid (Britain and Spain)
1631			
	Feb. Leipzig Assembly (to Apr.) 12 *Apr.* Leipzig Manifesto 20 *May.* Sack of Magdeburg		
	22 *June.* Brandenburg–Swedish alliance 4 *Aug.* Frankfurt convention (to Oct.) *Sept.* Saxony, Bremen and Hesse-Kassel ally with Sweden 17 *Sept.* ✗ BREITENFELD *Nov.* Swedes take Mainz (to 1636) *Dec.* Wallenstein recalled	15 *Nov.* Saxons take Prague (to 1632)	*Sept.* Revolt in Basque lands (to 1634)
1632	*Apr.* ✗ RAIN; Swedes occupy Bavaria 13 *Apr.* Göllersdorf agreement: Wallenstein restored to chief command		

France, Britain and Italy	Scandinavia, Poland and Russia	Transylvania and the Turks
17 June. Franco-Dutch subsidy treaty		
July. Imperialists take Mantua	*July*. Gustavus invades Germany	
13 Oct. PEACE OF REGENSBURG		
11 Nov. Day of Dupes (Paris)		
15 Nov. Peace of Madrid (Britain and Spain)		
23 Jan. Treaty of Bärwalde	*Jan*. Treaty of Bärwalde	
	13 Apr. Swedes take Frankfurt-on-Oder	
8 May. Treaty of Fontainebleau (France and Bavaria)		
19 June. Peace of Cherasco	*June*. Swedish–Brandenburg alliance	
	Sept. Swedish–Saxon alliance	
	17 Sept. ⚔ BREITENFELD	
	Apr. † Sigismund III; Władisław IV succeeds (to 1648)	

Date	Germany	The Habsburg Lands	Spain and the Netherlands
1632			*June.* Dutch capture Venlo, Roermond; South Netherlands revolt averted
	July. Siege of the Alte Veste (to 18 Sept.)		
			23 Aug. Dutch take Maastricht
	1 Nov. Wallenstein captures Leipzig *17 Nov.* ✗ LÜTZEN		
1633			
	23 Apr. Heilbronn League (to 1635)		
		June–July. Truce in Silesia	
	July. ✗ Hessisch-Oldendorf; Swedish army mutinies		
		Aug.–Oct. Truce in Silesia *Oct.* ✗ Steinau; Wallenstein reconquers Silesia	
1634	*25 Feb.* † Wallenstein *22 Apr.* Brandenburg demands Swedish evacuation of Pomerania		
		July. Saxons invade Bohemia (to Sept.)	
	6 Sept. ✗ NÖRDLINGEN		
			Oct. Cardinal-Infante governs South Netherlands (to 1641)
	1 Nov. French alliance with Heilbronn League *24 Nov.* Preliminaries of Pirna		

France, Britain and Italy	Scandinavia, Poland and Russia	Transylvania and the Turks
	Nov. ✗ LÜTZEN; † Gustavus; Christina succeeds (to 1654) *Dec.* War of Smolensk (to June 1634)	
19 Apr. Franco-Swedish treaty renewed *June.* France invades Lorraine	*19 Apr.* Franco-Swedish treaty renewed *23 Apr.* Heilbronn League; Swedish army mutinies	Turks attack Poland
Apr. France increases Dutch subsidy		
	June. Peace between Russia and Poland	Turks attack Persia
Nov. France occupies Swedish strongholds in Alsace; Heilbronn League allies with France		

Date	Germany	The Habsburg Lands	Spain and the Netherlands
1635			*8 Feb.* Franco-Dutch treaty renewed *26 Mar.* Spain occupies Trier
	Mar. Spain occupies Trier; Elector arrested (to 1645)		
	30 May. PEACE OF PRAGUE: emperor and Saxony *Aug.* Swedish army mutinies *6 Sept.* Brandenburg accepts peace of Prague	Peasant revolt in Styria	*19 May.* FRANCE DECLARES WAR ON SPAIN
1636	*Jan.* Sweden surrenders Mainz *Mar.* Emperor declares war on France		
			July. Army of Flanders invades France *15 Aug.* Army of Flanders at Corbie
	4 Sept. Regensburg Electoral meeting (to Jan. 1637) *Oct.* Congress of Cologne convened *4 Oct.* ✗ WITTSTOCK *22 Dec.* Ferdinand III elected king of Romans		
1637	*Jan.* Swedish army withdraws to Torgau *15 Feb.* † FERDINAND II; FERDINAND III succeeds *Mar.* † Bogislav XIV of Pomerania *June.* Swedish army withdraws to Pomerania (until Oct. 1638)	*15 Feb.* † FERDINAND II; FERDINAND III succeeds	John Maurice governs Dutch Brazil (to 1644)

France, Britain and Italy	Scandinavia, Poland and Russia	Transylvania and the Turks
8 Feb. Franco–Dutch treaty renewed		
Mar. France occupies Valtelline (to 1637)		
28 Apr. Treaty of Compiègne (France and Sweden)	28 Apr. Treaty of Compiègne	
19 May. FRANCE DECLARES WAR ON SPAIN		
	Aug. Swedish army mutinies	
	Sept. Swedish–Polish peace of Stuhmsdorf (to 1655)	
27 Oct. France engages Bernard of Saxe-Weimar		
Mar. Emperor declares war on France		
30 Mar. Treaty of Wismar (Sweden and France)	30 Mar. Treaty of Wismar (France and Sweden)	
	June. Oxenstierna returns to Sweden	
July. Army of Flanders invades France		
15 Aug. Army of Flanders at Corbie		
Sept. Imperialists invade Burgundy; Croquant revolt in France		
Mar. Revolt of Valtelline; Spanish reoccupation		

Date	Germany	The Habsburg Lands	Spain and the Netherlands
1637			
			Aug. Troubles at Evora *Sept.* French take Leucate (Catalonia) *Oct.* Dutch take Breda
1638	*Mar.* ✗ Rheinfelden		
	Dec. Bernard of Saxe-Weimar takes Breisach		*Dec.* Bernard takes Breisach
1639	*Apr.* ✗ Chemnitz		
		May. Swedes invade Bohemia (to 1640)	
	July. † Bernard of Saxe-Weimar; France inherits all his conquests		*July.* French capture Salces
			21 Oct. ✗ The Downs: Dutch navy destroys Spanish fleet
1640	*Jan.* Bavarian–French talks at Einsiedeln *Feb.* Nuremberg Electoral Meeting		
			May. Revolt of Catalonia (to 1652)
	Sept. REGENSBURG DIET (to Oct. 1641) *Dec.* † George William; Frederick William succeeds		*Dec.* Revolt of Portugal (to 1668)
1641			*Jan.* Catalonia accepts French protection
	May. † Baner; Swedish army mutinies		
			June. Dutch–Portuguese alliance
	24 July. Brandenburg–Swedish peace		
			Aug. Dutch take Angola (to 1648)
	Nov. Torstensson arrives in Swedish army		
1642	*Jan.* Peace of Goslar (emperor and Brunswick)		

France, Britain and Italy	Scandinavia, Poland and Russia	Transylvania and the Turks
	June. Swedish army withdraws to Pomerania	
Sept. French take Leucate (Catalonia)		
15 Mar. Treaty of Hamburg (France and Sweden)	*15 Mar.* Treaty of Hamburg (France and Sweden)	
Apr. Anglo-Danish treaty of Hamburg	*Apr.* Anglo-Danish treaty of Hamburg	
July. French capture Salces; Nu-pieds revolt in Normandy (to Nov.)		
Jan. Franco-Bavarian talks at Einsiedeln		
30 June. Treaty of Hamburg (Franco-Swedish alliance until war's end) *July.* Soissons conspiracy	*30 June.* Treaty of Hamburg (Franco-Swedish alliance until war's end)	

Date	Germany	The Habsburg Lands	Spain and the Netherlands
1642	Swedes occupy Saxony and invade Moravia 2 *Nov.* ✗ Breitenfeld II		
1643	*Feb.* Frankfurt 'Deputationstag' (to 1645) *May.* Sweden invades Denmark (to 1645) *Aug.* NEGOTIATIONS AT WESTPHALIA BEGIN (to 1648) *Nov.* ✗ Tuttlingen		*17 Jan.* Fall of Olivares *19 May.* ✗ ROCROI
1644	*Aug.* ✗ Freiburg; French occupy all Alsace		
1645	*5 Mar.* ✗ JANKOV *May.* ✗ Mergentheim *3 Aug.* ✗ ALLERHEIM; first full meeting of Westphalian peace conference *6 Sept.* Truce of Kötzschenbroda (Saxony and Sweden) *Nov.* Trauttmannsdorf arrives at Westphalia (to June 1647)	Swedish siege of Vienna	French capture ten towns in Netherlands
1646			*Jan.* Dutch Republic's negotiators arrive in Münster

France, Britain and Italy	Scandinavia, Poland and Russia	Transylvania and the Turks
Aug. English Civil War (to 1649); Cinq-Mars conspiracy *4 Dec.* † RICHELIEU; MAZARIN BECOMES FRENCH CHIEF MINISTER (to 1661)		
14 May. † Louis XIII; LOUIS XIV king of France (to 1715) *19 May.* ✗ ROCROI	*May.* Danish–Swedish war (to 1645)	
Nov. ✗ Tuttlingen		*Nov.* Swedish–Transylvanian alliance (to 1645) *Feb.* Rákóczi invades Hungary (to Aug. 1645)
July. ✗ Marston Moor; INNOCENT X succeeds URBAN VIII as pope		
	Nov. Cease-fire agreed in Danish–Swedish war	
June. ✗ Naseby		*June.* Turks besiege Crete (to 1668)
	July. † Michael Romanov *Aug.* Peace of Brömsebro	*Aug.* Rákóczi recalled
		Dec. Peace of Vienna

Date	Germany	The Habsburg Lands	Spain and the Netherlands
1646	*Apr.* Peace of Eilenburg (Sweden and Saxony) *Sept.* Franco-Imperial preliminary peace		*Oct.* French take Dunkirk
1647	*14 Mar.* Bavarian–French truce (to Sept.)		*Jan.* Spanish–Dutch truce (to 1648) *May.* † Frederick Henry; revolt of Sicily *July.* Revolt of Naples *Oct.* Spanish bankruptcy
1648	*17 May.* ✗ Zusmarshausen *6 Aug.* Sweden–Imperial preliminary peace *24 Oct.* PEACE OF WESTPHALIA	*Oct.* Swedish siege of Prague *24 Oct.* PEACE OF WESTPHALIA	*30 Jan.* PEACE OF MÜNSTER *20 Aug.* ✗ Lens
1649	*Jan.* Bavaria evacuated *Apr.* Imperial Cities admit religious parity		
1650	*26 June.* NUREMBERG AGREEMENT ON DEMOBILIZATION		

France, Britain and Italy	Scandinavia, Poland and Russia	Transylvania and the Turks

Sept. Franco-Imperial preliminary peace
Oct. French take Dunkirk

14 Mar. Franco-Bavarian truce
May. Revolt of Sicily

July. Masaniello's revolt in Naples (to 1648)

| | *Feb.* † Christian IV | |

May. Fronde begins (to 1654)
20 Aug. ✗ Lens

| *24 Oct.* PEACE OF WESTPHALIA | *24 Oct.* PEACE OF WESTPHALIA Chmielnicki's revolt in Ukraine (to 1654) | |

26 June. NUREMBERG AGREEMENT

Oct. Queen Christina's coronation

The
Thirty Years' War

CHAPTER I

Europe between war and peace, 1607–1618

The *History of the Voyages of Scarmentado*, set in the years 1615–20, is not one of Voltaire's best works. The author's vision of the seventeenth century as an unusually violent and unsettled period of history is better-developed and better-documented in his *Essay on Manners*; and much of his heavy irony, so telling elsewhere, here misses its mark. Yet the short story merits some attention from historians. Its hero and narrator, born in Crete and sent as a teenager to Rome by his parents, sets out on a 'Grand Tour' of Europe in search of truth, but instead finds only violence caused by religious and political disagreement. In Paris he is invited to dine on a morsel of flesh hacked from the fallen favourite of Louis XIII; in London he notes that 'saintly Catholics, for the good of the church' had recently tried to blow up the king, the royal family and the entire Parliament (the Gunpowder Plot). Next, Scarmentado visits The Hague, where he sees a venerable old man being led out for public execution. It is Johan van Oldenbarnevelt, chief minister of the Dutch Republic for forty years. Puzzled, the narrator enquires of a bystander if the old man is guilty of treason. 'Much worse than that,' comes the reply. 'He is a man who believes that we can achieve salvation by good works as well as by faith. You must realize that if such views become accepted, a state cannot endure, and severe laws are required to suppress such disgraceful horrors.' Disgusted, our hero moves on to Seville, where he is imprisoned and fined by the Inquisition for a careless word overheard while forty sinners are burnt at the stake for heresy. He counts himself lucky to escape to the relative peace and harmony of the Ottoman empire.

It is curious that Scarmentado never visited Germany. Some critics have suggested that Voltaire excised the passage which dealt (no doubt equally offensively) with that land, in order to spare the feelings of his ex-patron, Frederick of Prussia; but it may also be that the situation of Germany in the years 1615–20 was

1

simply too complex to be portrayed in a short story![1] Whatever the reason, there is a lot to be said for Voltaire's decision to concentrate on the periphery of Europe, for the religious and political passions which were to produce the Thirty Years' War did not in fact originate in Germany, but in the lands that surrounded it, and above all in the states governed by Europe's foremost dynasty, the Spanish and Austrian Habsburgs.

i The Habsburgs and Europe

Philip III, who succeeded his father as King of Spain in 1598, ruled an empire upon which the sun never set. He commanded subjects in fortresses and seaports around the coasts of Africa and southern Asia, in the Philippines, Mexico and Peru, in Spain and Portugal (united since 1580), in Lombardy, Naples and Sicily. But not in the Netherlands, although that country had formed an important part of the empire ruled by his father, Philip II. When he died, the South Netherlands passed to Philip III's sister, Isabella, and her husband Albert, universally known as 'the Archdukes' (see Table 1). In their satellite state, the Archdukes were sovereign in domestic matters; but in foreign and defence policy they were subject to Spain. The distinction was important, because Philip III seemed determined to continue his father's war against the Archdukes' northern neighbour, the Dutch Republic.

Born in the rebellion of the North Netherlands against Spanish rule during the 1570s, the young Republic had only survived the onslaught of Europe's greatest empire thanks to a combination of dogged defence at home and tireless diplomacy abroad. Treaties of friendship with England (1585), France (1589), the Palatinate (1604) and Brandenburg (1605) increased the supply of both men and money to the rebels until the Spanish government was forced to accept that victory in the Low Countries' Wars was no longer attainable. Early in 1607, despite some military successes the previous year, peace talks were begun. But after two years of discussion, the Archdukes, Spain and the Republic still could not agree on terms. Instead, a truce of twelve years was concluded, starting in April 1609; but even that applied only to the Netherlands. There was to be no withdrawal of Dutch warships or merchantmen from Spanish America or Portuguese Asia; and the Republic continued to seek alliances with anti-Habsburg forces

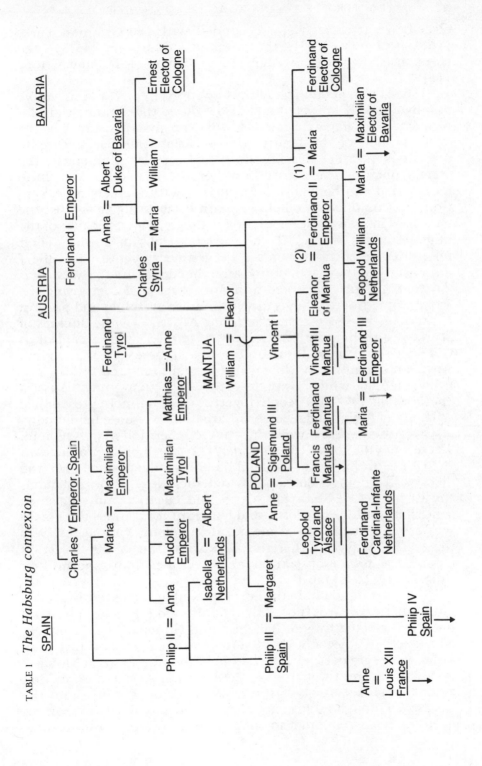

TABLE 1 *The Habsburg connexion*

elsewhere – treaties were concluded with the Ottoman Turks (1611), Algiers (1612), the German Protestants (1613), the Hanseatic towns and Sweden (1614), Savoy (1616) and Venice (1619).

The Dutch Republic had thus not only created an impressive patchwork of alliances; it had also secured the diplomatic isolation of its arch-enemy. Spain was not even given assistance by the other branch of the family, the Austrian Habsburgs. Despite numerous marriage ties – Philip II had been simultaneously the cousin, uncle and brother-in-law of Emperor Rudolf II, and Philip III married another Habsburg cousin – with scarcely an exception, Austria offered no help to Spain in her struggle against the Dutch.[1] This was most fortunate for the Republic, because of the huge resources over which the Austrian Habsburgs ruled. Their territories were (in the words of a seventeenth-century traveller) 'much larger than commonly apprehended'.[2] In the west was 'Further Austria', governed from Innsbruck and comprising the Tyrol, some isolated lands along the middle Rhine, and parts of Alsace; in the south-east was 'Inner Austria', as the duchies of Styria, Carinthia and Carniola were termed, with a capital at Graz and some two million subjects. Then there were the original Austrian duchies, the 'Upper' ruled from Linz, and the 'Lower' from Vienna, which were less populous than Inner Austria (perhaps only 600,000 people together) but far more prosperous, with many towns and a powerful aristocracy whose feudal powers over their vassals were the envy of their fellows elsewhere. These were the so-called Erbländer, the patrimonial provinces of the House of Habsburg. To them had been added, since 1526, the elective kingdoms of Bohemia (which included, besides Bohemia, the territories of Moravia, Silesia and Lusatia, and contained some four million subjects), and Hungary (or, rather, the north-western perimeter of the medieval kingdom, for the rest was under the sway of either the Turkish sultan or his Christian vassal, the prince of Transylvania) with perhaps one million inhabitants (see Map 1).

The turning-point in the development of this extensive Habsburg inheritance was the death of Ferdinand I in 1564. Ferdinand had been elected King of Bohemia and Hungary in 1526 largely because the subjects of those states, whose ruler had just been killed in the great Turkish victory over the Christians at Mohács, hoped to secure, through him, German and Austrian protection against the seemingly irresistible Turkish advance up the Danube. Throughout his reign, Ferdinand was able to exploit his need for defence in order to enhance his authority both in these new kingdoms, and in the Erbländer (where he was regent for his brother, the Emperor Charles V, after 1521). He successfully played off towns against nobles, acceptable non-Catholics (Hussites and, eventually, Lutherans) against unacceptable ones (Anabaptists, Bohemian Brethren and, eventually, Calvinists), and one state against another (the leaders of the Bohemian rebellion of 1547 were tried by judges from Moravia and Silesia). But this advantageous situation was transformed after 1564. In the first place, Ferdinand divided his lands at his death: Inner Austria went to his youngest son, Charles; Further Austria went to his second son, Ferdinand; only Upper and Lower Austria, with Bohemia and Hungary, were left for the eldest, Emperor Maximilian II. It was no longer possible to continue Ferdinand's practice of 'divide and rule'.[3]

Two other developments would probably have undermined that policy in any case: the creation of representative assemblies in all the Austrian duchies, each largely dominated by the aristocracy, after 1564; and the growth of a Protestant presence, especially among the nobles and the knights. By 1580, some 90 per cent of the nobles of Lower Austria were Protestant (almost all of them Lutherans), and the situation was similar in Upper Austria (except that several nobles became Calvinists). The Roman Catholic church in both duchies was moribund: parishes remained almost permanently vacant, congregations were abandoned, and the surviving establishments languished in an unedifying condition. Lower Austria in 1563 could boast 122 monasteries, with a total of only 463 monks and 160 nuns, but 199 concubines, 55 wives and 443 children.[4] They proved powerless to stem the Protestant tide. In 1568 and 1571, in return for substantial taxes to pay for defence against the Turks, Maximilian II granted freedom of Protestant worship in Lower Austria to all nobles and their vassals (although not to the towns). In 1578, the Protestant-led Estates of Upper Austria raised an army of 1,500 men in order to secure similar concessions from their new ruler, Maximilian's son Rudolf II. In the same year, the Estates of Inner Austria managed to extort extensive religious guarantees from their own sovereign, Archduke Charles, in return for voting taxes to support a permanent defence establishment along the Hungarian frontier. It was now the vassals, not the rulers, who exploited the Ottoman presence abroad in order to win important concessions at home. As the court preacher to Archduke Charles grimly observed: 'The Turkish threat is a blessing to the Protestants: if it were not for that, we would be able to deal with them in a very different way.'[5] The victorious Estates went ahead to make the most of their advantage, creating Protestant schools in the major cities, and a central standing committee to oversee religious affairs. The Austrians seemed bent on creating a territorial church on the lines of north German states such as Mecklenburg or Saxony.

But there was a crucial difference between the north German states and Austria: in the latter, the prince was not a Protestant. The entire process of securing guarantees and building up a *Landeskirche* was hollow and artificial. It flew in the face of a fundamental principle of early modern statecraft, that each sovereign secular ruler determined absolutely the faith of his subjects; it could therefore lead, ultimately, only to conflict. In 1579 the archdukes of Tyrol and Styria held a secret meeting at Munich with the duke of Bavaria at which it was decided to make no more concessions to the Reformed creeds, but to restore a Catholic monopoly, 'not with sound and fury, but surreptitiously and slowly; . . . not with words but with deeds'.[6] The process was easier in the outlying Habsburg duchies, for the Reformation had penetrated less deeply and the nobility was by no means solidly Protestant.[7] The progress of this first wave of the Counter-Reformation was halted by the death of Archduke Charles of Styria in 1590, and of the archduke of Tyrol shortly afterwards, but everyone realized that it was merely a truce. When Charles's son, the seventeen-year-old Ferdinand II, returned to Styria in 1595, after five years of Jesuit education at the university of Ingolstadt in Bavaria, he was given a paper drawn up by his advisers entitled 'A consideration of the way in which Catholicism may be restored'. In 1598, incognito, he paid a visit to Italy and was received in audience by the pope, to whom he no doubt explained his plan of campaign, for, as soon as he returned to Styria, he ordered all Protestant clergy and schoolteachers to leave. In 1599 a special 'Reformation Commission' set about closing down Lutheran establishments in the duchy (almost seventy were terminated within twelve months) and destroying all prohibited books (10,000 were burnt at Graz alone in a vast bonfire). In 1600, prominent Protestants and their families, including the Graz mathematician and schoolmaster Johannes Kepler, were obliged to leave. Perhaps 2,500 persons went into exile. After this success, the archduke and his Reformation Commission turned their attention to Carinthia and Carniola. Although one fearful bishop predicted the outbreak of rebellion 'on a Netherlandish scale', the archduke knew that fear of letting in the Turks (who had just captured Canissa, only 250 kilometres from Graz), and the Lutherans' reluctance to oppose a lawful prince, offered him a decisive advantage. Ferdinand II had managed to revive his grandfather's policy of divide and rule with startling success.[8]

There were some parallel moves in Lower Austria. In 1578 Rudolf II, then living in Vienna, ordered the closure of all Protestant institutions in the capital, including a notable grammar school run by the Estates themselves. There were complaints from the Protestant nobles as the churches and schools moved from Vienna to the nearby town of Horn; but there the matter rested. There was likewise no resistance from the nobles when the government, at the behest of Bishop Khlesl of Passau (and later of Vienna), began to force Catholic magistrates upon the towns of the duchy during the 1590s. In part, this compliance stemmed from the peasant revolt which paralysed much of Lower Austria in 1595 and 1596, and abated only thanks to Imperial intervention: the anti-aristocratic revolt had shown the landowners how dependent they were on government support. The powerlessness of the Lutheran pastors to stop the unrest had also shown that Protestantism was a poor guarantee of public order and, following the rebellion, several major landowners – Karl von Liechtenstein, head of one of the oldest families in the duchy, among them – converted to Catholicism.

It was much the same story elsewhere: from the 1590s onwards, scions of the major families of all Habsburg territories began to abandon the Reformed churches in favour of Catholicism – Wallenstein and Slavata in Bohemia, Eggenberg and Trauttmannsdorf in Styria, and many other figures later prominent in the Thirty Years' War among them. The spearhead of the Catholic offensive was formed by the colleges run by the Jesuit Order, of which there were four in the Habsburg lands by 1561, and some fifty by 1650, served by 870 full members of the Society. William Lamormaini, SJ, confessor to Emperor Ferdinand II, was not being over-patriotic when he later claimed that 'if there had been no schools of the Society founded by the prudent design of the emperors and archdukes in Vienna, Prague, Graz, Olomouc and elsewhere in Germany, there would have remained scarcely a vestige of the Catholic religion': the face of Catholicism in the Habsburg lands after about 1580 was moulded to an unusual degree by the stern, uncompromising, legalistic faith of the Jesuit Fathers.[9] As the more tolerant older generation was gradually removed by death, the temper of religious opinion became steadily more aggressive. The mannerist-humanist synthesis, with its defence of the old unity of Christendom, may still have attracted supporters, but too many of them were men of little substance, fugitives from fanaticism elsewhere. The Habsburg lands in central Europe had seemed their only refuge; now, there too they were threatened.[10]

These developments, which were apparent to all, should have alarmed the Habsburgs' Protestant subjects. But they did not. Those living in Bohemia and Hungary were particularly complacent, for both kingdoms possessed sound constitutional guarantees against princely absolutism – the Golden Bull of Hungary (1222) conferred particularly extensive rights on subjects – and both kingdoms had a long tradition of successful resistance to monarchical abuse (the Hussite rebellion of 1418–36 had defeated all efforts at repression by both Empire and Papacy). Moreover, both kingdoms elected their rulers, and regularly bargained with prospective candidates over concessions before coronation. But the coming of the Reformation to central Europe loosened the armour of these well-protected vassals. Admittedly the three major non-Catholic churches of Bohemia – Lutheran, Hussite and Bohemian Brethren (the radical wing of the Hussite movement) – agreed on a common creed in 1575, the *Confessio Bohemica*, and compelled Rudolf II to grant them official toleration in return for election as king; but his promise was only verbal and half-hearted. Almost at once, Rudolf reneged on the agreement by ordering the expulsion of the Bohemian Brethren (although it could not be carried out until 1602 for lack of resources). In Hungary, the situation was more uncertain still, since the major creeds there – Calvinist, Lutheran, Socinian – were unable to agree on a common declaration of faith.

The precarious position of Protestantism in both kingdoms under Habsburg rule was demonstrated during the 'Long Turkish War' (1593–1606) between Rudolf II and the sultan. Although the Turks had enjoyed success in the first years of the war, the sultan's Christian vassals in the Balkans – the princes of Transylvania, Wallachia and Moldavia – rebelled against him in 1597 and made common cause with the emperor. The Balkans might have been liberated had not Rudolf decided to use the opportunity to annexe Transylvania himself, and to exploit the presence of his armies both there and in Hungary to restore the Roman Catholic church to a position of supremacy. From 1602, special courts supplemented the actions of the troops, confiscating the lands of Protestant nobles (and indicting several for treason), expelling Protestant vassals, and restoring Protestant churches to Catholic use. In 1604 the Habsburg government declared that the local Estates were henceforth forbidden to discuss religious matters, and ordered that rigorous measures against heresy were to be strictly enforced.

This was pure folly: unlike Styria, there were scarcely any Catholics left in Hungary and Transylvania. Even papal agents could only find 300 Roman clergy in Hungary in 1606, most of them in the southern province of Croatia, flanking Inner Austria; in Transylvania there were less than thirty; and not a single Hungarian prelate had visited Rome since 1553.[11] There were no Catholic-controlled towns and virtually no Catholic nobles. So when, in 1605, the Imperial army was forced to march southwards to meet a major Turkish attack, there was no one left to prevent the rebellion of the Protestants of Hungary and Transylvania, led by the Calvinists Stephen Bocskay and Bethlen Gabor. When the Hungarian Estates had endorsed their revolt, Bocskay's forces invaded Moravia.

It began to seem as if the House of Habsburg was about to lose its grasp on the kingdoms acquired in 1526; yet the head of the family, Rudolf, whose ill-considered policies had unleashed the storm, seemed impervious to the risk and became more of a recluse than ever. He seldom emerged from the Hradschin, the massive palace complex above the 'New Town' of Prague which had been his home since 1581. Rudolf's closest relatives, fearing that he could no longer cope with the dangers facing the Empire and the dynasty, held a secret meeting at Linz in April 1605 to discuss what to do. They deputed the emperor's eldest sibling, Archduke Matthias, to take charge of affairs and urged him to make peace both with Bocskay and with the Turks; in return they promised to support his claim to succeed Rudolf as king of Bohemia and Hungary.[12] At first all went well: a hastily collected loyalist army, which included such important actors in future events as Count Thurn and the young Wallenstein, drove back Bocskay and enabled Matthias to conclude a cease-fire in January 1606. The following June, by the peace of Vienna, the archduke recognized Bocskay as prince of Transylvania, ceded him eight counties of royal Hungary, and promised full religious liberty to all the Protestants of the kingdom (although the Roman church was also offered protection). In November, thanks in part to Bocskay's good offices, Matthias also concluded a reasonably favourable treaty with the Turks at Zsitva Torok, which brought peace to the Turkish frontier – thanks to frequent renewals – for many decades.[13]

Rudolf, however, was not happy with these arrangements. Indecisive and uncertain, the emperor came to believe the suggestions of certain Catholics that the plague which was devastating

Bohemia, even driving him from his beloved Hradschin, was God's punishment for the toleration granted to the Protestants. Although he signed the peace of Vienna, he protested that his assent had only been extorted under duress, and he strove to prevent the concessions from being implemented. In 1607 he issued a 'List of charges', criticizing his brother's administration in Austria and Hungary, his direction of the war, and his concessions to the Turks and rebels.[14]

The Hungarian Estates and the archduke were thus almost forced, in order to defend themselves, to conclude an uneasy alliance: the former could offer to recognize Matthias as their king in return for firm guarantees that the peace of Vienna would be maintained; the latter could exploit the Hungarians' desire for constitutional security in order to achieve recognition of his succession claims. The bargain was sealed at a meeting of the Hungarian Diet at Bratislava early in 1608, and Matthias now set about securing similar recognition from the other Habsburg lands. His own provinces of Upper and Lower Austria presented no difficulty, for a delegation of their Estates was already at Bratislava, led by George Erasmus Tschernembl, a Calvinist nobleman partly educated in the West (whose library of almost 1,900 volumes included many Protestant works and a manuscript treatise of his own, concerning a subject's right to resist his sovereign).[15] In February the Austrian leaders, the Hungarian Estates, and the archduke signed an alliance to secure the enforcement of the treaty of Vienna. Moravia soon joined this union, and in May Matthias led a small army raised by the confederates towards Prague; but Rudolf still refused to recognize his brother's new titles. Only in June 1608, with Matthias and his army only five miles from Prague, did the emperor capitulate.

Now, however, the Estates had tasted the sweet fruits of blackmail, and they cynically increased their demands. The Estates of Upper Austria, led by Tschernembl, suddenly required from Matthias full religious liberty for the towns as well as for the nobles, and full parity of treatment with the Catholics, in return for coronation. When the archduke refused, the Protestant members of the Estates signed an alliance with their co-religionists from the Lower duchy pledging themselves to mobilize troops in order to secure these new concessions. In March 1609, since Rudolf remained intransigent, Matthias was constrained to accept the conditions and confirm the religious privileges of the Austrians in order to be recognized as reigning archduke.

Only Bohemia, Silesia and Lusatia were now left under the direct control of Rudolf. The events of 1597–1604 had shown that some form of confirmation of their religious privileges was advisable, and in January 1609 the Estates of the kingdom met in Prague to secure this. But Rudolf refused. In May, the Estates created an executive of thirty 'Directors' and authorized the levy of 4,500 troops, obliging the emperor to sign, on 9 July 1609, the famous *Letter of Majesty* which made official and legal the right of all Bohemians to choose either the Catholic faith or one of those comprised in the Confession of 1575. Protestant schools and churches could now be built by the nobles and towns; and even in the royal domain Protestants might open a church or cemetery, if these were not already in existence. One ambiguity remained, probably unperceived by contemporaries: there was no mention of the legal rights of Protestants living on ecclesiastical lands. Probably the Estates assumed them to be included in the provisions for the royal domain, although the government was later to deny this. But it was only a minor matter when set beside the enormous tangible gains. Rudolf had even agreed that a standing committee of the Estates, to be known as the 'Defensors', should become responsible for seeing that his concessions took effect. In 1611 these men were able to flex their muscles, when Rudolf inexplicably permitted his cousin Leopold (brother of Ferdinand of Styria) to invade Bohemia with some 7,000 troops. If he had hoped to overawe the Estates he was mistaken, for a considerable Bohemian force drove Leopold's men back from the suburbs of Prague, and the Defensors called upon Matthias to take over the government of their kingdom. Rudolf, cowering in his palace, alone and probably insane, was declared deposed; and in May 1611 Matthias, after confirming the Letter of Majesty, was crowned King of Bohemia. The power of the Estates in the Habsburg lands had rarely seemed so great. And yet it was bound to be impermanent: the Defensors only awaited an opportunity to secure more, while Matthias (according to his own admission) was equally anxious to revoke what he had conceded.

It is hard now to see these tumultuous events in true perspective. In the aftermath of the Bohemian rebellion of 1618 the gains of the Estates appear doomed from the start; but so did most of the other great political concessions of European history, when viewed only a few years later. Even England's Magna Carta, which by the seventeenth century was generally accepted as the corner-stone of the constitution, had been subjected to violations and attempted revocations during the century after the barons wrested it from King John at Runnymede in 1215. To make Bohemia's Letter of Majesty similarly immutable and respectable required only time. But time, as everyone recognized, was fast running out.

ii *Germany before the war*

I am very much afraid that the states of the Empire,
quarrelling fiercely among themselves, may start a fatal
conflagration embracing not only themselves . . . but also all
those countries that are in one way or another connected
with Germany. All this will undoubtedly produce the most
dangerous consequences, bringing about the total collapse
and unavoidable alteration in the present state of Germany.
And it may also perhaps affect some other states.[1]

The pessimistic assessment which Maurice, landgrave of Hesse-
Kassel, communicated to the French government in 1615, would
not have seemed extravagant to most of his contemporaries.
There was a widespread conviction, both inside the territories of
the Holy Roman Empire and beyond, that another major war in
Europe was imminent. All over Germany, governments had begun to spend heavily on defence. Travellers coming from the
Dutch Republic during the second decade of the century noted the
contrast between the Netherlands, where troops were seldom
seen, and the Empire, where every potentate seemed to boast a
private army, ostentatious in dress and obtrusive in presence.
Even Landgrave Maurice, patron of intellectuals (many of them
formerly attached to Rudolf II's court in Prague), musicians
(including the young Heinrich Schütz) and the theatre, created
in 1600 a new militia of some 9,000 men. The following year he
drew up in his own hand a 288-page directive on how it should be
employed in an emergency, and promptly used it to invade and
annexe Hesse-Marburg (page 21 below). In 1618 he created a
special 'military academy' to train officers for his regiments.[2]
    Some rulers concentrated upon improving territorial de-
fences in other ways. Thus, although the government of ducal
Prussia could not persuade the local Estates to pay for a militia,
taxes were voted in 1601 for new fortifications at the ports of
Pillau and Memel, and for two warships to patrol the Baltic
approaches. The Electors of Saxony created an Arsenal at Dresden which, besides being an architectural marvel, contained
enough military hardware to equip an army of (it was claimed)
10,000.[3] After 1600, the pace of defence-spending accelerated. The
Elector Palatine ordered expensive new walls, with bastions and
moats, to be built around Frankenthal and Heidelberg, and in
1606 he created at Mannheim an entire fortress-city which, with

its citadel and vast star-shaped chain of walls, was intended to be impregnable.[4] Between 1603 and 1618, the city of Hanau, allied to the Palatinate and ruled by a Calvinist count, was also given a completely new defensive network. The Catholic powers of the Rhineland, feeling threatened, soon undertook counter-preparations of their own. The Elector of Trier fortified Ehrenbreitstein, overlooking Coblenz at the junction of the Rhine and Moselle; Philip Christopher von Sötern, bishop of Speyer, built the great fortress of Philippsburg at Udenheim, on the Rhine south of the Palatinate (1615–23). The lords of Alsace built new walls at Benfeld, Breisach and Hagenau, while the duke of Bavaria added new fortifications around Munich, Ingolstadt, Rain and some frontier towns, at a total cost of almost 1 million thalers, between 1598 and 1618.[5] The scale of each of these enterprises must not be underestimated: millions of bricks were required to construct walls that might be as much as 40 feet wide, 30 feet high and several miles long. When John Taylor, the English poet, humorist and traveller, visited Hamburg in 1617, he was astonished by the size of the army of artisans at work on the walls.

> And when I perceived these fortifications I was amazed, for it is almost incredible for the number of men and horses that are daily set on work about it; besides, the work itself is so great that it is past the credit of report.[6]

By the summer of 1617, war certainly seemed to be in the air.

At the same time, it is possible to exaggerate the sense of gloom and impending destruction. The year 1617 itself saw an end to hostilities in France, Russia and Italy. The English ambassador in Turin, Dr Isaac Wake, was prompted to exult that 'the gates of Janus' had been shut, promising 'calm and Halcyonian days not only unto the inhabitants of this province of Italye, but to the greatest part of Christendome'.[7] Although the fortification and militarization of Germany caused the war there to last longer once it had begun, they did not of themselves make its outbreak inevitable. When Thomas Coryat, another itinerant English humorist, travelled to Venice and back in 1608, he walked alone most of the way from Basel to Mainz and yet only once met with any troops; nor did he have any unpleasant encounters with footpads or brigands. On the contrary, he frequently praised the orderliness, prosperity and peace of the upper Rhine valley, where bread and vegetables were so cheap that one could have a nourishing meal for a farthing and buy a year's supply of grain for £2. However, Coryat found it prudent to sail down the Rhine below Mainz on a passenger barge because the roads in that part were reputed to be infested with outlaws. He was wise: another English traveller of this period, Fynes Morison, was obliged to journey through Westphalia in disguise (on one occasion hidden under a wagon-load of goods) in order to escape robbers.[8] Germany was the largest country in Europe, and it was far from homogeneous!

> The dear old Holy Roman Empire,
> How does it stay together?

asked the tavern drinkers in Goethe's *Faust* – and the answer is no easier to find today than it was in the late eighteenth, or earlier seventeenth, century. The truth was that Germany, or 'The Holy Roman Empire of the German Nation' to give its proper title, was a land of many states and many economies. The prosperous south – the Palatinate, Alsace, Bavaria and so on – had always presented a contrast with the barren heaths and wastelands of the north-west, a prey to the armies operating in the war-torn Netherlands, and their irregular supporters. In 1599 the entire Spanish field army invaded neighbouring Westphalia in search of winter quarters. The local princes attempted to raise a force of their own to drive the Spaniards out, but it proved totally unsuccessful – and, to add insult to injury, the luckless troops then mutinied for their pay. The cost of failure was over 400,000 thalers. It was this débâcle, more than anything else, that initiated the headlong creation of separate territorial armies in the early years of the seventeenth century, for by that time the supra-territorial institutions of the Empire had become all but ineffectual.[9]

The 'Circles' (*Kreise*), responsible since the early sixteenth century for local defence, were no longer capable of mobilizing sufficient forces to guarantee the security of their members – the mutinous troops of 1599 were raised by the Rhenish and Westphalian Circle. Attempts at inter-Circle cooperation were few: the weaving regulations, common currencies, and grain controls agreed in 1564–72 between the Bavarian, Swabian and Franconian Circles were exceptional and impermanent. The main obstacle to cooperation was the extreme religious and political fragmentation of southern and western Germany. Swabia, more or less equal in area to modern Switzerland, included sixty-eight secular and forty spiritual lords, and also thirty-two Imperial Free Cities. All were represented in the Circle Assembly (*Kreistag*), which met regularly (sixty-four times between 1555 and 1599); and each was a direct vassal of the emperor. But they ranged in importance from the compact duchy of Württemberg, covering 9,200 square kilometres, down to the lands of the numerous

'Imperial Knights', who might each own only part of one village. Over half of the members of the Circle, and almost exactly half of its population, were Catholic; the rest were either Lutheran or Calvinist. It was the perfect formula for paralysis, and most of the Circles of south and west Germany were similarly divided by their confessional and political differences. In the Empire as a whole, with a population in 1600 of perhaps 20 million, there were some 1,000 separate, semi-autonomous political units, many of them very small. Yet even the tiniest polities were tenacious of their rights. The 400 or so Imperial Knights were organized into fourteen 'cantons' of their own, each with a Director, Treasury and Chancery, holding assemblies four or five times per year, and from 1590 their autonomy was guaranteed by a special Imperial ordinance. At a slightly higher level, the fifty or more 'Imperial Counts' also had their own organizations: perhaps the most important, in the Wetterau region north of Frankfurt, was led after 1565 by the Calvinist counts of Nassau (which helps to explain their importance in the politics of the Empire). The Imperial Counts even had two guaranteed seats in the Imperial Diet.[10]

But these minor potentates, although they insisted on exercising to the full their religious, economic and feudal powers, were of little weight when set beside the eight major states of the Empire. In the lead were Electoral Saxony, Brandenburg, and Bavaria, with over 1 million subjects each; the Palatinate with perhaps 600,000; and Hesse, Trier and Württemberg with 400,000 each. However, these large states, some equal in size and population to the kingdoms of Scotland or Sweden, were prevented by two serious disadvantages from achieving outright dominance in the Empire. First, they did not all accept the principle of primogeniture: Hesse, for example, was divided in 1567 between the four sons of Landgrave Philip the Magnanimous, Luther's patron, with a consequent loss of influence in the affairs of the Empire. Second, many of them were geographically fragmented. The Palatinate, most notably, was divided into two major units: the Lutheran upper county, which had once been part of Bavaria, adjoined the borders of Bohemia and contributed some 40 per cent of the Elector's revenues, while the Calvinist lower county, around Heidelberg, straddled the Rhine. Further, minor parts of the Palatinate were ruled by separate branches of the dynasty, such as Zweibrücken and Neuburg. Since the smaller principalities of the Empire were, if anything, more fragmented and fissiparous, it was sometimes very difficult for a traveller in Germany to know where he was. Only the borders of a few territories (such

as the confines of Lorraine, the Palatinate, Hanau and Zweibrücken) were marked by a series of special boundary columns.
More frequently, frontiers were represented by customs posts,
both on land and on water. For example, there were thirty toll
stations on the Elbe between Hamburg and Prague, and eleven on
the Rhine between Mainz and Cologne, each equipped with a
small cannon to sink ships attempting to run through without
paying dues.[11]

For all these reasons, no individual territory in Germany
could match the power of the Austrian Habsburgs, who had
monopolized the Imperial title since 1438. Yet their extensive
territorial and demographic base was insufficient to permit absolute control of the destinies of Germany. After 1601, many important territorial rulers ceased to accept the decisions of the Imperial Supreme Court (the *Reichskammergericht*), and by 1620 the
vassals of Saxony, Brandenburg and Bavaria were forbidden to
appeal to this tribunal without the consent of their prince. More
serious still was the refusal, after 1608, of an important group of
princes to attend the Imperial Diet. This assembly of all the
territorial rulers of Germany, or their representatives, had only
met six times between 1555 and 1603. Its members, divided into
three 'colleges' – Electors, princes and towns – deliberated separately on the propositions submitted by the emperor, then conferred together and, in due course, submitted a response. In a
prolonged Diet, there might be over 100 sessions and over twenty
joint conferences. Considerable delays were caused by the large
number of semi-autonomous participants: although there were
only seven Electors (including the emperor himself as king of
Bohemia), there were some 150 territories represented in the
princes' college, and fifty-two members in the towns' college. All
decisions depended ultimately on consensus, and therefore on
compromise; and it was because compromises could no longer be
reached on certain key issues, above all on religious equality for
Protestants and Catholics within the Imperial institutions, that
in 1608 the Diet ceased to function. Only one further meeting was
held between then and 1640 – in August 1613 at Regensburg – and
many Protestants boycotted even that.[12]

The paralysis of the major Imperial institutions – Circles,
Supreme Court and Diet – at this time was particularly unfortunate because the Empire was faced by a number of serious problems. Most important, perhaps, was Rudolf II's war with the
Turks between 1593 and 1606: without a Diet, he was unable to
secure taxes from the Empire to pay his forces in Hungary. The
extent of Rudolf's dependence upon German contributions

emerges by contrasting his demands for *Römermonate* (the basic tax voted by the Diet) with those of his great-uncle, Charles V (emperor 1519–58): whereas Charles had only asked for 73½ Römermonate, Rudolf asked for 409 against the Turks alone. The money could not be found: even as late as 1619, unpaid arrears of these wartime taxes still stood at almost 4 million thalers.[13]

But there was more to non-payment of taxes than a constitutional wrangle: many parts of Germany were suffering the effects of a serious economic recession. The rapid and prolonged growth of the population which Germany experienced (in common with the rest of Europe) during the sixteenth century created many difficulties. On the one hand, all available land had been cleared for arable farming, leaving less for pastoral use or industrial crops; on the other, the run of exceptionally high food prices during the 1590s caused a collapse in the market for manufactured goods – many consumers no longer had money to buy anything except bread. After this crisis, recovery was slow. Many towns, particularly in the south-west, experienced a fall in industrial output (as entrepreneurs turned increasingly to cheaper rural labour). Many more ran up heavy debts, either because economic recession reduced income or because the construction of new defences or new civic amenities increased expenditure. And almost all towns – whether Imperial or territorial – suffered increasing interference in their social, political and religious affairs from their princely neighbours.[14] What the territorial states desired from the towns, above all else, was money. The rulers of Germany, at the turn of the century were rarely solvent. Emperor Matthias owed almost 30 million thalers at his accession in 1612, while the Elector of Brandenburg owed 18 million, the Elector of Saxony over 3 million, and the Elector Palatine almost 2 million. It was no coincidence that this period saw a spate of 'household economy' books, advising princes on how best to cut their coats according to their cloth.[15]

Financial embarrassment brought many rulers into conflict with their Estates, whose consent (in almost all territories) was required before taxes could be levied. The composition of these representative assemblies differed from one territory to another. Some, particularly in south Germany, included nobles, clergy, towns and peasants; others had only towns and peasants; and the Estates of some smaller units had only peasants. All might claim to deal with legislation, taxation and declarations of war. But in the larger territories, where most people lived, there was no such 'democracy'. In a letter of 1598 to his father, who had just abdicated in his favour, Duke Maximilian of Bavaria wrote: 'I myself believe that we princes are only esteemed, by both spiritual and secular powers, according to "reason of state"; and I believe that respect goes only to those who have a lot of land or a lot of money.'[16] Throughout his long reign, Maximilian acted accordingly, aided to a surprising extent by his Estates. The *Landschaft* of Bavaria met thirty-three times between 1514 and 1579, six more times before 1612, and never again until 1669. At the 1612 assembly Maximilian, who had just issued a complex legal code without consulting his Estates, persuaded the 'representatives of the people' to vote him a handsome annual subsidy for seven years (equal by itself to double the revenues of the Elector of Saxony); to invest him with the power to make war and peace as he chose, and to raise all necessary taxes (in case of war) at his own discretion. Here was a relationship between prince and Estates that was quite unlike that prevailing in England, France or the Habsburg lands.[17]

Undoubtedly the principal reason for this cooperation was Maximilian's proven financial expertise. By 1612 he had halved the debts inherited from his father, and after that he carefully built up a surplus, so that even in wartime he could finance his army without recourse to his Estates. He also created a special fund (the *aerarium*) for the active defence of Catholicism in the Empire, whenever the need arose. These measures were only possible because Maximilian and his immediate predecessors had largely purged their domains of Protestantism. In the 1550s, the Bavarian Protestants had attempted to extort promises of toleration from the government against threats that, without such guarantees, they would vote no taxes. There was a confrontation on the issue in 1563, after which the dukes strained every nerve to expel all Protestants from their domains; and as they succeeded, so the Estates became more compliant.

The same development was taking place in other Catholic territories, under the terms of the 'Religious Peace of Augsburg' (1555), which put a temporary end to open confessional warfare in Germany. The Augsburg settlement created a layered structure of legal securities for the people of the Empire. At the top was the right of each secular territorial ruler, from the Electors down to the Imperial Knights, to dictate whether their subjects' religion was to be Catholic or Lutheran (the only officially permitted creeds: Calvinism and all other faiths were forbidden). This principle was later known as *cuius regio, eius religio*: that the religion of the governed should be the same as that of their territorial ruler, and that subjects who so desired were to be allowed to emigrate. The only exceptions to this rule were the

Imperial Free Cities and the Catholic ecclesiastical states. In the former, the Peace guaranteed that where both Lutheran and Catholic groups existed, both were to enjoy freedom of worship (in effect, this only applied to eight of the sixty or so Free Cities, because almost all the rest were either wholly Lutheran or wholly Catholic). The second exception was far more important, since it concerned the extensive ecclesiastical principalities. On the one hand, it decreed that 'territorial church lands' (i.e. those under the political authority of a territorial prince or city) in Protestant hands by the year 1552 were so to remain, but there were to be no more secularizations. Quite different was the fate of the 'Imperial church lands' (i.e. those under an ecclesiastical ruler – a prince-bishop or prince-abbot – subordinate politically only to the emperor), for if the *cuius regio* principle were to be applied there, the election of a Protestant bishop or abbot would produce the Protestantization of the entire principality. It was therefore agreed that if a prince-bishop or a prince-abbot embraced the Reformation, he was to resign so that a Catholic prelate could replace him. Not surprisingly, Protestant partisans at Augsburg did not accept this measure, known as the *reservatum ecclesiasticum*, and it was included in the Peace only by virtue of Imperial authority, not by vote of the Diet.[18] It could therefore be disputed, as happened after 1583 when the Archbishop-Elector of Cologne turned Protestant: a war lasting five years was fought between his supporters (who included the young Dutch Republic and the Palatinate) and his Catholic replacement, Ernest of Bavaria (aided by Philip II of Spain and by Ernest's brother, Duke William, who ran up debts of over 500,000 thalers in his successful attempt to uphold the *reservatum ecclesiasticum*).[19] But there were surprisingly few blatant attempts of this kind to challenge the terms of the Augsburg settlement.[20] More numerous were conflicts between rulers and ruled within the Imperial church lands because, during the heated discussions that preceded the Augsburg settlement, the Habsburg negotiators had made an undertaking (the *Declaratio Ferdinandei*) that if the cities or knights of an ecclesiastical prince had already practised Lutheranism for some time, they were to be allowed to continue. But this concession was not promulgated as part of the Peace, remaining secret for almost two decades. Not surprisingly, when it was eventually made public, many prelates treated it as spurious and thus provoked severe conflicts with their Estates.

At first, however, the Catholic rulers seemed unable or unwilling either to enforce religious uniformity in their domains or to prevent the rapid spread of Calvinism in the Empire (discussed below). Only after 1580, with support from Austria and Bavaria, did the ecclesiastical princes – most notably the abbot of Fulda and the adjacent bishops of Würzburg, Bamberg and Eichstätt – make serious efforts to end Protestant worship in their lands, in spite of the *Declaratio Ferdinandei*. Progress was particularly rapid after the War of Cologne (1583–8), which may be seen as the turning-point in the struggle between Protestantism and Catholicism in Germany. The war marked the first successful attempt to halt the Protestantization of an ecclesiastical territory; and it provoked an important treatise arguing that the Catholic cause was being lost in Germany by default and must be saved before it was too late – the anonymous *De Autonomia*, written in 1580 and published (at the duke of Bavaria's expense) in 1586.[21] The exodus of Lutherans from the *Pfaffengasse* (the Priests' Alley, as the ecclesiastical territories along the Rhine and Main were known) now became a flood. Most refugees sought a sanctuary as close to their former homes as possible, where they formed a militant and restless community of exiles: they left reluctantly, and they dreamed constantly of vengeance against those who had expelled them. There were many who, like the Lutheran exiles from Würzburg, driven into exile at nearby Ansbach in 1588, sang the psalm of bitterness 'By the waters of Babylon we sat down and wept' as they travelled in a body from their old home to the new and longed to return to their fatherland. But of this there was little chance, for Julius Echter von Mespelbrunn, bishop of Würzburg from 1573 to 1617, turned his territory into a showpiece of Counter-Reformation achievement. His capital was both beautified and enriched with a new university, a lavishly restored palace and many refurbished churches. Priests with concubines were exhorted to abandon them; and a special fund was created for renovating Catholic churches recovered from the Protestants (over 300 churches in the diocese were rebuilt in the 'Julius style'), for improving clerical standards, and for increasing clerical salaries.[22]

The impetus of the Counter-Reformation seemed irresistible, drawing strength from the creation of the *Congregatio Germanica* (Council for German Affairs) in Rome, in 1568, and of the diocesan seminaries, synods and schools all over Catholic Europe. Likewise, thanks to the presence of vigilant nuncios at the Imperial Court and at Cologne, and to the work of the religious Orders, Tridentine orthodoxy was defined with enhanced clarity and enforced with increased rigour. Many of the more active Catholic clergy were actually trained in Rome at the *Collegium Germanicum*, founded in 1552.[23]

Most of the Catholics' gains were made from the Lutheran church, which for some time had been in theological disarray thanks to the acrimonious internal debates between those who wished to maintain Luther's teaching unchanged in all respects (the 'Gnesio-Lutherans') and those (known as 'Melanchthonians' after their leader, Philip Melanchthon) who looked for certain changes. Between 1537 and 1577 there were ten major clashes on doctrinal issues between the two factions, and a continuing dispute over pedagogic and political attitudes; but eventually the Gnesio-Lutherans managed to have their views included in the so-called Formula of Concord, compiled between 1577 and 1580 by a committee of Lutheran court chaplains acting on their masters' instructions. This reunited about two-thirds of the Lutheran world on doctrinal matters, but left the Melanchthonians with little option but to merge into the Calvinist church. Defections from Lutheranism therefore became frequent and substantial, and they included several secular rulers. Among those who turned to Calvinism were Elector Frederick III of the Palatinate in 1559–60, Count John of Nassau in 1578, and Landgrave Maurice of Hesse-Kassel in 1603. The last conversion gave rise to a war, for the extinction of the Hesse-Marburg branch of the family the following year was exploited by the newly Calvinist landgrave: he occupied the vacant inheritance, and in particular the famous university of Marburg, which had become an important seminary for training Lutheran pastors. The students rebelled, but Maurice's troops prevailed. The Lutherans were forced to migrate to the academy of Giessen (in Lutheran Hesse-Darmstadt, made into a university in 1607), whence they conducted a violent and acrimonious debate with their Calvinist expropriators at Marburg.[24] Perhaps the Calvinist's greatest coup, however, was the conversion of two other Protestant Electors. Christian I of Saxony (1586–91) maintained close relations with the Palatinate and began to appoint Calvinists to senior positions in his schools and universities and at Court. In 1590 he offered to send military aid to assist Henry IV, the Calvinist king of France, against his Catholic enemies, and in 1591 he signed a military alliance with the Calvinist ruler of the Palatinate. In the same year, he introduced changes to the Saxon church order which brought it closer to Calvinism. Only Christian's sudden death, at the age of thirty-one, saved the Lutheran cause in Saxony. In 1613, much the same process threatened Brandenburg with major religious change: the new Elector, John Sigismund, openly embraced Calvinism, and tried to change the official creed of his territories according to the *cuius regio* principle. But there was rioting in the streets of Berlin and brawling in the Estates until a compromise, which tolerated both forms of Protestant worship, was agreed. A flood of pamphlets appeared – 200 are known for 1614–17 alone – discussing the change of religion in Brandenburg.[25]

Small wonder, then, that the Lutheran clergy cordially detested the Calvinists even more than they loathed the Catholics. The leading voice in the anti-Calvinist campaign was Matthias Hoë von Hoënegg, of Austrian descent, who became court chaplain to the Elector of Saxony in 1602, and chaplain-in-chief in 1613. Hoë was pugnacious. In the prologue to his *Prodromus* (1621) he wrote: 'I remain determined to make war for the Lord, and I thank my God that He has taught my hands to fight.' Even the titles of his numerous books bristle with aggression, from *A solid, just and orthodox detestation of Papists and Calvinists* (1601), to *A weighty (and in these dangerous times very necessary) discussion of whether and why it is better to have conformity with the Catholics . . . than with the Calvinists* (1620). Other works contrasted the Reformed religion unfavourably with Islam.[26]

But not all Lutherans were obsessed by Calvinism to the exclusion of their more ancient adversary. Most of the forty-six published sermons celebrating the Lutheran Jubilee of 1617 called for an immediate crusade against Rome, centre of idolatry, sodomy and other vices, and seat of 'the Beast of the Apocalypse'. Tensions between Lutherans and Catholics were most notable in the city-states of Germany, where social grievances were often added to religious division. There was rioting or rebellion in some twenty cities of the Empire between 1595 and 1618 (see Map 1), of which the most serious was that at Donauwörth in 1606–7.[27] Although Donauwörth was one of the eight Imperial Free Cities where both Lutherans and Catholics were officially tolerated, until 1605 the Catholic clergy had scarcely dared to hold open processions, carrying no insignia when they peregrinated on Holy Days and keeping to the backstreets. And with reason: for when, on St Mark's Day 1606, the clergy attempted to hold a proper procession, they were beaten up and their relics and banners were ridiculed and confiscated. Two months later, Father Laurence of Brindisi, a leading Capuchin (later canonized), arrived in the city en route to the Imperial Court and was himself mobbed by a Lutheran crowd chanting 'Capuchin, Capuchin, scum, scum.' He heard from the local clergy of their plight and promised to ask the emperor to provide redress.

He found Prague in the grip of plague, so that in September

even Rudolf II had to abandon his capital in order to escape the contagion. Laurence promptly preached a sermon blaming the plague on the concessions to the Protestants in Donauwörth and elsewhere. His tone gave grave offence, and he was only saved from unpleasantness by an urgent summons from Maximilian of Bavaria, who desired Laurence to exorcize his apparently deranged duchess. The successful treatment, which required several sessions, afforded the Capuchin a chance to engage Maximilian's sympathy for the cause of the Donauwörth Catholics, so that when he returned to Prague the following February, Laurence could assure the emperor that Bavaria was ready to enforce the Augsburg settlement on the city. Accordingly, Rudolf agreed to send an Imperial Commissioner to ensure that the Catholics had their full St Mark's Day procession in April 1607, and Maximilian sent a couple of agents, too. But to no avail: priests, commissioner and agents were virtually besieged by a Lutheran mob and could not leave the monastery where they had assembled. The magistrates, Protestants to a man, did nothing to prevent the disorders.

The emperor's authority had now been openly slighted and in August Rudolf ordered Donauwörth to allow the Catholics freedom of worship or be declared contumacious; Maximilian was empowered to use force if necessary to restore obedience. When requests failed, the duke raised an army and, despite countermobilization by some Protestant neighbours, his forces marched into the city on 17 December 1607 and restored Catholic worship. This act was manifestly illegal, for Donauwörth was in the Swabian, not the Bavarian Circle, and the Imperial Ban should have been enforced by the Swabian Director (the Lutheran duke of Württemberg). Further illegalities followed. In June 1609, in a move that was to be repeated in 1620 on a grander scale, the emperor granted Maximilian the city as a pledge for the expenses he had incurred in executing the Ban. At once the duke forbade Protestant worship there, according to the *cuius regio* principle, and expelled those who would not conform. Another pamphlet war began, this time between the Lutheran refugees (mostly in Württemberg) and Maximilian's apologists.[28]

On hearing of the occupation of Donauwörth, the prescient Duke Philip Ludwig of Neuburg lamented, 'Maximilian, Maximilian, you do not realize the consequences of what you are doing.'[29] He, like others, saw at once that the coup torpedoed all chance of cooperation between Protestants and Catholics at the Imperial Diet summoned to assemble at Regensburg in January 1608. Circumstances already favoured a confrontation there between the emperor, whose chief desire was for money to liquidate the debts incurred during the Turkish war, and the militant Protestants, led by the Elector Palatine, who demanded religious changes beneficial for Protestantism in general and for Calvinism in particular. The occupation of Donauwörth, scarcely 100 kilometres from Regensburg, drove normally moderate Lutheran rulers, such as the duke of Neuburg and the Elector of Saxony, into the Palatine camp. They demanded at least an increase in Protestant representation on the Imperial Supreme Court. But the emperor's representative, Archduke Ferdinand, remained ada-mant: the Catholics still possessed a majority in two of the three colleges of the Diet (four to three among the Electors, and thirty-three to fifteen among the princes; only the towns, who lacked a binding vote anyway, were predominantly Protestant). It was even rumoured that the archduke was plotting with Maximilian of Bavaria to launch an armed coup against the Diet if he failed to get his way. Although this did not materialize, in February 1608 the Catholics in the Princes' College introduced a motion calling for the restitution of all ecclesiastical lands se-cularized since 1552. This was intended to force the Protestants to offer concessions on other issues in order to have the measure withdrawn, but it in fact made their position untenable. In April the Palatine delegation, after submitting a formal protest to Ferdinand, walked out of the Diet. They were followed by the representatives of Brandenburg, Ansbach, Kulmbach, Baden-Durlach, Hesse-Kassel and Württemberg. Although the Saxon contingent, together with some others, remained, on 3 May Archduke Ferdinand reluctantly dissolved the Diet.

Nine days later, in the chapterhouse of the secularized monastery of Auhausen (near Nördlingen), six leading Protes-tant princes (the Elector Palatine, Neuburg, Württemberg, Ansbach, Kulmbach and Baden-Durlach) signed an alliance, known as the Protestant Union, to last ten years, pledging mutual support in case of attack. To a large extent, the battle-lines which divided Germany during the 1620s were thus drawn. Most of those who defied Ferdinand in 1608 were to do so again; those who hesitated at Regensburg were also to hesitate later; the archduke's supporters were already counted. It is a source of wonderment, to historians as to contemporaries, that a general conflict did not break out between the already embattled parties in Germany for a whole decade after the 'Donauwörth Incident', despite several serious clashes. The explanation is to be found in the policies of certain states outside the Empire.

iii The Union, the League and the politics of Europe

The foundation of the Protestant Union initiated a new phase in the politics of the Empire: despite the continued efforts of many princes to make the older Imperial institutions function, confessional alliances now dominated the stage. As the alliances turned for support to their co-religionists abroad, so the traditional opposition to the involvement of foreign powers in the Empire came under increasing pressure, and Imperial politics and the international balance of power became closely intermeshed. Yet the revolution was never a complete one: while some princes considered a full-scale war of religion to be inevitable, and others were frightened into confessional alliances by the apparent course of events, a few key figures (both within the Empire and without) still tried to prevent such a disaster. In consequence, the decade between the Donauwörth incident and the outbreak of the Bohemian Revolution was characterized by a complicated and confused mixture of open brinkmanship and cautious defensiveness.

The need for confessional politics was most unreservedly accepted in the Rhine Palatinate. The conversion to Calvinism of the Elector Frederick III (1559–76), and the continuation of his policies by his younger son, Johann Casimir (regent, 1583–92), had made Heidelberg one of the major centres of the Reformed religion. To the Palatine court a remarkable group of Calvinist freelances and former Melanchthonian Lutherans had been attracted, of whom the most ambitious, and ultimately the most notorious, was Prince Christian of Anhalt-Bernburg. Anhalt was appointed governor of the Upper Palatinate in 1595, and the alcoholism and infirmity of the Elector Frederick IV (1592–1610) soon gave him more or less unchecked control over the conduct of Palatine foreign relations. His immigrant protégés – such as Ludwig Camerarius, the brothers Christoph and Achatius von Dohna, Vollrad von Plessen and Hippolytus von Colli – became increasingly prominent as agents of Palatine diplomacy, and the distinction between Palatine policy and Anhalt's own steadily diminished.

These Palatine activists shared a starkly ideological approach to European politics. Since the late 1560s, Heidelberg had been convinced of the existence of an international Catholic alliance led by the Habsburgs and the papacy which, once it had established a position of strength, would embark on a campaign to extirpate heresy throughout Europe. To the Palatine leaders, a major religious war seemed inevitable: to defend the Protestant cause, the Catholic revival would have to be combated at every stage, not only within the Empire but also through the creation of an international Protestant alliance.[1] During the later decades of the sixteenth century the Palatines had repeatedly sought alliances with England, the Dutch rebels and the Huguenots of France; but by the end of the century their diplomatic effort had failed to achieve its end.

Their relations were closest with the Dutch Republic. Here the confessional bond was further cemented by personal and dynastic connexions on a number of levels and by a shared strategic interest in the Rhineland. In 1593 Frederick IV had married Louisa-Juliana, half-sister of Maurice of Nassau, the leader of the Dutch Republic. Her uncle, Count John VI of Nassau-Dillenburg, was a leading member of the Palatine Council until his death in 1606. John's brother-in-law, John Albert, count of Solms-Brauenfels, became Palatine court chamberlain in 1602. The dynastic link with the house of Nassau, which brought the Palatinate into the central nexus of European princely Calvinism, was supplemented by the service of a number of Palatine officers in the Dutch army.[2] The shared interest in the Rhineland had first emerged during the course of the war for Cologne and the Spanish invasion of Westphalia (page 14 above); by the beginning of the seventeenth century it had found a new focus in the disputed succession to the Catholic and childless John William, duke of Cleves-Jülich and Berg, count of Ravensburg and Mark.

The territories were divided in religion (Jülich was strongly Catholic, while Calvinists and Lutherans were plentiful in Cleves, Ravensburg and Mark); but both the leading claimants, Elector John Sigismund of Brandenburg and Philip-Ludwig, duke of Pfalz-Neuburg, were Lutherans. The duchess, Antoinette of Lorraine, and the Jülich Estates were determined to prevent a Protestant succession, and they had been given assurances of support by the Elector of Cologne and (in the 1580s) by Philip II of Spain.[3] The Dutch and the Palatines were equally anxious to prevent a Spanish occupation of the duchies. Owing to strained relations between Neuburg and the Palatinate, the candidate favoured by both the latter and the Dutch was Brandenburg: but the Elector was prevented from making a formal alliance by a long-standing compact with the ruling families of Saxony and Hesse (the *Erbverein*), which did not permit outside treaties.[4] The best that could be arranged was a private agreement between the three in April 1605, in which the Dutch, in return for loans of

100,000 thalers from Brandenburg and the Palatinate, promised to occupy Cleves-Jülich on John Sigismund's behalf when the duke died.

Anhalt's diplomatic endeavours were by no means confined to Germany, although Palatine relations with England and France were less encouraging. An invitation to James I on his accession in 1603 to become the head of an international Protestant alliance had been politely refused, and he displayed little interest in German affairs.[5] Relations with Henry IV had been complicated by his conversion to Catholicism (in 1593) and by the tension between the French crown and the Huguenots. In 1591, Anhalt himself had led a military expedition to Henry's assistance – and was still owed 1.3 million thalers for his expenses – but the king now regarded international Protestant connexions with suspicion.[6] The main aim of his foreign policy was the prevention of a new religious war in Europe that would jeopardize the hard-won and still fragile civil peace in France. While he was prepared to support the German princes against the emperor, he was less happy about the confessional trend in Palatine policy. His suspicions were confirmed by the Palatine protection of the Huguenot duke of Bouillon, an old friend of Anhalt's and the husband of another Nassau princess, who had fled to Heidelberg in 1602, following his implication in a conspiracy against the crown. When he returned to his seat at Sedan in 1606, Bouillon was accompanied by the future Frederick V, who completed his education there. In retaliation for this flagrant support of a rebel, Henry refused Anhalt's invitation to participate in the 1605 agreement over Cleves-Jülich.

With his ambitious diplomacy thwarted, Anhalt turned his attention to the creation of a purely German alliance. In 1607 he concluded a treaty between the Palatinate, his nephews the margraves of Ansbach and Kulmbach, and the city of Nuremberg – ostensibly for the protection of the Upper Palatinate against an attack from Bavaria. The occupation of Donauwörth six months later provided him with an opportunity to expand this alliance into something more significant. The Lutheran princes had previously been as much alarmed by Palatine activism as they were by the Counter-Reformation; but Elector Christian II of Saxony (1591–1611) had refused to sponsor a Lutheran confessional alliance. In the absence of the Saxon leadership, the most active Lutheran prince was Pfalz-Neuburg, whose uncomfortable proximity to Bavaria, claim to the Cleves-Jülich succession, and enmity to the Palatinate made him all the more anxious to see a firm stand taken. To counter the Palatinate–Netherlands–

Brandenburg agreement of 1605, he had created his own alliance with the duke of Württemberg and the margrave of Baden-Durlach, both for mutual defence and for the protection of his interests in Cleves-Jülich. This alliance was aimed as much against Heidelberg as against Munich: but the occupation of Donauwörth persuaded Philip Ludwig that Maximilian was the greater threat. After the collapse of the Regensburg Diet in April 1608 he agreed to Ansbach's proposal that he merge his alliance into a wider Union. Neuburg's 1605 treaty provided the basis for the constitution of the Auhausen alliance (page 24 above) – the main differences being the exclusion of any commitment to support the claimants to the Cleves-Jülich succession and the addition of clauses on the one hand discouraging theological controversy between Lutherans and Calvinists and on the other limiting the duration of the alliance to ten years.

Yet the future of the Protestant Union was by no means clear. Apart from an implicit commitment to mutual defence against Bavaria, the alliance did not embody a common political programme. Of the eight founder-members, only Ansbach and (more hesitantly) Württemberg and Baden shared the Palatine conviction that a major religious conflict was inevitable. A general invitation to all the Protestant states of the Empire had been issued from Auhausen; but by the spring of 1609 only the counts of Oettingen and the cities of Strasbourg, Ulm and Nuremberg had applied to join. Nor did Anhalt's simultaneous attempt to expand the Union into an international alliance get very far. The Union Assembly at Rothenburg in August 1608 rejected his proposal to include Henry IV, while further invitations to James I, the Dutch Republic and Christian IV of Denmark were deferred.[7] Thereupon, Anhalt – initiating what was to become a constant and ultimately disastrous trend in Union politics – decided to proceed independently. In the autumn of 1608 the Palatine council voted to seek a marriage between Prince Frederick and James I's daughter Elizabeth, while Anhalt himself encouraged his friend Tschernembl, leader of the Austrian Protestant Estates, to look to the Union for support against his Habsburg overlord, if required.

The long-awaited demise of John William of Cleves-Jülich on 25 March 1609, fifteen days before the Twelve Years' Truce brought the war between Spain and the Dutch Republic to a temporary end, presented the alliance with its first test. Neuburg and Brandenburg immediately sent representatives to the duke's seat at Düsseldorf to claim possession of the duchies. They were resisted by the widowed duchess (supported by the Jülich

Estates), and on 2 April Rudolf II ordered that she was to remain as regent until he had resolved the succession dispute. The confidence of Neuburg and Brandenburg (now known as the 'princes pretendant') in the emperor's impartiality had been destroyed by the Donauwörth affair, however, and in June they agreed to seek independent arbitration and to govern jointly in the meantime. Rudolf declared this agreement invalid and commissioned his cousin Archduke Leopold, bishop of Strasbourg and Passau, to assist the duchess, empowering him to call, if necessary, on military assistance from the Spanish Netherlands. Leopold took command of the Catholic garrison of the fortress of Jülich on 23 July but then found himself blockaded by troops raised by the claimants.

Neither side wished to initiate hostilities: but Leopold's mobilization of reinforcements in the diocese of Passau, his visit to Brussels in October, and the foundation of the Catholic League (see below), all convinced the princes of the Union that their fears of a second Donauwörth affair were justified. In May 1609 the Union had agreed that while the alliance was not committed to support the claimants, members should provide assistance individually if requested; in November a meeting of the leading princes agreed to recommend to the next full Assembly that the Union as a body should reinforce the princes pretendant with 5,000 men. The justifications for intervention were outlined by the Palatine councillor Michael Loefenius:

> Even if the Jülich affair does not in itself involve the Union, the members should still do something immediately to ensure that those lands be preserved for the Protestant princes. If the lands were held by those princes, a good part of the Rhineland would be joined to the Union, while great dangers would result if they fell into the hands of the Spaniards. If the princes were left helpless, great damage would be done to the Union's reputation. When Protestant estates, like Donauwörth, whom the Union is not pledged to assist, are threatened by dangerous practices, it is the case that all the Protestant estates are limbs of one holy body and that the illness of one will affect the others. Help for Jülich will, therefore, benefit the inhabitants of Donauwörth and others in similar situations.[8]

Earlier in the autumn Brandenburg and Hesse-Kassel had tried to persuade Christian II of Saxony to support the claimants. When he refused, they declared the *Erbverein* terminated and applied to join the Union. In December Anhalt himself went to Paris to discuss French intervention with Henry IV; simultaneously, other approaches were made to James I and the States-General.

The Union's intervention was confirmed by the Assembly held at Schwäbisch Hall in January and February 1610 – but not without some significant debate. Ansbach welcomed intervention with the confident assertion that 'with Donauwörth, the whole burden lay on us; but with Jülich, we will bring in France, the States-General, England and others'. But only he and Baden supported Anhalt's proposal that the Union commit itself publicly to the cause of the princes.[9] Hesse-Kassel, Württemberg and Neuburg, worried that a major conflict might result, wanted only an informal agreement to provide military assistance. On 4 February, Anhalt revealed Henry IV's offer to send troops to the siege of Jülich and to mount major diversionary campaigns in the Netherlands and northern Italy to prevent Spanish intervention. As he had hoped, this offer temporarily pacified those members who feared an open confrontation with Spain, and the Assembly in the end agreed to adopt the proposal to raise 5,000 men. The expenses incurred in the levy were to be considered a loan to Brandenburg and Neuburg.

The intervention of Henry IV transformed the Cleves-Jülich affair from an Imperial to an international crisis. At the time, the English diplomat Sir Ralph Winwood considered the king's decision to be 'a deeper mystery than every man's capacity can conceive and a project more strange than any man (I think) will easily believe'.[10] Henry's motives have remained the subject of considerable debate, but the theories most often advanced – the implementation of a Grand Design, or the flight of Charlotte de Montmorency to Brussels in November 1609 – provide less convincing an explanation of his decision than do the continuing dilemmas of French foreign policy. The crisis over Cleves-Jülich threatened to provoke the European religious war Henry feared so much; by intervening in force, he could regain control of the Union before the situation got out of hand. In this respect, the conditions attached to his offer of military support, which included a demand that the Union sever its contacts with the Huguenots, are revealing. In the event, the wider war did not take place. Spain decided not to endanger the Twelve Years' Truce by intervening in Germany, while the assassination of Henry IV on 14 May 1610 brought the more ambitious French manoeuvres to a halt. Military operations were limited to a short siege of Jülich by a composite army of French, Dutch, English and Union troops;

Archduke Leopold surrendered on 1 September. Nevertheless, the impact of the crisis, both upon the Union and upon the Empire as a whole, was considerable.

The willingness of the Union to resort to force in 1609–10 finally persuaded the leading ecclesiastical princes (who had resisted earlier appeals for a Catholic alliance from the bishop of Würzburg and the papal agent in Germany, the Palatine *émigré* Caspar Scioppius) to take measures for their own defence. During the sixteenth century the dukes of Bavaria had sponsored several confessional associations, but the last of these, the League of Landsberg, had been dissolved in 1599 as a consequence of the near-bankruptcy of Bavaria after the war for Cologne. Maximilian, made cautious by his father's experience, would only agree to a new alliance if he were provided with guarantees that the financial burden would be more equally shared. In the treaty of Munich, signed on 10 July 1609, the members of the new Catholic League gave Maximilian control over a centralized war-chest and command over any troops raised. The original members – Archduke Leopold, the bishops of Würzburg, Augsburg, Regensburg and Constance, the abbot of Kempten and the prior of Ellwangen – were all near-neighbours to Bavaria; but in the autumn, fear of war in the Rhineland brought in the bishops of Speyer, Worms and Bamberg and, most significantly, the three ecclesiastical Electors. At this point, both the Electors of Cologne and Mainz exchanged French for Spanish pensions.[11]

But the League hesitated over intervention in the Cleves-Jülich crisis. Despite Archduke Leopold's appeals for assistance and Maximilian's willingness to support him, the majority of the prince-bishops regarded the alliance as defensive in purpose and were unwilling to go to war unless directly threatened. Nor did the subsidies Maximilian had requested from Philip III and the papacy arrive until August 1610. In September, fear that the war might spread after the fall of Jülich caused the League to mobilize an army of 19,000; but on 24 October, when it became clear that the Union had no further military ambitions, Maximilian agreed to a truce. On the other hand, the foundation of the League inspired a dramatic expansion of the Union's membership. The January 1610 Assembly saw the addition of Brandenburg, Hesse-Kassel, the brothers of Christian of Anhalt, the duke of Pfalz-Zweibrücken and thirteen Free Cities from the south and south-west. The now numerically superior urban contingent provided a substantial reinforcement to the more cautious princes, for the cities were predominantly Lutheran and had joined primarily out of fear of Bavaria and the League; they were uneasy about Anhalt's adventurous politics and highly conscious of their vulnerability to retaliation. The constitution adopted at the Assembly to deal with the new composition of the Union – which gave them only eight votes to the princes' twelve – did little to assuage their fears.[12]

These fears were not unjustified, for Anhalt was led by his apparent success in the Cleves-Jülich affair to make some major miscalculations. Unlike the approaches to Henry IV, those made by the Union to James I and the Dutch Republic had met with a cautious response. The Dutch (like Spain) were unwilling to jeopardize the Twelve Years' Truce by a costly unilateral intervention, despite the 1605 agreement, and did not commit troops until after Henry IV had mobilized.[13] James I had initially intended to offer his services as a mediator; only after he learnt of the French decision did he offer the service of English troops in the Dutch army. Anhalt, however, had been listening to Winwood and other English diplomats who viewed the crisis in the same terms that he did. On 17 October 1609 Winwood had written to the earl of Salisbury that

> The issue of this whole business, if slightly considered, may seem trivial and ordinary, but duly examined with all the consequences necessarily ensuing (if freely I may deliver my poor judgement) doth, as it shall be carried, uphold or cast down the greatness of the house of Austria and the church of Rome in these quarters.[14]

Fortified by the belief that an international Protestant alliance was there for the making, the Union princes had rejected Henry IV's terms in February 1610 and had decided instead to offer the presidency of the Union, together with a Palatine marriage alliance, to James I.[15]

An initial embassy to England in the spring of 1610 met with a cold response; a personal mission by Anhalt himself in October was no more successful. What caused James to change his mind and revise his opinions about the utility of a Palatine alliance was the course of events in France following the death of Henry IV, particularly the Franco-Spanish marriage treaty of March 1611. For a brief period in 1611–12 he took seriously the possibility that an international Catholic conspiracy had been created, and resolved to counteract it. The Anglo-Palatine marriage was arranged by the duke of Bouillon in the spring of 1611, and in the autumn James agreed to make a six-year defensive alliance with the Union. Although he declined to become its president, he encouraged the Union to make similar alliances with the United Provinces and Christian IV of Denmark. The Anglo-Union treaty was signed at Wesel in April 1612, the Netherlands–Union treaty at The Hague in May 1613.[16]

These international alliances became the corner-stone of Anhalt's future diplomacy, but they were only achieved at the expense of increased tension within the Union. The brink-manship of 1610 had frightened the cities, and the Dutch treaty (which they feared would involve them in a renewed Dutch–Spanish war) was ratified by the princes in 1614 in spite of their objections. They were also unhappy about the tendency of Anhalt and his allies to conduct the Union's diplomacy secretly and informally.[17] Their fears were shared by the smaller Lutheran princes, particularly Oettingen, Kulmbach and Neuburg: by 1613 the latter were seriously considering resignation. Neuburg's dis-enchantment was reinforced by the open rejection of his claims to direct the regency of the Palatinate following the death of Frederick IV on 8 September 1610. Suspicious of the Brandenburg–Palatine association, he looked increasingly to Saxony, Bavaria and the emperor to protect his claims to Cleves-Jülich. In 1613 he finally broke with the Union by remaining at the abortive Diet of Regensburg after the departure of the other Union representa-tives. His son Wolfgang William went further and converted to Catholicism on 19 July 1613 – later in the year he married Maximilian's sister (see Plate 3). According to one contem-porary report, Philip Ludwig 'strongly regretted and detested the apostasy of his son, but, considering that he had thrown himself into the arms of the papists to obtain his rights and claims, he avowed all, as if he had done well'.[18] The Cleves-Jülich crisis had also converted Christian II of Saxony (who had been appointed Imperial arbitrator in July 1610) and his son John George into open enemies of the Union. The Electors' hostility now prevented the Union from recruiting any of Saxony's client states in the north and north-east. Only Brandenburg drew closer; the conver-sion of John Sigismund to Calvinism in 1613 was followed three years later by the marriage of his son George William to Frederick V's sister Elizabeth (see Table 2).

Despite the growing dissensions in its ranks, Anhalt still hoped to use the Union to exploit the weaknesses of Imperial authority. He had seen the long struggle between Rudolf II and his brother Matthias for control of the Habsburg lands as the oppor-tunity both to prevent the election of Rudolf's other brother, Archduke Albert, ruler of the Spanish Netherlands, as his successor – Albert was a particular *bête noire* of Anhalt's – and to create an Imperial interregnum, in which the Elector Palatine, as the senior prince of the Empire, would play a leading role in Imperial affairs.[19] But Anhalt was unsure whether it would be more advantageous to offer the support of the Union to the weakened Rudolf or to the ostensibly more accommodating Matthias. He vacillated between the two, and the sudden death of Rudolf on 20 January 1612 and the uncontested succession of Matthias took him by surprise.

The election of Matthias provided an opportunity for his new chancellor, Melchior Khlesl, bishop of Vienna, to attempt to halt the drift toward confessional confrontation by reviving the traditional Imperial alliance with Mainz and Saxony. Khlesl wished to see both religious alliances dissolved and the League then converted into a wider non-confessional body under Imperial presidency which would include the Lutherans and, hopefully, isolate the Palatinate. He tried to win over such discontented Union members as Neuburg and Kulmbach and even offered Ansbach the command of the Imperial army in Hungary. The Union, however, stood firm. The Assembly at Rothenburg in March 1613 voted not to disband while the League was still in existence, and to ensure that a number of long-standing grievances were rectified. These now included the abolition of the *reservatum ecclesiasticum* (page 19 above), the restoration of independence to Donauwörth, and the recognition of the religious liberty of Aachen – where in 1612, after several years of agitation supported by the Union, a Catholic magistracy installed by Spanish troops in 1598 had been overthrown.[20] The Union representatives walked out of the Diet at Regensburg in August 1613, immediately after it opened, when it became clear that, while some judicial reforms might be made, their main demands would not be met.

Khlesl's proposals had a more immediate impact on the League. The League's membership had further expanded following the election of pro-Bavarian prelates in Salzburg and Eichstätt in 1612, but at the same time Maximilian's presidency was being increasingly challenged. The ecclesiastical Electors were highly conscious of their constitutional position, particularly Johann Schweikart von Kronberg of Mainz, the Imperial archchancellor, and, under his influence, the other Electors demanded the decentralization of the League into an Upper German directorate led by Bavaria and a Rhenish directorate under Mainz. Maximilian regarded decentralization with mixed feelings; but he was decidedly more unhappy about Mainz's further demand for Habsburg participation, which Philip III of Spain had also made a condition for his subsidy. Habsburg involvement, Maximilian considered, would turn the League into an instrument of Imperial policy and commit it to the subsidizing of wider Habsburg interests.[21] At the League Assembly held simultaneously with the Diet of Regensburg in 1613, Khlesl and Mainz managed to persuade a majority of the members to accept both decentralization and Imperial participation: Archduke Maximilian, the emperor's brother, was admitted, and a third directorate, the Austrian, created for him. Maximilian of Bavaria had strongly opposed this step, for he now regarded Habsburg participation as a means for Khlesl to achieve his ambition of opening the membership to Lutherans.[22] To protect his own position, in March 1614 he formed a private alliance with his particular followers: the wealthy and geographically compact ecclesiastical principalities of Würzburg, Bamberg, Eichstätt and Ellwangen.

Decentralization made the League an ineffective instrument. During the second Cleves-Jülich crisis of 1614, its response was disorganized and hesitant. Moreover, there were also serious disputes between the two Maximilians over the membership of the new Austrian directorate, particularly regarding the wealthy Swabian bishoprics, which Maximilian of Bavaria wished to retain in his own directorate. As a consequence of these and other discontents, he resigned from the League at the beginning of 1616. His departure removed the League's guiding genius, and when Matthias issued a formal demand for the dissolution of both alliances, in April 1617, Mainz and Archduke Maximilian disbanded it with the agreement of the membership. In the following month, Maximilian of Bavaria, at the request of his allies of 1614, created a purely local and private defence pact for mutual protection against the Union.[23]

Yet by then, the Union's weaknesses had also been fully exposed by the revival of tensions over the Cleves-Jülich settlement. In May 1614, deteriorating relations between Brandenburg and Neuburg caused the Dutch commander of the joint Neuburg–Brandenburg garrison of Jülich, Colonel Pithan, to summon Dutch reinforcements. Wolfgang William, suspecting a Dutch–Brandenburg conspiracy, then seized control of Düsseldorf and Pithan dismissed the Neuburgers from Jülich. The States-General attempted to mediate, but in August, at Wolfgang William's request, 15,000 troops from the Spanish Netherlands entered the duchies to secure Neuburg's control over the other towns.[24] As in 1609, the Dutch were unwilling to intervene on their own, but this time neither England nor France was prepared to take

military action. Both James I (increasingly under the influence of
the new Spanish ambassador in London, Don Diego Sarmiento de
Acuña, the future count of Gondomar) and Marie de Medici
(unwilling to jeopardize the Franco-Spanish marriage treaty)
sought instead to mediate in the dispute. Only after the Spaniards
captured the important Rhine crossing at Wesel did the Dutch
mobilize. Neither side wished for a war, however, and a truce was
made quickly at Xanten; after English and French envoys had
intervened, the truce became a full treaty in November. The
government of the duchies, pending a final settlement, was now
divided: Brandenburg received Cleves and Mark; Neuburg secured Jülich and Berg. Less easy to arrange was the mutual
evacuation of the Spanish and Dutch armies and, despite repeated
efforts by James I in 1615 and 1616, the Dutch remained in Jülich
and the Spaniards in Wesel.

The second Cleves-Jülich crisis had a number of ramifica-
tions. For James I, it was a comparatively successful settlement of
a potentially dangerous dispute, in concert with France and
Spain, and he was encouraged to see himself as the mediator of
future crises rather than as the leader of a confessional bloc. For
others in England, the United Provinces and Germany, the price
of mediation appeared to be the surrender of Protestant interests.
Frederick V reminded James that Spanish occupation of the
duchies created an effective barrier to the military cooperation
between the United Provinces and the Palatinate upon which the
Union's security ultimately rested.[25]

Within the alliance, the crisis brought the tension between
the cities and the princes to a head. In 1615 the cities flatly refused
to support a war over Brandenburg's claims in Cleves-Jülich and
the Elector was advised to seek future military assistance from the
Dutch. The full effects, however, were felt two years later. In
April 1617 the Union held a major Assembly at Heilbronn to
formulate the terms for the renewal of the original treaty which
was due to expire the following year. Since 1610 the composition
of the alliance had stabilized: only two further small cities had
joined; Neuburg and one city had resigned; and a limited treaty
had been made with the princes of the Lower Saxon Circle – who
were growing increasingly worried about the security of their
secularized ecclesiastical estates. More significantly, many of the
princes, especially Brandenburg, Ansbach, Württemberg and
Baden, were heavily in arrears with their contributions and the
alliance was now financially dependent on those of the cities. Led
by Nuremberg, Ulm and Strasbourg, the urban representatives did
not hesitate to use their financial power to dictate the terms of

the new treaty. The cities were given a veto over future military action by the alliance; the Union was prohibited from providing support for claims to other than the existing territories of its members; and, expressly to prevent any involvement in a renewal of the Dutch–Spanish war, the alliance was to last only until 14 May 1621, rather than 1625 as the princes had desired.[26] Brandenburg's interests in Cleves-Jülich were thus clearly excluded, and the Elector resigned soon afterwards.

The loss of one of the two leading princes and the increased power of the cities made the Union a much less impressive alliance than it had previously been; but, to Anhalt, its weakness was counterbalanced by the demise of the League. In any case, his attention was drawn once more to the Habsburg menace. During the invasion of Jülich the Spanish commander, Ambrosio Spínola, had been granted an Imperial commission to restore the Catholic magistracy to Aachen – an action that confirmed the Palatines in their suspicion that no Habsburg emperor would hesitate to use Spanish troops within the Empire, and convinced them that a non-Habsburg successor to Matthias would have to be found.[27] Their conviction was reinforced in 1617 by the discovery of the Habsburg family compact to support the candidacy of Archduke Ferdinand of Styria (page 41 below): Anhalt later commented that he would rather see a Turk or the Devil elected.[28] He may at one stage have hoped to see Frederick V crowned: James I later claimed that a scheme for the election of Frederick had been proposed to him in October 1610.[29] But there was no possibility of obtaining a majority for Frederick in the Electoral College and, in the hope of dividing the Catholic Electors, the Palatines turned instead to sponsoring the candidacy of Maximilian of Bavaria. Between 1616 and 1618 a long series of discussions was held between Heidelberg and Munich. Maximilian, however, could not be persuaded to act as a front for the Protestants, while both James I and Louis XIII made it clear that they would not support interference with the election of a Habsburg.[30]

When the negotiations with Bavaria reached a stalemate, Anhalt returned to his earlier strategy of striking at the root of Imperial power by encouraging the Protestant Estates of Austria and Bohemia. During the winter of 1616–17 both Camerarius and Christoph von Dohna were sent to Prague to strengthen the contacts between Heidelberg and the Bohemian Protestants.[31] At the same time Anhalt had grown increasingly interested in forming an anti-Habsburg front in northern Italy with Venice and Savoy. His agents had been active in Venice since her great quarrel with the papacy in 1605–8; and, although Charles Emmanuel of Savoy had been distrusted in Calvinist circles since the 'Escalade' (his attempted assault on Geneva in 1602), the wars between Savoy and Spain over Montferrat between 1613 and 1617 suggested that he might be willing to join an anti-Habsburg alliance. Moreover, James I had been encouraging the Palatines to cultivate Savoy, while the attraction of closing the Alpine passes to Spain was difficult to resist.[32] In 1617, a former associate of Ansbach's, Ernest, count of Mansfeld, was permitted, as a gesture of good-will, to recruit a regiment for Charles Emmanuel in the territories of the Union.

By 1618, therefore, Anhalt was returning to the brink-manship of 1609–10, though this time he was not dealing with two small, if strategically important, duchies but with the future of the Empire. From his perspective, however, the challenge to the Habsburgs was not necessarily a desperate gamble. If recent events had exposed the weaknesses of the Union, he could take satisfaction from the collapse of the League amid internal discord. And if his foreign allies, particularly England and France, had proved to be less reliable than he had hoped, the dangers of acting in isolation could be set against the fact that a major war was due to recommence in the Low Countries on the expiration of the Twelve Years' Truce in 1621. England, if not France as well, would be forced to take the anti-Habsburg side. What he did not foresee was that the timing of his plans would be upset by the arrival, in May 1618, of unexpected and dramatic news from Prague.

iv The gathering storm

Rudolf II was broken in mind and body by his deposition in May 1611: in January 1612, barely sixty years old, he died. Later that year his brother and heir, Matthias, was elected Holy Roman Emperor and thus reunited under one sceptre all the lands and titles that Rudolf had once held. But his credentials for high office were not good. In 1577, despite the express prohibition of his family, he had journeyed secretly from Vienna to Brussels to become titular head of the Netherlands rebels against Philip II. But he found his position, in the words of a close adviser, 'a labyrinth, from which he expects his deeds to earn little thanks'. He was right: in 1581 he was forced by his own subjects to resign.

Next, Matthias went to Linz to serve as governor of Upper Austria for his brother. He was advised, to Rudolf's dismay, by several Calvinists, and in 1586–7 he went on a tour of northern Europe, including Protestant Denmark. In 1590 he moved his residence from Linz to Vienna, where his Reformed sympathies gradually declined as he came under the influence of Melchior Khlesl, bishop of Vienna; but he still lacked appeal in the eyes of hard-line Catholics. His conduct in 1608, playing off emperor against local Estates in order to win support for his cause, appalled Archduke Ferdinand of Styria: 'All Catholics very much lament it,' he wrote, 'but the Protestants are delighted.'[1]

Ferdinand, of course, had a vested interest in maintaining Imperial prestige: he regarded himself as next in line of succession, after the childless Matthias, both for the Imperial crown and for Austria, Bohemia and Hungary. But not everyone agreed, not even all members of the House of Habsburg. His relatives, and their advisers, found him too dependent on the Jesuits. The rector at Ingolstadt University, where Ferdinand's Bavarian mother had sent him, smugly observed of the young prince that 'nothing sown in this fertile soil seems to perish'; and in 1616 an exasperated Khlesl, trying to negotiate with Ferdinand over the succession, complained to Matthias that 'The court of Graz is ruled as much by the counsel of the Jesuits as by that of his advisers; they are with, around, and about the archduke day and night.'[2] And if this exemplary piety irritated his Habsburg cousins, it terrified the Protestants. Many of those expelled from Inner Austria in 1599–1600 had taken refuge in Bohemia and issued warnings of what Ferdinand's rule could mean; and before long the Court of Graz was in touch with beleaguered Catholics in other Habsburg provinces, encouraging firmness and welcoming converts. In Lower Austria, for example, the number of Catholic nobles rose from one-tenth to almost one-quarter of the total between 1580 and 1610, and in the latter year (much to Ferdinand's delight) sixty of them signed a league of association 'for the defence of God Almighty's faith and church'.[3] In the bishopric of Olomouc, covering much of Moravia, Cardinal Franz von Dietrichstein improved clerical standards, reformed monasteries and founded a seminary in order to strengthen the Roman church; he also strove ceaselessly to inconvenience the local Protestants. In all aspects of his Counter-Reformation he had the full support of the Court of Graz.[4] But after 1612 Ferdinand's religious zeal was tempered by three related political difficulties: the succession; the hostilities in northern Italy; and the threat of renewed war in the Netherlands.

At the centre of each problem was Spain. No sooner was Matthias crowned emperor than Philip III began discussions on the succession with his Austrian relatives. In October 1612, the king put forward his claim, as the only male grandchild of Maximilian II, to succeed to the Imperial title. He declared himself ready to waive these rights in favour of Ferdinand, but only in return for the cession of Alsace, Tyrol and certain Imperial territories in Italy. The price seemed too high to the archduke, and no agreement was reached; but when talks about the succession were resumed five years later, Ferdinand's bargaining position vis-à-vis Spain was far weaker. In 1615 a Venetian army with substantial Dutch and English reinforcements had begun the 'uzkok war' by laying siege to the archduke's city of Gradisca, and Ferdinand stood in desperate need of Spanish assistance.

The uzkok war was one of the more bizarre episodes of the earlier seventeenth century, yet it offered an alarming example of how a minor political conflict in a remote corner of Europe could threaten to engulf the whole continent with war. The defence of the Austrian frontier with the Turks was partially in the hands of refugees from the Balkans who had fled to the Habsburg lands: they were called 'uzkoks' (the Serbian word for 'refugees'). Some of them settled in the small ports of the eastern Adriatic, especially Zengg (Segna, captured in 1537), and kept the area free of Turkish shipping. Unfortunately for Ferdinand, his vassals kept the area free of Christian shipping, too: no one was safe from their piratical attacks, and Venetian merchantmen were a particularly frequent target. At first the Republic spent heavily on escorts for its fleets, on watch-towers, and on armament, appointing a special *capitano contra gli uscocchi* from 1575; but the cost soon became prohibitive (120,000 thalers annually in the 1590s, 200,000 in the 1600s, 360,000 by 1615). In addition, the uzkoks were now joined by others, including Spanish corsairs operating from the kingdom of Naples, so that, to a contemporary chronicler, it 'seemed as though all who sailed the sea had joined together in a plot to plunder Venetian shipping'.[5]

The Republic, somewhat unexpectedly, decided that the best form of defence was attack, and in December 1615 their forces crossed the Isonzo to besiege Gradisca. At the same time Venetian envoys abroad orchestrated a major diplomatic campaign for allies in the struggle against Ferdinand. In September 1616 Count John Ernest of Nassau-Siegen agreed to raise 3,000 men in the Dutch Republic for Venetian service against the archduke, and they arrived in May of the following year; six months later, some

2,000 more came, together with a contingent of English volunteers. Meanwhile a flotilla of ten English and twelve Dutch warships sailed into the Adriatic to prevent any aid from Spanish Naples reaching Ferdinand. No assistance could come to the archduke from Spanish Milan either, because of the outbreak of the 'war of Mantua'.

Mantua was an Imperial fief which could only be inherited by males so, when Duke Francis died in 1612 leaving a daughter but no sons, the state passed to his brother Ferdinand (see Table 1). But Montferrat, ruled by the Gonzaga dukes of Mantua for generations, apparently had no such restriction: succession through the female line was permitted. The state was therefore claimed by Francis's daughter, who solicited aid from the duke of Savoy (her grandfather).[6] Duke Ferdinand turned for support to the Habsburgs, but despite their assistance he was unable to secure all of Montferrat by the summer of 1615, when French diplomats negotiated a truce. But the following year, the French government (temporarily led by the bishop of Luçon, the future Cardinal Richelieu) and the Venetians offered to support Savoy if he should invade Montferrat again, thus tying down Spanish forces. The duke recruited widely, and his army eventually included 4,000 German Protestants, raised with the consent of the Union leaders by Count Ernest of Mansfeld, and perhaps 10,000 French volunteers. Although the governor of Spanish Lombardy managed to hold his own against this motley assortment until papal mediation secured a peace in October 1617, he was unable to assist Archduke Ferdinand against Venice.

So the archduke seemed set for a resounding defeat. With only 4,000 men in arms, beleaguered Gradisca seemed doomed unless he could find the money to raise more. In fact, only Spain could produce the subsidies that would avoid surrender, and the cession of Alsace and two Imperial enclaves in Italy (Finale Liguria and Piombino) now seemed a cheap price to pay in return for Spanish recognition of himself as heir to Matthias and a cash provision of almost 1 million thalers.[7] Accordingly, in March 1617, Ferdinand and the Spanish ambassador to the Imperial court, Count Oñate, concluded an agreement that formalized these terms. Next, with Spanish support in his pocket, Ferdinand joined the Emperor Matthias in Vienna, and together they travelled to Dresden to see John George of Saxony, 'to discuss something important concerning the welfare of the Empire' – namely the succession.[8] The Elector was obliging, and the Habsburg cavalcade proceeded first to Prague, and then to Bratislava, where Ferdinand was accepted in turn by the Estates of Bohemia and Hungary as 'king designate'. Things seemed to be going the archduke's way. Faced with Spain's military and diplomatic pressure, the Venetians reached an agreement with Ferdinand in the course of 1618, by which many of the uzkok pirates were executed or exiled, and a permanent Austrian garrison was installed in Zengg. Inner Austria was safe at last.

The uzkok war, although apparently minor, was important because it brought a general European conflict perceptibly nearer. On the diplomatic plane, it either cemented or occasioned alliances that favoured aggression: the easy cooperation of the Protestant Union with Savoy and Venice, and the apparent readiness of England and the Dutch Republic to send military assistance to distant allies, raised the spirits of militant Protestants everywhere; while the impressive and prompt support provided to Ferdinand by the king of Spain ended the decades of mistrust and misunderstanding that had divided the two main branches of the House of Habsburg. Even though Alsace never actually came into Spanish hands, the Oñate treaty created a framework within which Vienna and Madrid could work together to secure their joint interests both north and south of the Alps. Therein, however, lay a logistical problem: how could intention be turned into action? How could troops from Austria reach Lombardy, and vice versa? The western passes through the mountains were controlled by the hostile duke of Savoy; the central ones by the powerful but neutral Swiss cantons. Only the Alpine crossings controlled by the Protestant Grey Leagues (Graubünden), not yet a part of the Swiss confederation, seemed to offer a possible link between Spanish Lombardy and Habsburg Tyrol, thus affording access (if needed) to Alsace, Lorraine and eventually the Low Countries (see Map 2). There was, moreover, a major weakness in the Grey Leagues' position: the Catholic corridor of the Valtelline, which ran directly between Lake Como and the Inn. Already in 1572 and 1607 there had been revolts by the Catholics of the Valtelline against their Protestant masters, while in 1603 the Spanish government had constructed a major redoubt at the entrance to the valley: the 'Fuentes fort' (called after its founder, the count of Fuentes, who ruled Spanish Lombardy with a rod of iron from 1600 to 1610).[9] In 1618 there were further demonstrations by the Valtelliners against their Protestant masters which were so savagely repressed that many of the Catholic leaders were forced to flee to Innsbruck and Milan. There they set about convincing the representatives of both branches of the Habsburg family that a Catholic restoration was in their interest. They succeeded: in July 1620, while Habsburg troops sealed off both ends of the Valtelline, the Protestants of the area were massacred in a new rising and the Spaniards then marched in, creating a safe military corridor from Lombardy to Austria and northern Europe.

The new itinerary was urgently needed. The Twelve Years' Truce signed by Philip III in 1609 had not proved popular in Spain. Although the fighting ended in the Netherlands, enabling the Army of Flanders to be cut to a peace-time strength of 15,000, and although Dutch piracy in the North Sea virtually ceased, there was no reduction in the Republic's attacks on the Iberian overseas empires. Forts were established on the coast of Guyana in South America, on the Hudson river in North America, on the Gold Coast in Africa, and in many parts of southern Asia under the overall direction of the Dutch East India Company. In 1615–16 a fleet of six large warships sailed westabout to the Moluccas, raiding several Spanish colonies in America and destroying whatever Spanish and Portuguese vessels crossed its path. With the aid of such brutal tactics, the Dutch were soon able to export twice as much Asiatic pepper – the most valuable commodity in the spice trade – as the Portuguese. If these developments caused anger in Madrid, Dutch support for Spain's opponents in Europe produced outrage. As early as December 1616, the council of state had resolved that if Dutch troops were sent to aid the duke of Savoy, Spain would resume the war in the Netherlands.[10] Although this threat did not materialize, in March 1618 Philip III's ministers initiated an internal debate on whether or not to renew the Twelve Years' Truce when it expired, three years later. It was noted from the outset that the Dutch had prospered astoundingly, and there was a general feeling that there should be no renewal unless the terms of the truce, especially regarding overseas trade, could be changed in Spain's favour. In the oft-quoted (because cogent) formulation of Don Carlos Coloma, a commander of the Army of Flanders: 'If in twelve years of peace the Dutch have undertaken and achieved all this, we can easily see what they will do if we give them more time . . . If the truce is continued, we shall condemn ourselves to suffer at once all the evils of peace and all the dangers of war.'[11] It was thus becoming clear that a major war would start in Europe in the spring of 1621, and most political observers knew it. The events of 1618 in Bohemia merely anticipated that general conflict, bringing together the incipient but separate crises which had already polarized opinion in the Empire and in the Habsburg heartland.

In the winter of 1617–18, with Ferdinand safely – and unconditionally – elected king-designate by the Bohemian and

Hungarian Estates, the Imperial Court withdrew southwards to Vienna and left a committee of ten regents (seven of them staunch Catholics) to govern in Prague. Acting on orders from Ferdinand, the regents introduced a number of provocative measures: they established a censor's office in the capital to control printed literature; they prohibited the use of Catholic endowments to pay Protestant ministers; and they refused to admit non-Catholics to civil office. More inflammatory still, they ordered Protestant worship to stop in two towns – Broumov (Braunau) and Hroby (Klostergrab) – belonging to Catholic prelates (church lands were not specifically covered by the Letter of Majesty). Each of these measures increased the risk of a confrontation. Polyxena Lobkovic, wife of the chancellor of Bohemia, expressed the fears of many when she observed that 'Things were now swiftly coming to the pass where either the Papists would settle their score with the Protestants, or the Protestants with the Papists.'[12]

The leading roles in the gathering crisis were played almost entirely by members of Bohemia's landholding elite: some 200 nobles and about 1,000 knights. But this elite was neither united nor stable. It has been calculated that of sixty-nine families of peers holding lands in 1557, thirty-seven had entirely died out by 1615, making way for new men, such as Chancellor Lobkovic, Cardinal Dietrichstein, or the leader of the 1617–18 council of regency, Vilém Slavata. Much has been made of this 'biological failure' of the Bohemian aristocracy; but more important by far was the fact that the surviving families, and their new colleagues, acquired an increasing share of the lands of the kingdom. The peers had held less than half the total seigneurial lands in 1529; by 1619 they owned almost three-quarters.

It was amongst these great landowners that the Catholic church found most of its converts in the years before the revolt, and amongst them, too, that the Habsburgs' greatest supporters were numbered.[13] Those who stood up in 1618 for the Protestant religion and constitutional liberty tended to come from the ranks of the lesser nobles and the gentry, and they were acutely aware of their declining economic and political strength. Not least, they realized that their status under the Letter of Majesty was provisional. As Tschernembl, the leader of the Upper Austrian Estates, observed: 'what the prince can do, he can also undo.' It was to offset this inferiority that the Bohemian leaders began to search for allies abroad who would lend them moral – and, if necessary, political and even military – support. The list of contributors to the cost of building a new Protestant church in the Old Town of Prague in 1610 – one of the three to be erected in the city after the Letter of Majesty – gives a good idea of where the Estates were looking for support. James I of England headed the list, with a donation of over 3,000 thalers; then came the Electors of Saxony, Brandenburg and the Palatinate, the rulers of Brunswick, Hesse and Württemberg, and so on. The list reads like a roll-call of important Protestant princes, both Lutheran and Calvinist.[14] Nor was it merely religion that brought the Habsburgs' Protestant subjects into contact with foreign sympathizers: there was also the pursuit of education and learning. In 1622, Ferdinand blamed 'the subversive Calvinist schools' for the revolt of Bohemia, because the nobles of the kingdom had there, 'in their youth, imbibed the spirit of rebellion and opposition to lawful authority'.[15] In fact, well over 200 students from Bohemia and Moravia attended the universities of Heidelberg, Geneva and Basel between 1574 and 1620, 'imbibing' (among other works) Duplessis Mornay's *A Defence of Liberty against Tyrants* and Beza's *Rights of Rulers over Their Subjects*. It was a Moravian nobleman who in 1605 purchased Beza's entire library and took it home with him. Even more Bohemian students – over 300 in all – enrolled during the same period at the radical Lutheran universities of Jena (in Saxe-Weimar) and Altdorf (just outside Nuremberg): a dozen of them later became members of the rebel government. The professors of both institutions declared their support for the rebels' cause in 1619–20, and some even went so far as to criticize in public the pro-Habsburg stance of the universities of Leipzig and Wittenberg in Electoral Saxony. A degree from Jena or Altdorf must indeed have seemed to Ferdinand like a diploma in revolutionary studies![16]

The radical professors, however, were merely reflecting the prejudices of their powerful patrons. Jena constantly criticized Wittenberg because the dukes of Saxe-Weimar were implacable opponents of both the Habsburgs and Electoral Saxony.[17] Altdorf supported the cause of Bohemia because most of its students came from the nearby Upper Palatinate, governed from Amberg by Christian of Anhalt, the most active supporter of the anti-Habsburg cause, who propagated his policies by cultural as well as by political means. In 1617, at his suggestion, two literary societies with a distinctly Protestant bias were founded: the *Fruchtbringende Gesellschaft* (for the defence of the German tongue) at Weimar, and the *Ordre de la Palme d'Or* (for Calvinist nobles) at Amberg. Both soon came to include most of the supporters of Frederick V's bid for the Bohemian crown, many of them from outside the Empire.[18]

Naturally, the Bohemian leaders were much impressed by

Anhalt and his network of powerful and cultured friends. When, in 1618, they rashly decided to resist the emperor, without dobut they expected the mobilization of massive foreign support for their cause, much as had been done in 1616 and 1617 for Venice. But there was a fatal flaw in their calculations. Although viewed from Amberg, or Prague, a correspondent with similar tastes and beliefs might appear a political ally in peacetime, events were to show that there was a wide gap between intent and action when it came to war; and likewise it became clear that, whereas support for an independent state was permissible among the nations of Europe, support for rebels was not.

CHAPTER II

The indecisive war, 1618–1629

The events of the 1620s present historians of the Thirty Years' War with their greatest problem. On the one hand, the unprecedented success of the Catholic powers must be explained; on the other, the tortuous course of the Protestants' road to defeat must also be analysed. The latter task is the more difficult, because of the fragmentation of the Protestants' efforts. Until 1621, to be sure, there was a single focus to the struggle – the question of Bohemia; but, in that year, the war between Spain and the Dutch Republic resumed and Protestant Sweden attacked Catholic Poland. Although the progress of both these new conflicts was intimately connected with the evolution of the war in Germany, on the whole, until the end of the decade, they were conducted separately. Furthermore, in 1624, France intervened for the first time: she became involved in two of the existing wars, and she started an entirely new one of her own, in northern Italy and the Alpine valleys. But her participation was always intermittent and unpredictable. First there were the internal disorders caused by dissident nobles and militant Protestants; then there were the struggles of various power-groups for control of affairs. Both made a consistent foreign policy almost impossible to implement.

But France by no means stood alone in inconsistency. Most of the states which intervened in the war at this time also felt doubt about their grounds for doing so. Some political leaders perceived an international conspiracy ranged against them, drawn up along confessional lines and aimed at extirpating not only their liberty but also the entire religion to which they belonged. Others, however, claimed that the war was fought only for the sake of Frederick of the Palatinate – either to win him the title 'king of Bohemia' or, later, to win back his Electoral status. Factions which espoused these rival views could be found at almost every court of Europe. In France, the Catholic extremists (known as the *dévots*) called for intervention in favour of the emperor in order

47

to stem the Protestant tide, while in England, the Puritan leaders in Parliament urged their reluctant king to fight manfully for 'the Protestant cause'.[1] It was the same elsewhere: in Spain, in the Netherlands, in Sweden, in the princely courts of Germany (even in those of the principal antagonists, Frederick and Ferdinand) the interventionists and the isolationists wrestled. And since both interpretations were justifiable, and indeed seemed from time to time to be justified by events, no individual faction was able to monopolize the foreign policy of its government for long. That is why the course of European diplomacy in the 1620s (and to a lesser extent in the 1630s) is littered with repudiated negotiations and unratified treaties. That is also why the history of the first decade of the Thirty Years' War, which will be surveyed in this chapter mainly from the Protestants' standpoint, is so impossibly complicated.

i The war for Bohemia

The Defensors appointed in 1609 to maintain the precarious religious balance in Bohemia summoned a meeting of the Estates of the realm for 5 March 1618 to discuss the regents' anti-Protestant policies. There was particular concern about the grant of crown lands (protected by the Letter of Majesty) to Catholic prelates (who were apparently not bound by the Letter). Since 132 'royal' parishes had been transferred to the archbishop of Prague alone since 1611, the status of such lands under the Letter of Majesty was a question of some significance. The Prague assembly accordingly sent an urgent petition to the emperor asking for a change of policy. Matthias refused, and instead called on the delegates to disperse. Although they did so, it was agreed that a further meeting should be held in two months to consider developments. On 23 May, after only two days of debate, the assembly was again ordered to disperse at once. Since the command, which appeared to be unconstitutional (such meetings were certainly permitted by the royal concessions of 1609 and 1611), emanated from the council of regents which sat in the Hradschin, the incensed delegates marched to the palace, entered the council chamber, and (in conscious imitation of the events that began the Hussite revolution in 1418) hurled two of the most outspoken Catholic regents, and their secretary, out of the window. Next, the delegates appointed a provisional government of thirty-six Directors and authorized the levy of a small army, as had been done in 1611. For the third time in ten years, the Bohemians were in revolt.

News of the 'defenestration of Prague' struck most European courts like a bolt from the blue. All the diplomats attached to the Imperial court had followed Matthias from Prague to Vienna at the end of 1617, and so their dispatches over the winter contained scarcely a hint of the worsening crisis in Bohemia. When they heard the news, they tended to overreact. The Spanish ambassador, Count Oñate (who had only been in that post for one year), believed at first that 'The gravity of the offence, and the ease with which they have attained their object, will make them resolve to finish off what they have begun.' And his letters to Madrid – where news of the defenestration only arrived on 6 July – continued to exude an atmosphere of panic. By January 1619 Oñate had decided that only the arrival of a substantial Spanish army could save Bohemia: 'It seems to be necessary for Your Majesty to consider which will be of greater service to you,' he chided, 'the loss of these provinces or the dispatch of an army of fifteen to twenty thousand men to settle the matter.'[1]

It is unlikely that even these desperate pleas would have produced a favourable response in Madrid, had the king's council not come under the domination, at just this time, of the formidable Don Balthasar de Zúñiga. After distinguished service in the army (including the Armada campaign) and a long spell as ambassador in Brussels, Paris, Rome and (latterly) Vienna, Zúñiga had returned to Madrid in 1617, where he began to speak with unimpeachable authority concerning the affairs of northern Europe. Although his brief period of power appears, in the history books, as no more than an interlude between the more colourful supremacies of Lerma and Olivares, from early in 1618 until his death late in 1622 Zúñiga's first-hand knowledge of the terrain and the personalities involved were used to justify his own innovative foreign policy and to defeat that of his rivals, led by the duke of Lerma. For twenty years the duke had managed both Philip III and his government, but now his grip was failing. First he had yielded the role of royal favourite to his own son; now his decisions on Spain's overseas policies were being questioned. The man who had amassed a personal fortune of 44 million thalers (equivalent to Philip III's entire income for five years), and had built two palaces and founded eleven monasteries, three university chairs and two collegiate churches, was now publicly attacked for corruption. One of his principal advisers was arrested for murder and malversation of public funds. As protection against similar misfortunes, Lerma in the spring of 1618 decided to enter the church (securing a cardinalate), and he became anxious to retire from secular office. But before he went, he tried to salvage a project dear to his heart: the dispatch of a major naval expedition to Algiers.

The pirate kingdom of Algiers had been a thorn in Spain's side for almost a century, but in the early seventeenth century piratical attacks on shipping and raids on coastal settlements attained an unprecedented ferocity. The Madrid government therefore agreed that a major North African campaign would be undertaken in 1618; but now Zúñiga called for aid to Vienna instead. Clearly Spain could not afford both campaigns, especially not with the costly wars over Mantua and the uzkoks: a major decision on priorities became unavoidable. In July 1618, Lerma and his allies tried to prevent the dispatch of 200,000 thalers to the emperor, on the (entirely plausible) grounds that it would encourage him to take a firmer stand which might result in a prolonged war. Lerma lost. He lost again in September when, despite strong opposition, another 500,000 thalers were dispatched to Vienna; and he lost finally in January 1619 when the king reluctantly decided that the Algiers campaign would have to be abandoned in favour of aid to Vienna:

> Because it would be impossible to commit ourselves to both enterprises, and because of the risks involved, . . . if the aid to Bohemia is delayed, . . . it seems unavoidable that we must see to the latter.[2]

In May 1619 a force of 7,000 veterans from the Spanish Army of Flanders therefore marched across the Empire to Vienna, and by the end of Philip's reign (in March 1621) some 40,000 of his troops were assisting the Austrian Habsburgs. There was also a steady supply of money: 3.4 million thalers by July 1619; 6 million by the end of 1624.[3]

Spain's decisive stance, which was fully endorsed by the Archdukes in Brussels, encouraged the German Catholics to sink their differences and reactivate their League under the sole direction of Maximilian of Bavaria. Some Catholic princes declared their sympathies at once. The archbishop of Salzburg, for example, entertained Archduke Ferdinand in July 1619, on his way to the Electoral meeting at Frankfurt, with a military display, a waterfolly, a performance of Peri's *Orfeo* and – most important of all – a loan of 40,000 thalers.[4] But most other Catholics still hesitated to declare their support for Ferdinand in his struggle against the Bohemian rebels: most hoped to remain neutral, and only renewed fears that a 'Protestant international' existed forced their hand.

The wars over the uzkoks and Mantua, which were drawing to a close at the time of the defenestration of Prague, had already created important links between various anti-Habsburg powers. The news from Bohemia kept them in being. The duke of Savoy wrote, as soon as he heard the news, to the Elector Palatine to offer the services of the regiment Mansfeld had raised for him, through the good offices of the Protestant Union, the previous year. In August 1618 Frederick gratefully accepted and the Savoyard troops moved to Germany to await developments.[5] For a considerable period, they waited alone. The Protestant leaders – Frederick, Anhalt, Ansbach – were as surprised by the events in Bohemia as everyone else. Although they had considered the possibility of the Elector Palatine becoming king of Bohemia after Matthias, the pre-election of Ferdinand by the Estates seemed to settle the question of who ruled in Prague for at least another generation. Now, in mid-June, the Bohemian Estates wrote to the Protestant Union, asking to be admitted as full members and requesting military assistance. They hinted that the reward for timely aid would be the election of the Union's leader – Frederick – as their king, in place of Ferdinand. Unfortunately, this same hint was dropped to more than one aspirant – the hopes of the duke of Savoy, Bethlen Gabor of Transylvania, the Elector of Saxony and Frederick of the Palatinate were all raised – and the Bohemians' duplicity was gleefully made public by the Habsburgs, who seem to have intercepted and deciphered almost every letter leaving Prague for a foreign destination. But, for a time, indiscretion was immaterial: the rebellion prospered. In the summer of 1618, Lusatia, Silesia and Upper Austria joined Bohemia; and, in the summer of 1619, so did Moravia and Lower Austria. Only Hungary stood aloof, but the forces of Bethlen Gabor could be relied on to overcome loyalist elements there. In September 1618 Mansfeld and the duke of Savoy's regiment captured the stronghold of Pilsen. In May 1619 the army of the confederates, under Heinrich Matthias, Count Thurn (who had played a leading role in the defenestration) marched on Vienna and laid siege to it. At the same time, Christian of Anhalt visited Turin and persuaded the duke of Savoy to increase his financial support for the cause, while the Dutch and Venetian Republics talked about a mutual defence pact against Spain. But these successes alarmed the Catholics, and by June 1619 Ferdinand had secured enough support to permit an invasion of Bohemia.

The end of the uzkok war had freed the troops of the archduke for service further north, and throughout 1618 units were marched up to garrison the few towns that remained loyal. But there were still only 13,000 men, one-third of them in Spanish pay, and Ferdinand's principal commander, Count Bucquoy, urged his master to raise troops abroad – in the Spanish Netherlands (where Bucquoy had served his apprenticeship), in Lorraine, in Italy, in Croatia. Now, in the summer of 1619, with the aid of the subsidies from Spain and the papacy, the Imperial army numbered some 30,000 men, with reinforcements promised from Tuscany, Spanish Lombardy and the Spanish Netherlands. On 10 June, Bucquoy routed Mansfeld and his regiment at Záblatí in southern Bohemia, and cut off communications between Prague and Thurn's army around Vienna. The siege was lifted almost at once. Almost as serious for the rebel cause as these strategic reverses was the loss of their principal foreign supporter. Mansfeld's field chancery was captured by the Imperialists, revealing in detail the duke of Savoy's dealings with the Bohemians, the Dutch, the Venetians and the English. The embarrassed duke – already aware that he would not be elected king of Bohemia – hastily ended his subsidies (which had already cost him almost 40,000 thalers). But the rebellion continued without him. On 31 July 1619 the Estates of the crown of Bohemia signed a mutual pact of 100 articles, which created a federal union; shortly afterwards they signed a special treaty of alliance with the Estates of Upper and Lower Austria. On 22 August, the confederates solemnly deposed Ferdinand as their king and, despite support in some quarters for the rulers of Transylvania and Saxony, on the 26th they decided by an overwhelming majority to offer the crown to Frederick of the Palatinate.

It was in many ways an odd choice. Although part of Frederick's inheritance – the Upper Palatinate – bordered on Bohemia, it was a part he had rarely visited. Moreover Frederick was neither wealthy nor experienced. In 1622 a hostile observer, beleaguered for the Protestant cause in Frankenthal, questioned the wisdom of electing 'a man who had never seen either a battle or a corpse, . . . a prince who knew more about gardening than fighting'.[6] But three years previously this had seemed irrelevant: Frederick was one of the best-connected princes in Protestant Europe (see Table 2). It any ruler could mobilize confessional support, it was he.

Nonetheless, in August and September 1619, the young Elector was in a quandary, and his counsellors prepared conflicting papers of advice concerning the Bohemians' offer. The native

TABLE 2.1 *Frederick V of the Palatinate and his relatives I*

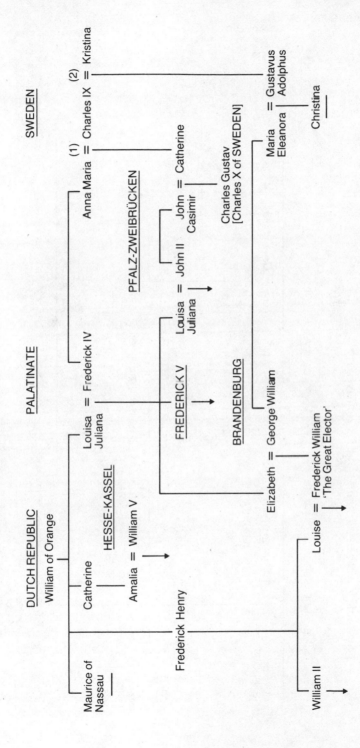

TABLE 2.2 *Frederick V of the Palatinate and his relatives II*

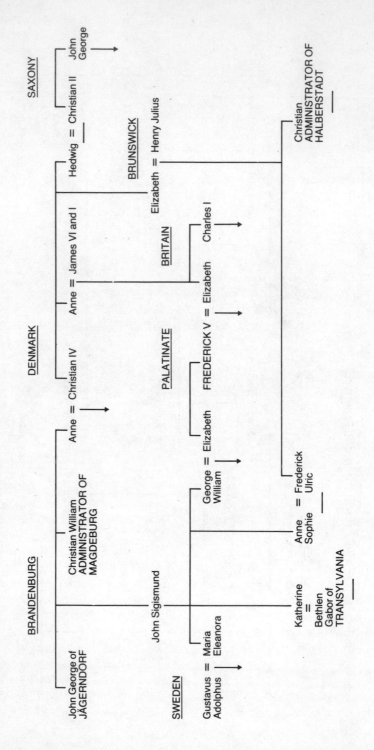

Palatine advisers on the whole concluded that, although there were several reasons in favour of acceptance, there were even more reasons against – including the probability that 'acceptance would begin a general religious war'. But the others, led by Anhalt and Camerarius, argued that war would come in any case: a general war seemed inevitable on the termination of the Twelve Years' Truce in the Netherlands, while everywhere there was evidence of a militant Catholic alliance, aimed at the destruction of Protestantism throughout central Europe. If the Bohemian revolt were suppressed, Camerarius and his friends argued, the kingdom's religious liberty would be ended; how long after that could the Protestants of Germany feel safe? It was a weighty consideration which was shared by many responsible foreign observers. Dudley Carleton, England's ambassador in The Hague, observed in September 1619 that 'this business of Bohemia is like to put all Christendom in combustion', and noted the Dutch leaders' deduction that 'since the revolution of the world is like to carry us out of this peaceable time, it is better to begin the change with advantage than with disadvantage'. For, if Bohemia were to be 'neglected and by consequence suppressed, the princes of the religion adjoining are like to bear the burden of a victorious army . . . Where it will stay', he added gloomily, 'God knows, being pushed on by the Jesuits and commanded by the new emperor, who flatters himself with prophecies of extirpating the reformed religion and restoring the Roman Church to the ancient greatness.'[7]

But by then the cause of Bohemia was again making good headway. Late in August, overcoming his chagrin at not being elected, Bethlen Gabor began the conquest of Habsburg Hungary. On 5 September he captured Kosiče, the capital of the eastern division of the kingdom, and was chosen 'protector of Hungary' by the Diet. News of this success seems to have tipped the scales for Frederick. Although he was, as he confessed to his wife at this time, 'in agony about what to do', on 28 September he accepted the Bohemian crown. The opportunity, he proclaimed, 'is a divine calling which I must not disobey. My only end is to serve God and His church.' And, for a time, it seemed as if the Lord had heard His servant. On 13 October, Bethlen defeated the last Habsburg army in Hungary, commanded by Ferdinand's brother Leopold, and soon afterwards entered the capital, Bratislava. From there, in November, the Transylvanians moved up the Danube, joining forces with Thurn's army in November to lay siege to Vienna a second time. Offers of further support arrived from several quarters. In December an envoy arrived in Bratislava from the new Turkish sultan, Osman II, offering military aid against the Habsburgs; and, after long arguments about the freedom of trade in the Adriatic, the Venetian and Dutch Republics signed a fifteen-year alliance during which each side promised to pay the other 30,000 thalers a month in case of attack.[8]

The political situation was now clearly out of hand, and many statesmen feared for the future. On 28 August 1619, at Frankfurt, the seven Imperial Electors decided to play safe and unanimously chose Archduke Ferdinand as the next Holy Roman Emperor. It was the most significant election since that of Charles V, exactly a century earlier, and the first since then to be seriously disputed. John George of Saxony, whose borders adjoined Bohemia and the Upper Palatinate, only agreed to vote for Ferdinand when, a week before the election, he was given a guarantee by the Brussels government that 'in case the Elector should be molested by the Bohemians, he will be aided and assisted by the troops that His Majesty [Philip III of Spain] has in Germany and, if it should be necessary, but some of the troops in this army also'.[9]

Some experienced observers hoped that the events at Frankfurt would bring about an end to the crisis in the Empire – and, indeed, in September the Army of Flanders stood down the troops which had been mobilized along the German frontier during the election. But Frederick's simultaneous acceptance of the Bohemian crown re-established the tension. So, from Frankfurt, Emperor Ferdinand went down to Munich, accompanied by the Spanish ambassador, Count Oñate, and a senior official of the Elector of Cologne, to discuss with Maximilian of Bavaria what assistance the newly reconstituted Catholic League could give to the Habsburg cause. Since the German Catholics were not prepared to intervene except with Spanish aid, the initiative rested almost entirely with Oñate; and he acted decisively. Without waiting to receive instructions from Madrid or Brussels, the ambassador promised the immediate dispatch of 1,000 cavalry troopers from the Netherlands to join the League, the transfer of substantial reinforcements from Spanish Italy to Austria, and the intervention in the Rhineland of a major army from the Low Countries. But Maximilian demanded still more, in return for a promise to commit the army of the League fully against Bohemia. So the ingenious Oñate persuaded Ferdinand to offer the duke not only a cash indemnity and a guarantee that the Habsburgs would play no part in League affairs, but also possession of any part of the Palatinate conquered by the League, and a promise that the Electoral dignity would be transferred from Frederick of the

Palatine to Bavaria. Since both men belonged to the Wittelsbach family, Oñate argued, and since Bavaria had some claim in law to both the land and the title, the transfer could be effected relatively easily. More practically, he added, Maximilian's armies would probably not make enough headway against the Protestant alliance to be able to claim these further rewards. So the treaty of Munich was signed on 8 October 1619, and on 5 December the leaders of the Catholic League authorized the levy of 25,000 troops, to be used as Maximilian thought fit.

Much had been promised by Oñate in the name of Spain, at a time when the governments in Madrid and Brussels were increasingly concerned with preparations for a new war with the Dutch. Zúñiga, at least, candidly admitted that he no longer knew whether the Twelve Years' Truce should be renewed or not. 'To convince ourselves that we can conquer the Dutch is to seek the impossible, to delude ourselves,' he lamented in April 1619, as he struggled to make the right decision.

> To those who put all blame for our troubles on to the Truce, and foresee great benefits from breaking it, we can say for certain that whether we end it or not we shall always be at a disadvantage. Affairs can get to a certain stage where every decision taken is for the worst, not through lack of good advice but because the situation is so desperate that no remedy can conceivably be found.

Spain's chief minister was scarcely more optimistic when he looked at the position in Germany:

> The situation demands [he claimed] that we should make all those supreme efforts that are normally made when one is confronted by total disaster, attempting to raise all possible resources to provide the archduke with what he is asking for, and attending to all the other matters in so far as it is humanly possible.

These and many other expressions of profound and complete disillusion in the last years of Philip III's reign read like quotations from a Calderonian tragedy.[10] For Zúñiga saw his dilemma all too clearly: unless Spain intervened massively in support for Ferdinand, the rebels would win, giving the Protestants control of the Empire and undermining Spain's position in Italy and the Netherlands; and yet, if massive aid were forthcoming, it might well provoke another conflict that would last as long as the Low Countries' War, if not (as some argued) for ever.[11]

But it was now too late for Spain to withdraw from Germany.

An agitated dispatch from Oñate, besieged in Vienna for a second time by the Transylvanian and confederate armies, arrived in Madrid early in 1620. The letter insisted yet again that, if the Austrian Habsburgs were to be saved, aid for Ferdinand was required on an unprecedented scale. Once more the ambassador's agitated voice could not be ignored, and it seemed to Philip III's council that the most effective way to take the pressure off Vienna was to mount a diversionary attack on the Rhine Palatinate. This would, in addition, make it more likely that the terms of the 'Oñate treaty' with Ferdinand would be implemented, delivering Alsace to Spain; and it would free the army of the League to campaign in Bohemia without fear of an attack from the rear. Accordingly, after some debate on size and timing, it was decided that, in the spring of 1620, an army of 20,000 veterans would march under the personal command of Ambrosio Spínola, from the Low Countries into the Palatinate. A crucial step in turning 'the revolt of Bohemia' into 'the Thirty Years' War' had been taken.

It was ironic that, because of the postal delays between Austria and Spain, Philip III's fateful decision was taken some time after the threat to Vienna had been lifted, On 27 November 1619, Bethlen Gabor received news that a large army from Poland had entered Upper Hungary and had cut his communications with Transylvania. In fact the report was greatly exaggerated, but it was enough to ruin the siege of Vienna: Bethlen hurried back to Hungary, so Thurn had to return to Bohemia. Although the Hungarian Diet at Bratislava elected the Transylvanian their 'prince' on 15 January 1620, his situation remained unfavourable. Bethlen had supported a large army for five months, although his principality was poor (it exported only cattle, salt and quicksilver, and a substantial portion of its wealth was surrendered every year in tribute to the sultan). To some, the prince's campaign had always seemed 'a torrent without a source'; and without urgent financial assistance from the rebel government in Prague, it was doomed to dry up.[12] But the confederates' resources were as depleted as Bethlen's own: they could not pay the 400,000 thalers that he demanded. Moreover the prince's chief asset had always been his vaunted role as mediator of Turkish aid to Ferdinand's enemies. Now Habsburg diplomats had persuaded the sultan to withdraw his support from the confederate cause, while the outbreak of hostilities between the Turks and Poland in 1619–21 prevented any Ottoman campaign up the Danube. So when an Imperial delegation offered a nine months' truce, which left Bethlen in temporary possession of his Hungarian conquests, the prince was pleased to accept (20 January 1620).

The neutralization of Transylvania was just one part of a careful campaign to isolate the rebels. Not only had Spain been persuaded to contribute men and money on a grand scale to the emperor (and, after April 1620, to the League, too); aid was also received from several Italian princes. The pope arranged a monthly subsidy of 8,000 thalers to Vienna from July 1618 and, by the end of the year 1620, 304,000 thalers had been dispatched; over the same period a further 204,000 were sent to the army of the League. Genoa also sent financial contributions and Tuscany sent troops. To be sure, Savoy and Venice were hostile but, alone, these two powers could do little. The only cause for alarm, in Habsburg eyes, was the promise of Dutch aid to Bohemia.

On several occasions in 1618 the States-General, the ruling body of the Dutch Republic, debated whether to accede to the confederates' request for assistance; but each time they declined. Their caution was well-founded: throughout the year, the Republic was paralysed by the struggle between the Estates of Holland, led by their Advocate, Johan van Oldenbarnevelt, and the Estates of the other provinces, led by Maurice of Nassau, the captain-general. Early in 1619 with Oldenbarnevelt arrested and his supporters scattered, the purged States-General resolved to provide a monthly subsidy of 25,000 thalers – but only for three months, and only as long as the Bohemians kept on fighting and the Dutch Republic remained at peace. In the event, the subsidy was continued (with great reluctance, and in the teeth of opposition from one or more of the inland provinces) until December 1620; but the States-General refused until it was too late to send troops into Germany either to aid Frederick of the Palatinate or to protect the Union. Worse still, although the States agreed that 'they will take such course by way of diversion that the Spanish troops in those provinces under the Archduke shall not be spared or have commodity to be employed into Germany', in fact they did nothing of the sort. Until almost the last moment they were fooled by Spínola into believing that his army's destination was Prague and not the Palatinate; and, when they realized the truth, the lack of support from England and the Protestant Union prevented any effective counteraction.[13]

After some hesitation, James I made public his distaste for the Bohemian venture of his son-in-law in the autumn of 1619. He refused to support attempts to collect money for Frederick's cause; he attempted to set himself up as a mediator between the two sides; and he urged the Union to remain aloof. But the Union was already in disarray. At a meeting in June 1619, the members resolved to raise an army of 11,000 men, but simply for defence against the League – 'to protect liberty and law' and 'to maintain our religion like true patriots'. But they would go no further, because 'one should not oppose the House of Austria lightly', especially not 'without either troops or money from England'.[14] At a further meeting of the Union in November, only the margraves of Ansbach and Baden supported Frederick's decision to accept the Bohemian crown (although others expressed readiness to defend themselves against the League). Other Protestant princes were equally cautious. Apart from the dukes of Saxe-Weimar, only the Calvinist Elector of Brandenburg offered encouragement, and he died at Christmas 1619. His young successor, George William, even though married to Frederick's sister, was unable to persuade the Lutheran Estates to continue his father's defiant policy. Since Brandenburg's public debt was one of the largest in Germany, without new taxes prudence was the only policy. The finances of John George of Saxony were scarcely better, a fact which the Catholic princes exploited to the full. At an Electoral meeting at Mühlhausen, called early in 1620 to prevent the 'Bohemian fire' from spreading into Germany, the Catholic Electors (including Ferdinand) promised that there would be no attempt to regain by force the secularized church lands in the Upper or Lower Saxon Circles until the princes in possession had received a legal hearing – always provided that those princes loyally supported the emperor. John George seemed reassured by the 'Mühlhausen guarantee' (20 March 1620), and so the emperor followed it with the offer of Lusatia as a pledge if the Elector would raise an army and capture it from the rebels. John George immediately agreed.

The final blow to the Protestant cause was dealt by France. Louis XIII had suffered rebellion and difficulties himself at the hands of his Protestant subjects, and he was therefore at first full of sympathy for Ferdinand's plight. At one point he impetuously offered to lead an army to aid his cousin. Although this resolve did not last, a high-powered diplomatic mission, led by the duke of Angoulême, was dispatched to Germany instead. Angoulême made first for Ulm, where the army of the League, under Maximilian of Bavaria's personal command, jockeyed for position with the troops of the Union under the margrave of Ansbach. Angoulême persuaded the two commanders to sign an undertaking to desist from mutual hostilities at once, and to withdraw their forces (the treaty of Ulm, 3 July 1620). He expected to negotiate a similar agreement between the emperor and Frederick, and moved on to Vienna; but here he was unsuccessful.

The cease-fire agreed at Ulm had given the emperor a decisive advantage, and he intended to use it: the Union army was compelled to meet Spínola's approaching host from the Netherlands; but the forces of the League, by contrast, were free to assist Ferdinand in the east. Accordingly, on 17 July, just a fortnight after the treaty of Ulm, an army of 30,000 League troops (which included many notable volunteers, the philosopher Descartes among them) was led by Count Tilly into Upper Austria. Within two weeks, the duchy had fallen and Tilly joined forces with the Imperialists under Bucquoy, now masters of Lower Austria. In the north, the Saxons occupied Lusatia with scarcely a blow (only Bautzen resisted – see Plate 4); while, in the west, Spínola made a leisurely progress through the Palatinate. The Union forces were heavily outnumbered and only small contingents reached them from England and the Netherlands. Small wonder that the duke of Angoulême's efforts to interest Ferdinand in peace talks fell flat: there was 'nothing more to be gained from treaties', the duke was informed, since the emperor was 'resolved to secure complete obedience from his subjects, and this could only be assured by the sword'.[15] Accordingly the troops under Tilly and Bucquoy, with the duke of Bavaria in attendance, advanced inexorably into Bohemia, seeking a decisive engagement with the enemy's main army (jointly commanded by Anhalt, Mansfeld and Thurn). On 8 November 1620 the rebels made a desperate stand on the White Mountain, just beyond the walls of Prague. It took only an hour for the Catholics to secure a total victory. The revolt of Bohemia was over.

ii Europe and the Palatine war

The loss of soldiers was not much unequal, but the loss of cannon, the baggage, reputation, is the Imperialists' victory who, as it seems, hold Bohemia now by conquest, and all immunities [and] privileges [are now] void. And if a new establishment by petition shall be obtained, it will be only the Law of the Conqueror, who doth already finely call those of the [Protestant] Religion to account for what they have, and put it into safe keeping; so that they taste already their condition to come.[1]

Sir Edward Conway's prophecy concerning the consequences of the Bohemians' defeat at the White Mountain was to prove entirely accurate: the Law of the Conqueror was indeed ruthlessly imposed on Bohemia (see Chapter III). But the 1620 campaign delivered more than just Bohemia into the victors' hands. Lusatia, Silesia, Moravia and Austria were all overrun, so was half of the Rhine Palatinate, while the Upper Palatinate lay defenceless. Yet these successes did not conclude the war: on the contrary they expanded it. Had the campaign resulted in a military stalemate, a compromise settlement might have been achieved. But, given the magnitude of his defeat and the implacable nature of Habsburg hostility, Frederick of the Palatinate had nothing to lose by continued resistance.

The emperor was therefore faced with the problem of eradicating all support for Frederick from the Empire, without provoking a general European war in the process. In 1619 and 1620, his military success had been assured by a careful diplomatic campaign which shattered the pattern of alliances built up by the Palatine party and isolated Frederick from his more powerful potential supporters; but whether this diplomatic feat could be continued in the future was another question. Skilful propaganda could easily arouse fears of boundless Habsburg ambition. It had been done before – within five years of Charles V's great victory over the German Protestants at Mühlberg in 1547, all Imperial gains had been lost – and a similar change of fortune was not considered impossible after the White Mountain.[2]

The chances of this, however, at first seemed slim. Frederick's active German supporters had never been numerous, and now some of these abandoned his cause – Anhalt and Ansbach led the way, making their peace with the emperor in 1621.[3] Only a handful of princes, of whom the most important were the dukes of Saxe-Weimar and Christian of Brunswick-Wolfenbüttel, administrator of the secularized bishopric of Halberstadt, still espoused the Palatine cause without reservation. Margrave George of Baden remained neutral in 1621 through fear that open defiance of the emperor would lead to his deposition in favour of the rival, Catholic, branch of the family (and he only went to war in 1622 because he became convinced that, whatever course he took, his deposition would follow Frederick's defeat). Similar considerations deterred the Calvinist rulers of Hesse-Kassel and Brandenburg from mobilizing in support of the Palatine cause: the former feared deposition in favour of the strongly Imperialist (and Lutheran) ruler of Hesse-Darmstadt; the latter was inhibited by his strongly Lutheran and neutralist Estates.

John George of Saxony, with Lusatia and the Mühlhausen Guarantee in his pocket, did his utmost to prevent all other Lutheran rulers from assisting Frederick's cause in any way.

This persistent failure to win over a significant body of German Protestant opinion made Frederick all the more dependent upon the same foreign allies who had failed him in 1619–20. His uncle, Maurice of Nassau, arranged a splendid welcome for the Elector when he visited The Hague in April 1621, and allowed him to establish his court-in-exile there. But at precisely this moment the Twelve Years' Truce ran out, and various half-hearted attempts to renew it proved unsuccessful. The States-General, therefore, only agreed to continue their monthly subsidy to Frederick on the understanding that he would also secure aid from England. With Spínola and his veterans returning victorious from the Palatinate, the States-General would take no chances: they might lend army officers, and advance credit for the purchase of arms, but they could not afford to become the paymaster of the Protestant cause.[4]

Christian of Denmark also maintained a prudent stance. Admittedly in 1618–19 he had allowed a number of his officers to serve the Bohemian Estates, while others later served with Mansfeld; and in 1620 he had loaned money to Frederick and his allies. But he faced substantial opposition from his council to any further action (see pages 72–4 below), and he had considerable misgivings about his nephew's rash attempt to 'overthrow kings and seize kingdoms'. At the assembly of the Lower Saxon Circle held at Segeberg in February 1621, he declared that he would only intervene if supported by England.[5]

So England served as the focus for Palatine – and, indeed, for all Protestant – diplomacy. There were many both at court and in Parliament who accepted the Palatine argument that on the success of Frederick's cause hung the fate of Protestantism. In June 1621 the House of Commons published a declaration supporting whatever military action would be necessary to defend 'the true professors of the same Christian religion professed by the Church of England in foreign parts . . . being touched with a true sense and fellow feeling of their distresses as members of the same body'.[6] The House looked for the creation of a coalition, based on an alliance between England and the Dutch Republic, to save the cause. James I, however, had no wish to see the Palatine issue turn into a general war of religion, and he had become convinced that the best way to preserve the peace was by a close alliance between himself and Spain, founded on the marriage of his son and heir, Prince Charles, to Philip IV's sister María. Although

James had indeed committed himself to the restoration of Frederick to the Palatinate, following the Spanish invasion in the autumn of 1620, he hoped to accomplish this as part of a wider diplomatic settlement. Paradoxically, therefore, England insisted on regarding the Palatine question as a purely German affair, yet at the same time attempted to link it to all sorts of other issues with which it really had no connexion.

At the beginning of 1621 James I attempted to negotiate a general suspension of arms in the Empire as a first step towards the desired full settlement, in which he hoped to obtain Frederick's restoration to the Palatinate in return for the surrender of his Bohemian claims. In April, a brief cease-fire was duly arranged at Mainz between the armies operating in the Palatinate, which lasted until July; but Frederick, encouraged it would seem by Maurice of Nassau, could not be persuaded to renounce his Bohemian pretensions unconditionally. The Habsburgs also proved obdurate. The death of Philip III on 31 March and of Archduke Albert on 15 July 1621 created something of a policy vacuum which left the initiative briefly with the Archduchess Isabella, Albert's widow, and her faithful general, Ambrosio Spínola. Both wished to complete the conquest of the Palatinate as soon as possible, and in this they received whole-hearted support from the emperor and the duke of Bavaria. The war was certainly going their way: as part of the Mainz armistice agreement, the Union had consented to disband its forces in return for an undertaking that their territories would not be attacked; and in May, the Union dissolved itself. This allowed Spínola to withdraw a large part of his army to the Netherlands, to meet any Dutch attack, yet still to leave some 11,000 men under Don Gonzalo Fernández de Córdoba to continue the conquest of the Palatinate. As soon as the Mainz armistice expired, they laid siege to Frankenthal, one of the three major fortresses (the others being Mannheim and Heidelberg) on which the retention of the Palatinate depended.

There were, at this time, still some forces loyal to the Elector in the east, but they did not survive for long. In the late summer of 1621, Tilly led the League army into the Upper Palatinate and occupied it with scarcely a struggle. Some of Frederick's troops decided to move eastwards and throw in their lot with Bethlen Gabor of Transylvania; but in January 1622 the prince made peace with the emperor at Nikolsburg. The rest of Frederick's soldiers, under Count Mansfeld, had marched to the relief of Frankenthal and in this they were successful. But Tilly was hard on their heels, and by the spring of 1622 the Catholics possessed overwhelming superiority in the Rhineland. Their advantage was consolidated when Spínola compelled the Dutch garrison of Jülich to surrender, thus blocking the route by which the Dutch Republic or England might send assistance to the Palatinate. But no such aid was in fact forthcoming. James I rejected his Parliament's demand for war against Spain in December 1621 and instead conducted a complex diplomatic quadrille designed to assemble all parties to the dispute at a general peace conference. At first, however, Frederick refused James's demands that he should cease fighting or else forfeit all English support.[7] Instead he allowed Mansfeld, in Alsace, to build up an army of 43,000 men by widespread recruiting among the Swiss Protestants and the French Huguenots. In April, they were joined by a further 11,000 men raised by George of Baden-Durlach. But the two armies failed to operate together and on 6 May, at Wimpfen on the Neckar, Córdoba and Tilly together inflicted heavy losses on Baden's army. The tables might have been turned, for Frederick could call upon a third army, raised by Christian of Brunswick in north Germany; but on 20 June the redoubtable Tilly intercepted this new force at Höchst on the Main and again caused heavy losses.

At last, Frederick was ready to negotiate. He dismissed Brunswick and Mansfeld on 13 July and retired to await the outcome of the general conference so desired by England, which had convened at Brussels.[8] The victorious Catholics, however, had now lost interest in negotiation. Tilly, under instruction from Maximilian, followed up his advantage: Heidelberg was stormed on 19 September; Mannheim surrendered on 2 November. The Brussels Conference broke up. Frankenthal was saved by the lateness of the season but, in March 1623, James I ordered its predominantly English garrison to hand the city over to officers of the Archduchess Isabella, who were to retain it until the peace conference reassembled.

James failed to realize that the Spaniards had no intention of surrendering their footholds in the Rhineland, for they offered an invaluable link between the Netherlands and the Alps. As long as the war with the Dutch lasted, the logistical problems of supplying the Army of Flanders with men, money and munitions made it imperative to preserve all reliable and secure military corridors between Lombardy, Spain, and the Low Countries (see Map 2). Exactly the same consideration made the Madrid government also reluctant to surrender control of the Valtelline, which had been occupied by force in 1620 (pages 42–3 above). But diplomatic pressure, this time from France, was building up for its restitution. From the first, Louis XIII had been begged to intervene by the Swiss Protestant cantons, Venice, and the Grey Leagues (the overlords of the Valtelline, to whose protection France had been committed by treaty since 1602). But the king was unable to help. He was compelled to concentrate on the revolt of some extreme Catholics, led by the Queen Mother (April–August 1620); afterwards, partly to placate these dissidents, he embarked on the forcible catholicization of the principality of Béarn in the Pyrenees (August 1620 – October 1622). By the time news of the Habsburg invasion of the Valtelline arrived, Louis had no resources to spare. At the end of 1621, the Grey Leagues therefore decided to act on their own, with some support from Bern, Zürich and Venice. They were totally defeated, and the victors occupied some of the Grey Leagues' lands as well. But French prestige was now at risk, and the 'Valtelline question' assumed much the same significance in Paris as the restoration of the Palatinate had acquired in London. In the autumn of 1622, following an agreement with the Huguenots, Louis XIII held a series of widely publicized meetings with the duke of Savoy and a Venetian embassy, from which emerged a triple alliance, known as the League of Lyons, pledged both to drive the Habsburgs out of the Grey Leagues' lands and to enforce Savoy's claims over Genoa and Montferrat (7 February 1623). Almost before the ink on the treaty had dried, Spain backed down. Her grip on the valleys had already been shaken by a new revolt during the summer of 1622, and in October the experienced Don Balthasar de Zúñiga died. His nephew and successor as chief minister, the count of Olivares, was not prepared to go to war with France for the sake of a remote Alpine valley. Accordingly, on 14 February 1623, he agreed that papal troops should take over the Valtelline for a transitional period of four months to allow Spanish forces to withdraw.[9]

By then, the attention of Europe had moved back from the Alps to the Palatinate. In the dark days of October 1619, with the prospect of defeat staring him in the face, the emperor had promised great rewards to Maximilian of Bavaria – above all, the transfer of both the Upper Palatinate and the Electoral title, in return for his military assistance against Frederick. The offer had been rashly made, on the assumption that Maximilian would never be able to mobilize an army strong enough to overcome the rebellion single-handed; but after the White Mountain, sooner or later the debt would have to be paid. By August 1621, Maximilian was already importunate and, as an English envoy in Germany noted, with Mansfeld still fighting in the west and Bethlen at large in the east, 'it may well be judged that this is not a fit season for the emperor to give the duke of Bavaria a pure negative'.[10] So

Ferdinand promised to effect the Electoral transfer at the next Imperial Diet, pending the approval of Saxony and Spain. But one of the couriers carrying news of this decision was captured by Mansfeld. The letters soon came into the hands of Frederick's principal counsellor, Ludwig Camerarius, who scored one of the publishing coups of the century by printing them in March 1622, with a damning commentary, in a book usually known under its Latin title, *Cancelleria Hispanica*.[11]

The popular outcry which followed this unsought publication of his plans persuaded Ferdinand that the transfer would have to be delayed, and in the meantime a remarkable task-force of diplomatic salesmen, all of them Capuchins, was provided by the papacy to convince the Catholic world, at least, that the transfer was in their best interests. Valeriano Magno was sent to Paris, Alexander of Hales went to Brussels, while Hyacinth of Casale engaged in ceaseless shuttle diplomacy between Munich, Vienna, Madrid and the Rhineland, covering almost 10,000 miles in the course of 1622. The importance which was attached to Hyacinth's work is revealed by the steady stream of letters the Capuchin received from the Bavarian chancery: nine between 25 November and 22 December alone, or more than two a week. And in the end, his efforts were successful. Father Hyacinth found the Spanish government opposed to the transfer (despite the fact that the idea had originally been suggested by its ambassador, Count Oñate); but the death of Don Balthasar de Zúñiga meant – as a Bavarian correspondent in Madrid was swift to note – that 'no one here has any understanding of German affairs'.[12] So the emperor felt able to overlook Spanish opposition to Maximilian's elevation to the Palatine Electorate, and in January 1623 a thinly attended assembly of princes (a *Deputationstag*) met at Regensburg to sanction the transfer. In view of the continuing opposition of Saxony and Brandenburg, however, after six weeks of heated debate the most that Ferdinand felt able to do publicly was grant Maximilian the dignity for his own life only, leaving the long-term future of the Palatinate unresolved.[13]

Yet even this was more than most European powers were prepared to stomach. Frederick deposed now found more supporters than he had ever done before. And he could make use of an army, still commanded by Mansfeld and Brunswick. After they had been summarily discharged from Palatine service in July 1622, the two commanders had entered Dutch employ and immediately performed useful deeds, first by defeating Córdoba's pursuing Spaniards at the battle of Fleurus (26 August) and subsequently by forcing Spínola and the Army of Flanders to raise

their siege of Bergen-op-Zoom (4 October). These successes persuaded the States-General to keep the allied army in being:
Mansfeld's troops were sent to winter quarters just across the
Dutch border in East Friesland, whose ruler had been flirting with
the Habsburgs. Mansfeld's unwelcome presence deprived Spínola
of a potential base in the north-east from which to invade the
Republic. Meanwhile, Frederick planned a new assault on the
emperor in order to recover his lands and titles. It was agreed that
Brunswick, with support from Mansfeld and the Dutch, would
approach Bohemia from the north while Bethlen Gabor, assisted
by a group of exiles under Count Thurn, would attack from the
east. The new campaign, however, scarcely got off the ground. In
May 1623, with the entire Palatinate finally under Habsburg
control, Tilly led his army northwards to the borders of Lower
Saxony, in order to block Brunswick's route to Bohemia. The
'mad Halberstadter' (as the Catholics called him) therefore
decided to lead his 21,000 men, most of them newly raised and
badly armed, to the Dutch Republic – as he had done, successfully, the previous year. This time, however, he was brought to
battle at Stadtlohn on 6 August and all but 6,000 of his troops were
wiped out. Tilly wanted to complete his victory by an attack on
Mansfeld, but the weather (together with the strength of Mansfeld's defences) frustrated him. Less impregnable, however, were
Mansfeld's finances. For most of 1623, he had existed on small
pensions paid him by the members of the League of Lyons as a
retainer, in case his troops should be required for a campaign in
the Valtelline. But when these ran out, at the beginning of 1624,
he had no alternative but to disband his army. Like Brunswick's
troops the previous year, most of his men immediately entered
Dutch service.

    Stadtlohn was the most decisive of all the Catholic victories.
Bethlen Gabor, abandoned by his allies, was obliged to make
peace again with the emperor; Frederick, on receiving the news of
his army's defeat, gave up all further military ambitions and
surrendered his cause without reservation to the mediation of
James I. But 'the English Solomon' was no longer prepared to
mediate. He had sought a 'Spanish Match' for his son Charles for
nearly six years, and had founded his hopes for a settlement of the
Palatine dispute upon this alliance with Spain. But in 1623 James
received a rude awakening. It came about through the romantic
secret journey to Madrid made in the spring by the young prince,
tired of the interminable diplomatic prelude to his marriage.
Accompanied by the duke of Buckingham (his father's chief
minister), Charles arrived at the Spanish court unannounced and

demanded a speedy conclusion of both the marriage treaty and the restoration of the Palatinate. The Spanish government was now forced to state its demands openly: the conversion to Catholicism of both Prince Charles and Frederick's heir. The English envoys were thunderstruck: such conditions had never been acceptable. In 1624 James therefore bowed to the demands of Parliament (and his son) that all negotiations with Spain should be broken off, and instead opened talks with the French government for a joint expeditionary force, to be led by Count Mansfeld, to regain the Rhine Palatinate for the deposed Elector.[14]

Frederick and his councillors, however, did not believe that this would be enough. Instead, Ludwig Camerarius was sent on a secret mission to Stockholm to discover whether the Swedish government was prepared to fight for the Palatine cause in Germany. King Gustavus was already known to be favourable: as early as 1618 he had begun to employ the Swedish clergy, through a regular series of days of intercession, to warn the population of the growing danger to the Protestant cause in continental Europe. Moreover the Palatine point of view was forcefully represented at Gustavus's court by Johan Casimir, duke of Pfalz-Zweibrücken, brother of the former administrator of the Palatinate and husband of the king's sister. But the desire for intervention was not shared by the rest of the Swedish council, led by Axel Oxenstierna: for them, the chief danger to Sweden came not from Germany but from Poland.[15]

Sigismund III of Poland, the emperor's brother-in-law, had become king of Sweden in 1592. After only a few years, he was deposed by a conspiracy led by his uncle, Duke Charles, who subsequently took the title of king and passed it on to his son Gustavus Adolphus. But Sigismund, representing the elder and legitimate Vasa line, never dropped his claim to the Swedish crown and aroused in the breasts of his younger cousins the sort of unease that, a century later, the Jacobite Pretenders to the British throne were to cause their Hanoverian relatives. However, whereas George I and his son waited to be attacked, Gustavus Adolphus took the war into the Pretender's camp. No sooner had Sweden made peace with Russia in 1617 than her army was directed into Polish Livonia. In autumn 1618 a truce was concluded, but only for two years; so a new Swedish assault in the spring of 1621 came as no surprise. The sophistication of the campaign, however, attracted international attention. The king crossed the Baltic to direct the siege of Riga in person, and he tried out several new military techniques – creeping barrage, total exclusion zones, all the latest techniques of siegecraft. The town fell. Gustavus seems to have hoped that he could barter Riga against Sigismund's claim to his throne and, to facilitate negotiations, a year's truce was agreed in July 1622, which was prolonged into 1624.[16]

It was during this hiatus that Camerarius arrived at Stockholm (November 1623) and was at once impressed by the personality of the young Gustavus – 'Gideon' he called him. 'I cannot praise adequately the heroic virtues of that king,' he wrote: 'piety, prudence, and resolution. He has no equal in Europe.'[17] Before Camerarius left the king's intoxicating presence, he believed the foundations of a general Protestant alliance under Swedish leadership had been laid, which would restore Frederick to Bohemia and install Gustavus Adolphus as the new Holy Roman Emperor.[18] But Sweden could not succeed alone, so the next targets for Frederick's diplomats were the Dutch Republic and France. Little could be expected from the former, for in the summer of 1624 the Army of Flanders began the siege of Breda in north Brabant and, for a whole year, the Republic's every effort was bent towards its relief. The Palatine court in exile therefore pinned its hopes increasingly on France, where in February 1624 the anti-Habsburg marquis of La Vieuville was appointed minister of foreign affairs. Almost at once, negotiations began between France and England not only for an alliance to restore Frederick but also for a marriage between Prince Charles and Louis XIII's sister, Henrietta Maria. Shortly afterwards, envoys were sent from Paris to the princes of Germany with offers of subsidies and promises of aid in case of need.[19] In June, the Franco-Dutch alliance, dormant since the execution of Oldenbarnevelt in 1619, was revived: by the treaty of Compiègne, in return for an immediate loan of 480,000 thalers, and the promise of further instalments, the Dutch agreed to continue their war against Spain for another three years.[20] Finally, the League of Lyons with Venice and Savoy was revived.

It did not escape the notice of Catholic extremists at the court of Louis XIII that the majority of these pacts were made with Protestants, and this was one reason why, in August 1624, La Vieuville was replaced by Cardinal Richelieu. But it needed more than a change of ministers to overcome the dilemmas of French foreign policy. While the Most Christian King might exploit the problems caused for the Habsburgs by the Protestant alliance being formed by Camerarius and his friends, he could not become a member. As Richelieu commented crossly to a confidant: 'We can neither contribute to [the restoration of Frederick of the Palatinate], because of our Catholic faith, nor deny it without being reproached by our allies'.[21] Likewise, Louis was obliged to reject the attempts of Maximilian of Bavaria (supported by the papacy) to place himself under French protection and thus become independent of the Habsburgs, because France could not yet bring herself to recognize Maximilian's new Electoral title. It was partly to escape these agonizing choices that Richelieu decided to concentrate on Italy rather than on Germany. In the autumn of 1624, using the pretext that papal forces had not been withdrawn from the Valtelline as agreed (page 66 above), French and Swiss troops invaded the lands of the Grey Leagues. They were surprisingly successful; so in the spring of 1625, with the Alps firmly under friendly control, Richelieu promised to send an army to join the duke of Savoy's siege of Genoa. Unfortunately, none of this was of much direct help to the opponents of Habsburg supremacy in Germany, and the Palatine politicians began to despair. However, at this critical juncture, a new power intervened to save them: the ambitious and wealthy Christian IV of Denmark.

iii The Danish intermezzo

Ever since the Augsburg settlement of 1555 the principal concern of Danish foreign policy had shifted from Germany to Sweden. Two major wars, in 1563–70 and 1611–13, had been fought to preserve Danish hegemony in Scandinavia and the *Dominium maris Baltici*, but by the second decade of the seventeenth century Sweden's expansion seemed to threaten both. After the 1590s the rulers of both countries abandoned attempts to settle their disputes by negotiation or mediation, and even in peacetime the Danish government spent heavily on defence and the fleet. During the first twenty-five years of the personal rule of Christian IV (from 1596), about 1 million thalers were spent on the fortifications of Copenhagen, Malmø and the fortresses along the Swedish frontier. Open conflict remained a permanent and immediate possibility.

Constitutionally, however, the king shared power with the council of state (*rigsraad*), representing in theory all Estates, but in fact exclusively recruited from the aristocratic élite. Basically, the balance of power and the chances of restricting monarchical emancipation lay with the council's right to vote or refuse extraordinary taxation, and its absolute veto concerning war. The core of the council's political programme, which in part reflected the interests of large-scale landowners, was the maintenance of peace with Sweden and the avoidance of any involvement in European alignments.

Of course, the council was equally worried by Sweden's Baltic expansion and by the Catholic victories in Germany after 1619, but it was reluctant to go to war over them. Although the council voted new taxes in 1624 to strengthen the garrisons along the Swedish frontier, it also prudently forced Christian to disband the small mercenary army raised to safeguard Danish neutrality against possible German infringements; under the circumstances it might have become a dangerous instrument in the monarch's hands. But aristocratic control over foreign policy had by then become an illusion. After the death of Frederick II in 1588 the regency government had succeeded in balancing the ordinary budget once more, and the favourable financial conditions laid the foundations for remarkable capital-formation in the royal Chamber over the following decades. By 1608 the ordinary budget surplus of Christian IV amounted to about 250,000 thalers annually (after all requirements had been met); more came from the tolls levied at Elsinore on international commercial shipping (200,000 thalers annually around 1620); but the largest single item was the war indemnity of 1 million thalers imposed on Sweden in 1613, and paid in instalments to the king in person until 1618.[1]

By 1618 Christian himself valued his assets at 1 million thalers, and he invested his profits prudently. In particular, between 1618 and 1624, a period of international economic crisis, the king lent over 400,000 thalers to noble landowners, thus binding the aristocratic council more closely to him politically. The formidable means at the king's disposal shattered the council's prospects of controlling royal foreign and military activities, for unless Christian remained dependent on their taxes, their power was at an end. By 1625 his total assets, including continental investments, approached 1.5 million thalers – enough to start a major war. With the exception of the queen-dowager Sophia's inexhaustible treasure chests (also accessible to her son), his only peer in Europe was, ironically, Maximilian of Bavaria, who could muster in 1618 around 4 million in cash. It was equally ironic that the Swedish war reparations contributed significantly to the formation of this royal fortune (see Plate 2).

Christian was drawn into the Thirty Years' War by two separate developments. First, his strong domestic position made him a valuable and important international figure. Initially, this counted against him: Sweden, fearful of further Danish aggression, signed in 1614 a defensive alliance with the Dutch Republic, whose ships made up over 60 per cent of the total traffic passing through the Sound. Dutch mercantile interests, ably championed by Johan van Oldenbarnevelt, therefore wished to weaken the Danish stranglehold on Baltic trade (amply demonstrated during the war of 1611–13) by increasing the power of Sweden. But in 1618, Oldenbarnevelt fell from power and the struggle in the Empire began; in 1621, the truce between the Dutch and Spain expired. The Republic now placed politics above trade, and chose to make a determined effort to enmesh Christian in the Protestant cause, lending tacit support to his dynastic ambitions in Germany. The king needed little encouragement; he was already deeply involved.

In his capacity as duke of Holstein, Christian exerted a not inconsiderable influence within the Lower Saxon Circle and he was anxious to extend it. In particular, he cast avaricious eyes on the secularized bishoprics of Bremen, Verden and Osnabrück (south-west of Holstein), not only because they would provide a handy appanage for his younger sons, but also as a means of establishing political and fiscal control over the estuaries of the Weser and the Elbe; furthermore, they would serve to counterbalance Sweden's expansion in the eastern Baltic, intensified since the peace of Stolbova (1617). In 1616, Christian scored an early success by constructing the fortress-port of Glückstadt above Hamburg; five years later, Hamburg was forced to recognize the suzerainty of the Danish crown. Next, the king spent at least 135,000 thalers from his private fortune 'to see that my son Frederick should come to the see of Verden'. This was achieved in 1623. The prince was already coadjutor of the archbishopric of Bremen.[2]

It would seem, therefore, that Danish foreign policy had achieved all its immediate aims by 1624. The Dutch–Swedish alliance had been broken; the king's position in north Germany was strong; and Denmark had, apparently at least, avoided engagement in the European maelstrom. Yet by the beginning of 1625, Denmark found herself at war with the emperor and his allies, in spite of the council's flat refusal to countenance armament and hostilities. Why?

The explanation should be sought principally in the policies of the ally-hungry supporters of Frederick of the Palatinate, who managed to exploit Scandinavian rivalries, and Christian's German ambitions, to the point where the king had to throw in his lot with them in order to safeguard the very structure of his political system in Scandinavia and north Germany. At first, Christian refused, at a conference convened at Segeberg (February 1621), to intervene alone against the emperor. He himself was willing, but he failed to enlist sufficient powerful allies abroad. So he merely loaned money: 300,000 thalers at James's request for the support of Frederick in 1621–2; a further 1 million thalers to other leading German Protestants (such as the Elector of Brandenburg and his nephews the dukes of Brunswick).[3] But most of these transactions were kept secret: the full range of the king's financial and political commitments, which so endangered the policy of non-intervention desired by the council, only became manifest in 1623–4. At first the council steadfastly persisted in its position, drawing a clear-cut line of demarcation between the 'engagements of the realm' and those of the king personally; but the situation changed totally in 1624, when the Dutch, English, Brandenburg and Palatine leaders resolved to invite Gustavus Adolphus of Sweden to lead a coalition army into Germany.

In November 1623, Gustavus had agreed with Ludwig Camerarius (page 70 above) that Sweden, backed by a general Protestant alliance, should descend the Vistula in order to invade Bohemia, restore Frederick and depose Ferdinand. However, the Elector of Brandenburg (Gustavus's brother-in-law) pointed out that a direct challenge to the emperor might alienate more support than it gained. Instead he proposed that Sweden intervene in the west and regain the Palatinate. Gustavus was prepared to accede to this change of strategy, provided that he was supplied with an army of 40,000 men (to which England, Sweden and the German princes would each contribute a third) and bases in the Lower Saxon Circle. But the king refused to allow France to become a full member of his proposed Protestant coalition, despite the fact that James I had already agreed to send a joint Anglo-French expeditionary force, led by Count Mansfeld, to the Palatinate; and he also refused to take part in any campaign in which he was not given full command of the armies.

These developments thoroughly alarmed Christian, for Denmark's relations with Sweden were strained at this time because of alleged or real Swedish violations of the treaty of 1613, and he feared that if his rival were entrusted with a large army, perhaps supported by the Dutch fleet, the Baltic would be turned into a Swedish lake. Accordingly, in January 1625, Christian offered to intervene himself, provided England would send 7,000 men to Denmark as part of an invasion force, and dispatch a diversionary campaign in the Low Countries (if necessary, led by the 'odious and suspect' Mansfeld). Still James hoped to secure the participation of both Sweden and Denmark, and it was to resolve their differences – as well as to make sure of continued French support – that he asked for a major conference of the allies to be held at The Hague in April 1625. But the death of both Maurice of Nassau and James in that month intervened and the conference was postponed until November.[4] None of this deterred Christian: he pressed ahead on his own, rashly assuming the role of Defender of the Protestant Faith. Early in 1625 he entered the war, in his capacity as duke of Holstein, without having secured binding promises of political and financial support from anyone.

Danish historians have traditionally labelled the intervention the product of the king's 'foolhardy' or 'childish' schemes. But neither this explanation nor recent attempts to argue that the royal enterprise was basically sound, failing only because of the council's systematic – and economically selfish – sabotage, can be maintained without serious reservations. It was more that the king's extraordinary freedom of financial operation left the way open for extensive activity beyond the range of constitutional control; and the fusion of Scandinavian rivalry for Baltic hegemony with the tortuous yet disruptive diplomacy of England, the Elector Palatine and the Dutch, played upon Christian's confessional conviction and personal ambition in a way that was hard to resist.

In defence of his decision to invade Germany, it must be said that the military situation in the spring of 1625 seemed disarmingly simple. The forces of the Catholic League and the emperor were on the borders of the Lower Saxon Circle; only the French (in the Valtelline), Mansfeld (in the Netherlands), Bethlen Gabor of Transylvania, and Charles Emmanuel of Savoy seemed prepared to take the field. Christian convinced himself that he must act before it was too late. In spite of the opposition of his council, he secured election as *Kreisoberst* of Lower Saxony in April 1625, pledged to defend the Circle against Imperial or League aggression. In June he led some 20,000 mercenaries, paid for the time being mainly by the king's personal fortune, across the Elbe and marched south to Hameln.

However, by a bizarre coincidence which is often overlooked, Christian had in fact chosen the worst possible moment to invade. So far, the Protestants' main enemy had been Tilly's army, financed largely by the Catholic League and billeted in Westphalia and Hesse. But in the spring of 1625, at the suggestion of the League's leaders, the emperor decided to raise a major campaign army of his own, entrusting the supreme command to a

Czech nobleman who had made enormous profits from the sale of confiscated estates in Bohemia: Wallenstein. With the aid of the resources from his new domains, of loans arranged by the Antwerp banker Hans de Witte, and of contributions extorted by his own troops, Wallenstein had by the summer raised some 30,000 men. This force, about which the Danes knew nothing, moved northwards into the territories of Magdeburg and Halberstadt. So now Christian, far from his home-base, had to face two armies, not one. Inevitably he was forced to fall back, only avoiding disaster because Tilly and Wallenstein quarrelled about the limits of their authority.

Christian now stood in desperate need of help, but his allies melted away. First came the collapse of the Anglo-French alliance. By the end of 1624, even before Christian intervened, Richelieu had withdrawn his support from the Mansfeld expedition. When the count landed in the Netherlands with 12,000 English levies in January 1625, he brought with him no plan of campaign other than the strict orders of James I that he was to engage in no military action outside the Palatinate. The dispute over Mansfeld coincided with the revolt of the Huguenot duke of Soubise in western France. Richelieu demanded naval assistance from England and the United Provinces as the price of his continued support for the anti-Habsburg cause, but cooperation in the repression of Protestants provoked a major public reaction in both countries. Trapped by the dilemmas of confessional politics, Richelieu changed course and abandoned the war: he refused to honour his commitment to the duke of Savoy, who had rashly invaded Genoa (Spain's ally and a crucial link in her Imperial communications), and he agreed to abandon the Valtelline to Spain, retaining only nebulous rights of transit for French troops (peace of Monzón, 5 May 1626). A few months later, the French government formally refused to join the anti-Habsburg alliance and, worse still, in March 1627 concluded an alliance with Spain to make war on England (page 105 below). In retaliation, Charles I offered support to Soubise, the Huguenot leader, and in July sent an expedition under the duke of Buckingham to foment rebellion in La Rochelle. For over a year, the siege of the port-city was a focus of European attention: England supported the Huguenots; Spain (briefly) and the Dutch (even more briefly) lent their aid to Louis XIII and Richelieu, who directed operations in person. Until La Rochelle surrendered, on 28 October 1628, France was powerless to intervene in affairs elsewhere.

In the summer of 1625, Gustavus Adolphus also deserted the coalition and embarked on an independent campaign against the king of Poland, first overrunning the rest of Livonia and then attacking Polish Prussia. In view of Gustavus's decision, Branden-burg returned to neutrality. More serious still, the new king of England, Charles I, also offered less to his allies. Although in April, just after his accession, he agreed to provide Christian IV with a monthly subsidy in lieu of an English contingent for his army, the dissolution of Parliament in 1625 gravely weakened his financial position. In the event, most of the available funds were used to equip the fleet sent to raid Cadiz in November, and even that was a miserable failure. Ninety Dutch and English ships, carrying some 9,000 men, failed to capture the treasure fleet from America, failed to destroy any Spanish shipping of note, and failed to take any enemy town. The return of the battered expedi-tion to England in November, having lost thirty ships and many men, did nothing to raise the level of enthusiasm in the country for another foreign venture.

So, in the autumn of 1625, it was only a rump of the grand alliance – England, Denmark and the United Provinces – which actually sent delegates to The Hague to discuss the next cam-paign against the Habsburgs. At first the English delegation, led by the duke of Buckingham, concentrated on trying to shift some of the financial burden on to their allies.[5] But in October Jacob Ulfeld, the chief negotiator for Denmark, made it plain that the appearance of Wallenstein's army had completely changed the nature of the problem, for if the theatre of war should move into northern Germany, the Danes might well have to arrange a separate peace with the emperor. A compromise was reached on 9 December 1625: the Hague Convention. England and the Dutch Republic each promised to pay 144,000 thalers to Denmark every month, and Mansfeld's army was to become a part of Christian's forces.[6] It was hoped that Bethlen Gabor – so far not in contact with Christian IV – would attack the emperor again, and France promised to pay the prince a subsidy should he do so.

Although coordinating and supplying trans-continental op-erations in the seventeenth century was not easy, the allies decided on an ambitious campaign for 1626. Mansfeld would advance down the Elbe into Silesia, ravage the Habsburg lands and join up with Bethlen Gabor; their united forces would draw Wallenstein after them, and defeat him. The Imperial victory at the Desssau Bridge in April 1626 delayed Mansfeld's departure, but in June he resumed his campaign and, according to the information relayed back to Christian's headquarters, succeeded in drawing Wallenstein after him. In July the king was greatly encouraged to learn of the widespread peasant revolt in Upper

Austria (page 93 below), which required the intervention of regular units of the Imperial and Bavarian armies before it could be contained. So in August, confident that only Tilly's army – equal to his own in quality and strength – lay between him and Vienna, Christian set out from Wolfenbüttel. His forces were to form one arm of a giant pincer movement towards the Habsburg heartland; Mansfeld and Bethlen were to be the other. But Christian was outnumbered and outgeneralled: Wallenstein had in fact left considerable forces behind in Lower Saxony, and Tilly had all the advantages of recent military experience. When, on 26 August 1626, after several days of heavy skirmishing in the rain, Christian brought Tilly to battle at Lutter-am-Barenberg, the laconic entry in the king's diary for that day reads: 'Fought with the enemy and lost. The same day I went to Wolfenbüttel.' To his army, retreating chaotically under constant enemy pressure and abandoned by their commander, his comment must have seemed something of an understatement.[7]

What exactly happened at Lutter is obscured by the plethora of pamphlets produced immediately after the battle by Tilly's field chancery – all of them stressing the inevitability of defeat for heretics who opposed the rightful emperor and his loyal host. By contrast, Protestant propaganda seems to have blamed – for internal political reasons – the defection of the cavalry at a crucial moment, and the ambushes laid behind Christian's lines. As far as one can see, Tilly's victory was due not so much to the superior quality of his troops as to tactical blunders on the side of the king. What is not in doubt, however, is the significance of Lutter: the fragile unity of the Lower Saxon Circle collapsed, and there was now nothing to stop the Catholic forces from invading Denmark. If the decisive campaign was delayed until 1627, that was merely to allow Wallenstein and the new Imperial army to get a share of the spoils.

Mansfeld had been no more successful than Christian. When he heard on 3 September 1626 of his colleague's defeat, he was in Silesia, with Wallenstein in hot pursuit. Deprived of his avenue of escape northwards, he resolved to join forces immediately with Bethlen Gabor. This he achieved within a week. Shortly afterwards, some contingents supplied by the Ottoman government arrived, and on 30 September the unlikely allies turned to face the Imperialists. But there was no battle, because Wallenstein (whose troops had suffered severe privations on their rapid march to Hungary) had not enough men and Bethlen Gabor (who had taken the field late) had not enough guns. It was the Transylvanian's last chance of a great victory: a few weeks later, news reached him that the Turks had suffered a massive defeat in the Near East – despite a siege lasting almost a year, the Ottoman army failed to recapture Baghdad, taken by the Persians in 1624. Bethlen realized at once how significant this reverse was for his own plans. 'I see that I must make peace' was his immediate comment: deprived by Lutter of aid from the west, and now deprived by Baghdad of support from the east, he could not afford to face the Habsburgs alone. The peace of Bratislava was signed early in 1627 and Wallenstein moved north-westwards into Mecklenburg, Pomerania and ultimately Jutland.

The emperor now demanded an awesome price for peace. The dukes of Mecklenburg, who had supported Christian, were summarily deprived of their titles, and Wallenstein was given the escheated duchy. Christian was required to cede all Jutland, to make extortionate reparations, and to renounce forever his territories in the Empire. Such extreme demands went too far. Christian was unwilling to accept them, and his allies could not afford to let him. England and the Dutch, who regarded a separate peace between Denmark and the emperor as a prelude to the collapse of their cause, sent fresh (though limited) supplies of men and money. Gustavus Adolphus signed a defensive alliance with his former rival, and even held an awkward personal meeting with him on their common frontier in February 1629, apparently with a view to frightening the enemy. But by then it was clear that the Imperial position, so impressive at the end of 1627, had begun to crack. Wallenstein's efforts to create an Imperial fleet in the Baltic, with Spanish aid, foundered when neither Poland nor the Hanseatic ports would cooperate. His attempt to dig a canal between the Baltic and the North Sea, which would allow shipping to avoid the Sound tolls, remained a pipe-dream. More important, the Imperial army failed to take the Danish islands – the necessary precondition of complete surrender; and it proved unable to capture the port of Stralsund, which contained a ready-made fleet, despite a prolonged siege (see page 99 below).

While Wallenstein strove unsuccessfully for his objectives, the cost of his army became intolerable to the German states. It was clear that the Empire needed peace as much as did Denmark, and negotiations therefore began in earnest at Lübeck. Now there was no question of war reparations or the cession of territory. At the peace, in May 1629, Christian regained all the territories he had lost and was confirmed in his right to levy tolls on the river Elbe. In return, the king promised never again to interfere in the internal affairs of the Empire, a purely personal bond that did not affect the political parameters within which he could – and did – operate on behalf of his successors.

So ended the Danish intermezzo. Exactly how much it cost is hard to estimate. Christian IV, who did not even attempt to make his forces live off the land like the armies of Wallenstein or Tilly, spent correspondingly more of his own money and that of the realm. 2.6 million thalers passed through his treasury during the two years of continental war alone. Most of it was raised in Denmark: the foreign subsidies only began to arrive in spring 1625, and were only paid reluctantly and in part (only 547,000 thalers of the English subsidy were ever paid). This figure does not include the subsidies paid either by Christian himself, or by the Western powers, to allies such as Mansfeld. In 1628 the council re-established its financial tutelage over the king: taxes for war purposes were voted only on condition that they should be administered by special commissioners elected by the council. This applied to the 700,000 thalers (or so) raised to pay the arrears of, or to disband, units in Denmark. When all the bills were paid, the government was faced with not inconsiderable debts both at home and abroad, so that Christian's German adventure might have cost his kingdoms between 6 and 8 million thalers in all.[8]

This was a serious blow, but its long-term consequences must not be exaggerated. True, Jutland (in particular its forests) had been devastated, and its population had been required to pay 2 million thalers, over only four months, to the Imperial army of occupation. The war therefore left much poverty and a legacy of social tension, not least directed against the nobles who had 'safeguarded' themselves by flight to the islands. Poor harvest, epidemic diseases and heavy taxation made a bad situation worse. But the post-war crisis did not last long. The continuing war in Germany created a market for Danish agricultural produce that enriched both merchants and large-scale cultivators, until Christian's anti-Swedish diplomacy provoked Lennart Torstensson's lightning attack upon Denmark in 1643 (see page 174 below).

If the war thus did little permanent damage to Denmark, what were its effects on her king? Again, the assessment must be negative. In international terms, Christian's defeats discredited him, while Sweden's victorious intervention after 1630 (with French, Russian and Dutch support) secured her the *Dominium maris Baltici* and allowed her to encircle Denmark – precisely the development that Christian had fought to avoid. The war had proved the vulnerability of Denmark's southern frontier for the first time; before long, others would exploit its weakness. On the domestic front, king and council recognized that there would now have to be more spending on defence, 'since . . . the impending danger is coming ever closer to our borders'; but they could not agree on who was to direct their foreign policy and control taxation.[9] In 1629, Christian blackmailed the council into approving taxes worth 1 million thalers, 'to repay his expenses on behalf of the realm during the war', by threatening that otherwise he would not ratify the peace of Lübeck. Apparently, the king had intended to restore by this manoeuvre his pre-war financial independence; he failed due to the council's systematic obstruction. By 1637 his 'ten barrels of gold' – as it was called by contemporaries – had vanished, and the need to establish a standing army for the first time enabled the Estates, resisting the explosive growth of taxation, successfully to insist that they should supervise the collection of tax revenues for military purposes through elected noble commissioners.[10] In 1645, after a second and far more fatal war, the commissioners also gained control of military expenditure. These developments – aided by economic depression from the 1640s – rather than the immediate consequences of the Danish intermezzo, started the country's period of decline.

What, then, had the Danish intermezzo achieved? Christian was discredited and defeated; Charles I, whose starving troops surrendered in April 1628, effectively withdrew from the war; Mansfeld and Bethlen Gabor, although technically undefeated, had been forced to withdraw from the war and both were dead by 1629. By then the Protestant cause was in ruins, but at least it had survived. It had also been transformed. Those who had argued that the Palatine cause was the same as the Protestant cause were vindicated; the leaders of Europe, whether Protestant or Catholic, were now convinced that the troubles of the 1620s were caused by more than the ambition and obstinacy of Frederick V. This changed vision was not, however, entirely due to the propaganda of the Palatine exiles or their allies. It owed far more to the actions and statements of the victorious Habsburgs, and their supporters, who left Europe in no doubt that they intended to exploit their successes to the full. After a century of standing on the defensive, the Catholics of Germany had many scores to settle.

CHAPTER III

The Habsburgs victorious

Never since the Reformation had all the major Catholic states of Europe combined effectively to extirpate heresy. Charles V had been consistently opposed by France and occasionally by the papacy; Philip II had been almost as much at loggerheads with his fellow-Catholics as with the Protestants. After 1619, by contrast, Ferdinand could count for a time on the active support of Spain, France, Poland, the German Catholics and the leading states of Italy in his wars against rebels and heretics alike. Gradually, it is true, these allies peeled away – Poland and France in 1621; the papacy and most of the Italian states in 1623 – but the Vienna–Brussels–Madrid axis, aided only by the German Catholic League, nevertheless continued to defeat their Protestant enemies. Eventually they were even able to mount impressive joint operations in both the Netherlands and Italy – although many of Ferdinand's councillors entertained profound doubts about the wisdom of such open aid to Spain.

Although it has become the convention, in histories of the Thirty Years' War, to examine the events of the 1620s mainly through the eyes of the defeated Protestants, such a view is both distorted and deceptive. It fails to take into account the patient labours of the victors to turn their temporary triumph into a permanent achievement, first in the reconquered lands of the rebels, and later in the Empire at large. It therefore also fails to explain how these activities, pursued for a full decade, eventually caused the isolation of the Habsburgs so that they could be decisively defeated. Re-examining the first decade of the war from the Catholic point of view is therefore essential, even though it means looking again at certain events, such as the crucial sieges of La Rochelle and Stralsund in 1628; for the same occurrence might take on an entirely different significance when seen through Catholic rather than Protestant eyes.

i The Imperial vision

The year 1620 represents a turning-point in Central European history. Yet it was not the brief and confused encounter on the field of the White Mountain which made that so, nor even the breathless and craven withdrawal of Frederick of the Palatinate. Rather, Emperor Ferdinand II took a series of personal decisions in the wake of his victory, which markedly altered the nature of Habsburg sovereignty in his own territories, as well as rendering a prolonged war in Germany much more likely.

In Bohemia his lieutenants instituted a programme which blended persecution with reorganization. However chaotically implemented at times, the plan bore the mark of an underlying consistency. First, the active participants in the rebellion were brought low, then the most dangerous ideological opponents, the Calvinist ministers, were expelled, followed closely by the Lutherans. Next came an assault on the Protestant towns, and finally, by 1627–8, the whole nobility faced a choice between conversion and exile. Meanwhile, trusted Imperial advisers hammered out a revised constitution for Bohemia and Moravia to enshrine and perpetuate the new royal powers: hereditary Habsburg rule, with enhanced legislative and judicial rights; the abolition of religious tolerance; officials made responsible to the sovereign rather than to the Estates; an exclusive royal prerogative to ennoble, and hence to bring foreigners into the administration; equality of the German language, which predominated at court, with Czech, which predominated among the people. And though Bohemia, as the main focus of contumacy, received the severest treatment, moves were afoot throughout the Habsburg lands to proscribe Protestants and enforce adherence to the new lines of policy. In Upper Austria a combination of Bavarian occupation and Imperial Counter-Reformation unleashed in 1626 the most violent peasant disturbances of the Thirty Years' War.

The man behind this policy has always puzzled historians. Not surprisingly, since contemporaries themselves formed very diverse judgments of Ferdinand. Some found him friendly and mild of manner – he was certainly not unsociable and could charm even those who disapproved of his actions; others stressed rather his toughness and inflexibility. Some saw him as self-reliant; others pointed to the role (benevolent or malignant, according to taste) of his confidants. But on one matter all could agree: the emperor's Catholic convictions amounted to a consuming passion. He attended Masses at all hours of the day and night; he revered the Blessed Virgin and the relics of saints; he showed conspicuous favour to the priesthood and to the institutions of the Church, especially its monasteries; he went on pilgrimages and endured self-abasement; his private life was a model of piety and familial virtue. This devotion was not merely common knowledge: it was publicly paraded, most of all at the end of Ferdinand's life in a celebrated homiletic tract by his Jesuit confessor, Lamormaini. Indeed, the ascetic faith lies at the root of all the emperor's political activity. Not for nothing did he restore the clergy to first place in Bohemia's constitutional hierarchy after the White Mountain. While he certainly thought that heresy would always breed insubordination in his realms, the resolve to extirpate it came first.

To understand the drama of the 1620s we need to return to Ferdinand's political origins. For, only a few years earlier, this international warlord, the king-emperor linked by family marriages with Spain and Poland, Bavaria, Mantua, and Tuscany, had still been merely a junior archduke, ruling in provincial Styria under the general aegis of the Habsburg house. There can be no doubt that Ferdinand was moulded by that experience, and that the capital of Inner Austria, Graz, continued to occupy pride of place in his affections: he personally supervised the building of a mausoleum there, where his remains were interred in 1637. As a youth, he had witnessed the fierce struggle of his parents, especially his zealous, formidable Bavarian mother, against the overbearing and self-righteous leaders of the Styrian Protestant Estates. He had observed how, in these circumstances, princely consolidation might march hand in hand with Catholic consolidation, splitting the ill-knit opposition camp of nobles, burghers, and preachers, leaning on the faint-hearted with multifarious forms of spiritual and material suasion, helped above all by a freshly established Jesuit university. On reaching his majority, fortified by a visit to the shrine at Loreto and a meeting with the pope, Ferdinand set out to perfect the methods of political Counter-Reformation. Between 1599 and 1602, his commissioners, lay and clerical, toured towns and villages, enforcing adherence to the Roman Church. The citizens had to swear a Catholic oath, to present evidence of absolution, to abandon all sectarian books and schooling. Those who proved intransigent were forced to accompany their Protestant ministers on the road into exile.

The gamble paid off triumphantly. Henceforth Austria's southern province remained obedient to the Habsburg will; the nobility, though still predominantly Lutheran, stood isolated and

pacific. Neither the heady events of 1608–9, nor the subsequent
insurrection, provoked it to any disloyalty. For his part, Ferdinand, confident now of a mission in the service of Mother
Church, bided his time, and intrigued with the extremer,
Spanish-Bavarian faction at the courts of his Imperial cousins,
Rudolf and Matthias. On gaining the succession, he removed to
Vienna eager to enforce a similar code of godly discipline upon a
wider homeland. Significantly, many of his closest associates had
likewise risen to political maturity in Graz: the chancellor Wer-
denberg, the confessor Lamormaini, above all the shrewd and
supple chief minister, Eggenberg. Within a very few years the
whole pattern was repeated: commissioners, confession-slips and
oaths, Jesuit-dominated education and censorship, pressure for
conformity, mixing blandishments towards those of higher social
standing with an unyielding assault on dissenters. Now the last
heretics in Styria too, however refined their pedigree, had to
make a choice; hundreds of them followed their consciences into
emigration in Germany.

The resulting solution has frequently been called 'confessional absolutism'. The term may serve, but we must rather define it
in negative terms, by demonstrating what it was *not*. In the first
place, it was no abstract political ideal. Ferdinand's notions
could be thoroughly legalistic, a kind of radical conservatism,
claiming that Protestant Estates in Central Europe had never
owned constitutional rights, and might therefore be dispossessed
at their sovereign's will. But one would search in vain amid the
thousands of pages compiled by the emperor's faithful diplomat
and chronicler, Count Khevenhüller, for any theoretical statement of such a principle, just as Vienna found no one in 1619 who
could adequately refute the well-argued *Apology* of the Bohemian rebels. Besides scraps from Jesuit authorities picked up
during his impeccably orthodox training at the Bavarian university of Ingolstadt, Ferdinand's mind was innocent of philosophy. He won through by determination married to practical
resource.

In the second place, confessional absolutism was not
theocracy. For all that he might trust in divine intervention, the
emperor kept his earthly clerical supporters on a tight rein. In
particular the stories from his enemies about domination by the
Jesuits were much exaggerated, and such power as Ferdinand
devolved upon them and their kind he devolved consciously and
willingly. Throughout his life he was made aware of the insepar-
ability of Church and politics when matters like sovereignty over
ecclesiastical lands were at stake. His Bavarian cousins ruled in a

string of German sees, his younger brothers Leopold and Charles both became bishops at an early age. The immediate cause of the revolt in Bohemia lay precisely at this intersection of clerical and lay spheres: if Protestants could now (since the Letter of Majesty) build churches on lands belonging to the crown, were they therefore entitled to build on monastic estates? Whereas Ferdinand backed to the hilt the claim that Catholic possessions were in this respect inviolable, he had no doubt about the practical corollary (however inconsistent in theory): that a *Catholic* sovereign could interfere with them. When Melchior Khlesl, long-serving councillor of Matthias and strongest arm of the Austrian Counter-Reformation till that time, tried as an elder statesman to negotiate a settlement with the insurgents, Ferdinand had him apprehended and forcibly detained in a distant abbey. Nor was he loath to pick a fight with Rome itself (whither Khlesl at length withdrew in dudgeon). The alienation between Ferdinand and Pope Urban VIII became a major international factor during the 1620s and 1630s. The Edict of Restitution made perfect sense, to Vienna at least, as an expression of the sovereign Imperial will, though it caused almost as much annoyance among some Catholics as among the Protestants.

Finally, confessional absolutism did not involve any consistent centralization of government or any clear view of a free-standing 'Habsburg Empire'. The 1620s indeed saw the creation of one new administrative organ, the Austrian court chancery. But its title did not (at this stage) imply any new political entity – the purpose was to circumvent the authority of Germany's arch-chancellor, the Catholic Elector of Mainz – still less any radical new conduct of business. In the Tyrol and Alsace, Ferdinand happily allowed his brother Leopold (now released from clerical vows) to rule with almost plenary powers; and when Leopold died in 1632, his widow, an Italian princess, took over. Even in Bohemia, once the dust had settled, the former institutions of government were seen to remain in practice largely intact. Everywhere local Estates, provided they adopted a Catholic and loyal stance, survived and even prospered.

Despite all the expulsions and the wave of ennoblements during the 1620s, the Habsburg system of government created no new social élite. Few military adventurers or court favourites gained a lasting foothold, while fresh titles largely adorned families already powerful somewhere within the Monarchy. Habsburg policies continued to be executed primarily by local notables (just a little more oligarchic than before), who adapted them to suit their own essentially provincial circumstances. Ferdinand might well reflect, as he remembered the dangerous Protestant confederations of the years before 1620, that efficient and central-ized government of such multifarious realms could easily call forth a correspondingly cohesive and international opposition. Besides, two further elements, vital for any royal absolutism worth the name, were lacking in the Habsburg lands. There existed no advanced network of financiers or entrepreneurs. Indeed, the emperor had already done his best to cripple commer-cial life by his destruction of the Protestant burgherdom (though he did show some favour to the Jews). Towards the end of his reign Ferdinand even nominated two abbots to be president of his treasury: the Counter-Reformation state was still conceived rather like a gigantic monastic latifundium. At the same time the army exercised no decisive public influence. Ferdinand himself hardly possessed better credentials as a soldier than his immedi-ate Imperial predecessors. The whole Wallenstein episode shows a lack of established channels of military control, as well as the fact that Imperial troops (like those of other countries) tended to win battles despite – and not because of – attempts to impose any religious or moral authority upon them.

The revived Habsburg Monarchy thus underwent only a moderate amount of structural change. By the 1630s the new ideological sanctions of the civil power, together with its triumphs abroad, tended to conceal the still shallow roots of the edifice. But one Achilles' heel was evident enough: royal Hun-gary. In Hungary the Turkish threat had faded for the time being, and been replaced by a national revolt against Austria on broadly Protestant lines. The princes of Transylvania, Bethlen Gabor and George Rákóczi, Calvinists with good Ottoman connections, found little difficulty in securing the allegiance of the ruling class over most of the Habsburg-controlled area, despite Ferdinand's election as king in 1618, just a few weeks after the defenestration of Prague. The Counter-Reformation in Hungary, which had done much to precipitate this disaffection, managed to stem the tide of rebellion during the 1620s, thanks to firm leadership from the indefatigable palatine, Nicholas Esterházy, and from the buoyant controversialist, Archbishop Pázmány. But the situation remained fragile: even the Catholic Church could not always be relied upon, and Esterházy and Pázmány stood at odds with each other on matters of principle. In the absence of deep reserves of loyalty, obedience to Ferdinand's regime was still conditional on good behaviour. Hungary might nevertheless have been pacified (plans were ready, to be drawn on later) if only the Habsburgs could disengage in Germany. But that antithesis was an unreal one for Ferdinand II. His greatest act of faith, faith in his own divine calling, involved claiming the patrimony of the Christian emperors undiminished. Beside the splendour of Charlemagne's legacy, the thorns in the holy crown of St Stephen seemed a mere provincial irritant.

Any account of the rebuilding of Catholic Austria must concentrate on Ferdinand II. But what of his talented son, Ferdinand III, whom posterity has so consistently neglected? The younger Ferdinand was reared in the struggle: born in the year when Matthias took up arms against Rudolf; crowned king of Hungary during a pause from the campaigns against Bethlen Gabor; king of Bohemia in the year of the new constitution; then the first Austrian Habsburg for generations personally to direct, at Nördlingen, a major military victory. Following his accession in 1637 he had to cling to the task, despite his private commitment to intellectual and artistic pursuits (he was, for example, the founder of his family's tradition of practical musicianship). Yet Ferdinand III proved even less of a genuine innovator in government than his father. Changes in emphasis were hesitant and slight. In his unspectacular way the new emperor simply confirmed the gradual shift towards a more Danubian, orthodox, Vienna-based Monarchy, self-sufficient as a whole and interdependent in its several parts.

Of course, Germany was still worth fighting for. Now, however, the most crucial aim became to secure existing Counter-Reformation gains by seeing off the Swedes, with their own Central European designs and their continued backing for émigré Protestants. Ferdinand settled in the end for minimum demands abroad, to be sure of a free hand nearer to home. By 1648 the Habsburgs were left with institutions of state half-consolidated vis-à-vis Germany on the one hand, where their sphere of influence contracted, and Bohemia and Hungary on the other, where it was correspondingly enlarged. But if the House of Austria still lacked the substance of absolute rule, it could now at least pursue the shadow unhindered.

ii The practice of absolutism I: 1621–1626

The first consequence of Ferdinand II's victory over his rebels to be felt by most ordinary people was the collapse of the currency. It began, like the revolt itself, in Bohemia. Even under the government of the Estates, the coinage of Bohemia had been debased in order to make the same amount of silver go further. But the scale of the operation was modest in comparison with the next regime, headed by Ferdinand's lieutenant, Karl von Liechtenstein: during the year 1621, a 25 per cent devaluation took place. But this, too, was modest in comparison with 1622. On 18 January of that year, a contract was signed between the Imperial treasury and a consortium of fifteen prominent subjects of Ferdinand who agreed to lease all the mints in Bohemia, Moravia and Lower Austria, and to control their coinage for one year. The consortium, whose composition was kept so secret that even today only five members can be identified with any certainty, managed to destroy the Bohemian economy totally within its brief period of office. The market was flooded with 34 million thalers of consortium coins, their face value cried up by 25 per cent, their silver content drastically reduced. A debasement of about 90 per cent was effected, which made it almost impossible to exchange the consortium's money (called 'long coins') outside the Habsburg lands. Whereas an Imperial thaler had been obtained for 90 Bohemian kreuzer in 1618, by 1623 the commercial rate of exchange was 675 kreuzer. Nor did matters end here, for some members of the consortium were also members of the 'Confiscations Court', created late in 1620 to determine the guilt of those accused of supporting rebellion. Over 1,500 landowners were tried, and almost half were condemned to lose all or part of their estates. The court invariably confiscated the entire property of those suspected of involvement in the revolt, and when only a portion – one-half, one-quarter and so on – was judged forfeit, the remaining land was not returned. Instead, its value was assessed and the equivalent paid in 'long coins'. This meant the ruin of even those nobles whose property was only partially confiscated (perhaps 600 in all) and the loss of almost all town land. By the time the consortium and the court were dissolved, in the autumn of 1623, the power of both towns and nobles in Bohemia was broken, while the economy of the kingdom was so crippled by the lack of reliable currency that students were forced to stay away from schools and universities, those dependent on money wages or pensions became destitute, and craftsmen and tradesmen would only barter their wares ('We will not sell good meat for bad coin,' the butchers protested). In his *Republic of Bohemia*, published in 1633, Pavel Stránský wrote:

It was then, for the first time, that we learned from

experience . . . that neither plague, nor war, nor hostile foreign incursions into our land, neither pillage nor fire, could do so much harm to good people as frequent changes in the value of money.[1]

The monetary confusion caused by these developments could not be confined to Bohemia. Everywhere, the 'long coins' of the consortium were imitated by rulers anxious to increase their profits from coining. From 1621 until 1623, the currencies of the Empire were in total disarray. In some places, even the government could not cope. The clerks of the city treasury at Nördlingen in Swabia, for example, were no longer able to calculate any totals for municipal income and expenditure: so rapidly did the value of coins change that, after 1621, they merely made individual entries and tried to keep as many silver coins in their coffers as possible.[2] In several areas, especially in Saxony, there was rioting against those public authorities which failed to maintain a stable currency. And, all over Germany, popular songs and poems preserved the memory of the *Kipper- und Wipperzeit* (the 'see-saw era'), when, for over two years, the Empire had perforce to maintain a copper standard.[3]

While their economic position was thus under heavy attack, people in many parts of the Empire were also subjected to pressure of another type: recatholicization. The pace of this operation was slower than the recoinage, although its effects lasted longer. In the Upper Palatinate, for example, conquered by the troops of Maximilian of Bavaria in 1621, Catholicism had not been practised since the 1540s, so that the first priests to celebrate Mass again – two Jesuit chaplains with the Bavarian army – had difficulty in finding the necessary accessories, such as a chalice. Recatholicization proceeded slowly until 1625, not least because the administration remained in the hands of Frederick V's officials, many of them Calvinists; but eventually they were purged, and Catholic churches, a school, and a Jesuit mission were opened in Amberg, the territorial capital. Then, in 1626, Calvinist ministers were expelled; in 1628, even Lutherans were given six months either to convert or to leave, and the Catholic clergy introduced compulsory catechism classes for all. The following year, a plan for a permanent hierarchy was adopted by the Bavarian authorities and implementation began immediately. The Catholic congregation at Amberg rose from 1,000 in 1625 to 5,000 in 1629 and (after some losses in the 1630s) to 10,000 and more by 1645.[4]

Progress across the border in the Habsburg lands was likewise slow. Although the Catholics, supported to the hilt by Ferdinand, proved highly successful at closing down the churches of their Protestant rivals, for some time they seemed incapable of replacing them. Even in the 1640s, about half of the parishes of Bohemia lacked an incumbent, and Polish priests (whose language was not always intelligible to their Czech congregations) had to be brought in to help. In Moravia, in 1635, there were still only 257 resident clergy (most of them regulars) to serve the 636 parishes, while in Hungary the normal requirements for ordination often had to be waived in order to secure a respectable number of priests.[5] In Upper Austria, as we shall see, the government found it necessary to import Italian priests to augment the small number of local Catholic clergy.

It was the same story further west. Recatholicization in the Rhineland was led by Philip Christopher von Sötern, bishop of Speyer, an early supporter of the League who had been driven into exile in 1621 by the armies defending the Rhine Palatinate for Frederick V. Apart from the disgrace and inconvenience, he estimated that the Palatine war had caused losses to his domains worth 8 million thalers. Now he resolved to exact his revenge, and his elevation as Elector of Trier in 1623 increased his power to do so. The primary aim of Sötern and his fellow-prelates was to reclaim all the church lands in the Rhine Palatinate which had been secularized; their second was to root out Protestant worship there and replace it with Catholicism. At first all went well: In February 1623 the Bavarian governor of the Palatine territories to the east of the Rhine ordered the expulsion of all Calvinist preachers; two years later the Spanish governor of the far more extensive west bank territories did likewise. At the same time, the Elector of Mainz's officials prepared a programme for recatholicizing the Calvinist county of Nassau. It was put into effect in the autumn of 1626, and the pace of restitution was accelerated the following year when Tilly's forces were quartered in the area.[6] But, as in the Habsburg lands, it was one thing to destroy and quite another to rebuild. Once again, there were simply not enough priests available to take over all the regained parishes: by the end of 1630, scarcely 20 per cent of the livings in the Palatinate had a Catholic priest, and congregations everywhere were small. Neither was the restitution of church lands pressed home with much enthusiasm, for the 5,000 Spanish troops quartered in the area often retained the church's former lands for their own sustenance.[7] Perhaps, however, a gradual approach in this matter was the best policy. At least such moderate recatholicization in the Palatinate provoked little or no popular opposition; in Upper

Austria, by contrast, there was a major revolt.

In 1620 the Estates of Upper Austria, led by Tschernembl, had openly endorsed the cause of Frederick of the Palatinate. Within weeks, Maximilian of Bavaria put down the insurrection, leaving behind a garrison of 5,000 men, whose wages he tried to meet from the payments of the local taxpayers. In 1621, Ferdinand agreed that the Bavarians should continue to hold Upper Austria and the Upper Palatinate, as a pledge, until Maximilian's considerable war-expenses had been repaid.[8] In lieu of interest on this debt, Maximilian was allowed to levy taxes yielding 240,000 thalers annually from each occupied territory. The arrangement worked well in the Palatinate, whose ruler was outlawed; but in Upper Austria, the Bavarian occupation forces were supposed to act in the name not only of Maximilian but of Ferdinand, as archduke, as well. There was an important conflict of interest between the two overlords. To Maximilian, Austria offered an important source of revenue with which to pay his army: he therefore desired to maintain peace and prosperity in the duchy at all costs, so that taxes would be paid promptly and in full. Ferdinand, on the other hand, was interested not in money but in loyalty: he wanted the duchy purged of traitors and heretics, and as territorial prince, under the *cuius regio* clause of the peace of Augsburg, he felt entitled to do this. Reluctantly, the Bavarian occupation authorities, led by the well-meaning Adam von Herberstorff, in October 1624 ordered the expulsion of all Protestant pastors and schoolteachers, and allowed Catholic creditors to foreclose on Protestants in order to force the sale of their property. In October 1625, the government created a Reformation Commission charged with recovering all secularized church lands and endowments, and it was decreed that, by Easter 1626, residents of the duchy must either attend Catholic worship or leave. Only the nobles were spared: they were allowed up to fifty years to convert.

The final catalyst for the revolt was provided by the Congregation for the Propagation of the Faith, founded in Rome by Gregory XV expressly to derive maximum benefit for the Catholic Church from the victories of Ferdinand and his allies beyond the Alps. In 1625, the Congregation authorized the dispatch of numerous Italian missionaries to the Empire to carry out the work of recatholicization – partly because there were not enough German-speaking priests of suitable quality, partly because the Italians' Latin was excellent, and partly (in the Congregation's own words) 'because the Italians are not so addicted to wine and drinking' as the natives. But these virtues were less apparent to the Austrian laity, who offered some opposition to the foreign priests installed in formerly Protestant parishes. Under pressure from Ferdinand, Governor Herberstorff decided to make an example of one area: the men of several parishes were summoned to Frankenfeld castle, and on 15 May 1626 were reproved for their unruly and disrespectful behaviour towards the new priests. Then Herberstorff accused the local officials of causing the trouble and ordered the immediate execution of seventeen of them, chosen by lot.[9]

This frighteningly arbitrary behaviour, albeit forced on Herberstorff by the emperor, provoked a group of Protestant lay officers, led by Stephen Fadinger (a modest farmer and an assistant of the local magistrate), to organize a general revolt which all but succeeded in driving out both Bavarian and Austrian overlords. Unlike earlier peasant uprisings, which were anti-seigneurial, this time the rebels' objective was Linz, the government's capital. Support for Fadinger was widespread, and it came from Catholics as well as Protestants: all had suffered from the fourteen-fold increase in taxation required to pay for the Bavarian forces of occupation, and from the collapse of the currency between 1621 and 1623. In May 1626 a small army under Herberstorff was routed by the rebels, and a regular siege of Linz began. But Fadinger was killed in the trenches in July and the siege was abandoned. The peasants also failed to secure foreign aid, although contact was made with Scultetus, a Palatine court preacher who acted as ambassador for Christian IV, then also in arms against the emperor. The rising soon became more a guerrilla war than a peasant revolt. It nevertheless required some 12,000 regular troops and a series of pitched battles before the situation was brought under control (see Map 2). The only successes which the rebels could claim were the end of Bavarian occupation and the removal of the Italian priests. In May 1628, after prolonged negotiations in which Count Max von Trauttmannsdorf made his diplomatic début for the emperor, the Upper Palatinate was sold to Maximilian for 10 million thalers, the exact amount agreed as Ferdinand's debt to Bavaria and the League. In return, Austria was restored to Habsburg control. At the same time, in place of the unpopular Italians, the papacy gave permission for 300 regular clergy in Upper Austria to serve in formerly Protestant parishes (for there were still not enough Catholic priests to go round).[10]

None of this, however, deterred the emperor and his allies in their crusade against the heretics. 'God is on our side, not on theirs' was the jubilant refrain of Father Hyacinth of Casale (who had done so much to bring about the Electoral transfer) in the spring of 1624.[11] Unknown to him, at much the same time in Vienna, Emperor Ferdinand took a solemn vow in the presence of his confessor, that 'he would undertake whatever the circumstances seemed to permit' for the good of the Catholic religion. The confessor, William Lamormaini, entertained no doubts about the implications of this declaration: 'great things can be accomplished by this emperor', he triumphantly informed the Vatican. 'Perhaps even all Germany [may] be led back to the old faith, provided . . . [pope and emperor together] take up the matter vigorously and see it through with persistence.'[12] Events were to show how perfectly Lamormaini knew his man.

iii The practice of absolutism II: 1626–1629

It seems strange that the gains of the Habsburgs and their Catholic allies in the five years after the White Mountain provoked so few protests from the Lutherans. There were some critics of Imperialism, of course, but they carried little weight.[1] More typical, and more influential, was the Elector of Saxony, who in 1626 tried to convince his neighbours in the Lower Saxon Circle that they were wrong to oppose the emperor. In a lengthy argument, John George accused his co-religionist, King Christian IV of Denmark, of foreign aggression, and his fellow Germans, Christian of Brunswick and the dukes of Saxe-Weimar, who had joined the Danes, of treason. He argued that Ferdinand was waging a just war against rebels and not a religious war of conquest; that fears of Spanish Habsburg domination of Germany were crude exaggeration; that the conspiracy theory of a Jesuit reconversion of Lutherans was disproved by Ferdinand's moderate actions (this was in 1626!); and that Luther's injunction to 'Obey the powers that be' still applied to Ferdinand, since he had offered no cause for resistance. What the emperor chose to do in Bohemia and Austria, according to John George, was covered by the *cuius regio* principle. And, as if all that were not enough, the Elector even claimed that Tilly was a patriotic general, defending loyal Germans against the Danes and the Dutch-paid freebooters of Mansfeld, and that the Army of the League should therefore be supported by all Lutherans in a concerted campaign for peace, justice and obedience in the Empire.[2]

Saxony's argument amounted to a conservative plea for peace and unity, with loyalty to Ferdinand as duly-elected emperor. Its flaw lay in the assumption that Ferdinand was thinking along exactly the same lines. It is nevertheless the most confident statement that we have of German Lutheran pacifism, quietism, legalism and xenophobia just before the emperor's maladroit and militaristic policies forced even Saxony to consider opposition. But even in this lengthy policy statement of 1626, John George was ominously silent about the two new Habsburg armies – one Spanish, one Imperial – which had begun to operate in the Empire.

The members of the Catholic League had become alarmed, over the winter of 1624–5, by the persistent rumour that Christian of Denmark was preparing to invade Germany. They feared for the League's forces, vulnerably encamped in north-west Germany. 'Tilly cannot gain superiority alone', Maximilian of Bavaria was warned. 'The Danes hold great advantages: they will act first and overwhelm us.'[3] The new Elector took the matter up with the emperor. Some reinforcement was all he desired, but to Ferdinand the matter was not so simple. In the first place, there were also rumours that Bethlen Gabor of Transylvania was mobilizing for another attack on the Habsburg heartland. Spain, which had offered help in the past, could spare no troops; on the contrary, of the sixteen Imperial regiments then in existence, six were in the Netherlands assisting at Spínola's siege of Breda and one was in Spanish Lombardy. There were not enough men left to defend Vienna, let alone to reinforce Tilly. So on 7 April 1625, Ferdinand signed a patent naming Albert of Wallenstein (duke of Friedland in Bohemia since 1623) to be 'chief over all our troops already serving at this time, whether in the Holy Roman Empire or in the Netherlands', and ordering him to create 'a field army, whether from our existing units or from newly raised regiments, so that there shall be 24,000 men in all'. In September 1625 the 'Friedlandsche Armada', leaving a skeleton force to defend Vienna, moved northwards from Bohemia to the borders of Lower Saxony, to take up position on the right of Tilly's army.

On Tilly's left were detachments from the Army of Flanders. After the triumphant capture of Breda, in June 1625, some 11,000 troops from the South Netherlands were sent into garrisons along the Rhine, Ems and Lippe to enforce a strict economic blockade of the Dutch Republic, by land and sea. They remained until 1629. At the same time, a new body – the *Almirantazgo*, or Admiralty – was created in Seville to check that no Dutch goods were brought into Spain and (to a lesser extent) that no Spanish wares were shipped to the Republic. These measures were not popular in Germany. The Hanseatic ports protested long and loud about the rigorous scrutiny to which their cargoes were subjected by the officials of the *Almirantazgo*; and the river blockade was denounced by the territorial rulers of the Rhineland, whose subjects were deprived of valuable trading contacts as well as being required to quarter and placate the ill-paid troops of Spain. The Elector of Cologne's bishoprics of Münster, Osnabrück, Paderborn and Minden were in the front line of this economic warfare, and he complained bitterly that 'The Spaniards have no respect for the Imperial Constitution; . . . they are always claiming that their alleged "necessity" or "commodity" must prevail.'[4]

In 1627, the Spaniards gave further offence when they enforced a judgment of the Imperial Chamber Court concerning the partition of Hesse. In 1604, upon the extinction of the Marburg line, Maurice of Hesse-Kassel had occupied the entire inheritance (page 21 above); now, by Imperial decree, he was compelled to hand most of it over to his cousin, George of Hesse-Darmstadt, and in addition to pay just over 1 million thalers in damages for wrongfully holding Marburg.[5] The outrage caused in Germany by this exercise of Imperial power was surpassed, however, by the simultaneous deposition of the dukes of Mecklenburg, again by the decision of the Imperial Supreme Court, on the grounds that they had supported Christian of Denmark. This time the confiscated estates were transferred, not to a relative, but to Wallenstein. At first (February 1627) they were only given as a pledge for the money owed by the emperor to his general; but the following year Wallenstein was recognized as duke and began to reside, with a court of over 1,000 persons, in the great palace at Güstrow.[6]

There will never be agreement about the character and role of Wallenstein, but his alleged treason and murder in 1634 have tended to turn the matter into a historiographical hornets' nest, thus overshadowing his real importance as an unscrupulously innovatory but loyal Habsburg military entrepreneur during his first Imperial generalship, 1625–30. These were the crucial years of his life; this was the period of his truly significant influence on events. But even so, in these years, Wallenstein did not make major policy decisions; he merely executed those made by his master. On matters of religion, for example, he remained as calculating and pragmatic as any modern business executive running a multi-national company.[7] When his pro-Danish enemies, Christian of Brunswick and John Ernest of Saxe-Weimar, tried to gain the support of Lutheran Magdeburg in 1626 by saying that the Imperial army which wished to occupy the city was

taking the first step in a religious war of aggression to recatholi-
cize all Germany, Wallenstein requested the emperor[8]

> To be so good as to assure the city of Magdeburg that this is
> not a war of religion in any way; but that as a loyal and
> devoted city, their privileges of religious and secular peace
> will not be harmed in the slightest, rather that they will be
> protected graciously and also defended against anything to
> the contrary.

But Magdeburg's fears were well-founded. Three years later the
city was suffering from the attentions of Franz Wilhelm von
Wartenburg, bishop of Osnabrück, acting as a special Imperial
commissioner, who made a bid to infiltrate the traditionally
Lutheran Cathedral Chapter by confiscating ten key prebends in
order to facilitate the election, for the first time in almost a
century, of a Catholic ruling bishop. Having tried to get that far,
the plan in July 1630 was to apply *autonomia*, i.e. the constitutional right of a Catholic ruler to impose religious uniformity on
his territorial subjects.[9] Nor was this an isolated case: the events
at Magdeburg were part of a grand campaign waged all over the
Empire to recover church lands for the Catholic cause once and
for all (see Plate 5).

The operation was planned at Mühlhausen in the autumn of
1627, when the Electors (or their representatives) met to discuss
the implications of the defeat of Denmark. The emperor's envoy
to the meeting was instructed to say that, after nine years of war,
the time had come to reconsider the religious state of Germany,
and in particular the restoration of church lands illegally taken
from the Catholics. This, according to Ferdinand, was 'the great
gain and fruit of the war' on which he had his eye, and he assured
the Catholic party at Mühlhausen – who clamoured for some
action – that 'just as up to now we have never thought to let pass
any chance to secure the restitution of church lands, neither do
we intend, now or in the future, to have to bear the responsibility
before posterity of having neglected or failed to exploit even the
least opportunity'.[10]

But for months no concrete steps were taken, and in September 1628, five south German prelates sent a joint letter beseeching
the emperor to keep his promise. The next month a preliminary
draft of the document known as the Edict of Restitution was sent
to the Imperial Privy Council, and to the Electors of Mainz and
Bavaria, for comment. Ferdinand claimed, in the preamble, that
he was merely restoring the status quo of 1555, immediately after
the peace of Augsburg, and that the Edict was thus designed

merely to enforce respect for the laws of the Empire. The opening sections of the draft Edict seemed to confirm this: all church lands seized since 1552 (the 'normative date' in the Augsburg peace) were to be restored. But the Edict also declared that ecclesiastical princes had the same right to enforce religious conformity on their subjects as secular rulers. This went far beyond the settlement of 1555 because it effectively rendered the *Declaratio Ferdinandei* (page 19 above) invalid. Yet even this was not enough for the Catholic prelates: they proceeded to demand the inclusion in the Edict of a new prohibition of Calvinism, and the application of its terms to the Imperial Free Cities, too. After five months of discussion, the emperor and his advisers finally decided to include the ban on all Protestant sects other than Lutheranism, but to leave the cities out. The rest of the document remained more or less as it stood.

Five hundred copies of the Edict were secretly printed in Vienna and distributed to the Directors of the Imperial Circles and the major princes, with instructions to publish multiple copies simultaneously on 28 March 1629. The document looked disarmingly simple – a single sheet of paper bearing four columns of small print and the emperor's signature – but appearances were deceptive. On a version printed in Würzburg, a contemporary hand has added to the title page the words *Radix omnium malorum*: the root of all evils.[11] For a whole year, the Edict and its execution became the central issue of German politics. The bishoprics and archbishoprics of Lower Saxony and Westphalia were immediately affected, as were some 500 monasteries, convents and other church properties secularized by a host of Protestant rulers since 1552. The duke of Württemberg alone was to be deprived of the lands of fourteen large monasteries and thirty-six convents; the dukes of Brunswick faced demands only slightly less exorbitant (see Map 2 and Plates 6–7).

Although as yet the territorial church lands in Brandenburg and Electoral Saxony seemed safe, having been secularized long before 1552, there were reasons to fear that another Edict might one day challenge their immunity. In the first place, some of the former church properties claimed in other areas had become Lutheran before 1552: thus, out of forty-five Imperial cities affected by the commissioners' demands between 1627 and 1631, only eight had clearly broken the post-1552 moratorium on further Protestantization (indeed one – the Imperial city of Lindau – had been Protestant since 1528). In the second place, the appearance of the Edict was closely followed by publication of an influential tract which seemed to reveal in detail the philosophy which underlay Ferdinand's decree: Paul Laymann's *Pacis Compositio*. The author – a Jesuit – argued that 'Whatever is not found to have been explicitly granted, should be considered forbidden', and that therefore the Protestants should restore everything they held unless a valid title to it could be produced. The pamphlet, not surprisingly, caused a sensation. When Gustavus Adolphus arrived in Germany the following year, he announced that he intended to execute three men whose names began with 'L' – one was Laymann.[12] The third reason for disquiet in Brandenburg and Saxony arose from more practical matters: the size of the Catholic armies massed close to their borders, and their role in enforcing the restitution of church land. Tilly and his League troops assisted the Imperial commissioners in the dioceses of Osnabrück, Bremen, Verden and Hildesheim, as well as in key cities like Augsburg. If the forces of Wallenstein were as yet less forward, it was only because they had to undertake major operations against the Danes and against the Hanseatic port of Stralsund, one of the places designated to receive an Imperial garrison in the treaty of submission signed with Wallenstein in 1627 by Duke Bogislav of Pomerania.

Stralsund, a town of some 15,000 inhabitants, had been on bad terms with the dukes of Pomerania for some time. In 1612 a ducal army had occupied the defiant city in order to impose more effective control, but there had been rioting against the new order almost immediately and disputes between duke and magistrates continued for some years thereafter. In 1627, fearful of Wallenstein's approach, the city magistrates employed a team of Swedish engineers to construct a new chain of powerful fortifications, and the militia was increased to almost 5,000. They refused the ducal order to admit the Imperialists. This defiance was welcomed by Christian IV, but he had few troops to spare; he therefore signed an agreement with Sweden guaranteeing that both powers would defend Stralsund if she were attacked. No sooner had the siege begun (May 1628) than seven companies of Scottish veterans in Danish service arrived, and 600 Swedes followed the next month. Together, these foreign troops beat off the Imperialists' assaults on 27–29 June, and more reinforcements – Scottish, Swedish, Danish and German – poured in. The siege was lifted on 24 July.[13]

The successful defence of Stralsund did not create a state of war between the emperor and Sweden, whose king was still campaigning in Poland, although Ferdinand was encouraged to send the Poles substantial military aid in 1629 (page 122 below). Nor did the Imperialists' failure seriously affect their overall

military position – Denmark was still losing the war. But it was
nevertheless a devastating political blow. Already in September
1628 Wallenstein warned Ferdinand, from his camp at Breiten-
burg in Holstein, that his presence was so unpopular that he could
only continue to operate if he possessed such a great number of
troops that they could coerce the native inhabitants into providing tribute at fixed rates every week. Wallenstein's advice to the
emperor was to recruit and arm more and more men, and to
occupy as much of the Empire as possible. Only in that way, he
argued, would territorial princes like Saxony and Bavaria be
forced to remain loyal and give up any plans to call upon foreign
support, or to offer assistance to the Palatine exiles.[14] But it was
simply not possible to continue troop-raising indefinitely: there
were already too many men in arms for the Empire to support.
Wallenstein's own army lists indicate the scale of the problem he
had created (see Table 3). And, on top of this, the Empire also had
to pay for the forces of Spain and the Catholic League in the
north-west.

TABLE 3 *Wallenstein's army lists, 1625–30*[15]

Year	Foot	(% of whole)	Horse	Total	% increase over previous year	% German troops
1625	45,300	(73)	16,600	61,900	—	61
1626	86,100	(77)	25,000	111,100	79	72
1627	83,100	(74)	29,600	112,700	1	79
1628	102,900	(79)	27,300	130,200	16	74
1629	111,000	(86)	17,900	128,900	−1	80
1630	129,900	(86)	21,000	150,900	17	87

The first concerted political attack on Wallenstein and his
system was delivered at the same Electoral meeting of Mühlhausen, in November 1627, at which the Edict of Restitution was
planned. The Catholic Electors criticized both the level of taxes
raised by Ferdinand's general, and the way they were distributed:
'His war taxes guarantee exorbitant rates of pay to regimental
and company staff officers', they claimed, asserting that
Lieutenant-General Arnim alone received 3,000 florins a month.
They also censured Wallenstein's practice of selling commissions
'for up to four regiments at a time to anyone offering his services,

including criminals, foreigners and those ignorant of military administration', and the poor discipline that he kept. They mentioned the recent mutiny of the duke of Saxe-Lauenburg's regiments in the Wetterau. But, of course, their main grievances were the destruction and depopulation that the army caused, and their inability to control the Imperial forces stationed in their own domains. 'Territorial rulers', they lamented, 'are at the mercy of Colonels and Captains, who are uninvited war profiteers and criminals, breaking the laws of the Empire.'[16]

The Electors demanded that Ferdinand should stop all new recruitment, and instead reduce the strength of Wallenstein's army (especially in the Rhineland, where both Habsburg troops and the League's members were numerous). They also asked that he provide a new system of command which would inspire the confidence of territorial rulers in the Empire; and that, in order to save 'the poor widows and orphans', the Imperial army be deprived of the right to levy its own taxes by the so-called 'Contributions system', and instead be put under civilian economic control. Wallenstein was to be forbidden to levy more troops without the approval of Imperial commissioners, and was no longer to raise war taxes without the consent, administration and audit of those territorial rulers who were his hosts.

As long as there was a war to fight, the emperor was prepared to ignore the complaints. But in December 1629, with Denmark defeated, the new Elector of Mainz, Anselm Casimir von Wambold, organized a meeting of the Catholic League at Mergentheim, and for the first time openly insisted that Wallenstein be dismissed:

> Since the Duke of Friedland [Wallenstein] has up to now
> disgusted and offended to the utmost nearly each and every
> territorial ruler in the Empire; and although the present
> situation has moved him to be more cautious, he has not
> given up his plans to retain Mecklenburg by virtue of his
> Imperial command.

According to the Elector, as long as Wallenstein remained in charge of the Imperial host and in possession of Mecklenburg, there would never be peace in the Empire.[17] In March 1630, acting as arch-chancellor of the Empire, Wambold summoned the seven Electors to meet at Regensburg on 3 June in order to resolve the problem.

This time, Ferdinand had to listen to the complaints of his German allies, for he now had few others. Urban VIII, who had been elected pope in August 1623, did not share the pro-Habsburg stance of his predecessors. He ended the subsidies sent by Rome to Ferdinand and the League, preferring to concentrate on what he perceived as the interests of the papal states in Italy – a task which he believed required the neutralization of Habsburg influence in the peninsula. Sigismund of Poland, another sometime supporter of the emperor, was also now deaf to his appeals for help. In the summer of 1629, his kingdom exhausted, Sigismund had gratefully made a six-year truce with Sweden which left Gustavus free to intervene in the Empire, if he chose: he already possessed a bridgehead at Stralsund. France, with her Huguenot rebellion crushed at last, was also free to offer support to the emperor's opponents once again – and was already doing so in Italy. Worse still, Spain was at this point obliged to withdraw her aid from Ferdinand's cause by serious reverses in the Low Countries' Wars. In 1628, a Dutch task force captured the entire treasure fleet sailing from the Caribbean to Spain, thus simultaneously providing the Republic with the resources to launch a major assault on the Spanish Netherlands and depriving Philip IV of the means of mounting an effective resistance. Early in 1629, confident of success and with the unprecedented number of 128,000 men at his disposal, the Dutch commander-in-chief Frederick Henry (Maurice's brother) laid siege to the important city of 's Hertogenbosch. The Habsburgs retaliated by sending two columns – one of 10,000 Imperialists, the other from the Army of Flanders – deep into Dutch territory. In August they captured Amersfoort, only 40 kilometres from Amsterdam. Sadly for the Habsburgs, in the same month the Dutch took Wesel by storm, and in September they forced the surrender of 's Hertogenbosch thus compelling the Habsburg forces at Amersfoort, now uncomfortably isolated, to retreat in disorder. Nor was this all. Over the winter of 1629–30 the Dutch chased almost all the Spanish garrisons out of north-west Germany. The river blockade collapsed, and in July 1630 Spain handed over the remaining strongpoints to Tilly's League forces.[18]

The truth was that Tilly now shouldered the burden of defending the Catholic cause in Germany almost alone, since the Army of Flanders was now too weak to defend any place outside Philip IV's patrimonial lands and the troops of Ferdinand II were too involved elsewhere to help. The principal reason for both developments was simple. In the course of 1629, both branches of the House of Habsburg, thanks to the tireless diplomacy of the count-duke of Olivares, had become fatally involved in a major war with France in Italy.

iv Spain and the war

'God is Spanish and fights for our nation these days.' There must have been moments in 1625, that *annus mirabilis* for Spanish arms, when even Spain's enemies may grudgingly have conceded that the count-duke of Olivares was not entirely unjustified in his confident assessment of the divinity's national affiliation.[1] During the course of that year Breda surrendered to the Army of Flanders under the command of the incomparable Spínola; the republic of Genoa, Spain's ally and client, was rescued from the onslaught of the combined forces of France and Savoy; a joint Spanish–Portuguese naval expedition drove the Dutch from Bahía in Brazil; and an English expeditionary force was humiliatingly defeated when it attempted an attack on Cadiz. Add to this the Habsburg victories in Central Europe, and it certainly seemed that, if God was not Spanish, at least He had a strong predilection for the House of Austria.

Yet to Olivares, poring over the maps of Europe in his map-room in Madrid, the victories of 1625, although immensely encouraging, offered little more than a breathing space. Spain needed peace – needed it to restore the exhausted crown finances and the shattered Castilian economy, and to undertake those great reforms which he saw as essential to his country's survival. Yet peace was painfully elusive. The king of France, although temporarily embarrassed by the problem of the Huguenots, presented a permanent threat to that *pax austriaca* which Madrid regarded as indispensable for the survival of Catholicism and the maintenance of stability through large parts of Europe. The attack on Cadiz in November 1625 (page 77 above) had initiated a state of war between England and Spain. The condition of Italy was precarious, with Venice forever engaged in anti-Habsburg machinations, Charles Emmanuel of Savoy hopelessly volatile, and the Barberini Pope Urban VIII not to be trusted. But above all, the problem of the Dutch seemed consistently to evade solution. It was not only that the war in the Netherlands imposed a continuing and almost intolerable strain on Spain's resources in manpower and money, although this was bad enough. It was also that the hand of the Dutch was to be found behind every new anti-Habsburg coalition; that the activities of the Dutch East and West India Companies imperilled the overseas possessions of the crown of Castile and Portugal; and that the economic life of the Iberian peninsula was being remorselessly undermined by the success of Dutch mercantile and entrepreneurial activities.

Olivares entertained no illusions about the possibility of bringing back the United Provinces of the Netherlands into allegiance to the king of Spain. The days for that were long since passed. But he believed, and with some justification, that the terms on which the 1609 truce had been negotiated had proved disastrous for the Spanish Monarchy, and he hoped that it might be possible to induce the Dutch, by means of military and economic pressure, to negotiate a new, and more permanent, peace settlement on terms with which Spain would be able to live. But to achieve this, Spain needed help – help that could only come from the Empire.

It was the central axiom of the count-duke's foreign policy that 'not for anything must these two houses [the Austrian and Spanish branches of the Habsburgs] let themselves be divided'.[2] The breakdown of the English marriage negotiations made it possible for him to strengthen the existing ties between the two houses by arranging for a marriage between Philip IV's sister, the Infanta María, and Ferdinand, king of Hungary, the emperor's son. But he also believed that a more formal arrangement was needed, which would guarantee to both parties mutual assistance in time of trouble. It was in 1625 that the council of state in Madrid first discussed the possibility of a formal alliance between Spain, the emperor and the princes of the Empire, Protestant as well as Catholic, since it was considered essential to divide the Lutherans from the Calvinists.[3] In the following years Olivares pursued with tenacity this plan for an offensive and defensive military alliance between Madrid and Vienna, which he regarded as the only effective key to permanent stability in Central Europe and to the solution of the Netherlands problem. If he could once involve the emperor in Spain's war with the Dutch, perhaps by persuading Ferdinand that a final peace in Germany depended on the pacification of the Netherlands, those rebellious vassals might yet be brought to heel.

The Habsburg victories in Germany created what seemed an ideal opportunity for united Spanish–Imperial action. From 1625 Olivares had been actively negotiating with the emperor and with Maximilian of Bavaria about the possibilities of realizing a great 'Baltic design'. The intention of this design was to provide Spain with a naval base in the north. This would serve as the home port for a new trading company, which would be well placed to wrest from the Dutch their control of the lucrative Baltic–Mediterranean trade – a trade which Olivares correctly identified as the foundation of their economic prosperity and

military resilience. One way of realizing this ambitious design
would be for the armies of the emperor and the Catholic League to
expel the Dutch from the territory of East Friesland, adjacent to
the Republic, which had good ports available. But Maximilian of
Bavaria, who was congenitally suspicious of Spanish ambitions,
showed no enthusiasm for associating the League with this
scheme, and Madrid was forced to look for alternative solutions.

The spectacular rise of Wallenstein gave Olivares another
chance. The count-duke's overtures to Wallenstein in 1627
evoked an encouraging response: it seemed that he would be
happy to lend help against the Dutch. There were two ways, by no
means mutually exclusive, by which this help could be provided.
He could send his army to occupy one of the Baltic ports, and he
could order his forces into East Friesland and invade the Dutch
provinces across the Ems, which might subsequently be used to
satisfy his territorial ambitions. If at the same time the Army of
Flanders could bring pressure to bear on the Dutch from the south,
then surely the Republic would be forced to accede to a settlement which would guarantee peace with honour for Spain.

The prospects for Spain improved in June 1627 with the
outbreak of hostilities between France and England. Hoping to
capitalize on Richelieu's difficulties, Olivares switched course
abruptly, and held out to Paris the bait of a Franco-Spanish
rapprochement. The Spanish ambassador in Paris was instructed
to win Louis XIII's support for an alliance against all mutual
enemies: the French Protestants, the English and, if possible, the
Dutch. As a token of good faith, Spain's Atlantic fleet moved up
from Cadiz to the Gulf of Morbihan to assist Louis with the siege
of La Rochelle, whose Huguenot population, counting on promises of English aid, had rebelled against their king. Nevertheless
the Franco-Spanish alliance, though eagerly welcomed by the
papacy, was never easy. There was opposition in Madrid – where
one of Philip's councillors warned that 'there is nothing in theology which obliges Your Majesty to send his armed forces against
heretics everywhere' – and there was suspicion in Paris of Spain's
motives.[4]

The situation deteriorated dramatically in 1628. The emper-
or gave his approval to the 'grand design' in the Baltic, but almost
at once Wallenstein's army was forced to raise its siege of the port
of Stralsund, and all immediate hopes for the project were dashed.
But worse was to follow, for almost simultaneously an ill-considered
venture on which Olivares had embarked in Italy jeopardized,
and then wrecked, his plans for ending the war with the Dutch,
and brought about a transformation of the international scene.

The renewal of the dispute (see page 41 above) over the succession to Mantua and Montferrat, following the death of Duke Vincent II in December 1627, created dangers in Italy which Olivares was unable to ignore, and temptations which he was unable to resist. If the French-born duke of Nevers, the strongest claimant, succeeded to Duke Vincent's inheritance, the French would be in a position to outflank Milan, the base from which Spain dominated northern Italy. Milan was also the starting-point of that vital strategic system of military corridors which ran by way of the Valtelline (see Map 2) to Central Europe, or up the Rhine to the Netherlands. It was unfortunate for Spain that the duke of Nevers, forewarned of his kinsman's impending death, managed to arrive in Mantua in mid-January 1628 and at once took over the government. He immediately sent an envoy to Vienna to convince the emperor (whose new wife, the late duke's sister, was already sympathetic) of his right to succeed.

Alarmed by these dangers, and under heavy criticism at home for the alleged failures of his government, Olivares authorized Don Gonzalo Fernández de Córdoba, the commander of the army of Milan, to lay siege to the fortress of Casale in Montferrat. The capture of this almost impregnable stronghold would represent a brilliant coup, enhancing the reputation of Spanish arms and consolidating Spain's hold over the Lombard plain. But Don Gonzalo's army, ill-provisioned in spite of all the count-duke's efforts to send it money, became fatally bogged down outside the walls of Casale, and what had originally been planned as an overnight triumph turned instead into an interminable nightmare. It was the one political act for which Philip IV later expressed regret: 'If ever I have erred and given God cause for dissatisfaction', he admitted to a confidante in 1645, 'it was in this.' Pope Urban VIII, for his part, lamented in 1632 that the war of Mantua had caused the downfall of the Catholic cause, 'for everyone knows that, before the war, the Habsburgs, the French and all the other Catholic princes were in accord on foreign matters, and that the . . . progress of the Catholic religion proceeded most favourably in Germany, in France, everywhere.'[5]

The long siege of Casale imposed heavy new demands on the finances of the Spanish crown, and made it necessary to divert scarce resources from the Army of Flanders to the forces in Italy. This in turn had disastrous repercussions on the war in the Netherlands at a moment when peace negotiations with the Dutch were under way. As noted above, reinforced by the windfall of Spanish silver seized off the treasure fleet from America in 1628, the Dutch were able to move over to the offensive in 1629

against the Army of Flanders, now weakened by the departure of
Spínola, who had gone to Madrid to argue the case for a peace
settlement with the Republic. Once again, therefore, Madrid
found itself confronted in 1629 with an age-old dilemma: Flanders
or Italy? After agonized debate, the council of state, under the
influence of Spínola and against the count-duke's wishes, authorized the Archduchess Isabella in Brussels to reach an agreement
with the Dutch, so that the war in Italy could be given priority.
The consequences of this decision were just as Olivares feared.
The Republic, perceiving Spain's new weakness in the north, lost
any immediate interest in a peace settlement, while the loyal
provinces of the southern Netherlands, desperately war-weary
and demoralized by a string of defeats, came within an ace of
revolt.

This, however, was only one of the many troubles that nearly
overwhelmed Olivares during those critical years of the Mantuan
war between 1628 and 1631. The economic condition of Castile
steadily deteriorated. 1627 had been a particularly bad year:
prices rose sharply under the combined pressure of poor harvests
and the effects of the minting by the government of excessive
amounts of debased *vellón* (copper) currency during the first years
of the reign, in an effort to meet its financial needs. The productive forces of Castile were crippled by an inequitable system of
taxation; soaring prices threatened to provoke unrest in the
towns; and the reform programme on which Olivares had
embarked with such high hopes in 1621 had virtually come to a
halt, paralysed by the resistance of the Cortes, the urban oligar-
chies, and the governmental machine itself. The regime was
deeply unpopular, and its various contradictory attempts to
grapple with the problems of inflation only served to increase its
unpopularity and add to the general distress. The involvement of
Spain in a costly and apparently unsuccessful war in Italy gave
further ammunition to Olivares's enemies. Manifestoes and sa-
tires circulated in Madrid during 1628 urging Philip IV to get rid of
his favourite and become a real king.

Philip showed no immediate inclination to accept the advice
of the count-duke's enemies, but there were signs of tension
betweeen king and minister in the spring and summer of 1629, as
the king leant towards the majority of his council of state, and
even began to talk of leading an army in person to Italy. In
according preference to Italy, and approving the idea of a settlement with the Dutch, the council of state had succumbed to
Spínola's arguments in favour of peace in the north. But a major
consideration was the behaviour of the French. Olivares had

always gambled that Don Gonzalo de Córdoba would capture
Casale before Louis XIII defeated the Huguenots of La Rochelle;
but once again he miscalculated. In October 1628 La Rochelle
surrendered; in January 1629 Olivares warned the papal nuncio,
with uncanny prescience, that if a French army crossed the Alps,
France and Spain would be involved in a war which would last for
thirty years. A month later, ignoring the warning, Louis XIII led
his army over the Mount Cenis pass through heavy snows, and
Don Gonzalo, shaken by the approach of the French, was forced
to raise the long and abortive siege of Casale.

As the count-duke had foreseen, Louis XIII's decision to
follow Richelieu's advice and lead an army across the Alps set
France and Spain on a collision course. Neither side was ready for
a full-scale war, and the Mantuan confrontation was therefore
contained. But from the spring of 1629 the requirements of an
assertive foreign policy were assuming precedence in both Paris
and Madrid over all considerations of domestic reform. Both
Richelieu and Olivares now struggled to mobilize their resources
of money and manpower with an eye to the impending conflict.
Both hastened to make peace with England – France in April 1629,
Spain in November 1630 – and assiduously courted potential allies
while they engaged in a complicated game of political chess for
control of that strategic section of the board running from northern Italy to the Netherlands frontier.

In his search for allies Olivares turned once again to Vienna
for help, and this time with some success. But the price of success
proved high. The presence of the French in Italy was a source of
greater concern to Ferdinand than the course of the war in the
Netherlands, and in the summer of 1629 he revoked the permission he had given Wallenstein to deploy part of his army against
the Dutch in Friesland. Instead, his troops were ordered to Italy.
This diversion of Imperial forces across the Alps redressed the
balance in Mantua (at a terrible cost to that unhappy duchy) but
it also destroyed a probably unrepeatable chance to realize Olivares's plans for a combined Imperial–Spanish operation against
the Dutch. And, even in Italy, the presence of some 50,000
Imperial soldiers did not bring the clear-cut Habsburg triumph for
which Olivares had hoped.

Relations between Madrid and Vienna were dangerously
soured over the Mantuan question, which once again made it
painfully clear that the two courts did not possess identical views
and priorities. Olivares deeply distrusted the influence wielded
over Ferdinand by his Gonzaga wife and by his confessor, Lamormaini, and felt that, of the Imperial councillors, only Eggenberg

was a true friend of Spain.[6] The count-duke regarded the peace of Regensburg of 1630 (page 113 below) as an Imperial betrayal of Spain's interests – 'the most discreditable peace we have ever had' – and was not sorry to see it repudiated by France.[7] But he could do no better himself. When the Mantuan question was finally tidied up by the peace agreements of Cherasco in the spring of 1631, the duke of Nevers still retained his inheritance; the French contrived to keep for themselves the fortress of Pinerolo as a military base on the Italian side of the Alps; and the Spaniards failed to get their hands on Casale.[8]

The final phases of the Mantuan question were inevitably overshadowed by the apparently irresistible advance of the Swedes. Olivares, looking anxiously at Europe in 1631 and 1632, detected a great international conspiracy against the House of Austria – a conspiracy in which those who professed loyalty to the Catholic cause, France, Bavaria and the pope himself, were unleashing forces which would submerge large parts of Christendom beneath a tidal wave of heresy. It was for Spain, as the true champion of the faith, to stem this tide as best it could. But the conflict of the giants which was precipitated by Olivares's intervention in Mantua was only to prove irrefutably that God, after all, was not Spanish, but French.

CHAPTER IV

Total war

Although he was emperor for almost eighteen years, Ferdinand II never convened an Imperial Diet. Instead he chose to rule the Empire by decrees issued either on his own authority, or after consultation with the Electors and other sympathetic rulers. This might have proved acceptable had the emperor been content to pursue non-controversial policies; but he was not. The deposition of rulers such as the Elector Palatine or the dukes of Mecklenburg, the Electoral transfer, the maintenance of Wallenstein's army, the Edict of Restitution – these were issues that would have excited debate and opposition under any circumstances. But because no Diet assembled between 1613 and 1640, the legality of these (and other) measures taken by the Imperial government became subjects of controversy at every ruler's court: political advisers and academics circulated countless pamphlets, or position papers known as *Denkschriften*, which either justified or criticized a given decision in terms of the 'Public Law' of the Empire ('public' because it involved relations between corporate states).

The audience for these publications was huge. Law was, after theology, the commonest intellectual pursuit in Germany, and almost half the 8,000 or so young men entering the universities of the Empire each year in the early seventeenth century studied it.[1] Moreover, the arguments of the *Denkschriften* and the learned pamphlets filtered down to other classes of society by means of illustrated flysheets and chapbooks, of which thousands were printed during the war. In effect, this created an informed 'public opinion' which, on certain issues, came to exercise a considerable influence. The degree of support manifested for the Bohemian rebellion, to take the outstanding example, was affected to a high degree by the opinions expressed in popular literature. Of the 1,000 surviving flysheets from the war in the Gustav Freytag Collection at Frankfurt, almost 400 were published between 1618

110

and 1621. There was only one more similar burst of literary activity during the war: between 1629 and 1633, as the major participants in the struggle sought to win the support of the uncommitted. Some 229 items in the Freytag Collection come from these years.[2]

Since all the items under discussion were published in Germany, and for the edification of the people of the Empire, it is tempting to argue that the Thirty Years' War remained, despite appearances to the contrary, very much a German affair. It has even been suggested that 'The "Thirty Years' War" should really be called "The German religious war" '.[3] But this viewpoint is highly misleading. The last date at which the political leaders of Germany were free to determine their own destiny was the interlunary period between July 1630 and March 1631, the months that separated the Electoral Meeting at Regensburg from the Protestant Colloquy at Leipzig. Both assemblies, and several smaller meetings in between, attempted to create a realignment of forces within the Empire that might preserve the peace – for, as long as the German princes remained neutral and unattached, there was still a chance for peace. But in the spring of 1631, Sweden's shotgun marriage with Brandenburg and the Franco-Bavarian treaty of Fontainebleau broke the unity and led the statesmen of Europe headlong over the edge of the abyss. A general European war became unavoidable.

i On the edge of the abyss

Both the emperor and his League allies welcomed the Electoral meeting (*Kurfürstentag*) at Regensburg in the summer of 1630, since it offered an opportunity to resolve the differences that had recently developed between them. Its importance in the eyes of all participants is shown by the roll-call of those who attended in person: the emperor, all the Catholic Electors, the papal nuncio, with diplomatic representatives from France, Spain, Venice, Tuscany and England. The Electors of Saxony and Brandenburg refused to appear in person because of their opposition to the Edict of Restitution, but they did send delegates. In all, there were some 2,000 participants and observers.

Ferdinand needed to win the Electors' approval for his

financial and military aid to Spain in the war against the Dutch
Republic. He also needed their support against the threat of
French and Swedish aggression and, more immediately, for the
election of his eldest son as king of the Romans, heir apparent to
the Imperial crown. The prime concern of the Electors, on the
other hand, was to secure the dismissal of Wallenstein, which
they formally demanded on 16 July, after only a week of delibera-
tion. In this they were aided by the sphinx-like posture of the man
himself, who spent the summer at Memmingen, not far from
Regensburg. He was tired and depressed by the deepening financial crisis in which he found himself: indeed, the cost of his army
so far exceeded the income received from the emperor that
Wallenstein simply could not afford to remain as commander-in-
chief. He seems to have been almost relieved when, on 13 August,
the emperor bowed to the vociferous demands for his dismissal.
The general retired to his estates in Bohemia; his chief financier,
Hans de Witte, committed suicide. It was left to Count Tilly, still
general of the army of the League, to reduce the Imperial host by
75 per cent and merge the surviving units with his own. But Tilly
was denied the means to maintain even these reduced forces,
which required some 5 million thalers for their annual sustenance: payment was now to come from the Circle Assemblies,
and the territorial governments represented there consistently
failed to produce their quotas on time. The army's problems were
increased when the bulk of its forces were concentrated at the
siege of Magdeburg, a city which openly defied the emperor after
August 1630. Local resources were quickly consumed; without
Wallenstein's contributions system, the troops became restless.

A thorough military reformation was not the only concession
wrested from the emperor at Regensburg. The Electoral meeting
in effect turned into a court of enquiry concerning Ferdinand's
foreign and domestic policies. Its verdict was devastating, and
several innovations of the 1620s had to be abandoned: the Imperial Supreme Court at Speyer came back under the general
supervision of the territorial rulers, rather than of Vienna; and
the emperor was made to promise that, in future, 'no new war
will be declared other than by the advice of the Electors'. In
return for all this, Ferdinand gained virtually nothing: no king of
the Romans was elected and no League support for the Habsburg
armies in the Netherlands was pledged. His only victory was to
maintain the Edict of Restitution in its pristine form, even though
several of his Catholic allies (led by Bavaria) considered some
relaxation advisable. According to an account of an interview
between Maximilian (who favoured minor concessions to the

Protestants) and the emperor's confessor, Lamormaini (who did not), the full implementation of the Edict was equated with Imperial salvation:

> [Lamormaini] closed his eyes and answered . . . the Edict must stand firm, whatever evil might finally come from it. It matters little that the emperor, because of it, lose not only Austria but all of his kingdoms . . . provided he save his soul, which he cannot do without the implementation of the Edict.[1]

Instead of solving the problems confronting Empire and emperor in 1630, the Regensburg Electoral meeting had thus only made them worse. By sacrificing Wallenstein, Ferdinand lost the one man whose ability and power might conceivably have enabled him to consolidate his recent gains and unite a weak and divided Germany under a strong Habsburg monarchy. By retaining the Edict of Restitution, the emperor and the League princes further alienated the north German Electors, thereby exacerbating existing Protestant–Catholic divisions. The events at Regensburg had, in effect, created a power vacuum. No one was now in control of the empire.

It was precisely at this moment of weakness and crisis that France and Sweden, in their different ways, were sucked into the struggle. A French delegation had been sent to the emperor in the summer of 1630 with orders to seek a solution to numerous points: control of the Valtelline (still disputed despite the peace of Monzón in 1626); sovereignty in the three Lorraine bishoprics (seized by France in 1552 and still claimed by the Empire); and the duke of Nevers's title to Mantua and Montferrat. Talks dragged on throughout July and August, with the French diplomats using their spare time to foment opposition to the emperor (for example, by encouraging the Electors to refuse recognition to Ferdinand's son as heir-apparent). But then sensational news reached Regensburg: on 18 July the Imperialists had taken the city of Mantua, and the duke of Nevers with it. A swift solution to the war in northern Italy now seemed a pressing necessity to the French negotiators, before the situation deteriorated further. They appealed to Paris for immediate powers to conclude a settlement; but none came. Eventually, with considerable misgivings, on 13 October, they signed a treaty which not only stipulated joint French and Imperial evacuation of northern Italy, but committed Louis XIII to refrain from offering support to anyone who opposed the emperor.

It is not hard to imagine the impact of these concessions at

the French Court. The king had hitched his wagon to the star of
Mantua since the capture of La Rochelle in October 1628. To
permit the speedy relief of the duchy, the French government had
made extensive concessions to the defeated Huguenots (the
'Grace of Alais', June 1629); it had swallowed its pride and made a
peace with England which brought no direct benefits (the treaty
of Susa, April 1629); and it had renewed its expensive alliance
with the Dutch Republic (June 1630). In all these compromises
with Protestant groups, France had enjoyed the active encouragement of Urban VIII, because they were done for the sake of
liberating Italy from the 'Spanish yoke' – an issue dear to the
pope's heart.[2] Now, thanks to the unauthorized initiative of the
envoys in Regensburg, all this had been signed away: instead
Louis was required to refuse support to the Habsburgs' enemies.
The king's prestige and credibility were gravely compromised and
he was livid. The extent of his fury shows in a letter written to his
ambassadors a week later:

> This treaty is not only contrary to your powers, to the orders
> in the Instructions you took with you, and to those I have
> sent you at various times since, but it even contains several
> items that I have never even thought about, and that are so
> prejudicial that I could not hear them read out to me except
> with extreme displeasure.[3]

In the event, the king refused to ratify the peace of Regensburg,
and a few weeks later, since Richelieu's authority appeared to
have been compromised by this episode, a major attempt was
made to remove him from power. The 'Day of Dupes' (11
November 1630), engineered by the extreme Catholic faction at
Court, came within an ace of success. Mantua remained, for the
time being, in Habsburg hands.

And yet, in the long term, French diplomacy could hardly
have been more successful: by appearing to agree at Regensburg,
and then reneging, France caused far more damage to the Imperial cause than refusal at the outset would have done. Temporarily fortified by Louis's apparent withdrawal from the struggle,
Ferdinand II not only declined to moderate the Edict, but decided
that he could tackle the small Swedish army, which King Gustavus Adolphus led ashore in Pomerania on 6 July 1630, without any
attempt to render his policies more acceptable to German Protestants. It was a fatal miscalculation for, by the time the Imperialists realized that their troops could not be withdrawn from Italy,
the Swedes could no longer be dislodged from Pomerania.

The principalities most immediately affected by the Swedish

invasion were the north German Protestant states. How their rulers, especially the two Electors, would react was crucial for the future course of the war. John George of Saxony and George William of Brandenburg, the one a Lutheran, the other a Calvinist, had seldom maintained cordial relations in the past. As the Empire's 'foremost Lutheran prince', John George saw himself as 'the protector of the cradle of the Reformation' and, like most of his co-religionists, he distrusted Calvinists more than Catholics. As a political conservative, he had generally supported the emperor. The role of the Elector of Brandenburg was more difficult. Although, after the disgrace of Frederick of the Palatinate, George William was as much the leader of the German Calvinists as John George was of the Lutherans, in reality his position was far weaker. The Elector would have chosen the course of armed neutrality during the 1620s, but Brandenburg's powerful Lutheran Estates, fearful that they might be drawn into the conflict, refused to grant their Reformed ruler the necessary support for such a policy. Then, in 1626, with both Danish and Imperial troops crossing the Electorate with impunity, a choice between the two sides had to be made. Although the majority of George William's councillors were (like him) Calvinists, his principal adviser, Count Adam of Schwarzenberg, was a Catholic and he played upon the desire of the Lutheran Estates for economy and security in order to bring his Elector into an alliance with the emperor (the treaty of Königsberg, May 1627). But the Imperial alliance was not a happy one: the Brandenburgers soon complained about the harsh treatment that they suffered at the hands of the Imperial troops who came streaming into the country in pursuit of the Danes.

The two Protestant Electors met for a week in April 1630, at Annaburg in Saxony, to discuss recent political developments and the coming Electoral meeting in Regensburg. Reaffirming an earlier decision not to attend the meeting in person, they agreed to provide their delegations with similar instructions. George William's Reformed advisers would have preferred the Electors to have taken a more definite stand against the emperor – they even contemplated the possibility of a Protestant defensive alliance – but the Saxons were not yet ready for such joint ventures. By early September, however, when the two Electors and their advisers met again, this time at Zabeltitz castle (Saxony), the Saxon attitude had changed considerably. John George was deeply disturbed by the Swedish invasion and the proceedings at Regensburg, particularly the Catholics' uncompromising stand on the Edict of Restitution, and this provided the Brandenburgers with an ideal opportunity to resubmit their proposals and receive a more favourable response. George William's privy councillors, who were already advocating a more resolute stand vis-à-vis the emperor, now called for a similar strategy towards the Swedish king. Indeed, their Swedish policy must be seen as the direct corollary of their Imperial policy: both aimed to preserve the integrity and the constitution of the Empire in general, and the rights and liberties of Protestant states in particular; both were designed to create a neutral third force between king and emperor to keep the war from spreading further. At Zabeltitz, the Brandenburgers' proposals carried the day and John George announced that he would call a meeting of all German Protestant rulers at Leipzig in the very near future to discuss their grievances and to consider appropriate counter-measures.

John George's resolve, however, was short-lived. As a Lutheran, and a firm believer in the Imperial constitution, he continued to oppose a direct confrontation with the emperor. Not surprisingly, therefore, the combined pressures of the Catholic Electors and of his fellow-Lutherans (particularly his son-in-law, the arch-conservative Landgrave George II of Hesse-Darmstadt) soon convinced John George that bilateral negotiations with the emperor would be more fruitful than any multilateral efforts made with other Protestant rulers. Then in November the Catholics, alarmed by the French repudiation of the peace of Regensburg, suddenly let it be known that concessions on the Edict of Restitution might still be possible, and they proposed a meeting with the Protestants early in 1631, at Frankfurt, to discuss the execution of the Imperial Edict. 'We sensed', the Catholic Electors explained later, 'that the complete denial of all gestures of kindness on our part would have endangered the Holy Roman Empire, especially the . . . Catholic faith.'[4] The Frankfurt meeting, in other words, was deliberately scheduled to keep the Protestants from pulling together (see Plate 8).

That the gathering of Protestants at Leipzig eventually took place at all was due mainly to Brandenburg's Calvinist councillors, who kept on prodding the Elector of Saxony, insisting that a meeting of Protestant rulers was needed, if for no other reason than to devise a joint evangelical strategy for Frankfurt. John George, despite the objections of some of his own advisers, was eventually persuaded, and in January 1631 notices went out to some 160 states informing them that the long-expected conference would finally commence on 6 February. The response was overwhelming: except for George of Hesse-Darmstadt, every major Protestant prince attended and several Imperial cities also sent representatives.

Stürmung der Judengasse zu Franckfurt am Mayn.

1 *The Fettmilch uprising in Frankfurt (1612–1616)* The revolt of the citizens of Frankfurt which began in 1612, during the celebration of Matthias's election as emperor, was both anti-patrician and anti-semitic in character. At first the burghers, led by the charismatic pastry-baker Vincent Fettmilch, called for a more democratic city council and for the expulsion of the city's large Jewish population (which, many thought, derived unfair advantage from the protection provided by the council). In 1614, since the councillors refused to mend their ways, the citizens deposed them and looted the Jewish ghetto (as seen in this print). All the Jews were driven from the city. These new disorders, however, forced the emperor to intervene and, eventually, Fettmilch was seized by his fellow-citizens and his movement collapsed. In 1616 he was executed and the patricians returned to power. The disorders in Frankfurt were but the most extreme example of the tension between councils and citizens which erupted into violence in a score of German cities in the years before the war (see Map 1).
From J. L. Gottfried, *Historische Chronica* (Frankfurt, 1633), p. 1142. Courtesy Historisches Museum, Frankfurt-am-Main

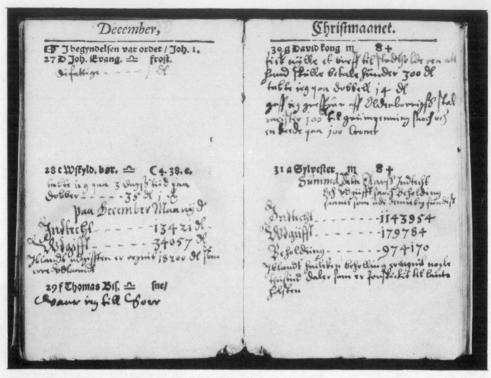

2 *The finances of Christian of Denmark (1618)* The holograph diary of Christian IV, for New Year's Eve 1618, summing up his capital assets (in Danish *daler*). In translation the text runs:

Totals of this year's revenue and expense as well as the reserve, recorded in this book:

revenue 1,143,954
expense 179,784
reserve 974,170
This reserve includes some thousand *daler,* which have been sent to Holstein.

This astonishingly healthy financial position—of which the king's diary is the only record—helps to explain why the king of Denmark was to be so assiduously courted by the supporters of Frederick of the Palatinate.
From Copenhagen, Rigsarkivet, Kongehusets arkiv: Christian IV

3 *The Neuburg Wedding (12 November 1614)* If the Protestant 'Wedding of the Year' in 1613 was that of Frederick of the Palatinate with Elizabeth Stuart in London, the Catholic equivalent was unquestionably between Wolfgang William, heir to the duchy of Pfalz Neuburg, and Anna Magdalena, sister of Maximilian of Bavaria, in Munich. This print, one of a set of twelve (by Wilhelm Peter Zimmermann of Augsburg) commemorating the festivities, shows the newly married couple proceeding out of the church to the accompaniment of a volley of muskets. The wedding cemented Wolfgang William's adhesion to the Catholic cause—he had only left the Lutheran faith the previous July—and also served as a guarantee of Bavarian support for the Neuburg claim to the Cleves-Jülich succession.
From Munich, Staatliche Graphische Sammlung 94.451

Abbildung der Statt Budißlin oder Baußen, wie dieselbe von Ch. F. Durchl. zu Sachsen erobert worden im Sept. Anno 1620.

Jgne Jau.

Anweisung der Ziffer. 1. Das Schloß. 2. S. Nicolaus. 3. Schules Thor. 4. Schellenthurm 5. Becker gassen. 6. Haupt Kirch S Peter. 7. Das Rahthauß.
8. Reichenthor. 9. Mühlthor. 10. Alte Wasserkunst. 11. die grosse Bastl. 12. Lauwenthor. 13. die Neue Wasserkunst. 14. F. Ch. F. Durchl. 15. gesangne.

Der Jeſuiter, Sampt des General Tilly.
Newliche Zuſammenkunfft, in einer ſünckel ſtuben. Zu Aug.

4 (above) *The surrender of Bautzen to John George of Saxony* (1620) Although the support of Bavaria for the Habsburg cause in 1620 is the more famous, the campaign of Saxony to assist Ferdinand II was also important. It was, however, largely bloodless. Where Maximilian had to fight his way through Upper Austria and Bohemia to Prague, John George occupied Silesia and Lusatia with scarcely a blow. Only the Lusatian capital, Bautzen, put up serious resistance and (as this engraving shows) even that did not last long. The defenders were soon compelled to make their formal surrender to the stout Elector.
From J. P. Abelinus, *Theatrum europaeum*, I (Frankfurt, 1639), pp. 421–2

5 *General Tilly joins the Jesuits in the spinning-room* (1632) It was Tilly rather than Wallenstein who symbolized, for Protestant propagandists, the Imperial and Catholic threat; and he became the butt of endless satirical prints and broadsheets, especially after his fortunes began to fail with the battle of Breitenfeld. This savage lampoon, for example, shows the aged general surrounded by Jesuits and monks in a decrepit spinning-room. No longer able to spin their plots, they are now reduced to spinning flax in the manner of old village women.
From Wolfenbüttel, Herzog-August-Bibliothek, *Sammlung Illustrierte Einblattdrucke JH 170*

6 *The Edict of Restitution (1629)* Seldom has a scrap of paper proved so controversial as the Edict on religion, issued by Ferdinand II on 6 March 1629. It contained only four columns of text, yet it was to prove the downfall of all his ambitious plans. This copy, signed by Ferdinand himself, was sent in advance to Maximilian of Bavaria, as Director of an Imperial Circle, with orders to have it reproduced and distributed widely in his area by the official date of publication, 28 March.

From Munich, Bayerisches Hauptstaatsarchiv, *Kasten Schwarz* 60 fo. 106

Der Röm. Käys. auch zu
Hungarn vnd Böheimb Kön. Mayst.

FERDINANDI II.

Außspruch/Decision/vnd Käys. Edict/

Radix omnium Vber malorum.

Etliche Puncten den ReligionFrieden/sonderlich
die Restitution der Geistlichen Güter betreffendt.

Auß dem Original mit fleiß nachgedruckt.

Gedruckt in der Fürstl. Hauptstatt Wirtzburg/
bey Stephan Fleischmann.

Anno M. DC. XXIX.

7 *The Edict: 'root of all evil'* This edition of the Edict was reprinted in pamphlet form from the copy sent to the bishop of Würzburg. It was one of the thirty-five different versions known and bears the handwritten judgment of an anonymous (but certainly Catholic) contemporary: *Radix omnium malorum.*
From Nuremberg, Stadtbibliothek, Hist. 494. 4°

8 *The Leipzig Colloquy (1631): a Protestant Plot* To the Catholics, the meeting of the Protestant states of the empire in the spring of 1631 seemed to presage an international conspiracy involving England, France, Sweden and the Dutch as well as German Lutherans and Calvinists. A 'restless spirit' (*unruhiger Geist*)—in fact the Devil himself—is shown as the conference secretary and is blamed for sowing opposition to the lawful authority of the emperor (on the right) and the true church (on the left). This is one of only three known pamphlets hostile to Gustavus Adolphus of Sweden. Broadsheets of a Catholic persuasion were rare in the years after 1629: however they fared in battle, the Protestants retained a crushing superiority in the propaganda war.
From Munich, Bayerische Staatsbibliothek, Einblattdrucke V, 8a, no. 37

9 *The Swedish progress (1630–1632)* The rich allegorical content of this broadsheet from 1632 is typical of the period. The victorious king of Sweden is shown advancing towards the Holy Roman Empire in a chariot pulled by animals symbolizing the magnanimity, speed, forthrightness and exalted ancestry of the charioteer; these beasts are, in turn, guided by the hand of God. A team of dispossessed Protestant princes helps to push the chariot forward, while Imperial peace overtures ('Pacem') are spurned so long as 'Religion' (G) points accusingly at the gagged and bound true church ('R').
From British Library, Call no. 1750, b. 29/47

10 *The siege of Smolensk (1632)* Sweden had been at war with Poland throughout the 1620s, and Gustavus Adolphus was concerned that his cousin Sigismund III might, despite the six-year truce of Altmark (1629), launch a further attack designed to recover some of his losses while Sweden was fully occupied in the German war. It was to counter this threat that Gustavus encouraged the Russians to declare war on Poland, weakened by the death of Sigismund in the spring of 1632. The Russian army, aided by English and Scottish volunteers, laid siege to Smolensk and besieged it over the winter of 1632–3 with all the latest military techniques (shown in this print by Hondius). Nevertheless, partly due to quarrels among the British mercenaries, the siege failed and peace was concluded early in 1634. Poland was now free to work towards the removal of the Swedes from the Baltic when the truce of Altmark expired the following year.
Courtesy Dr Paul Dukes

11 *The Swedish Hercules (1631)* Another, rather more obvious allegory concerning the amazing king of Sweden, whose embodiment of the Protestant cause was a feature of almost all the propaganda of these years.
From Wolfenbüttel, Herzog-August-Bibliothek, *Sammlung Illustrierte Einblattdrucke:* 'Der Schwedische Hercules'

12 *'The Saxon Sweetmeats' (1631)* At a meeting between the Elector of Saxony and representatives of General Tilly, the former was said to have warned the Imperialists that if they tried to devour the hitherto untouched 'confection' of Saxony, they would find that it contained some hard nuts to crack (see page 126). This exchange gave rise to a whole series of broadsheets. Here we see Tilly trying to seize the tasty dishes labelled 'regio' and 'religio' while John George fends him off with the staff of 'clear conscience' and Gustavus Adolphus brandishes the chalice of justice. The Saxon stands on solid blocks entitled 'just cause' and 'sure hope', while Tilly balances precariously on balls labelled 'malice' and 'falsehood'!
From British Library, Call no. 1750.b. 29/32

13 *Swedish progress continues* Some broadsheets were closely linked to the changing daily news. Here we see Gustavus Adolphus forcing the pope, as a symbol of the Catholic cause, to disgorge cities and fortresses captured from the Protestants during the 1620s. The sequence, almost resembling a strip-cartoon, includes the places taken or relieved by the Swedes on their march from Stralsund on the Baltic to Kreuznach in the Rhineland. Space has been left for the insertion of further victories in later editions of the print!
From British Library, Call no. 1750.b. 29/67*

14 *Gustav Adolphiana* After the great victory at Breitenfeld a veritable 'Gustavus industry' grew up. Some items were individually crafted, but others were mass-produced: ivory reliefs, silver statues, gold rings, pendants and medallions were made in the likeness of the Swedish king. The ceremonial beaker offered yet another way to commemorate the Protestant hero.
From London, Victoria and Albert Museum, item 1885A–1898

15 *Gustavus redivivus (1633)* The king's death did not immediately bring to an end the flood of broadsheets associated with his achievements in Germany. This print of 1633 presents in maudlin fashion the king's apotheosis: borne up by the 'three crowns' (Sweden's national emblem), Gustavus rises indestructible from the waves. The title reads: 'The Swede lives on'.
From Munich, Bayerische Staatsbibliothek, Einblattdrucke V, 8a, no. 89

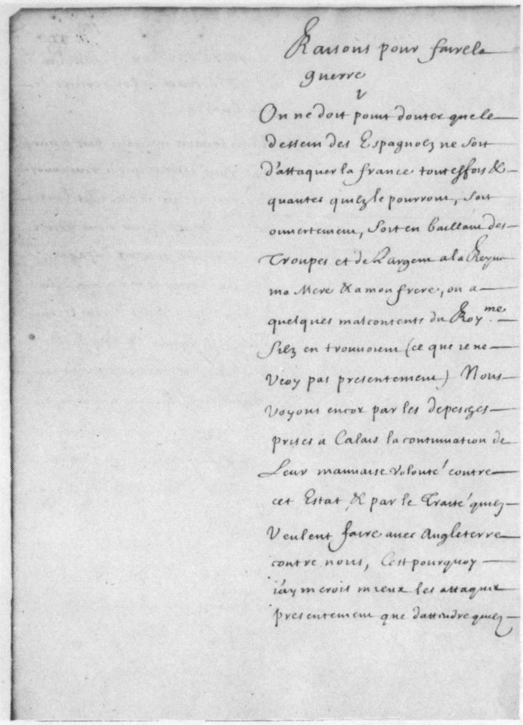

Raisons pour faire la
guerre

1

On ne doit point douter que le
dessein des Espagnolz ne soit
d'attaquer la france, tout effort &
quantes qu'ilz le pourront, soit
ouvertement, soit en bailleant des
Troupes et de l'argent a la Reyne
ma Mere & a mon frere, on a
quelques malcontens du Roy, me
silz en trouvoient (ce que ie ne
voy pas presentement) Nous
voyons encor par les depesches
prises a Calais la continuation de
leur mauvaise volonté contre
cet Estat & par le Traité qu'ilz
veulent faire avec Angleterre
contre nous, C'est pourquoy
i'aymerois mieux les attaquer
presentement que d'attendre qu'ilz

110

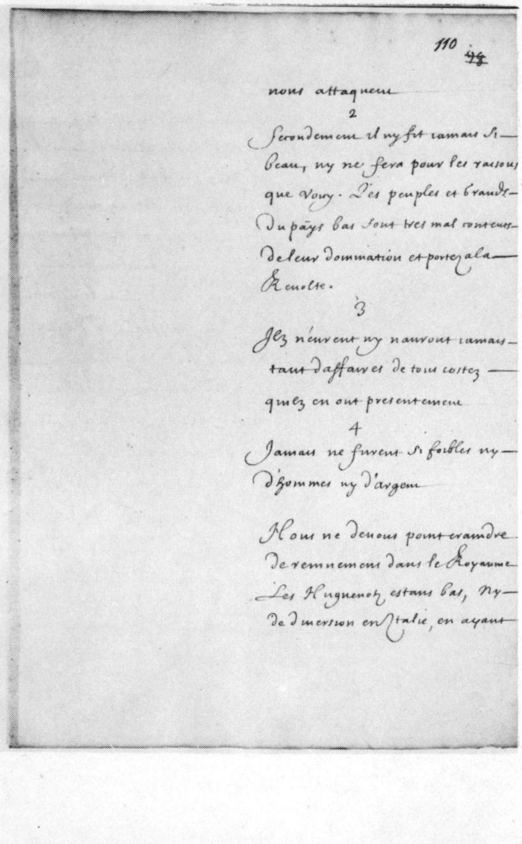

nous attaquent
2

Secondement il ny fit iamais si
beau, ny ne sera pour les raisons
que dessus. Les peuples et brandt
du pays bas sont tres mal contens
de leur domination et portez a la
Revolte.

3

Ilz n'eurent ny n'auront iamais
tant d'affaires de tous costez
qu'ilz en ont presentement

4

Iamais ne furent si foibles ny
d'hommes ny d'argent

Nous ne devons point craindre
de remuement dans le Royaume
Les Huguenotz estans bas, ny
de diversion en Italie, en ayant

16a and b *Louis XIII prepares for war (1634)* On
4 August 1634 the king of France wrote a top
secret memorandum ('Not a living soul has seen
it' according to the document) to his chief
minister, Cardinal Richelieu, concerning the
correct policy to be followed towards the
Habsburgs. At this stage, Louis's view was
primarily defensive. He argued that France could
not afford to be left isolated if the Dutch signed a
new truce with Spain, or if the Swedes and their
Heilbronn allies made peace with the emperor. A
French declaration of war against Spain, on the
other hand, would forestall a Dutch truce and
give new heart to the German Protestants. The
underlying assumption was that the Spanish, not
the German war would be the central concern;
after Nördlingen, just a month later, this
viewpoint had to be considerably amended.
From Paris, Archive du Ministère des Affaires
Etrangères, *Correspondance politique:
Allemagne*, vol. 23, fos 338–40

17 *Amore Pacis (1648)* This enormous broadsheet incorporated a map prepared on the orders of Quarter-Master-General Cornelis van den Büsch and accompanied by details on the leading battles of Sweden's war (1630–48), the location of the various garrisons of Sweden and her allies at the end of the war, and other useful military information. It served both to advertise Sweden's successes and to locate her far-flung garrisons ready for evacuation.
From Stockholm, Krigsarkivet, *Hist. Plan. 1648*: 24 fol.

Groß Europifch Kriegs Balet/getantzet durch die Könige vnd Potentaten Fürften vnd Refpublicken/
auff dem Saal der betrübten Chriftenheit.

18 *The Great European War-Ballet (1647–1648)* This simple satire on the seemingly endless diplomatic quadrille
at Westphalia shows the various European rulers trying to move in unison, as angels scatter olive-branches and
apples of discord before them. On the right, watched by the Turkish Sultan and the prince of Transylvania, the
infant Louis XIV holds hands with John IV of Portugal, the prince of Orange and General Torstensson (an
interesting choice to represent Sweden). They dance in front of the coffin of Frederick of the Palatinate while
Gustavus lies dead on the ground. On the side, the emperor and his allies are watched by a group of Italian
princes, while Saxony and the Swiss cantons seek advantage in the foregound.
From Munich, Bayerische Staatsbibliothek

Secundum et ultimum Prælium à Meridie usq; ad Noctem apud Ianckau 24.Febr. 6.Mart. A 1645. factum, in quo Cæsarianos et Bauar. relicto campo Suecis Victoriæ concedere oportuit.
Das Andere vnd Letste Treffen so nach mitag biß in die nacht den 24.Febr. 6.Meth Anno 1645. bey Jancowitz geschehen, daben die Schwedischen das feldt erhalten.

Lanckau

19 *The battle of Jankov (1645)* One of the superb engravings by the Frankfurt engraver and bookseller Matthaeus Merian (1593–1650), published in the volume *Theatrum europaeum* as a sort of contemporary history, printed as the war proceeded. The perceived importance of Jankov is reflected in the fact that four separate illustrations of the battle were included in the work, as against two for Breitenfeld and three for Lützen.
From M. Merian, *Theatrum europaeum*, V (Frankfurt, 1647), pp. 716–17

20 and 21 *Nuremberg: the end of the war (1650)* Although the peace of Westphalia brought the fighting to an end in October 1648, it took almost two more years before a formula for demobilizing the army was agreed by all parties. The leading role was played by Prince Charles Gustav of Pfalz-Zweibrücken, commander-in-chief of the Swedish army and heir apparent to the Swedish throne (to which he ascended in 1654 as Charles X). Here (*above*) he sits to the left of the Imperial commander, Ottavio Piccolomini, at the end of the table (left foreground), awaiting the feast which celebrated the final agreement, while outside a firework spectacular takes place (*opposite*). At last, Germany was at peace.

From M. Merian, *Theatri europaei oder historischer Beschreibung . . . sechster und letzter Teil* (Frankfurt, 1652), pp. 939 and 1076

Abriß deß Kaÿsserlichen Fewerwercks Schlosses: vnd BARRAQUEN,
worinen daß Fried vnd: freudenmahl gehalten werdt: vor Nurnberg auff eᵐ Joh: Schüßplatz. Aᵒ1650.

A. Die Haupt Barraque
B. Trumeter vnd Heerpaucker Standte
C. Iho Fürstl: Durchl: Reven: Generalissim, welcher :

Das Fewerwerck zu Erst angezündet
D. Die Seule, worauff das Friedens Bild gestanden.
E. Porta: des Fewerwercks: Schlosses auf welcher das Bildt Diuercke

vnd dar unter das Bildt Martis gestanden.
F. Ein Vorständiges Stucklein, welches nebenst einer Raqueten oder
mahl, so offt eine Gstund bei getruncken worden Laßung geben.

woraußdan die oben gesetzte Stuck auf beyden seiten zu:
gleich in gebührender Ordnung geantwordet
G. Ein Theil der Statt Nürnberg. H. Barren.Schmid.J.Schöttn. bau zu.Nᵒ65

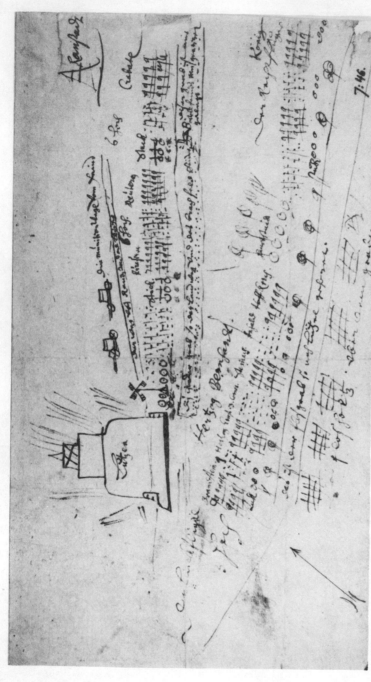

22a and b *Contemporary sketches of the battle of Lützen (1632)* The Catholic defeat at Breitenfeld arose because the Swedish battle order—with thinner, longer lines, more field artillery, and more musketeers—proved superior to the traditional way. Therefore the defeated Imperialists, directed by Wallenstein, now adopted the Swedish technique. At Lützen, both sides were deployed more or less in the same new fashion, and the result was a draw. By a happy chance, two contemporary sketches of the battle lines at Lützen have survived: one (*above*) from the Protestant side (although anonymous, Wallenstein's '*munitionslager*' is described as '*vom Feind*'—'of the enemy'); the other (*below*) perhaps drawn up by Wallenstein himself and given to Pappenheim (it was found on the dead count, stained with his blood, after the battle). Wallenstein's right flank is shown to have been anchored on Lützen village and the windmills, while Gustavus's position ('*König*' in top map at bottom right) was on the opposite flank, which is why his funeral monument is today located some two miles away from the village. The massed artillery of the Swedes, which caused such heavy losses among the Imperialists, is shown in the centre of their line ('*Sämptstücke*') in the more schematic 'Protestant sketch'.

Top from Stockholm, Krigsarkivet, *Sveriges Krig*, 3 : 86; bottom from Vienna, Heeresgeschichtiches Museum (Kat. Erben/John 1903), nr 75/3

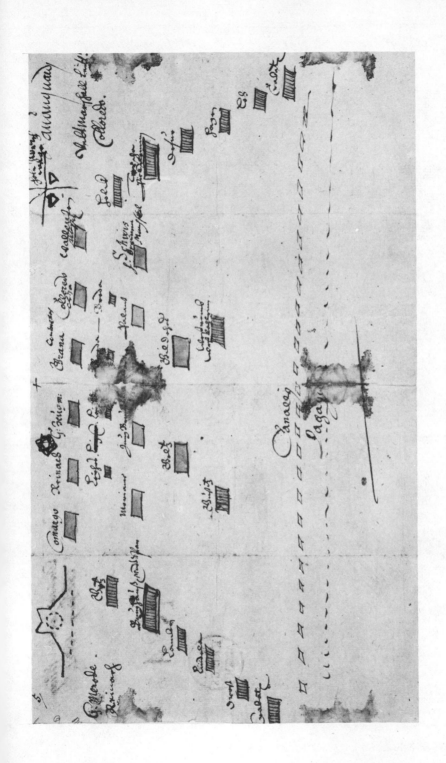

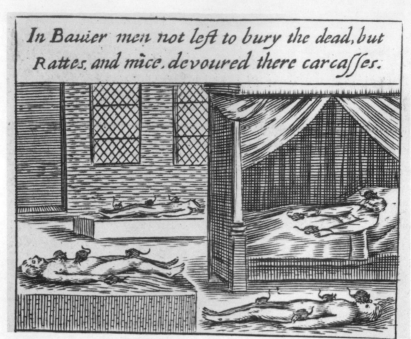

In Bauier men not left to bury the dead, but Rattes, and mice, devoured there carcasses.

Haue pittey vpon me, haue pittey vpon me, o yee my frends, for the hand of the Lord hath touched me.

GERMANY

23a, b and c *The lamentations of Germany* An English booklet on the war published in 1638, entitled *The lamentations of Germany*, included letters from some Protestant ministers in the Palatinate to their exiled colleagues in London. But the main text was a long report on 'the miserable estate of Germany' compiled by the refugee G. R. Weckerlin with chapter-headings such as 'Of tortures and torments   Of rape and ravishing', 'Of bloodshed and killing' . . . These are but a few of the less horrifying illustrations to his chilling account of man's inhumanity to man.
From *The lamentations of Germany* (London, 1638), plates facing pp. a2, 26, 61

Priests slaine at theire Altars

Croats eate   Children

Noses & eares Cut of to make hatbandes

Snalles and froges eagerly eaten

Eatinge dead mens guts and Interalls

A divines wife saw 6 of her Children ley starued before her eyes. Corne 3 pounds 18 shilling a bushell.

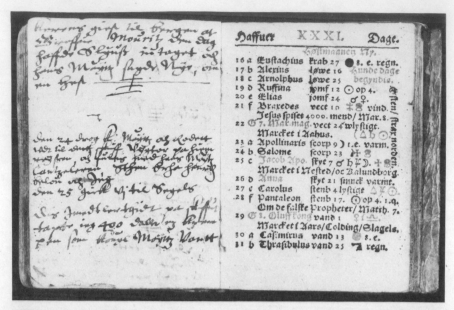

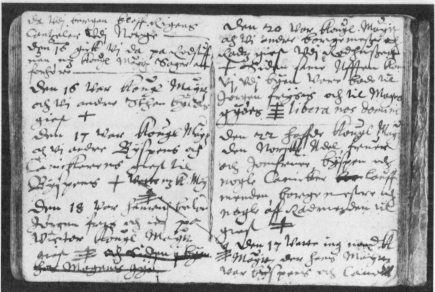

24a and b *At the court of Christian IV* An extract from the diary of Christian's councillor, Esge Brock, during the king's visit to Norway by sea in 1604. The crosses at the end of each entry register the degree of intoxication at the end of each evening. The entry for 20 July, on the lower right hand page, runs 'His Royal Majesty and ourselves were the guests of the mayor and the council (of Bergen) at the city hall. Later the same night we entered the city and the lodgings of Jørgen Friis and Mogens Gøye. Libera nos domine!' The four crosses, and the prayer, appear to indicate a night of unparalleled excess which left even the hard-drinking Brock with a hangover. The royal court set the tone for heavy drinking which became fashionable in so much of Protestant Europe. From Copenhagen, Rigsarkivet, Privatarkiver no. 5212: Esge Brock C: Dagbøger 1604–1622

But the main problem remained the attitude of John George: would he insist that the Leipzig conference must remain merely a preparatory meeting for the coming Frankfurt talks? Or would he also support defensive measures? Five days before the conference began, Ferdinand II had sent a threatening letter to the Elector which forbade the Protestant rulers to arm. But others were urging him to consider joint defensive measures, among them the influential Saxon court preacher, Matthias Hoë von Hoënegg, who in years past had distinguished himself by his vociferous anti-Calvinist polemics (page 22 above). The Edict of Restitution, however, had changed his tune. Only a few weeks before the Leipzig conference, Hoë had told John George that if the Edict were not repealed, it would be the Elector's duty as a Lutheran to fight the emperor. Similarly, in a sermon that he delivered on the first day of the convention, Hoë urged the assembled rulers to unite and to defend themselves against the arbitrary rule of Ferdinand and his allies.[5]

The Calvinist pastors at the court of Berlin welcomed Hoë's sentiments. For years they had urged, without much success, greater cooperation with the Lutherans, and their more militant policies received ideological support from Reformed irenicism whose leading spokesman in the 1620s and '30s was John Peter Bergius, Hoë's counterpart in Berlin. Bergius's studies in Heidelberg, Strasbourg and Cambridge, and his visits to France and Holland, had brought him into contact with international Protestantism. As a theological moderate he was convinced that most Lutheran–Calvinist disagreements could be overcome, since the two Protestant churches agreed on the 'fundamental articles' of the Christian faith. His views reflected the official confessional position both of Brandenburg's Calvinist church and of the Elector and his councillors. Like Hoë, he urged the princes at Leipzig to unite and defend themselves.[6]

While the politicians met, the theologians held their own colloquy. Hoë and two of his Lutheran colleagues from Saxony met with Bergius of Brandenburg and two other Calvinists from Hesse-Kassel. Using the Augsburg Confession as the basis for their deliberations, these six men demonstrated an almost unprecedented harmony. To be sure, the major issues dividing Lutherans and Calvinists – the doctrines of the Lord's Supper and predestination – were not resolved; but the two sides agreed to consider these differences further at later meetings. They also promised to 'show each other Christian love in the future'. The religious colloquy was important because it helped to create an atmosphere of good-will and thus provided a valuable ideological basis for the political and military cooperation that the princes were seeking in their own meeting at Leipzig.[7]

Yet the surprising harmony which existed on the theological front did not entirely prevail in the political deliberations. Initially, John George and his more timid secular advisers seemed prepared to talk about nothing apart from the coming meeting at Frankfurt. But the Brandenburgers were obviously expressing a common concern when they raised on 15 March the question of military resistance.[8] A Protestant defensive alliance, they suggested, could be organized without violating the Imperial constitution. Such an alliance would not be aimed against anyone in particular, but it would safeguard the princes' rights against anyone who might endanger them, regardless of whether this was the Emperor Ferdinand or the king of Sweden. The response was so encouraging that the Brandenburgers decided to draft a formal proposal for the creation of a defensive alliance. This became the basis for the Leipzig Manifesto – the final resolution issued by the princes on 12 April 1631 which created a defensive association, the *Leipziger Bund*, with an army of 40,000 troops to be used for defensive purposes only. Their recruitment and financing was left to individual Imperial Circles, whose defensive efforts would be coordinated by a committee over which John George of Saxony presided. The purpose of this armed association was clearly stated: it was to protect and 'uphold the basic laws, the Imperial constitution, and the German liberties of the Protestant states'.[9]

The Leipzig Manifesto was an eleventh-hour attempt to protect the religious and political interests of the Protestant rulers. It served clear notice on Ferdinand II and his allies that the Protestant princes would resist military oppression and further recatholicization. It also warned Gustavus Adolphus that the Electors of Brandenburg and Saxony, and most other Lutheran states, would not willingly become his allies. In short, the Manifesto sought to defend the constitution of the Holy Roman Empire by creating a neutral third force between the Imperial, the League, and the foreign armies whose aggression threatened to turn the war in Central Europe into a major international conflict.

Maximilian of Bavaria, too, was deeply disturbed by developments in the summer of 1630. At first glance, his anxiety may appear somewhat unwarranted, for more than any other German prince he had benefited from Wallenstein's dismissal. Tilly, the League general, now also commanded the Imperial army, and the way seemed clear for Maximilian to regain that military dominance over Ferdinand which he had possessed before 1625. But, besides safeguarding his rights and interests as a German prince and a Roman Catholic, Maximilian was concerned with protecting the Electoral title and lands he had recently acquired. And for this he needed a period of peace. The growing divisions within the Empire and the widening conflict in 1630 seemed to threaten his gains, forcing him to explore new ways to safeguard his rights and interests. Maximilian's predicament was exacerbated by his support for the Edict of Restitution (which kept him from making common cause with any of the Protestants) and even more by France's geographical proximity and growing hostility to the Habsburgs.

The French and the Bavarians had already conducted negotiations for a possible alliance in the mid-1620s. In an effort to weaken the power of the Habsburgs, Richelieu had tried to persuade Maximilian to organize and lead a confessionally mixed group of princes, but the Bavarian, eager to preserve his political independence, looked to France only to protect his Electoral title and land. Since the French government could not bring itself to do this, negotiations had been broken off in 1627 (page 71 above). However, the threat of a Habsburg absolutist regime in the Empire, posed principally by Wallenstein's army, made Maximilian again more receptive to French overtures. The arrival of Hercule de Charnacé, Richelieu's agent, in Munich on 16 March 1629, set the stage for another round of negotiations.

For a while it looked as if once more the talks would lead nowhere, and Charnacé moved on. However, by October 1630, Father Joseph, at Regensburg, could report that Bavaria was now ready to discuss the alliance seriously. There were several reasons for this change of heart. One was Maximilian's fear that Spain had secretly promised Charles I of England that both the Palatinate and the Electoral title would eventually be restored to Frederick.[10] Another was the deepening political crisis in the Empire: fear of Wallenstein and opposition to involvement in Mantua were now replaced by fear of Gustavus Adolphus. Although the extent of Sweden's involvement in the war was not immediately evident, Gustavus's presence on German soil, perceived as a serious threat to the Imperial constitution and to Bavaria's interests, inexorably pushed Maximilian in the direction of a French alliance. An agreement with France was desirable in the autumn of 1630 because of the still uncertain attitude of Sweden and the Protestant princes; it became urgent for Maximilian after the treaty of Bärwalde (January 1631), which allied France and Sweden in the cause of 'the restitution of the suppressed Estates of the Empire'.

Yet, as was the case with the Protestant Electors, religion also underpinned Maximilian's political outlook. His confidant and confessor, the Jesuit Adam Contzen, had urged a treaty with France since the spring of 1629 in the hope that such an alliance would further the Catholic cause in the Empire. He dreamed of a Europe-wide Catholic front (a very unrealistic scheme as long as Habsburg–Bourbon rivalry continued), but Contzen's pro-French arguments – backed to the hilt by papal diplomats – clearly did influence Maximilian and his secular advisers, especially when it became evident that Sweden's Lutheran king would use his military might to roll back the Catholic position in the Empire.[11]

The major stumbling-block in the Franco-Bavarian talks was Richelieu's refusal to commit himself on two points which Maximilian deemed basic for the protection of his own rights and the Imperial constitution. Bavaria wanted France to accept his family's hereditary right to the Electoral title which he had acquired; but Richelieu would only acknowledge Maximilian's personal claim and declined to guarantee it for his descendants. In addition, the Elector wanted a special clause in the treaty recognizing his constitutional obligations to the Empire and the emperor; Richelieu, who wanted to enlist Bavarian support against the Habsburgs, refused. Eventually, in order to secure an alternative ally to the Swedes, and to appease his Catholic critics, Richelieu gave in: Maximilian received the guarantees and the recognition he sought. The treaty of Fontainebleau was signed in May 1631. It was to last for eight years, and it was to remain entirely secret. Both parties agreed not to attack each other or to assist each other's enemies. However, the League princes were not included in the treaty – an omission that was to have grave consequences the following year.[12]

The treaty of Fontainebleau can be seen as the Catholic counterpart to the Protestants' Leipzig Manifesto issued only a few weeks earlier. Both were direct responses to the failure of the Regensburg Electoral meeting to restore order. Both sought to protect the constitution of the Empire and the rights and liberties of the princes. Both aimed at the creation of a neutral third force that would stand as a buffer between the emperor and his foreign enemies in order to prevent the war from spreading further. But both efforts – and this was Germany's great tragedy – in the end failed because neither could stop the Swedes, who had their own idea of what the Empire wanted, and had the strength to trample underfoot all whose opinion on the subject differed from theirs.

ii 1630–1632: The intervention of Sweden

An anonymous English pamphlet of 1638, entitled *The civil wars of Germany*, offered to readers a useful guide to both the war and its commanders. There were twenty-one portraits of the military leaders on each side, together with a succinct *curriculum vitae*; and the war itself was divided into 167 numbered 'episodes', each one briskly narrated and bristling with facts. It was significant, however, that only thirty-two of the selected episodes occurred during the first twelve years of the war: for the English spectators, as for most Germans, the war only began in earnest with 'episode 33', the arrival in the Empire of King Gustavus Adolphus of Sweden, and his army, in July 1630 (see Plate 9).

The king did not arrive at Peenemünde with the express intention of plunging Europe deeper into war. His *Declaration* of June 1630, which had the widest circulation of any known pamphlet of the time (twenty-three editions in five languages) was couched in modest terms. It opened, innocently enough, with a list of minor personal grievances: 'His Majesty of Sweden has suffered many outrages and injuries without being able to receive any satisfaction for them, such as having his letters [to other princes] intercepted, opened, falsely deciphered and interpreted', or being refused permission to participate in the peace of Lübeck or send an embassy to the emperor. Then came a denunciation of Wallenstein's aid to the king of Poland in 1629 – '[the emperor] has caused whole armies to march into Prussia against His Majesty and the kingdom of Sweden'. Next, Gustavus complained of the Habsburgs' 'Baltic design', which, he argued, was directed against the maritime supremacy currently enjoyed by Sweden. Only at the end, and with some reticence, did the Manifesto note the oppression of German liberties by the emperor as a motive for invasion. There was no mention at all of what Sweden hoped to gain by her intervention, nor of any desire to save the Protestant cause from extinction at the hands of Imperial troops.[1] As late as August 1630, the king was still protesting that his campaign was 'in no way directed against his Imperial Majesty . . . but only and solely for defence against the disturbers of the public peace, both ecclesiastical and secular'. This constitutionalist stance was clearly designed to appeal to public opinion in Germany – the king well knew the value of fighting a war that contemporaries considered to be 'just' – but Gustavus probably himself believed his Manifesto to be a true statement of his mission. In 1636, four

years after the king's death, his close collaborator, the chancellor
Axel Oxenstierna, still denied that the invasion of 1630 had been
primarily a Protestant crusade. It was, he reminded the council of
state (to whom there was little point in lying), 'not so much a
matter of religion, but rather of saving the *status publicus* [the
general political situation], wherein religion is also
comprehended'.[2]

And the *status publicus* of northern Europe in the summer of
1630 certainly gave Sweden's leaders cause for concern. Three
years previously, following the defeat of Christian IV and his
allies, the armies of Tilly and Wallenstein had advanced northwards to the Baltic. The Jutland peninsula was entirely occupied;
the dukes of Mecklenburg were deposed, and Wallenstein installed
in their place; the duke of Pomerania was compelled to admit
Imperialist garrisons to his territories. Although Stralsund held
out against the Imperialists' siege, in September 1628 a new
offensive by Christian IV, reinforced by the Scots from Stralsund,
was heavily defeated at Wolgast. This left Wallenstein free to
loan 12,000 of his troops to the emperor's brother-in-law, Sigismund of Poland, who had been fighting off a Swedish invasion
since 1625 (page 77 above). At first Gustavus's forces had prevailed: Dorpat was taken almost at once and all Livonia fell to the
Swedes; in 1626 several ports in Prussia were captured. But here
the Swedish advance stopped. Whereas the gentry who controlled
the Polish state were not prepared to fight for Livonia, a recent
acquisition which they regarded as bringing benefit only to the
crown, Prussia was a part of the Commonwealth for which they
were prepared to fight to the end. Gustavus and his men were
therefore pinned down by the Baltic shore, steadily exhausting
the lands they controlled and draining the Swedish treasury.[3]
They were no match for the Polish–Imperial army which advanced down the Vistula in the summer of 1629. At the battle of
Honigfelde (or Stuhm) on 27 June, the Swedes suffered a heavy
defeat from which Gustavus was lucky to escape with his life.

He was also fortunate that, shortly after this defeat, a French
envoy arrived at the Swedish camp. Hercule de Charnacé, Riche-
lieu's special envoy in Germany, having failed either to persuade
Maximilian of Bavaria to break with the emperor or to convince
Christian of Denmark to continue his war, was now instructed to
extricate Gustavus from the Polish conflict as a preliminary to
Swedish intervention in Germany. This time he succeeded. At
Altmark, between the two hostile camps, French diplomats
(aided by Sir Thomas Roe representing Charles I) persuaded the
Vasa cousins to sign a six years' truce on 25–6 September, which

confirmed Swedish control of Livonia but involved the restitution of all other gains except a few ports in Prussia. Sweden only accepted these harsh terms in return for the grant, for the duration of the truce, of all tolls on shipping using the ports of Poland and Prussia. This was an extremely lucrative source of revenue, for most of the 1,500 or so ships entering the Baltic annually at this time were bound for the ports of Danzig, Königsberg and Elbing. The tolls produced, in fact, a sum equal to one-third of Sweden's total revenues. When the concession expired in 1635 Oxenstierna exclaimed petulantly to his brother: 'I assure you that Sweden is not more than half the kingdom she was last year.'[4]

But that lay in the future. In the autumn of 1629, with peace in Poland, a new source of wealth in his pocket, and the promise of future French support, Gustavus Adolphus was ready to intervene in Germany. He was, in many ways, well-equipped to do so. He commanded a disciplined and experienced army; he ruled over an orderly and loyal country; he possessed important reserves of war material – particularly iron and copper. On two separate occasions, the Swedish Diet had declared its support for a campaign in Germany, agreeing to leave the timing of operations entirely to the king's discretion. Gustavus chose, as we have seen, to use Imperial intervention in Poland as his principal *casus belli*, but it left no time to find allies beforehand. When he landed in Germany in July 1630, Sweden's sole ally in the Empire was the city of Stralsund. Over the next few months, the situation scarcely improved: only the dispossessed (the dukes of Mecklenburg and Saxe-Weimar), the expectant (one of the claimants to Brunswick-Lüneberg), or those directly threatened or occupied by Imperialist troops (Hesse-Kassel and the secularized bishopric of Magdeburg) declared for Gustavus. Among the foreign powers, only Russia offered practical assistance – and that only amounted to a licence to export large quantities of grain from Narva to Amsterdam duty free, so that it could be sold at a profit to finance Sweden's war effort. In the course of the year 1630, the Swedish treasury only received 78,000 thalers from this source.[5]

This uncoordinated concert of allies was scarcely a match for the victorious Catholic armies facing them, and at first Gustavus's cause advanced but little. His diplomats secured neither an agreement with the major states of north Germany nor a firm promise of continued financial aid from France, and without these vital supports his troops proved unable to break out of their Baltic bridgehead. The reason for the neutrality of the German Lutherans was no secret: the princes made it clear to everyone that they were anxious to avoid open treason, preferring instead

to use the Swedish threat to wrest concessions from Vienna
without themselves breaking with the emperor. Their hopes were
pinned on the discussions at Leipzig and Frankfurt, not on the
restless armies in Pomerania and Mecklenburg. The reason for
French reticence was, however, rather less visible to the anxious
watchers by the Baltic shore. France, like Sweden, had been
engaged in a full-scale war for several years, and her leaders could
see clearly enough the advantages which peace and demobilization would bring. Had the emperor weakened and made concessions – whether over the Lorraine bishoprics, the Valtelline or
Mantua – in the summer of 1630, Richelieu might well have
abandoned Sweden; but after the Imperialists' capture of Mantua, an alliance with Gustavus seemed inescapable. The severe
challenge to Richelieu's personal power in the autumn of 1630
(page 114 above) delayed an immediate agreement, but on 23
January 1631, by the treaty of Bärwalde, France undertook to
provide 400,000 thalers annually for five years to subsidize
Sweden's war for German liberties and the freedom of Baltic
trade. It was agreed that Catholic worship would be allowed to
continue in conquered areas where it already existed, and that
the territory of members of the Catholic League would be treated
as neutral, unless they themselves provoked aggression.[6]

The French subsidy was not large – substantially less than the
yield of the Prussian port tolls – but it came at a critical moment
for Sweden's war-finances. Gustavus's treasury now had to support 50,000 men in Germany and Livonia, with a further 20,000 in
Sweden and Finland, and the cost was exorbitant: 2.3 million
thalers from the royal treasury were actually spent in 1630 – far
more than the entire year's revenues – but it met less than half of
the troops' needs. The king had gone to war in the expectation
that the majority of the army's needs would be met by the
occupied territories; but until August 1631 these were simply not
extensive enough to support such a concentration of troops (in
the second half of 1630 they provided only 35,000 thalers a month,
and in the first half of 1631 only 75,000). Nor could the Baltic
provinces, already picked clean by successive armies of occupation, shoulder the burden for long. Even a previously unscathed
area, the county of Memel, which was temporarily ceded to
Sweden in 1629, was devastated within a year by the seventeen
cavalry companies billeted on it. Where, before the occupation,
there had been 154 horses, 236 oxen, 103 cows, 190 pigs and 810
sheep, there were in 1631 just 26 oxen and 1 cow: all the rest had
gone, either killed or taken by the soldiers. Even the Swedish
authorities described the area as 'laid waste'. Richelieu's gold

could hardly have arrived at a more opportune moment.[7]

Yet if the French subsidies alleviated the immediate cash crisis, they did not, by themselves, win allies. In the west, Tilly's forces still had Magdeburg under siege and Hesse-Kassel under occupation; Gustavus's army was still 150 miles away at Stettin, his 30,000 men hemmed in by a superior force of Imperialists. In the east, the Protestant princes' meeting at Leipzig showed no interest in an alliance with Gustavus. Sweden would clearly have to undertake some 'rough wooing'.

Accordingly, in April 1631, the Swedish army advanced southwards into Brandenburg, taking and sacking the towns of Küstrin and Frankfurt-on-Oder (which were defended by Imperial garrisons). But it was too late to save Gustavus's sole ally-in-arms, Magdeburg, which was captured by the Imperialists on 20 May. The entire city was promptly sacked by the enraged soldiery, who had suffered terrible privations in the siege trenches. A large part of the population was massacred, and even more perished in the fire which broke out soon after capture. Only a few, like the inventor Otto von Guericke, managed to save themselves. There was nothing special about the level of brutality at Magdeburg – to sack a town that resisted was standard practice during the war – but the scale of the slaughter was unusual. A village or market town plundered or burnt was one thing; the annihilation of a city of 20,000, and a capital of Protestantism at that, was quite another. No less than twenty newspapers, 205 pamphlets and forty-one illustrated broadsheets describing the horror were published, circulating all over Europe, so that observers in London, Paris, Amsterdam, Stockholm, Rome and Madrid, as well as in the princely courts of Germany, were made aware of how the emperor treated his Protestant subjects. Unquestionably, the widely publicized fate of Magdeburg, just across Brandenburg's borders and administered by the Elector's uncle (Margrave Christian William), helped convince the reluctant George William to throw in his lot with Gustavus (21 June 1631).[8]

The pact with Brandenburg was most opportune for Sweden. The peace of Cherasco (ratified by Ferdinand on 19 June) at last freed the large Imperialist army in northern Italy for service within the Empire, encouraging Tilly to move north-eastwards from Magdeburg to confront Gustavus. The key to the military situation was now held by Saxony, trapped between the Swedes and the Imperialists, for each side had to cross the rich lands of the Electorate, so far untouched by war, in order to attack the other. In August, Tilly asked permission for his army, which was running short of food, to cross the frontier, but John George refused (see Plate 12). He declared: 'Now I see that the Saxon sweetmeats, so long spared, are to be eaten; but you may find that they contain hard nuts that will break your teeth.'[9] When, on 4 September, Tilly led his army to feast on the 'Saxon sweetmeats', John George at once joined forces with the Swedes, adding his 'Leipziger Bund' army of 18,000 untried recruits to Gustavus's 23,000 veterans. An alliance between the two rulers was signed a week later, and they determined to give battle to Tilly at Breitenfeld, a little to the north of Leipzig. The allies enjoyed a clear numerical superiority over the Imperialists, who only had 31,000 troops, including 7,000 tired men just arrived from Mantua (a further 5,000 were on the way, but were still 200 miles to the south). The Protestants were thus 30 per cent stronger than their adversaries, and they possessed a crushing superiority in artillery: whereas Tilly had twenty-seven standard field pieces, the Swedes disposed of fifty-one, supported by a battery of four mobile (and highly effective) 3-pounders attached to every regiment. The Swedes were also more flexible: although in the battle on 17 September the Saxon infantry broke when the Imperialists charged, the Swedish formations, only six men deep (compared to the thirty-deep Imperial formations), quickly extended to fill the gaps. It took a mere two hours for the cannonade, the continuous musketry salvoes and the superior tactics of Gustavus's army to force Tilly's troops into headlong flight. Seven thousand six hundred Imperialists lay dead on the field, most of them killed by Swedish gunfire; 9,000 others were captured, or else deserted; still more fell in the retreat. Two-thirds of the Imperialist army, previously undefeated, was lost, together with all its artillery and 120 regimental and company standards.[10]

Breitenfeld was the first major Protestant victory in the field since the war began. But how was it to be exploited? Gustavus had intended to make the Baltic safe for Sweden by driving the Imperialists from its southern shore, and this he had triumphantly done. But the king had made no contingency plans for a victory on this scale – indeed, he did not even possess any detailed maps covering the lands south of Brandenburg or west of Magdeburg.[11] So Gustavus may perhaps be forgiven if he failed to eliminate his principal enemy, Tilly (who withdrew beyond the Saale and Weser), preferring instead to lead his tired veterans southwestwards into luxurious quarters amid the Catholic lands along the Rhine and Main, while his Saxon allies moved southeastwards through Silesia into Bohemia. Frederick V and the dukes of Saxe-Weimar accompanied Gustavus to winter at Mainz, while most of the Bohemian exiles travelled with the

Saxons and entered Prague again on 15 November 1631.

This strategy at least ensured the destruction of the 'third force', whether led by Protestant Saxony or Catholic Bavaria. The Frankfurt Convention had eventually assembled on 4 August, but only thirteen Catholic states (ten of them ecclesiastical) and a handful of Protestants (led by Saxony) attended. The Brandenburg delegation only appeared in September and scarcely any business had been transacted when, on 14 October, the Catholic participants fled, rather than fall into the hands of the advancing Swedes. The Elector of Mainz, who had vainly reinforced the garrisons of his state, fled to Cologne, closely followed by the bishop of Würzburg, who had equally vainly created a militia of 1,700 men. Their subjects fled to wherever they could find refuge – to Westphalia, to French Lorraine, to the Swiss cantons.[12]

Yet, strangely enough, the Swedish standard continued to attract few supporters except those with little to lose. Thus the first – and for some time the only – potentates to declare for Gustavus in Franconia were the Imperial Knights, lords of minute estates. More substantial rulers were less enthusiastic about the king's great victory, for the arrival of the Swedish host was invariably followed by demands that princes abandon their neutrality and declare war on the emperor. Margrave Christian of Brandenburg-Kulmbach, for example, a staunch Lutheran, had managed to keep neutral throughout the early phases of the war: although a leading figure in the Protestant Union (page 24 above), he refused the requests of the Elector Palatine for help; and although a loyal subject of the emperor, he likewise refused to assist the Imperial armies as they moved north against Denmark. He attended the Leipzig Colloquy (one of his many visits to Saxony for political discussion), and afterwards raised a militia of 1,200 men to protect his frontier. But it was all in vain. Within a month of Breitenfeld, a letter arrived from Gustavus asking if he were friend or foe. With the Swedish host advancing, there was no choice: on 31 October, Margrave Christian had an audience with the king, swore to be his ally against the emperor, and agreed to provide quarters and contributions for the army. The margrave's subjects were thereby subjected to unprecedented hardship at the hands of troops, quartermasters and tax-collectors. When the peasants attempted to drive out the intruders, in November 1632, they were massacred: a chronicler who visited the site of the peasants' last stand was appalled to find the vineyards and fields red with blood, with corpses scattered in bizarre positions over a three-mile radius. Meanwhile the margrave locked himself in his only defensible castle, the

Plassenburg, and waited for the storm to subside. Such were the consequences for the former 'neutrals' of Sweden's victory at Breitenfeld.[13]

All over the Empire the same agonizing choice confronted Protestant princes. George of Hesse-Darmstadt was in particular difficulty because his title to the Marburg inheritance rested exclusively upon Imperial goodwill. Early in 1632, forced to decide between the Lutheran Swedes at the gate and the Catholic emperor in far-away Vienna, Landgrave George summoned a meeting of his counsellors and court theologians to answer the pressing question: 'If his princely Grace is forced to choose between one of the two warring parties in the Empire, . . . with which side must he unite himself?' Incredibly, the theologians inclined more to the Imperial side than to an alliance that included Calvinists and – worse still – William of Hesse-Kassel. But in the end the Edict of Restitution, and the example of the landgrave's father-in-law, John George of Saxony, tipped the scales: George too threw in his lot with Sweden.[14]

Thanks to the resources of these reluctant new allies, the troops of Gustavus were at last adequately provided for. The efficiency of the Swedish supply system was unconsciously reflected in the report from their camp early in April 1632, printed by an English weekly newspaper. There was an abundance of livestock, the account began: a horse for £1, an ox for half that, and geese and poultry for almost nothing; indeed, all over Franconia, where the army was quartered, the troops found abundant and cheap food. Clearly this situation was the consequence of massive extortion. Only wine was in short supply, the reporter noted, speculating that the Catholics had 'cherished their fainting hearts . . . withall before their doleful departure'.[15]

Actually, with or without the comforts of alcohol, the Catholic army was busily re-forming beyond the Weser. The garrisons in the north-west, under the direction of Count Pappenheim, harassed Sweden's communications; the main army, under Tilly, moved in November to the safety of Bavaria and recruited reinforcements for the new campaign. In theory, under the terms of the treaty of Bärwalde, Gustavus was obliged to regard all the territories allied to France as neutral, but Tilly seems to have lost his nerve. Now aged seventy-three, according to a Bavarian councillor at headquarters, the commander-in-chief was 'Wholly perplexed and seemingly cast down, wholly irresolute in council, knows not how to save himself, abandons one proposal after another, decides nothing, sees only great difficulties and dangers – but has no idea how to overcome them'. In

March he rashly forfeited the protection afforded by Bärwalde by driving a Swedish detachment out of Bamberg. Within three weeks Gustavus was advancing southwards with 37,000 men against Tilly's 22,000. Remorselessly he forced his way across the river Lech at Rain, in the teeth of the main Bavarian army: beneath a Swedish barrage of seventy-two heavy guns, a bridge was built, over which Gustavus sent his men. In the slaughter that followed, Tilly was mortally wounded.[16]

With Tilly dead and his army routed, there was now nothing to stop the plundering of Maximilian's beloved duchy: many towns, even forty and fifty miles away, made haste to surrender to the victors; many more were pillaged; only a few places escaped. 'Your Grace would no longer recognize poor Bavaria', Maximilian wrote to his brother, Ferdinand of Cologne; 'such cruelty has been unheard of in this war.' Gustavus and Frederick V held a triumphal entry into Munich on 17 May, reviewed their victorious troops, played tennis together on the ducal courts, surveyed the ducal art collection, and plundered it as thoroughly as the Bavarians had plundered Heidelberg ten years before. They also captured over 100 pieces of artillery, much of it formerly belonging to Frederick and his allies. Maximilian was unable to return to his capital for three full years (see Plate 13).[17]

The Catholic cause now appeared to be in ruins. The army of the League was shattered; its mainstay, Bavaria, in ashes. For a moment, it seemed that Spain might come once more to the rescue, for her forces regained Speyer and some other minor places along the Lower Rhine in the spring of 1632; but then Philip IV all but lost control of the South Netherlands. In June the Dutch army captured, in rapid succession, Venlo, Roermond, Straelen and Sittard, forcing the recall of a Spanish relief army sent to defend the Palatinate against the Swedish onslaught. But it was not enough to prevent the Dutch from laying siege to the great fortress of Maastricht, commanding all communications between Brussels and the Catholic party in Westphalia. At this point, a small group of Netherlands nobles, led by Count Henry van den Bergh, fled to join the Dutch army in Limburg and called upon their compatriots to throw off 'the Spanish yoke'. Nobody stirred, save only the Dutch who carried their siege of Maastricht to a successful conclusion on 23 August, in spite of the desperate assault of an Imperial relief army under Pappenheim on the siegeworks, less than a week before. Somewhat shaken by these developments, a second group of conspirators, who (unaware of the first group's existence) had intended to call in the French, decided not to act.[18] Spanish rule over the South Netherlands was thus, almost

Following page: **25** *The battle at Rain (1632)*

A. Ihr kön May zu Schwed Armee.   C. Tranchee an dem Waßer.   E. die Bruck über den Lech.   F. Finländische Reuter so
B. Schwedisch Batterien vnd geschuz. D. Ein großer Rauch darunter die Brück geschlag worde   durchs Waßer geßetzt

miraculously, preserved – but it was some time before Brussels could again come to the aid of Vienna.

Italy, too, was unable to offer assistance to the emperor in 1632. The end of the war of Mantua coincided with a plague epidemic which devastated the northern half of the peninsula with unprecedented ferocity. In April 1631, the governor of Spanish Milan complained that 'The plague has left [this province] so reduced in population that it is impossible to raise any troops', and thus it remained for some time.[19] The papacy, too, pleaded hardship when asked by the emperor for support. Although subsidies to the German Catholics were resumed in December 1631, they amounted to a mere 5,000 thalers per month: during the whole quadrennium 1631–4, only 550,000 were sent, and even that sum was remitted solely on condition that 'If peace is made with the Protestants . . . His Holiness will withdraw his aid, the more so because, since the eruption of Mount Vesuvius, the collection of tithes has become more difficult.'[20] The Imperial cause was indeed in desperate straits. As a Viennese courtier wrote in April 1631, just after the Swedes took Frankfurt-on-Oder: 'We cry "Help, Help", but there is nobody there!'[21]

As the tide of Swedish success approached Munich and Vienna, even Maximilian had to recognize that salvation could only come from the creation of a new Imperial army, and that only Wallenstein was capable of raising, maintaining and leading it. Accordingly, in April 1632, after three months of recruiting, the general was restored to full command. His tactics during the new campaign were extremely cautious: he was aware that, with all Ferdinand's allies out of action, and another peasant uprising in Austria (fomented by exiles in Swedish service), the Imperial cause could not survive a further defeat. So, in July, he moved into a heavily fortified position around a medieval castle, called the Alte Veste, just outside Nuremberg, which the Swedes were besieging. Gustavus and his men were tied down in a fruitless confrontation there for two months while Wallenstein's lieutenants drove the Saxons out of Bohemia and Silesia. The Swedes launched several costly yet unsuccessful assaults on the Alte Veste, but the siege continued into October, until the area around Nuremberg was totally devastated ('For three months we were besieged by our enemies; for four months we were eaten out by our friends' was the terse verdict of the Nuremberg patrician Lukas Behaim on the year 1632).[22] Eventually Gustavus led his dispirited and depleted army back towards the north-west, while Wallenstein moved north-east and overran the lands of Sweden's crucial ally, the Elector of Saxony. Leipzig fell on 1 November.

But now Wallenstein made the most serious error of his professional career. After holding his army at battle stations for two weeks, he apparently concluded that the campaign was over: on 14 November he gave orders for his host to disperse into winter quarters. The very next day he received reports that the Swedes were advancing on his headquarters at Lützen. Hastily, he recalled all units. But on the 17th, when battle commenced, he still only had 19,000 men, exactly the same number as the Swedes, after all their losses over the summer. As usual when the two sides were equally matched, the battle was prolonged and losses were heavy. Nevertheless, when dusk fell, both sides remained at their posts. After dark, according to the English captain Sydnam Poyntz, who was in Wallenstein's army, 'wee were scarcely laid down on the ground to rest and in dead sleep, but comes a command from the Generall to all Coronells and Sargeant Maiors to give in a note how strong every regiment was found to be'. The replies were discouraging. Poyntz had only three officers left out of twelve, and casualties in other units were equally high, so that Wallenstein felt it prudent to withdraw from the field, abandoning baggage and artillery to the enemy, relinquishing his Saxon conquests and withdrawing to Bohemia. He also left behind some 6,000 dead, including his lieutenant-general, Pappenheim. But he took with him the conviction that victory had been forfeited through the treachery or desertion of some of his hastily raised Lutheran troops. After the battle he had seventeen of them (including twelve officers) executed for cowardice, gave seven officers a dishonourable discharge, and put a price on the head of forty others – actions that did much to alienate the army from its mercurial commander and thus made it easier, at a later date, to eliminate him.[23]

On the Protestant side there were also reprisals – the commander of the Leipzig citadel was executed for precipitate surrender – but Gustavus Adolphus took no part in the proceedings. He had died in the battle on 17 November, shot three times – in the arm, in the back and in the head. For some weeks, news of his death was not believed. Wallenstein himself was not convinced until 30 November; in England, £200 was wagered at Court in December that Gustavus was still alive. The intervention of Sweden had captured the popular imagination to such an extent that even Frederick of the Palatinate, who also died in the autumn of 1632, was later remembered in England as 'the prince for whom Gustavus fell'; and when, in the same year, the grandson of Axel Oxenstierna and the nephew of Gustav Horn were given honorary degrees by the University of Oxford, the

Following page: **26** *The battle of Lützen (1632)*

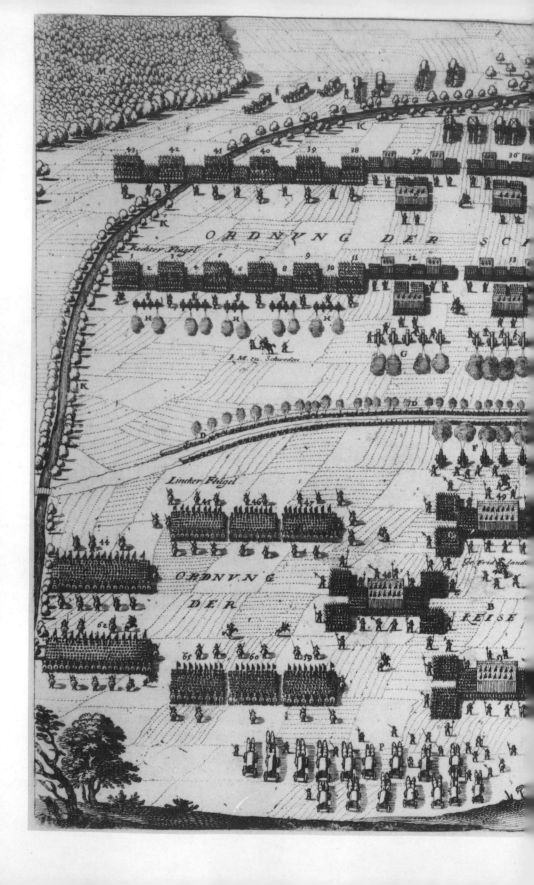

In Tesseram Militarem Prusg
Exercitus
Qui Regi erat
GOTT MIT VNS.
Fridlandie vero
IESVS MARIA
Orat uterg Ducem, nec vincit uterg salute
Fortis hic est hominum, fortior ille Dei.

34   33   32   31   30   29   28   27

DISCHEN ARMEEN Linck er Flügel

14   15   16   18   20   22   24   26
            17   19   21   23   25

H   H   H   H

G   Hertzog Bernhard

N   D   Lutzen

F

Rechter Flügel   57

52   50

ISCH   N ARMEEN

P

Delineation
Der Schwedischen
vnd Keyserischen Schlacht
ordnung den 6. Nouemb: 1632.
bey Lützen gehalten.
Matthæus Merian sculpsit.

vice-chancellor's laureation compared their illustrious relatives to 'two thunderbolts of war, . . . [who] to the terror of the house of Austria, have now for long been conspicuous in fighting for the hearth and home, the religion and indeed the liberty of the whole of Germany'.[24] (See Plates 14 and 15.)

It was because it put an end to the brief Protestant tide of success that Lützen, although a drawn battle, was so important. Another Swedish victory like Breitenfeld or Rain would have destroyed the Imperial cause beyond all hope of recovery. Now the two sides were again more or less equal, leading each combatant to seek desperately for more foreign support which might tip the scales – the hopes of Sweden pinned ever more firmly to France, those of the emperor fixed increasingly on Spain.

iii 1633–1635: Oxenstierna versus Wallenstein

The Swedish campaign of 1631–2 had been disastrous for Spain as well as for the German Catholics. The troops of Philip IV were driven from the Palatinate, those of her allies were expelled from Alsace: the 'Spanish Road' was blocked. At first the count-duke of Olivares had hoped that the link between Lombardy and the Low Countries might be restored by the Army of Flanders; but the crisis of 1632 in the South Netherlands (page 129 above) prevented this. So in the summer of 1633 a force of some 20,000 men under the duke of Feria, governor of Spanish Lombardy, marched through the Valtelline to south Germany and began to restore Habsburg influence: Constance and Breisach were relieved; Bregenz and Rheinfelden were recaptured. The road through Alsace was again secure. But that was no longer enough: even as Feria marched, the French invaded the duchy of Lorraine, occupying Nancy and all other major strongholds and driving the duke into exile. In desperation, the Spanish government authorized Feria to proceed from Breisach to recapture Nancy, thus in effect sanctioning a new war with France; but the campaigning season was over, and the duke retired to the apparent safety of the Alpine foothills, where both he and most of his army died of plague in the course of the winter.[1]

Yet the war in south-western Germany was just a sideshow in 1633: it was fought by small armies campaigning largely independently of the main protagonists further east. The same was true of operations in the north-west, where William of Hesse-Kassel had joined his private army to a Swedish force under Duke George of Brunswick-Lüneburg. Together, they occupied the ecclesiastical territories of Paderborn and Fulda, captured several minor towns on the Weser, and defeated an Imperial army at Hessisch-Oldendorf.[2] But this too was a sideshow; it seemed important only because the main armies scarcely fought. The central problem was the vacuum created by Gustavus's death at Lützen. His heiress, Queen Christina, was aged only six, and the direction of Swedish foreign policy therefore came into the hands of the late king's closest collaborator, Axel Oxenstierna. This remarkable man, now aged fifty, commanded a prestige in Europe enjoyed by few mere subjects before him. He treated princes as his equals and spoke freely in the presence of kings; he was in sole charge of the operations and supply of some 100,000 men, and of the cumbersome administrative machine which had been set up in Germany in the wake of the Swedish conquests. And, as if that were not enough, as chancellor of Sweden and head of the regency government he was also besieged by requests for innumerable decisions on domestic matters (often minute, such as the selection and dispatch of Rhine wine for the Court in Stockholm, the precise regalia to be placed on Gustavus's catafalque, or the correct policy to be followed by the Mint). The range of precise information displayed in his vast correspondence, on an incredible variety of public business concerning Sweden and her neighbours, is overwhelming. But his skills, great as they might be, were not equal to the challenges that he faced in 1633; it is indeed doubtful whether any human faculties could have overcome them.[3]

At first, the outlook did not seem too bleak. The outbreak of war between Poland and Russia in 1632, the 'war of Smolensk', offered a respite in the danger from that quarter which might allow the conclusion of a permanent settlement of the German question that was favourable to Sweden.[4] Early in 1633 Oxenstierna submitted a lengthy memorandum to the regency council in Stockholm concerning the correct foreign policy to be followed, now that the king was dead. Out of thirty-six clauses, only six dealt with Germany, but those laid down a clear line of action. The chancellor advocated a double-security arrangement: first, making permanent the Swedish presence in Pomerania and Prussia, in order to secure the Baltic against both Poland and the emperor, but keeping only a few outposts further south; and, second, organizing a confederation of friendly princes in central Germany to serve as a buffer in case of further Imperial aggression. He therefore proposed to dissolve the main field army and move most of the Swedish national units north into Pomerania. But not all units were to be withdrawn; not all the southern conquests were to be abandoned. In particular, Oxenstierna had no intention of surrendering Mainz, which had served as Gustavus's headquarters in the winter of 1631–2. The strategically placed Electorate was given a separate government, staffed largely by the Imperial Knights who had been Sweden's earliest supporters in the area, and there was a major redistribution of Catholic land to loyal Protestants. A programme of economic regeneration was drawn up, a new currency was issued, and a Lutheran hierarchy and church order were introduced. But the cornerstone of 'Swedish Mainz' was a vast fortified camp, the 'Gustavsburg', at the junction of the Main and the Rhine, with bridgeheads across both rivers and enough room to shelter 17,000 men if necessary. The fortress, adjoining the reconstructed walls of Mainz, was intended both to guarantee control of the area and to serve as a refuge in case of need – a military bulwark to underpin Swedish power in western Germany. It was the fulcrum of the elaborate balance of power that Sweden sought to create by 'atomizing' Germany into a host of loosely organized but mutually suspicious independent units. From Mainz, Oxenstierna could ensure that no one else won the upper hand in the west.[5]

But how were the garrisons of these Swedish outposts, far from their home base, to be paid? And what of the other troops in Swedish service, who still numbered over 100,000 fighting men? Oxenstierna was determined that the cost to Sweden would never again approach the level of 1630–1, when expenditure on the German war exceeded the country's ordinary revenues ten-fold. For a time, at least, there were the toll revenues from Prussia, Pomerania and Mecklenburg, and the subsidies from France and the Dutch, which enabled him to reduce the immediate pressure on Sweden still further. But the former were due to expire in 1635, while the latter arrived, after 1632, tardily and sometimes not at all. Other expedients of the first years of conquest – indemnities from towns spared from sack (100,000 thalers from Nuremberg, for example) and gratuities from princes restored to their lands by Swedish arms (60,000 thalers from the Elector Palatine; 220,000 from Baden-Durlach) – were likewise inapplicable after Lützen. Yet the army could not be supported by Sweden and Pomerania alone. Gustavus had made his soldiers swear an oath of loyalty to the Swedish crown in return for an undertaking to pay their wages; Oxenstierna therefore resolved to transfer both loyalty and financial obligation to other shoulders.

As early as October 1632, the king had deputed his chancellor to convene a meeting of the Franconian, Swabian and Rhenish Circles at Ulm, to discuss the formation of a defensive League, in alliance with Sweden. The meeting actually took place the following January. Those present debated ways of creating this association, raising an army, and paying for it. In March, after the Circles had discussed the various matters separately, the assembly reconvened at Heilbronn (a safer place than Ulm) and on 23 April 1633 signed the league that Sweden desired. They agreed to fight, and to go on fighting, until three goals had been achieved: first, 'until such time as the liberties of Germany, and a respect for the principles and constitution of the Holy Roman Empire, are once again firmly established'; second, until 'the restoration of the Protestant estates is secured, and a certain and just peace, in spirituals and temporals . . . is obtained and concluded'; and, third, 'until the crown of Sweden has been assured of an appropriate satisfaction'. Moreover, the achievement of these aims was placed firmly in the hands of Chancellor Oxenstierna: in respect (so the allies handsomely affirmed) of his 'God-given, exceptional qualities', he became sole Director of the Heilbronn League.[6]

But the political organization of the new alliance was better than its financial base. The League agreed to maintain an army of 56½ infantry regiments and 216 cavalry companies, at an annual cost of almost 10 million thalers; to this effect the French and Dutch subsidies were diverted into the League treasury. But over and above this commitment – and here lay the fatal weakness – the allies also agreed to pay the arrears of the units already in service. These were so monstrous, stretching back in some cases to 1627, that it proved impossible to agree upon a total figure. Moreover, even before the ink was dry on the treaty of confederation, the army in south Germany mutinied. In this emergency, Oxenstierna made over to the local commanders the right to levy contributions directly, under the general supervision of a military entrepreneur, Colonel Brandenstein. Thus Bernard of Saxe-Weimar, in Franconia, was allocated the bishoprics of Würzburg and Bamberg for the satisfaction of his troops' arrears: it was more or less a licence to plunder. In addition, the commanders were allowed to purchase lands under Swedish control at nominal prices, and officers in Gustav Horn's Swabian army were given cash rewards for the Swedish treasury. These measures solved the short-term crisis, although the campaigning season had largely slipped away by the time the mutiny subsided in August; but it created a serious long-term obstacle for the Heilbronn League, which was now deprived of many taxable areas required for the current remuneration of the troops. The problem grew worse almost daily for, as more areas were allocated to settling arrears, less remained to meet present pay. Before long the troops took to exacting their wages directly, with all the inevitable brutality and devastation. By the end of 1633, it was clear that the League was unequal to the burden of the army; to survive it must expand.

For a time, Oxenstierna pinned his hopes on Brandenburg, whose Elector was Queen Christina's uncle and whose Calvinist advisers still seemed to favour a policy of active anti-Imperial aggression. But George William remained under the influence of the Catholic, pro-Imperial Count Schwarzenberg, and he also had a private grievance against Sweden that overrode all other motives. In 1529 the Estates of Pomerania, Brandenburg's northern neighbour, had recognized the then Elector, and his heirs, as eventual successors to their duchy should the ruling line die out. Now, that situation seemed near: Duke Bogislav XIV (who died in 1637) was indeed the last of his line. But in 1630, the duke had been forced to sign a treaty which granted Sweden total control of the duchy as long as the war lasted: so what would happen if Bogislav died before the peace? Sweden made it clear that she could not surrender Pomerania, and the evacuation of her national units from central Germany to the duchy, after Lützen, confirmed George William's worst fears: that Sweden intended to annex Pomerania in spite of Brandenburg's rights. The Elector sent his son and heir, Frederick William, to reside at Bogislav's court in Stettin in 1633–4, but to no avail: the Swedes proved immovable.

George William was already convinced that a reconciliation with the emperor was the only way to achieve peace, and thus free his states from foreign occupation. In January 1633 he sent envoys to Dresden to persuade John George to join him in a peace initiative. But the Saxon capital was already seething with diplomats and foreign dignitaries, all trying to win the Elector's support. Oxenstierna arrived first, and spent Christmas 1632 persuading his host to participate in a new invasion of the Habsburg heartland. Shortly afterwards, Landgrave George of Hesse-Darmstadt came to invite John George to join him in formal discussions with an Imperial delegation on the terms of a possible peace settlement. In the event the Habsburgs' terms proved too harsh, and John George (like Brandenburg) threw in his lot with Sweden for another campaign. But he exacted a high price for his participation: above all, he ensured that the main Protestant offensive would be launched in the east, into Silesia, under commanders chosen by himself.

The tension between Sweden and her German allies could not be kept secret for long. As Wallenstein shrewdly observed: 'I believe that Sweden wants peace, that she wants to bring her forces home, and to leave the two Electors [Brandenburg and Saxony] to find their own way out of the labyrinth.'[7] The Imperial general therefore concentrated his attention on exploiting the rift. First he tried to seduce the Czech exiles at the court of Saxony, leading them to believe that he – also a Czech – might be able to secure for them a favourable settlement with the emperor. It was to parry this threat, and to keep a finger on the exiles' pulse, that Oxenstierna was forced to take the unpalatable step of accepting John George's nominee, Count Thurn, the unsuccessful general of the Bohemian confederation a decade before, as Swedish commander in Silesia. But in June 1633 Wallenstein managed to split the Saxon and Swedish units in Silesia when he arranged a cease-fire of one month to allow peace negotiations with Arnim, once his subordinate and now the Saxon commander. The talks proved inconclusive and, to the chancellor's relief, hostilities resumed in July. But in August Arnim agreed to a second truce to allow further negotiations, and when, on 27 September, fighting resumed, Wallenstein suddenly launched a massive attack on Thurn's Swedish force at Steinau, cut them off and forced 8,000 men to surrender within a week. Thurn himself was captured and agreed to surrender all the towns in Silesia held by his fellow-exiles in return for his freedom. These were devastating blows, and Wallenstein followed up his success by making renewed offers of a peaceful settlement to both Saxony and Brandenburg. Oxenstierna found it necessary to make a personal visit to George William early in 1634 in order to secure their rejection.[8] But on 25 February, the chancellor was unexpectedly saved from further difficulties by the assassination of his principal adversary.

Although a full-scale investigation of Wallenstein's last days was mounted by Imperial Commissioners soon after his murder, and although literally thousands of poems, plays, pamphlets and books have subsequently been published on the subject, the labyrinthine process by which the general was removed is still obscure. But this was the intention of the conspirators, one of whom explained to a close colleague: 'Put briefly, dissimulation is the alpha and omega of this business.'[9] Nevertheless, certain reasons for the assassination can be discerned. In the first place, the emperor was clearly incensed that he had paid for the upkeep of an enormous army throughout the year 1633 which, in military terms, had achieved very little: Bavaria was still partly occupied by Protestants; Heidelberg and Regensburg had been lost; Silesia was only liberated in October. Furthermore, Wallenstein insisted on quartering his hordes on the Habsburg provinces once more, over the winter of 1633–4, creating a severe risk of peasant revolts against the exactions of the troops. Then there was the Spanish dimension. It had been decided by the governments of Madrid and Vienna that in 1634 a large army would cross from Lombardy to the Empire, under the personal command of Philip IV's brother, the Cardinal-Infante Ferdinand, and join with the Imperial army to clear southern Germany of all enemies. According to Wallenstein's commission, the cardinal-infante and his men would have to serve under the commander-in-chief's orders, and Spain made it clear that this was unacceptable. However, probably none of these arguments led the emperor to contemplate assassination. More damaging to Wallenstein's standing in his master's eyes were the quasi-independent diplomatic manoeuvres with Saxony and Brandenburg. Yet for these he appears to have had full authority. In April 1632, after he had assumed control of Ferdinand's armies, unusually broad powers were conferred on Wallenstein. At a secret meeting at Göllersdorf, half way between his headquarters and Vienna, it was agreed that the commander-in-chief might quarter his troops wherever he wished, even within the Habsburg hereditary lands; that he was to control all Catholic troops fighting for the Imperial cause (thus including any units sent from Spain); and that he was to exercise authority 'in absolutissima forma'. Since the original text of the ten-point Göllersdorf agreement has not survived (if, indeed, it was ever written down) it is impossible to say what, precisely, this last clause meant. Certainly Wallenstein behaved as if it conferred power to negotiate cease-fires and even a peace with his enemies, and he kept in constant contact with Dresden, believing that Saxony (certainly) and Sweden (possibly) wished to end the war; but he did so with minimal reference to Vienna.[10]

Wallenstein had always had his enemies at the Imperial Court and, although in 1631 they failed to prevent his recall, they maintained throughout his second generalship a constant barrage of criticism, aimed at the general's personal habits almost as much as at his public policy. Both seemed more extravagant than before. For example, Wallenstein could now not endure any noise. On arrival in any town, it was alleged, he ordered all dogs and cats to be killed; he forbade the wearing of boots and spurs in his presence; and he punished severely and arbitrarily those who talked loudly or shouted. His behaviour towards his entourage varied between excessive generosity and frightening cruelty (penalties were carried out instantly by his household executioner). His utterances on politics ranged from inscrutable forecasts to brutal threats. As a pamphlet written after his death observed, he was 'a subject become a soveraigne'. He had been 'advanced to supreame charge, such as formerly hath not binn conferred on any other'; and the experience of supreme power no doubt encouraged exaggerated behaviour.[11] Certainly, his enemies had no difficulty in finding, among his boastful or careless words and his extravagant actions, ample grounds for impugning his loyalty to the emperor. Wallenstein had consistently criticized (and had sometimes thwarted) Vienna's efforts to assist Spanish ambitions in Italy and the Netherlands; he had also shown a marked lack of enthusiasm for the Edict of Restitution. Moreover, he had often argued in favour of a negotiated settlement between the emperor and at least the Lutherans. Now he conducted his own diplomatic offensive towards this end, refusing to take the military actions ordered by Vienna because they might jeopardize his peace initiative. As if all this were not enough to spread alarm at the Imperial Court, in January 1634 Wallenstein exacted an oath from his colonels that they would be loyal to him before all others. The emperor and his entourage may be forgiven for seeing this as open treason, and acting accordingly.[12]

Whatever the reasons that finally determined Ferdinand to get rid of his overmighty vassal, it proved relatively easy to do so. By the end of 1633 no one trusted him: not Sweden, whose troops he had captured, by a ruse, at Steinau; not Saxony or Brandenburg, who were unsure how far his promises had Imperial backing; not Bavaria, whose lands were left unprotected; and not the Bohemian exiles, who by now realized that Wallenstein had no interest in restoring the lands he (and his colleagues) had taken. In February 1634 the emperor issued a secret order that his general should be brought to Vienna for questioning. Realizing that it might not prove possible to take him alive, permission was given to kill if necessary. Even so, the risk of failure seemed high, and Ferdinand begged his confessor to seek the prayers of Jesuits throughout the world for a favourable outcome. The Order took this appeal very seriously indeed. Its Superior-General decided to apply 'another one thousand Masses weekly for the safety of the emperor and the happiness of the Empire', and later noted (with satisfaction) that at just that moment 'marvellous deeds were done by the arm of the Most High'. 'The more intently I look,' he boasted, 'the more clearly I see that the merciful God was moved by our prayers.'[13] He referred, of course, to the brutal murder of Wallenstein and his escort, as they fled towards Saxony after hearing about the emperor's order, on the night of 25 February

1634. And perhaps it was indeed miraculous that there should have been virtually no unrest among the Imperial troops after the general's assassination. Supreme command was now assumed by the emperor's son, Ferdinand, king of Hungary, aided by a triumvirate of senior officers: Piccolomini, Gallas and (for the Catholic League's forces) Aldringen.

Nevertheless, the murder of Wallenstein offered Sweden a moment in which to repair some of the divisions that had appeared in the Heilbronn League. Oxenstierna convened a meeting of the Protestant states of the Empire at Frankfurt which, he hoped, would expand the League to include Saxony, Brandenburg and the other territories of the north-east, and would also determine in precise terms which German lands Sweden would retain after the war. The meeting went well until, in April 1634, George William took the crucial step of insisting that, unless Sweden renounced her claim to Pomerania, he would not join the League. In June, the members of the Lower Saxon Circle agreed to support him. Next the Elector of Saxony, affecting to be above such mundane matters, tried to win support for the peace talks begun by Imperial officials at Leitmeritz with George of Hesse-Darmstadt.

So the Protestant cause was deadlocked even before hostilities recommenced in July with, once more, two separate theatres of operations: the Saxons under Arnim pushing into Silesia, while the Swedes and their Heilbronn allies, under the joint command of Gustav Horn and Bernard of Saxe-Weimar, sought to conquer south-eastern Germany. At first the campaign went well: Arnim invaded Bohemia and soon arrived once more before the walls of Prague, while the Heilbronn forces took Landshut in Bavaria by storm, killing Johann von Aldringen, Maximilian's commander-in-chief, in the process. But these successes were counterbalanced by the recapture of Regensburg and Donauwörth by the Imperialists, under Ferdinand of Hungary, who thus restored contact between Bavaria and the Habsburg lands. Arnim deemed it prudent to withdraw from his now exposed position before Prague. Next, Ferdinand laid siege to the Protestant city of Nördlingen and awaited the arrival of his cousin, the Cardinal-Infante Ferdinand, and his 15,000 men from Spain and Spanish Italy. They arrived on 2 September, just ahead of the forces of Bernard and Horn. The two Ferdinands realized that a confrontation would probably be to their advantage and they prepared a heavily fortified camp in the hills south of the city. Their confidence was not misplaced. When the two armies met in battle, on 6 September, the Habsburg armies numbered 33,000 and the Protestants only 25,000. By the end of the day, after 'the greatest victory of our times' (as Olivares jubilantly termed it), some 12,000 Protestants lay dead on the field and some 4,000 more, including Gustav Horn, were captured. Nördlingen fell at once, and the remnants of the defeated army, under Bernard of Saxe-Weimar, retreated into Alsace while Sweden reluctantly withdrew all her garrisons from south of the Main.[14]

Oxenstierna's spirits at last began to flag. In November 1634 he wrote to Johan Baner, the only capable Swedish general left in Germany, 'I will struggle no longer, but drift where the tide may take me . . . We are hated, envied, harassed.' At home there was open criticism of his policies by the regency council, prompting him to lament to his brother, 'Such proceedings make me weary of my life.'[15] Abroad, the diplomatic situation was fast changing for the worse – and not all due to Nördlingen. Although in 1633, to Sweden's delight, both the Turks and the Russians had attacked Poland, the following year, as the Turks once more concentrated their forces against Persia, Poland and Russia made peace. A serious risk now existed that, when the truce of Altmark, so favourable to Sweden, ran out in 1635, it might not be renewed – or, at least, not renewed on the same advantageous terms. Sweden's position in the Empire also became critical. The members of the Heilbronn League, who were now exposed to the Imperialists' undivided attentions, mounted a mission to Paris in November 1634 without Oxenstierna's knowledge. They offered extensive concessions in return for a declaration of war against Spain and the emperor (see page 148 below for details). The following month, Oxenstierna withdrew from the League, never to return. Even to Sweden's oldest ally, William of Hesse-Kassel, it had become clear that only Catholic France was now capable of saving the Protestant cause. In November 1634 he wrote:

> The House of Austria wishes to subjugate all Germany, extirpating liberty and the Reformed religion. So in this extremity we must look to France.

The landgrave even wanted to elect the king of France as emperor because, he considered, only that would guarantee the continuation of 'German liberties'.[16]

But these defections from the cause were as nothing compared to the loss of Saxony. A mere ten weeks after Nördlingen, the negotiations of Hesse-Darmstadt and Saxony with the Imperialists (moved from Leitmeritz to Pirna in the course of the summer) produced an agreement. The 'Preliminaries of Pirna' offered major advantages to both sides: Saxony gained full rights

to Lusatia (ceded in 1620 as security for the Elector's aid to
Ferdinand during the Bohemian revolt) and the territory of
Magdeburg; a single army of Saxon, Bavarian and Imperial troops
was to be formed for use against all foreign forces in the Empire;
and the transfer of the Palatine Electorate to Bavaria for all time
was accepted. Above all, the 'normative date' for the restitution
of church lands and the exercise of permitted faiths was taken as
November 1627 – a crucial compromise which allowed the Catholics to retain their gains in the south and south-west but offered
complete security to the secularized lands of the northern princes
(the Edict of Restitution itself was declared suspended 'for forty
years').[17]

The further military successes of the Imperial army over the
winter of 1634–5, weakened the negotiating position of the Saxons, however. A Protestant pamphleteer later claimed to have
noted 371 changes detrimental to his faith between the text of the
'Preliminaries of Pirna' and that of the final agreement, signed at
Prague in May 1635. John George eventually agreed to the withdrawal of the amnesties promised to the Palatine family, to
Hesse-Kassel and several others, and to the enforcement of the
Edict in many additional areas. There might have been still more
concessions, had French troops not invaded the Empire, in the
winter of 1634–5, to defend Heidelberg against the emperor's
forces. Although there was no declaration of war, almost everyone at the Imperial Court realized that peace must be made with
Saxony before further support for the Protestant cause material-
ized. Even the papal nuncio in Germany, who consistently
opposed any settlement that sacrificed the Edict of Restitution,
noted that 'If the French intervene in Germany, the emperor will
be forced to conclude peace with Saxony on whatever terms he
can.' So it made sense to settle more advantageously beforehand.
The pragmatic primate of Hungary, Cardinal Pázmány, declared
himself content to accept any settlement with Saxony 'so long as
the Catholic religion is preserved in the patrimonial provinces
without allowing any other creed'.[18]

In February 1635 Ferdinand put his peace proposals to a panel
of twenty-four theologians, including his trusted confessor.
Lamormaini, true to the providentialist philosophy he had always advocated where the emperor's affairs were concerned,
argued that the great victory at Nördlingen was yet another sign
of God's continuing favour, and called for a rejection of any peace
with the Protestants. But this time, only six members of the panel
voted with him. The rest saw Nördlingen as a narrow escape, and
the emperor agreed with the majority. Later the same month, a

cease-fire was concluded not only with Saxony but also with Brandenburg, still resentful towards Sweden over Pomerania. The peace of Prague was published, amid general rejoicing, on 30 May 1635. The Saxon army, still occupying parts of Silesia, now became part of the Imperial host (as did the troops of Bavaria, much to Maximilian's regret), and most Lutheran states hastened to make peace with the emperor on the same terms as the two Protestant Electors. Colonel Brandenstein, whose allocation of Catholic lands to the Protestant armies had caused such misery, was imprisoned, and died, in 1640, a debtor in a Saxon jail. Those who, like William of Hesse-Kassel, rejected reconciliation, and instead accepted the promises of aid freely given but poorly performed by France and the Dutch, were mercilessly attacked and hunted down by the new, enlarged Imperial armies. The Calvinist landgrave was driven out of his territory by a force led by his Lutheran rival, George of Hesse-Darmstadt. He died, penniless, in exile. Later in the year, the great fortified camp outside Mainz, the Gustavsburg, came under siege and in January 1636 the 5,000-man garrison surrendered. Now only Hanau held out for the Protestant cause in the Rhineland, and in 1637 that too fell, in spite of its formidable defences and desperate resistance. Already the Swedes had abandoned Bremen and Verden, in the northwest, to their old rival Christian IV of Denmark.

The peace of Prague marked a significant turning-point in the Thirty Years' War. On the one hand, it brought about a notable scaling-down in the religious aspect of the struggle. No longer were Protestants ranged against Catholics in almost monolithic blocs; no longer did the ultra-Catholics monopolize Imperial policy. The rejection of the advice so explicitly and tenaciously proffered by Lamormaini was, in this context, of crucial importance: the formation of Imperial policy was now in the hands of pragmatists, such as Trauttmannsdorf (Director of the Imperial Privy Council from 1637), who realized that sacrifices would be required if the gains of the 1620s were to be recovered. Yet the making of peace with the German Lutherans was not only a triumph for the pragmatists; it was also a vindication of the policies of Olivares who had, for over a decade, urged the emperor to make an agreement with his domestic foes in order to destroy his remaining foreign enemies and deploy his resources against the Dutch and, if necessary, France. But Spanish rejoicing at the peace of Prague proved short-lived. The destruction of the Swedish army at Nördlingen, swiftly followed by the defection of so many of her allies, seemed to call into question Oxenstierna's ability to orchestrate successful opposition to the Imperialists –

particularly if they could count on further aid from Spain. In the same month that the peace of Prague was signed, therefore, the king of France declared war on Philip IV.

iv France's 'war by diversion'

The French declaration of war against Spain in May 1635 followed the arrest on 26 March of the Elector of Trier, a French ally, by a column of Spanish soldiers. The council of state of Louis XIII, discussing the event, concluded that 'The king cannot avoid taking up arms to avenge the affront which he has received by the imprisonment of a prince who has been placed under his protection.'[1] The Spaniards argued that the issue of the Elector of Trier was simply a pretext, and that the French intended to make war in any event. In a sense they were right: a secret memorandum from Louis XIII to Cardinal Richelieu, dated 4 August 1634, argued at length the case for a 'vigorous open war against Spain in order to secure a beneficial general peace'.[2] For his part, however, Louis XIII was genuinely convinced that the Spaniards intended to invade France whenever it suited them, and he too was right. The Spanish council of state had discussed on 13 April 1634 whether or not to declare war on France, and although they decided against it, an alliance was signed a month later with Gaston of Orléans, the French heir presumptive who was in exile in the Spanish Netherlands.[3] In such a tense situation, there were strong arguments in favour of a pre-emptive French strike, making the Habsburg territories the field of battle rather than fight a defensive war 'in the bowels of France'.[4] (See Plate 16.)

Both sides were thus more or less ready for hostilities to commence. Between 1630 and 1635, the French government had made commitments to a disparate collection of allies which were almost certain, at some point, to produce international conflict. The most famous of these alliances were with the Dutch Republic (a subsidy arrangement had existed since June 1624; it was renewed in June 1630 and the amount of subsidy increased in April 1634), and with Sweden (after January 1631; it lapsed temporarily with the death of Gustavus Adolphus, on the grounds that it was an agreement between two kings and was abrogated by the death of one of them, but it was renewed in April 1633). The purpose of these alliances was to fight the Habsburgs by proxy and to avoid open French intervention in the Thirty Years' War, since this was a bitterly contested issue in domestic politics. At the 'Day of Dupes', Richelieu's opponents had almost succeeded in ousting him from power, and criticism of his foreign policy – particularly the intervention in the war of Mantua – had figured prominently in their grievances. The threat posed by domestic conspiracy and faction was a powerful element in delaying direct French intervention in the German conflict.

Among the other strategic considerations were the vulnerability of the French frontier to invasion, and the proximity of two Habsburg client states (Savoy and Lorraine) whose dukes had on occasion given refuge to, or otherwise assisted, aristocratic critics of the French government. Louis XIII and Richelieu decided to strike first at Charles Emmanuel of Savoy, who made the fatal mistake in 1628 of trying to partition Montferrat with Spain, at the expense of the French candidate, the duke of Nevers. With the connivance of the papacy, the French army invaded Savoy twice in 1629–30 and retained first the fortress of Susa and later the more considerable one of Pinerolo. Victor Amadeus I, who succeeded his father as duke in 1630, agreed to the permanent transfer of Pinerolo to France (contrary to the terms of the peace of Cherasco, which stipulated that both France and Spain should withdraw from all their conquests), and in 1635 Savoy was one of the few states to join a French-inspired league against Habsburg power in Italy.

The quarrel with Charles IV of Lorraine was more complex. In part, it was a struggle for jurisdiction: the duchy of Bar was claimed as a fief of the French crown for which Duke Charles had failed to pay homage (he did not do so until 1641); other territories were claimed to have been 'usurped' from the sovereignty of the French king; while the emperor claimed that the duchy of Lorraine was purely and simply a fief of the Empire. These disputes would not have assumed such importance had not Duke Charles given Gaston of Orléans refuge in his lands on two occasions in 1629–32 and allowed him to marry Marguerite of Lorraine, the duke's sister, without Louis XIII's permission. Moreover, in February 1630 the duke had allowed Imperial troops to occupy the two fortresses of Vic and Moyenvic, which dominated the road from Strasbourg to Nancy. In December 1631, Louis XIII issued an ultimatum for the withdrawal of these Imperial troops: when it was ignored, three French invasions followed in the space of the next two years. Each time, the duke submitted, agreed not to assist the Habsburgs, and handed over territorial guarantees; each time he went back on his word. Finally in 1634 all resistance to Louis XIII's army of occupation collapsed, a French administration was installed and the duke took up permanent exile as a Habsburg general. Except for a brief interlude in 1641, the exile was to last for twenty-eight years.

In Savoy and Lorraine the French king strengthened his borders by neutralizing, or evicting, an unreliable neighbour. From December 1631, however, much more was attempted: Louis XIII would protect all Catholic princes who needed his help, against either Spanish or Swedish troops. Of the three ecclesiastical Electorates in the Rhineland, only Trier took up this offer, but the territory was of the greatest strategic importance. The key points were the great fortresses of Coblenz and Ehrenbreitstein, together with Philippsburg which belonged to the Elector in his capacity as bishop of Speyer. In April 1632 Gustavus Adolphus recognized the neutrality of the Electorate and agreed that the key strongpoints should be occupied by the French (the first two were taken over in May and June 1632; Philippsburg was not obtained until August 1634, and its recapture by Habsburg forces in January 1635 was one of the factors precipitating French intervention in the war). Trier was merely a testing-ground for the principle of French protection, however: once the war was over, it would revert to its former status within the Empire. Likewise, in the subsequent treaties of protection with the mostly Protestant territorial rulers in Alsace in 1633–6, this was also to be the case. But the complexity of the rival territorial jurisdictions in Alsace, the competing interests of France, the Swiss cantons, and the Habsburgs, and the power vacuum resulting from a distant archducal authority, facilitated the gradual installation of French political, as well as military, control. Until Nördlingen, France desired only enough authority in Alsace to guarantee access to the Rhine; afterwards she urgently needed the power to keep the Habsburgs beyond the east bank of the river. Therefore Richelieu enforced French protection over the states of Alsace more energetically between 1634 and 1636, and then took steps to consolidate the rights he had acquired into a compact lordship.

The exact timing of the declaration of war between France and Spain was determined by tactical considerations: the successful campaign of the Cardinal-Infante, which caused Spain to keep the peace in 1634, provoked France to break it in 1635. The defeat and dispersal of the Swedish army at Nördlingen, and the collapse of the Heilbronn League, necessitated decisive intervention by France in order to prevent Swedish capitulation. But, at first, the French intended their intervention to be both limited and indirect. France would make a powerful 'war by diversion' but keep its commitment in Germany to a minimum. The assumption behind this strategy was that it was the king of Spain, not the emperor, who constituted the most serious threat to European security: if Philip IV's power was decisively weakened, the French believed that the emperor would no longer make war 'according to the appetite and passion of the Spanish'.[5] Of course, the French were committed to 'freedom and peace for Germany', just satisfaction for all interested parties at a free Imperial Diet (in which the French would be full participants), and an inter-confessional alliance against the attempt to establish a Habsburg monarchy in Germany; nor had Richelieu lost sight of his objective of enticing Maximilian of Bavaria away from the Habsburg alliance in return for his retention of the Electoral title. But the French declaration of war was directed against Spain, not the emperor. The French fought under the nominal authority ('sous le nom') of Sweden in Germany in 1635, and a tight rein was kept on the actions of the French troops within the Empire.[6]

From the death of Gustavus Adolphus, Richelieu had always envisaged overall command in Germany going to Bernard of Saxe-Weimar as the most experienced general with a mercenary army at his disposal; yet, as a Lutheran with his own territorial and dynastic ambitions, he could not be entrusted with the command of French troops. The French forces in Lorraine and Germany in 1635 therefore had their own commanders (respectively the duke of La Force and Cardinal de la Valette, with the viscount of Turenne as a secondary commander), their own supply system, and independent finance controlled by French army intendants. A volte-face by Duke Bernard would thus be a serious blow to the French war effort, but not total disaster. Different estimates have been produced of the size of the French forces on all fronts in the years 1634–6. The lowest figure was 9,500 cavalry and 115,000 infantry, but it is difficult to be sure that even these forces were actually mobilized, because no series of muster roles survives. Since 6,000 cavalry and 20,000 infantry were committed to the Low Countries' campaign of 1635, and other forces were sent to Savoy and the Valtelline, it follows that the French armies operating in Lorraine and Germany were relatively small. Twelve thousand men had to be levied to defend Lorraine from a threatened Imperial offensive in 1635, and it was hoped to raise 15,000 cavalry and 35,000 infantry to relieve Corbie in 1636. Most of the French troops were fighting outside Germany in the early years of the war, and the losses on some fronts were catastrophic: in the Low Countries' campaign of 1635, the French force fell from 26,000 to 8,000 men.[7]

In view of these large commitments on several fronts, the French were naturally cautious in Germany itself; indeed, the declaration of war on the emperor was delayed until the Franco-Swedish pact was renewed at Wismar in March 1636. None of this was much to Sweden's liking. The French still remained committed to maintaining the Swedish alliance, to ensuring that Sweden obtained Pomerania in order to 'keep a tight hand over . . . the House of Austria', and even to bolstering up Sweden's position after the peace, if that proved necessary;[8] but they were not prepared to give Sweden a free hand in the conduct of a war that was waged with such massive French contributions of men and money. It is true that Feuquières, the French ambassador extraordinary in Germany, offered greatly augmented French assistance at one point; but even after Nördlingen, the Heilbronn League's envoys to Paris found in November 1634 that what they were being offered fell far short of a French declaration of war against the emperor. In return for a guarantee of assistance in case of attack for twenty years after the peace, Sweden was to surrender the supreme direction of the war effort and the French subsidy. Not surprisingly, Oxenstierna refused to ratify the arrangement, and Feuquières was instructed to withhold French support until he did. When even Sweden's special envoy, Hugo Grotius, failed to obtain concessions from the French, Oxenstierna was forced to visit Louis XIII and his chief minister in person in the spring of 1635. Richelieu found the Swedish chancellor 'a bit gothic and very wily',[9] and the upshot was the treaty of Compiègne on 28 April, by which both parties undertook to assist the Protestant party in Germany by force of arms, with neither concluding a separate peace or armistice. Yet the size of the French army and subsidy alike was left unspecified, and it remained so until the treaty of Wismar in March 1636. Moreover, Richelieu sought to attract former Swedish commanders into the service of France, and by the summer of 1635 he had already won Bernard of Saxe-Weimar over. A formal arrangement was signed on 27 October, by the terms of which Bernard was to receive 1.6 million thalers a year (about four times the annual French subsidy to Sweden), in return for his keeping an army of 18,000 men in the field. From that time onwards, military operations in southern Germany were firmly under French control.

The relative ease with which Bernard was suborned from the Vasa to the Bourbon allegiance (and by the spring of 1636 he was receiving his orders at Paris) demonstrates both the strength and the weakness of the French position. The weakness was the lack of experienced commanders and battle-hardened troops. Montglat, a secondary commander who served in most of the campaigns and whose memoirs provide a good account of the fighting, records that in 1636 a Frenchman who had served in the Low Countries was listened to as an oracle. The French, he concluded, had forgotten the arts of war in a long period of peace.[10] His comments may seem surprising when one considers the French civil wars in the 1620s, the intervention in the Valtelline in 1624–6, the participation in the Mantuan war in 1628–31, and the occupation of Lorraine in 1632–4; but each campaign had been of short duration, and few had been an overwhelming success. The French had to wait until 1643 for their first great victory against the Spaniards in a straight fight (at Rocroi).

Nevertheless, the great strength of the French position arose, at least in part, from her relatively passive role in the German conflict between 1618 and 1635. France came into the conflict fresh, and with an ability to finance war on several fronts at the same time. Indeed, one reason why Richelieu had delayed intervention in the Thirty Years' War for as long as possible (apart from the need to deal with domestic criticism of his policy and aristocratic rebellion) was precisely to improve the financial position of the French monarchy and its capacity to sustain a long war. Thus in 1635, at the lowest point in the fortunes of the Swedish and Protestant cause in Germany, a powerful new war fund was provided which neither the emperor nor the king of Spain could match (see Table 4). At the prevailing rate of exchange, French war expenditure on all fronts (including the Mediterranean) in 1635 was the equivalent of 16.5 million thalers. The average expenditure in the years 1636–9 was just under 13 million a year, and just under 16 million annually in the years 1640–5.[11] This was indeed a powerful 'war by diversion'. It should not be supposed that military success necessarily follows upon an influx of funds; but in a long war of attrition, such as the German war had proved to be, an influx of funds late on in the conflict was well worth having. It constituted a new factor in the balance of power.

In fact, virtually nothing went right in the first two French campaigns. In 1635 it was hoped that a sudden strike against the Spanish position in the Low Countries, Italy and the Valtelline would decisively weaken the position of Philip IV and encourage a rebellion by his disaffected subjects, particularly in the Spanish Netherlands (as had almost occurred in 1632). However, no rising comparable to that of the Burgundian lands in 1477 took place; when rebellion eventually broke out, in 1640, it unexpectedly took place in the Iberian peninsula. The Franco-Dutch campaign

TABLE 4 *French military expenditure, 1618–48*

Date	Military expenditure in millions of thalers	Internal political event	External war
1618	3.2		
1619	4.5	⎰ Revolt of the	
1620	5.2	⎱ Queen Mother	
1621	7.5	⎰ Revolt of the	
1622	9.0	⎱ Huguenots	
1623	4.8		
1624	4.6		
1625	6.9	⎰ 2nd Revolt of	⎰ Valtelline
1626	4.9	⎱ the Huguenots	⎱ War
1627	5.7	⎰ 3rd Revolt	English invasion
1628	7.8	⎱ of the	⎰ War of the Mantuan
1629	7.4	⎱ Huguenots	⎱ Succession
1630	9.2		
1631	6.0	⎰ Revolt of Gaston	
1632	7.4	⎱ d'Orléans	⎰ Occupation
1633	6.7		⎱ of Lorraine
1634	9.9		
1635	16.5		War against Spain declared
1636	13.5		⎰ Habsburg invasions
1637	11.0		⎱ of France
1638	12.8		Breisach
1639	12.8	Peasant revolt (Normandy)	
1640	12.5		
1641	13.4	Revolt of Count of Soissons	French assistance to Catalans
1642	13.0	Cinq-Mars conspiracy	
1643	19.4	Cabal of the *Importants*	Rocroi; Tuttlingen
1644	19.0		Freiburg
1645	18.0		Allerheim
1646	15.4		
1647	15.8		
1648	13.0	Beginning of Fronde	Zusmarshausen; Lens

Source: R.J. Bonney, *The King's Debts. Finance and Politics in France, 1589–1661* (Oxford, 1981), appendix two, table 2.

of 1635 was a total failure – none of the objectives was attained, least of all partition of the Spanish Netherlands – and it ended in mutual recriminations among the allies. The Spanish Army of Flanders managed to recapture several towns as well as repulsing the French invaders (who had to be evacuated, by sea, by the Dutch). In 1636, when the Army of Flanders invaded France, the Dutch army did nothing to distract them. And little of importance was achieved in Italy, either, until the French managed to relieve Turin in 1639 and take the war to the borders of Lombardy. The French occupation of the Valtelline, under Rohan (the erstwhile Huguenot leader), started quite auspiciously until, in 1637, the failure to pay subsidies regularly provoked a general rising in the valleys against all foreigners. Bernard of Saxe-Weimar and Cardinal de la Valette led a coordinated French invasion of southern Germany in September 1635, but the Imperial commander Gallas almost succeeded in cutting off their lines of communication near Frankfurt-on-Main and the invaders had to endure a forced march of thirteen days before they reached safety again in Lorraine.

It was scarcely surprising that Richelieu could not disguise his displeasure at the lack of success in the first French campaign. He is said to have been 'astonished' at the military failure despite 'many millions' spent on the war effort.[12] In February 1636 he accused the finance ministers of unwarranted delays in the transfer of funds: 'I say this . . . without [seeking] a quarrel but with great resentment and displeasure: . . . matters are not proceeding as the king's service and the good of the state require . . .'[13] The ministers replied that they could do no more and feared a general bankruptcy which would force France out of the war on disadvantageous terms and spell an end to 'war by diversion'.[14] The king had to choose between his ministers, since Finance Superintendent Bullion blamed Abel Servien, who had served as war minister for nearly six years, for the failure: in March 1636 Servien was forced to resign. His replacement, who remained in office until April 1643, was François Sublet des Noyers. He had already acquired considerable experience of financial and military administration (as intendant of the army he had helped to plan a new line of defence in northern France), which was to prove invaluable in the crisis of 1636.

France's second campaign started quite differently, with Bernard of Saxe-Weimar seeking to advance into Alsace, where the French already enjoyed protectorates, and Condé besieging Dôle in Franche-Comté. By the late autumn, the fighting had turned into a rout: Condé was forced to retreat in late October in order to save Dijon from capture by an invasion force under Gallas, and the Imperial advance was halted less by French resistance than by the Swedish victory at Wittstock and the flooding of the river Saône. In northern France, the Habsburg advance was equally spectacular, partly as a result of the precipitate capitulation of three fortress commanders who were subsequently condemned to death for cowardice (Le Bec of La Capelle, Saint-Léger of Le Câtelet and Soyecourt of Corbie). This invasion force, of Spanish and Imperial units combined, swept down from the South Netherlands and reached Corbie, a town situated on the river Somme about eighty miles from Paris, on 15 August. It was not retaken until 9 November (see Map 3). Had the planned invasion of Languedoc from Spain taken place then, instead of being delayed until 1637, the kingdom of France might have been forced into ignominious surrender. But the great opportunity for the Habsburg cause in 1636 was lost. By comparison with the *année de Corbie*, the subsequent invasions of France were half-hearted affairs.

But for the next three years, the outcome of the war hung in the balance. The French combined an over-ambitious strategy with poor generalship and an unprepared military machine.[15] The great French commanders – Harcourt, Condé the younger, Turenne – had either not yet risen through the ranks or else were not given the resources with which to make an impression. One of the few French successes of the first four years was Bernard of Saxe-Weimar's capture of Breisach in December 1638; but even that would have proved an illusory gain for the French had not the victor died the following July without a son, for France was committed to allow Bernard to establish his own dynasty in the parts of Alsace that he captured with the aid of Louis XIII's money. His death without an heir presented France with all the benefits and few of the dangers of this policy.[16] Bernard's successor, Erlach, was also a Lutheran, and there were fears that he might revert to the Swedish alliance;[17] but his loyalty never wavered, because the French paid his subsidies regularly, and in any case he was not allowed the dynastic rights accorded to Bernard.

Although the great French victories in the war against the Habsburgs only came after the revolt of the Catalans in May 1640, the years of 'war by diversion' had thus not been entirely fruitless. To be sure, France proved unable to impose her own solution in the war for German liberties: that would require both a resurrection of Swedish military power and renunciation of the peace of Prague by the German Protestant princes. But France did provide, albeit at an awesome cost in taxation at home and destruction of life and property abroad, important tactical support for the Protestant party through the creation of 'gateways' into Germany, such as Ehrenbreitstein, Philippsburg and, most important of all, Breisach. The real achievement of the 'war of diversion' was to ensure that there could never be another Nördlingen: a joint Habsburg military solution to the Thirty Years' War.

CHAPTER V

Countdown to peace

There were three critical stages in the transformation of the revolt of Bohemia into a major European war. The first was the involvement of Frederick of the Palatinate and Spain in 1619; the second was the Swedish invasion of Pomerania in 1630; the third was, paradoxically, the peace of Prague. Although the peace of May 1635 reconciled the emperor with so many of his enemies, opposition to the Habsburgs thereby fell almost exclusively into the hands of foreigners. It was not, as Table 5 shows, that more foreign countries were involved in the war than before – on the contrary there were less. It was the attitude of the interventionists that had changed. Few outside the Empire now spoke sincerely of the 'Protestant cause'; not many more felt genuine enthusiasm for 'German liberties'. The statesmen who now dominated the war saw Germany primarily as a theatre of operations. The costs and consequences of their policies to the Empire caused these men little or no concern; what mattered was their own advantage and prestige.

It is natural to see Richelieu and (after 1643) Mazarin as the arch-exemplars of the new *Realpolitik*, but they were less influential in this respect than Oxenstierna. France fought on several fronts, dividing her strength almost equally between Italy, Spain, the Low Countries, and the Empire; her inferiority to Sweden in the German war was manifest. It emerged most clearly in the size of the armies opposing the emperor: Oxenstierna controlled roughly twice as many men as Mazarin. Even in 1648, at the war's end, there were 127 Swedish, 52 French and 43 Hessian garrisons in the Empire, representing, together with the field armies, a total of 915 Swedish, 432 French and 224 Hessian companies.[1] Sweden held the initiative in the later stages of the war just as surely as the emperor had done in the 1620s. After the peace of Prague, if not before, her aims and her demands were central both to the making of war and to the making of peace. A

154

TABLE 5 *States involved in the Thirty Years' War*

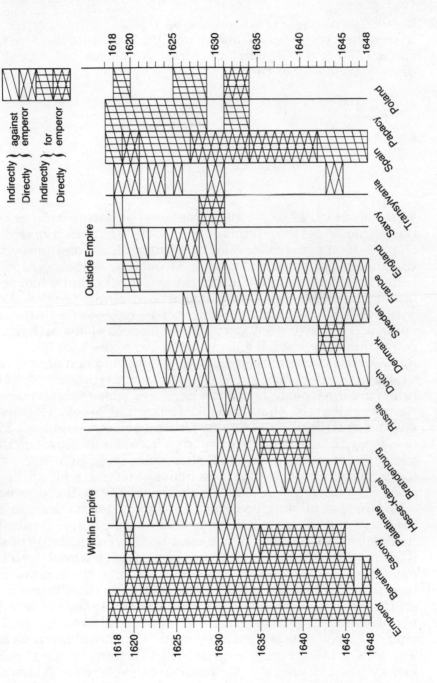

knowledge of the internal debate on foreign policy, carried on with some bitterness for almost ten years within the Swedish council of regency, is therefore crucial to a proper understanding of the second half of the war.

i The Swedish dilemma

With the death of Gustavus Adolphus, the nature of Sweden's involvement in the German war underwent an immediate change. Such plans as he may have entertained for altering the constitution of the Empire were at once abandoned. Already before his death members of the council in Stockholm had been saying that Sweden's war aims had been attained, and that there was no point in fighting any longer. This was not Oxenstierna's opinion. He did indeed share with his colleagues at home a conviction that Sweden must now get out of the war; but he did not always agree with them as to how this could best be effected. Granting that the objective was now peace, two important questions remained: peace by what means? and peace on what terms? He never doubted that he must if possible negotiate from a position of strength; and though circumstances would force him to infringe that principle, he departed from it only provisionally, and with deep chagrin. Sweden, then, must go on fighting, as the surest road to peace; but she must fight by methods which differed from the old. Early in 1633 Oxenstierna began the complete withdrawal of all purely Swedish units from central Germany to the coast; and he had laid it down as a principle that in future the task of carrying on the struggle must be the responsibility of the German princes themselves. Henceforth Sweden would 'lend her name' to the war; but if possible no more than that. Hostilities were to be conducted by proxy.[1] The overriding consideration for Sweden must now be to secure herself against possible attacks by her neighbours: attacks from Denmark, but above all from Poland. 'The Polish war', wrote Oxenstierna a little later, 'is *our* war; win or lose, it is our gain or loss. This German war, I don't know what it is, only that we pour out blood here for the sake of reputation, and have naught but ingratitude to expect.'[2] It followed that 'we must let this German business be left to the Germans, who will be the only people to get any good of it (if there is any), and therefore not spend any more men or money here, but rather try by all means to wriggle out of it'.[3]

It was an appreciation which was warmly endorsed by Oxenstierna's colleagues at home. But if peace were to be concluded, they were all agreed that it must embrace three main elements: first, that 'recompense and debt of gratitude' which they considered was due to them from the Protestant states they had delivered, and which they envisaged in terms of large territorial acquisitions in Germany; next, security against invasion, which meant a Swedish command of the ports of the Baltic; and finally, a wider concept of security which implied the destruction of Habsburg pretensions to a real sovereignty in Germany. Gustavus Adolphus had expressed this idea when he said, 'While an Elector can sit safe as Elector in his land, and a Duke is Duke and has his liberties, then we are safe.'[4] Germany, then, must be restored to the 'free' position of 1618 – not only, or even mainly, for the sake of the Protestant cause, but for Sweden's sake. It was a programme which conveniently forgot that in the Germany of 1618 there had been no place for a Swedish territorial recompense.

The Heilbronn League (see Map 3) seemed to take care of most of these objectives: it was pledged to fight for German liberties, and to go on fighting until Sweden had obtained her due compensation; it was firmly under Oxenstierna's direction, and represented the defeat of Richelieu's plan to launch John George as Gustavus Adolphus's successor; and in theory it provided the means to fight the war by proxy. But for the League to be equal to performing all that Oxenstierna expected of it, it was essential to expand it: the four Circles of Upper Germany were too weak, militarily and financially, and above all politically, to carry the burden he designed for them. Hence the attempt, at the Frankfurt Convention of 1634 (page 140 above), to persuade the Upper and Lower Saxon Circles to adhere. That attempt revealed a fatal clash between the need for security and the desire for compensation. For Sweden's refusal to drop her claim to Pomerania ensured that George William of Brandenburg would refuse to join the League, and his refusal in turn entailed that of the two Saxon Circles. From that moment, the Heilbronn solution was doomed. Before the Frankfurt meeting ended, the League's military effectiveness was dealt a crushing blow at Nördlingen; before the year was out the Preliminaries of Pirna opened the way to its disintegration. Oxenstierna could no longer save it.

It now became urgently necessary to find some substitute for Heilbronn. Central Germany seemed as good as lost; Sweden's truce with Poland was due to run out within the next year; and the government in Stockholm, in panic at the prospect of a renewal of war in that quarter, clamoured for peace on any terms, or even on none at all. For Oxenstierna it seemed clear that in the immediate future the only substitute for Heilbronn was France. His object now became to involve Richelieu in Germany and, while avoiding binding commitments, to use France as Sweden's proxy, as once he had used the League. After the peace of Prague Sweden's position appeared desperate: by the end of 1635 almost all her former allies had accepted it, and her military resources in Germany had dwindled to Baner's small army in Pomerania. She was now confronted with a resurgence of German patriotism under the emperor's leadership, with a universal desire for peace, with a fierce hatred of the foreigner: a situation more menacing by far than that of 1629. It was no wonder that the Regents were ready to pay what Oxenstierna bitterly condemned as a disastrous price for the renewal of the truce with Poland at Stuhmsdorf (20 September 1635). The overwhelming majority of the 'Swedish' forces in Germany (and their officers) were Germans, threatened now with proscription if they resisted the emperor's summons to return to their allegiance. Where now could they look for their massive arrears of pay? In August 1635 their mutinous officers kept Oxenstierna a prisoner in their camp near Magdeburg, as a hostage and a bargaining-counter in negotiations with John George of Saxony; and before he escaped he had been driven to promise that if he did not at the peace obtain sufficient cash to pay their arrears, they might come over to Sweden to collect them. It was an appalling prospect, a pledge impossible to redeem. From this moment, 'the contentment of the soldiery' became an essential element for Sweden in any peace settlement.

The government at home was now plainly defeatist. Already in 1634, under the impact of Nördlingen, one prominent member of the Council had cried, 'What good does it do us to acquire many lands and spend all our money on it?'; a year later, another pronounced the whole idea of territorial recompense to have been a mistake from the beginning; and in April 1636 even Oxenstierna's brother declared, 'It is intolerable to go on fighting in a war in which we have no interest.'[5] In the face of this attitude, Oxenstierna was driven in the autumn of 1635 to explore the possibility of peace through the intermediary of Saxony. The exploration exposed him to intolerable humiliations and rebuffs: John George demanded Sweden's immediate evacuation of Germany and her adherence to the peace of Prague (which meant sacrificing her last ally, William of Hesse-Kassel), and only then was he prepared to offer a quite inadequate cash payment, with no territorial concessions; furthermore, he made it clear that no guarantee could be given that the emperor would ratify any peace that might be concluded. Such terms meant the end of Sweden's search for security, the end of her hope of financial recompense, the end of any prospect of a Baltic naval base, and no prospect for the contentment of the soldiery.

It might now seem that the only hope of salvaging anything from the wreck was a French alliance. But a French alliance would bar the way to any separate peace for Sweden if the military situation should improve sufficiently to make it possible to get out of the war on relatively tolerable terms. It was this dilemma which continued to confront Oxenstierna until his final decision in 1641. For the moment, his solution was to try to have it both ways. On the one hand, he concluded in March 1636 the treaty of Wismar, which assured to him – subject to ratification – the French alliance. On the other hand, he took care not to ratify it. And on his return to Sweden in July he succeeded, by sheer force of personality, in stiffening the morale of his colleagues and rallying them to his delicately balancing, procrastinatory policy. They would not, they said, sacrifice Sweden's liberty of action for 'a squirt of money'; and perhaps they realized that, in the year of Corbie, France needed Sweden almost as much as Sweden needed France. So they would keep the French option open; they would, if possible, get their hands upon French gold; but they would try again for a negotiated peace in Germany. They had long since abandoned the grandiose ideas of territorial gains which they had entertained in 1633; and some of them believed that if they made no such demands at all, if they renounced even the claim to Pomerania and asked only for the contentment of the soldiery, the chances of peace were reasonably good. Even so, the idea of security was not simply to be jettisoned; but it now took a new form – the demand for an amnesty for those princes and towns excluded from the peace of Prague: Sweden must, if at all possible, keep alive a party in Germany committed to the defence of 'German Liberties'. But in July 1636 the military situation was such that in the last resort even this must be sacrificed: as Per Brahe remarked in the Council, 'Amnesty is honourable; compensation is useful; but the contentment of the soldiery is essential.'[6] Still, if they could realize even a part of this programme, an alliance with France seemed decidedly a second best.

The limiting factor in regard to this policy, however, was the doubt whether, if Sweden went on fighting until she obtained a negotiated peace, war could be made to sustain war, as in the great days after Breitenfeld. It could hardly do so if Sweden was penned into a narrow and exhausted base in Pomerania and Mecklenburg. For negotiations to have any teeth in them, war must be waged offensively; a break-out from the base must occur; fresh supply – and recruiting – areas must be brought under Swedish control. And the question was whether this could be achieved without French money, and hence without the French alliance. Baner's great victory at Wittstock in October 1636, and his vigorous offensive campaign in the opening months of 1637 (see page 163 below), seemed to show that the trick could be done. The decision to fight and negotiate, and in the meantime keep France on a string – the decision to which Oxenstierna committed the Regents in August 1636 – seemed to have been the right one. But it was speedily contradicted by events in the second half of 1637. Baner's offensive was followed by his brilliant but disastrous retreat from Torgau; and by the end of the year the Swedish armies were fighting with their backs to the sea, clinging with the utmost difficulty to the last shreds of Pomerania. There was now only one way out. The negotiations with the French were resumed, and in March 1638 the treaty of Wismar was at last ratified by the treaty of Hamburg, which bound each party not to make a separate peace for the next three years, and provided Sweden with the subsidies of which she stood in urgent need.[7] The option which Oxenstierna would have preferred was now closed to him, at least for the present. It was a diplomatic defeat. But the French subsidies immediately transformed the military situation – though not before Oxenstierna, violating the principle upon which he had been conducting the war since 1633, sent 14,000 troops from Sweden to Baner's assistance. A military revival duly occurred; and with batteries thus recharged Baner could embark on campaigns so successful that for the first time since 1632 it was possible to dream of ending the war by the capture of Vienna.

In this happier situation, the temptation presented itself to violate the terms of the French alliance while the going was good: the idea was canvassed in the Council more than once, and derived some support from Swedish indignation at France's 'debauching' of the army of Bernard of Weimar (recruited by Gustavus Adolphus, and bound to Sweden by oath) after Bernard's death in 1639. But even though so gross a breach of faith was avoided, it still seemed a fair question whether in the existing, relatively favourable, military situation it would really be wise to renew the French alliance after it expired in 1641. What put an end to all such ideas (at least for Oxenstierna) was another formidable outbreak of mutiny, which paralysed the Swedish armies immediately after Baner's death in May 1641. The basic cause of the trouble was, once again, the question of arrears of pay; and French money now seemed absolutely essential if the new commander, Lennart Torstensson, were to be enabled to restore the army as an effective fighting force. And so, when in 1641 the alliance was in fact renewed, Sweden bound herself, in exchange for subsidies at an increased rate, to fight alongside France – not for a limited period, but for the duration of the war.

The attempt to regain a free hand had failed. In 1641 Oxenstierna had made his final option; and the outcome would prove that he was justified in sticking to it. But by this time he had made another option, too. Territorial compensation was now firmly relegated to a subordinate place among Sweden's war aims. Some hold on the Baltic coast must indeed be retained; but if Sweden could keep a few naval bases, the acquisition of German land was now a minor consideration: what mattered was amnesty and restoration. Oxenstierna was now ready to forget about Pomerania, if only the Germany of 1618 could be restored.[8] In April 1641 he defined his main objectives as the prevention of the enslavement of the Empire, and the contentment of the soldiery: 'These points are *real*; but our compensation is not to be so regarded.'[9] The essential war aim was now the destruction of the peace of Prague, rather than the enlargement of Sweden's territories. At Westphalia it turned out that the attainment of the essential made possible the attainment also of the desirable, and Sweden secured terms such as could never have been obtained by Oxenstierna's balancing tactics of 1635–8: the peace of Prague destroyed, German 'liberty' restored, a comprehensive restoration and amnesty, Sweden herself an Estate of the Empire. It was a full security. But it also brought with it, as 'compensation', territorial gains which seemed to make strategic and economic sense, a large cash indemnity, the contentment of the soldiery firmly placed on German shoulders – and incidentally (though this had long since ceased to be a major preoccupation) the Protestant cause upheld. All this without Sweden's having been trepanned (as Oxenstierna always feared that she might be) into serving as a catspaw for the slippery French.

ii 1635–1642: The deadlock broken

At the time of the peace of Prague, Ferdinand II was already fifty-seven years old. He had faced opposition from many quarters since he first exercised power in 1596, but he had, by and large, overcome it. In the course of his term as emperor he had deposed an Elector and a number of dukes, margraves and counts. He had restored Imperial power to a level unequalled since the reign of Charles V. But he had failed to persuade the Electors to recognize his son Ferdinand, the victor of Nördlingen, as emperor-designate. Now, the chances seemed better: Ferdinand himself was Elector of Bohemia; Saxony and Brandenburg, newly reconciled to the emperor by the peace of Prague, were anxious to please; the anti-Habsburg Elector of Trier, Philip von Sötern, languished in prison (where he was to remain until 1645) for openly placing himself under French protection. This left only the Wittelsbach brothers, Electors of Bavaria and Cologne, and the refugee Elector of Mainz, Anselm Casimir von Wambold, who had been in exile at Cologne since 1631. Ferdinand felt confident that he could secure recognition of his son's title to succeed from these men, and a meeting of the Electoral College was summoned to Regensburg for September 1636.

The power of the Electors, however, was formidable. In the absence of Diets, they were able (in the caustic phrase of David Chytraeus, a Protestant constitutional lawyer) to 'deck themselves with an eagle's plumage' and usurp certain functions of both the Diet and the emperor. Although, in 1636, young Ferdinand was effectively the only serious candidate – French efforts to run first Wladislaw of Poland and then Maximilian of Bavaria came to nothing – the Electors managed to postpone acknowledging him until December while they attempted to force the emperor into making peace with his enemies. There was some success on the internal front: Ferdinand reluctantly agreed that he would pardon any prince who was prepared to submit to him. He also promised to hold an international peace conference to settle the claims of the foreign powers involved in the war, but further progress on this score was prevented by the extreme demands of the Electors themselves. Maximilian of Bavaria required that France should evacuate Lorraine and restore his dispossessed cousin, Duke Charles IV; George William of Brandenburg, still obsessed by the Pomeranian question, insisted that Sweden 'should not retain one foot of territory on Imperial soil, still less any town or fortress'.[1] In the end, the Electors had to be content with Imperial promises that negotiations would soon begin. But on 15 February 1637, Ferdinand died. No serious talks with foreign powers took place.

The war therefore continued. While the French tried unsuccessfully to overrun the South Netherlands and the Rhineland (pages 149–51 above), the Swedish main army under Johan Baner prepared to meet the forces of the emperor, uneasily combined since the peace of Prague with those of Bavaria, Saxony and Brandenburg. In the autumn of 1635, Baner fought a number of engagements against the Saxons, in preparation for a major thrust down the Elbe and Saale to Naumburg in the spring of 1636. As he had intended, this drew upon him an attack by the Imperialists which Baner defeated decisively at Wittstock on 4 October 1636. The Swedes captured their enemies' supplies, equipment and over 100 field guns. This victory effectively eliminated Brandenburg from the war: Elector George William cowered henceforth at Königsberg in East Prussia, one of the few places still under his control, while the Swedes extended their authority to the Elbe.

Baner now had three aims: to keep his enemies away from Sweden's newly acquired Baltic possessions, to provide support (if needed) to his allies George of Brunswick-Lüneburg and William of Hesse-Kassel, and to overawe – if not to overrun – Electoral Saxony. But he was outmanoeuvred. In January 1637 his siege of Leipzig failed, and he withdrew to Torgau on the Elbe. In June he was driven from there too, and Imperial and Saxon forces compelled him to retreat to Pomerania. Here, short of money and munitions, the Swedish army remained confined for over a year. The only actions of the 1638 campaign which attracted international attention were Bernard of Saxe-Weimar's victory at Rheinfelden and his capture of Breisach.

On the local level, however, the war never seemed to stop. Large armies starved and small ones were beaten, but nothing could check the marauding of garrison commanders and freebooters. The account of William Crowne and the engravings of Wenceslas Hollar, both of whom accompanied Charles I's ambassador to the Electoral meeting at Regensburg in 1636, provide a horrifying picture of war-torn Germany. Although they only passed through one actual battle zone (at Ehrenbreitstein on the Rhine, where there had to be a pause in the siege to allow the embassy's barges to pass upstream), devastation was apparent everywhere. They found the entire territory between Mainz and Frankfurt to be desolate, with the people of Mainz so weak from hunger that they could not even crawl to receive the alms that the travellers distributed. At Nuremberg, the ambassador (Thomas Howard, earl of Arundel) purchased the fabulous Pirckheimer library, with manuscripts illustrated by Dürer and other masters, for 350 thalers because its owner was short of money 'in consideration of the hard times and the difficulty of obtaining food'.[2] Beyond Nuremberg, as far as the Danube, there was again total devastation: the English party came across one village that had been pillaged eighteen times in two years, even twice in one day. In several other places there was no one left to tell what had happened, and the company had to camp amid the abandoned ruins and live off the supplies it had prudently brought along, washed down with rainwater. Elsewhere their approach, with eighteen horse-drawn wagons and cavalry escort, was mistaken for an enemy attack and provoked panic defence measures. Finally, in Linz, capital of Upper Austria, they witnessed the execution of Martin Laimbauer, the leader of yet another peasant uprising against the Habsburgs, which had achieved considerable local support earlier in the year.[3]

The English were lucky to be spectators only. Others were less fortunate. 'Men hunt men as beasts of prey, in the woods and on the way,' wrote one observer, and there are even well-documented cases of cannibalism from the Rhineland in 1635.[4] No one was safe from attack. In January 1638 a column of Nuremberg merchants, with seven wagons, was returning from the Leipzig Fair when it was ambushed by some cavalry. The soldiers demanded 1,000 thalers in cash; the convoy leader offered only 300, and the troops attacked and plundered the wagons. They killed several of the merchants and took perhaps eighty horses which they loaded with booty, spoiling what remained. The loss was estimated at 100,000 thalers yet the identity of the attackers was never established (although many suspected the Bavarian army). That was the seventh convoy to be lost by the merchants of Nuremberg in less than two years, and the city now launched a diplomatic mission to all major combatants, and to the other free cities of the Empire, demanding better protection for trade.[5] It was, of course, fruitless.

The plight of Nuremberg was typical. Between the battles of Breitenfeld and Nördlingen the territories of central Germany suffered appallingly, as the Swedish troops demonstrated how far they could make war pay for itself. The bishopric of Würzburg between 1631 and 1636 suffered losses estimated at over 1 million thalers. During the same period the city of Mainz, under continuous Swedish occupation, lost perhaps 25 per cent of its dwellings, 40 per cent of its population and 60 per cent of its wealth. The Elector's library was broken up, most of his books going to Västerås in Sweden and some of the manuscripts ending up (thanks to the intervention of Archbishop Laud, Chancellor of Oxford University) in the Bodleian Library.[6] After Nördlingen, it was the turn of the Protestants to suffer. In the three months immediately following the Habsburgs' great victory, according to the ministers of George of Hesse-Darmstadt (then lurking in Dresden), 30,000 horses, 100,000 cows and 600,000 sheep had been lost, and damage worth 10 million thalers inflicted on the territory. In 1635 the counts of neighbouring Nassau also abandoned their lands, taking refuge in Metz from what the chronicles later referred to as 'The year of great destruction in the land'.[7] The duchy of Württemberg, occupied by Imperial and Bavarian forces between 1634 and 1638, suffered damage estimated at 34 million thalers and its population fell to less than a quarter (from 450,000 inhabitants in 1620 to less than 100,000 in 1639).[8] Admittedly, Swabia was ravaged with particular severity during the 1630s, but matters were scarcely better further north. In Mecklenburg, a partial survey of the duchy in 1639–40 revealed only 360 cultivated farms where, before the war, there had been almost 3,000. In Brandenburg, Werben (once the headquarters of Gustavus Adolphus) sank from 267 occupied houses to 105 during the same period; while the Elector's capital, Berlin, with a population of 12,000 in 1618, could boast only 7,500 inhabitants twenty years later, and the demographic decline of several rural areas – whether through war, famine or plague – exceeded 40 per cent.[9] At the Elector of Saxony's capital, Dresden, which was never captured, the ratio of burials to baptisms changed from 100:121 during the decade before 1630, to 100:39 during the decade following. Only immigration maintained the city's population.[10] And to these misfortunes must be added the heavy taxation levied by all governments to pay for defence: it was seldom enough to guarantee security, but it was always sufficient to create hardship.[11]

All these reports of misery and cruelty, generalized and impersonal as they may seem, in fact concerned countless individuals, whose personal suffering was not reduced because it was shared. The autobiography of Johann Valentin Andreä, writer of Rosicrucian and Utopian tracts in his youth and supervisor of the Lutheran churches in Calw (Swabia) in the 1630s, reminds us of the agony endured even by survivors. In 1639, he wrote despondently that of his 1,046 communicants of 1630 only 338 remained. 'Just in the last five years [that is, since Nördlingen], 518 of them have been killed by various misfortunes.' Among these, he noted five intimate and thirty-three other friends, twenty relatives, and forty-one clerical colleagues. 'I have to weep for them', he continued, 'because I remain here so impotent and alone. Out of my whole life I am left with scarcely fifteen persons alive with whom I can claim some trace of friendship.'[12]

Dr William Harvey, who accompanied Arundel's embassy to Regensburg in 1636, noted the dangerous implications of such extreme war-weariness and desperation. 'This warfare in Germany', he wrote to a colleague, 'threateneth in the ende anarchy and confusion'; and he commented on 'The necessity they have here of making peace on any condition, where there is noe more meanes of making warr, or scarce of subsistence'.[13] It was only a short time after this that Pope Urban VIII took the first steps towards the organization of peace talks to bring the war to an end. A papal legate arrived at Cologne in October 1636 and invited all interested powers to send representatives to a general peace congress. But nobody came: neither France nor Spain trusted the pope to be impartial; and the Protestants rejected papal mediation altogether, convening a conference of their own at Hamburg instead. This meeting arose from an agreement between France and England in March 1637, under which Charles I promised to allow French recruiting in England and the loan of thirty ships for a new campaign against the emperor. In return, Louis XIII undertook to conclude no settlement that did not involve the restoration of the Palatine family to their lands and titles, and to convene a peace conference at either Hamburg or The Hague where Sweden, Denmark, the Netherlands and France could prepare articles to present to the emperor for redress. Although France eventually refused to ratify the treaty, she did send envoys to Hamburg, where Swedish diplomats were already engaged in talks with the Imperialists. France soon stopped this (by the subsidy treaty noted on page 160 above), and, in the end, the Hamburg protocol was only signed by Denmark and England – states no longer actively involved in the war – in April 1639.[14]

The German territorial rulers, however, were bound to take more seriously the prospect of 'anarchy and confusion' unless a formula for peace were found. As the prospect of a general settlement temporarily receded, several princes attempted to make a separate, local agreement. Wolfgang William, duke of Neuburg and Jülich, concerned about the unrest in his Rhineland duchy caused by the presence of large Imperial forces over the winters of 1635–6 and 1636–7, proposed to an assembly of the Lower Rhenish Circle that the entire area should be declared neutral. In 1639 he opened direct negotiations with the local commanders – Imperial and Protestant – to this end, even asking the Dutch Republic to guarantee his neutrality. But this peace initiative, like many others, came to nothing: the duchy of Jülich, with its Rhine crossings, presented strategic advantages that the rival armies could not afford to neglect.[15]

All these developments – the victories of his enemies, the widespread destruction and demoralization of Germany, and the attempts to make a separate peace – were warning signals that the new emperor, Ferdinand III, could not ignore. Therefore, in February 1640, he held another Electoral meeting at Nuremberg. When this failed to make headway, he proposed that the Imperial Diet should meet again, for the first time since 1613, in order to clear the way for a general peace. The opening ceremony took place at Regensburg in September 1640 and for more than a year the three colleges of the assembly discussed intensively the disputes that kept their country at war. The Electors held 185 formal sessions, and the princes 153; there were also twenty-six joint meetings. Naturally the territorial rulers themselves did not attend for the entire year – some dared not come at all – so there were innumerable delays for correspondence between the princely courts and their delegations in Regensburg; letters from Munich took two or three days, letters from Mainz and Vienna took between five and eight days, and letters from Königsberg (where the Elector of Brandenburg now resided) took three weeks in summer and five weeks in winter. Some rulers did not even send delegations: Ferdinand excluded the Protestant administrators of dioceses affected by the Edict of Restitution, and those princes in arms against the emperor. Indeed, one of the weightiest problems to be solved by the Diet was the readmission of these rulers. In the end only Brunswick, the Palatine family and Hesse-Kassel refused to stop fighting and accept Imperial authority again; the rest were reconciled. The difficulty of this issue was dwarfed, however, by the problem of secularized church lands. Again the emperor gave way. In spite of papal protests, which were formally tabled at the Diet by the nuncio in April 1641, the emperor abandoned the Edict of Restitution: ecclesiastical property which had been in secular hands on 1 January 1627 was so to remain. Although the papacy continued to condemn all future settlements, including the final peace, that included this abrogation of the Edict of Restitution, in effect the issue was resolved for ever at Regensburg.[16]

Ferdinand had no choice but to make these substantial concessions, for he was losing the war. Late in 1638, after a year on the defensive in Pomerania following his retreat from Torgau,

Baner – with Swedish reinforcements at his back and French subsidies in his pocket – drove the Imperialists into Silesia again. The next year, while Bernard of Saxe-Weimar overran Alsace and attacked Spanish Franche-Comté, Baner defeated the Saxons at Chemnitz (April 1639) and threatened Prague. The Swedes were obliged to withdraw from Bohemia in June, but the following year, for the first time, they were able to mount a combined operation with their French allies. Baner was joined in Saxony by the troops formerly commanded by Bernard of Saxe-Weimar (who had died in July 1639) as well as by contingents supplied by Brunswick and Hesse-Kassel (the latter now directed by William V's widow, Amalia, countess of Hanau). The combined force of 40,000 men campaigned on the Weser somewhat ineffectually, but in January 1641, as the Diet sat in conclave, they appeared before Regensburg and briefly shelled the city. It was a fearful reminder of the need for a settlement. Shortly afterwards there came another: Brandenburg made a separate peace with Sweden.

Ever since the peace of Prague, by which George William had exchanged a Swedish for an Imperial alliance, Brandenburg had become a war-zone. After the battle of Wittstock the following year, his lands had come almost entirely under Swedish control: Cleves and Mark were entirely occupied; Brandenburg was regularly fought over; only Prussia remained free, although Sweden levied tolls even there. The Elector's army numbered scarcely 6,000 men, all of them in garrisons. When George William died in December 1640, after over a year of semi-inertia (euphemistically termed 'melancholy' by contemporaries), his son Frederick William (aged only twenty-one) lost no time in proposing a separate peace with Sweden to the Brandenburg Estates (or what was left of them). Following the death of his father's chief adviser, the pro-Imperial Count Schwarzenberg, in March 1641, envoys were sent to Stockholm to arrange a ceasefire. In July, almost precisely ten years after Gustavus Adolphus had brought his army to Brandenburg, the fighting there stopped. The 'Great Elector' was not prepared to see his patrimonial lands destroyed by the Swedes simply because he was allied to an emperor who could offer him no protection.

Another successful disengagement from the war was made shortly afterwards by Brandenburg's western neighbours, the dukes of Brunswick – the several members of the Welf family who jointly dominated the lands between the middle Elbe and the Weser. They had been inconstant allies of both sides in the past. Led by Duke George of Brunswick-Lüneburg, they had supported Ferdinand II until 1630, when Imperial commissioners demanded the surrender of the secularized bishopric of Hildesheim. Rather than return it, Duke George and his cousins signed an alliance with Sweden and formed an army which kept the Imperialists at bay. In 1635, Duke George quarrelled with Oxenstierna and eventually accepted the peace of Prague, but the emperor still insisted on the return of Hildesheim so George signed a new alliance with Hesse-Kassel and Sweden. It was as he led his forces south to do battle with the Imperialists again that, in April 1641, he died. His cousins lacked the same diplomatic and military agility, and in the course of the summer the emperor's troops overran large areas of Brunswick. Then, in the winter, the Swedes returned, and heavy fighting in the duchies took place. It was this, above all else, that persuaded the Welf dukes to sign a preliminary accord with the emperor in January 1642 (the peace of Goslar), even though it meant the return of the secularized lands of Hildersheim, duly handed over a year later to the bishop, Elector Ferdinand of Cologne. In return, the Protestants were granted toleration (even in Hildesheim, where six churches were reserved for Lutheran worship) and the whole of Brunswick was henceforth regarded as neutral.[17]

These developments brought relative peace to consider-able areas of the north-east and north-west of Germany, but the war continued elsewhere just the same. The death of Baner in May 1641, followed by the mutiny of some units of his army for their pay, provided a brief respite for the Imperialists. But on 30 June Oxenstierna's envoys at Hamburg concluded a final alliance with France, to last until the peace, and Lennart Torstensson, one of Sweden's most successful commanders, was sent to Germany to win the war. In the spring of 1642 the new commander-in-chief invaded Saxony, defeating the forces of John George yet again (at Schweidnitz), and advanced through Silesia into Moravia. He captured the capital, Olomouc, in June and threatened Vienna before withdrawing his main army to Saxony, where he laid siege to Leipzig. There, on 2 November, the Imperial army (under the personal command of the emperor's brother, Archduke Leopold William) challenged the Swedes to battle. Torstensson withdrew a little northwards to Breitenfeld, and there won a victory almost as complete as that of Gustavus, on the same terrain, eleven years before. The Imperialists lost 5,000 men on the field, and a further 5,000 as prisoners – as well as forty-six field guns, the archduke's treasury and chancery, and the supply train. Leipzig fell a month later, paying an indemnity of 400,000 thalers. It remained in Swedish hands until 1650.[18]

This sequence of disasters terrified the emperor's Catholic

allies in western Germany, especially Bavaria. In January 1640, even before the Electoral meeting at Nuremberg, secret talks with French representatives had been held at Einsiedeln at which Maximilian offered to make a separate peace with France on three conditions: recognition of the Electoral title for himself and his descendants; French withdrawal from Alsace; and a repudiation of France's alliance with Protestant Sweden. These haughty terms were angrily brushed aside by Richelieu, who had already decided to renew the Swedish treaty. Soon, however, the success of the allied army under Baner and the resolution of so many issues at the Regensburg Diet led Maximilian to try a different tack. This time he hoped to enlist the support of the pope and of the other Catholic Electors in order to persuade the French that they could accept the compromises reached at Regensburg and make peace, even if Sweden could not. In April and May 1642 he held discussions with the Electors of Mainz and Cologne in order to prepare a common platform for the intended negotiations, after which a deputation was sent to Paris for discussions.[19] After almost a quarter-century of war, the emperor had at last been abandoned by almost all his German allies. The deadlock in the struggle, which had prevailed since Lützen, was at last broken; now it only remained to compel the Habsburgs to bow to the inevitable.

iii 1643–1647: The defeat of the Habsburgs

Ferdinand III was encouraged to respond positively to calls for peace by the sudden and apparently total collapse of Spanish power. Ever since Nördlingen, Philip IV had given his brother-in-law extensive aid. He maintained garrisons in the Palatinate; he provided a subsidy worth around 500,000 thalers a year; and by supporting armies in Lombardy, the Low Countries and Catalonia, he tied down the major part of French military strength.[1] His brother the Cardinal-Infante, who governed the Spanish Netherlands until his death in 1641, even managed to threaten Paris (page 152 above). The French, however, were not Spain's only enemies. The Cardinal-Infante was still forced to commit most of his troops against the army of the Dutch Republic (which in 1637 recaptured Breda, lost to Spínola twelve years before); and Philip himself deployed important resources on the defence of the overseas possessions of his Spanish and Portuguese crowns (especially in South America, where the Dutch had held the northern province of Brazil – Pernambuco – since 1630). In October 1639, a great fleet of warships carrying troops and supplies from Spain to the Netherlands was intercepted by the Dutch in the Channel and almost totally destroyed (the battle of the Downs); another, sent to relieve Brazil, met the same fate off Recife three months later.

As if this were not enough, the year 1640 saw even worse defeats. In May the province of Catalonia rebelled and at once attracted French aid; in December, the kingdom of Portugal followed suit, securing immediate support from both France and the Dutch. Philip IV was reluctantly compelled to divert his attention from northern Europe to the troubles in the peninsula. Some of his advisers – including the once bellicose count of Oñate – urged Spanish withdrawal from overseas commitments; but to no avail.[2] Instead there were losses on all fronts: Arras and most of Artois in 1640; Salces and Perpignan in 1642. The count-duke of Olivares, who had survived many defeats, could not now withstand the campaign of criticism waged against him. In January 1643, he resigned. But the change of ministry did not affect Spain's foreign policy: no talk of peace was countenanced. Then in May the Army of Flanders was decisively defeated at Rocroi. Although the battle was perhaps less influential than has sometimes been claimed – for it had no immediate effect on Spain's control over the South Netherlands – it did bring to an abrupt end all chance of launching another invasion of France from the Low Countries. With Trier, Alsace and Lorraine in French hands, and with the Dutch in command of Limburg, the Channel and the North Sea, Philip IV's government was now physically unable to send reinforcements to the Low Countries. The 'Spanish Road' was blocked; the Spanish Netherlands were therefore unable to resist effectively the progress of French and Dutch arms – Gravelines was lost in 1644, Hulst in 1645, Dunkirk in 1646.

But France was by now also experiencing grave difficulties in maintaining her war effort. A succession of serious popular rebellions broke out between 1636 and 1643, affecting both towns and countryside, and detachments of the regular army had to be withdrawn from the front to put them down. There was also opposition from the royal bureaucracy, which either refused to collect taxes or else pocketed the proceeds, while a series of aristocratic plots were hatched against the chief minister, Cardinal Richelieu. In 1641 a conspiracy, led by the king's cousin (the count of Soissons) and advocating a programme of peace and disengagement abroad, rapidly attracted a great following. Only the accidental death of Soissons saved the government. It was followed the next year by a plot led by the king's favourite, the marquis of Cinq-Mars, who had rashly promised Spain that he would make peace as soon as Richelieu fell. But, three months after Cinq-Mars's execution, Richelieu died; and though there was no policy change at first, in May 1643 – just before the great victory of Rocroi – death also claimed Louis XIII. Power was now left in the hands of the Spanish-born regent, Anne of Austria, sister of Philip IV of Spain and the Cardinal-Infante, and sister-in-law of Ferdinand III. She was, naturally, somewhat less opposed to peace with her Habsburg relatives than Louis had been, but in matters of foreign policy she accepted the advice of the chief minister who succeeded Richelieu, Cardinal Jules Mazarin. Although born a subject of Philip IV and educated partly in Spain, Mazarin's training as a diplomat under first Urban VIII and then Richelieu had made him a convinced enemy of Habsburg power. His overriding aim was to weaken, and if possible to divide, the Austrian and Spanish branches of the family; and in this he was ultimately successful. But in 1643, newly installed, Mazarin was inclined to be cautious. He could not ignore the risk that eterna-lizing the costly war might provoke a revolution that would topple the monarchy – as seemed to have happened across the Channel, in the states ruled by Charles I and his French queen, Henrietta Maria. The English Civil War, which broke out in August 1642, was a fearsome warning: it encouraged prudence amongst princes.

In Sweden, too, the government was conscious of the intense hostility towards the war – and its attendant taxation and con-scription – felt by the population at large. 'The common man wishes himself dead,' noted Oxenstierna's lugubrious brother, whose long, despondent reports on affairs of state were one of the many crosses the chancellor had to bear. 'We may indeed say that we have conquered our lands from others, and to that end ruined our own.' 'While the branches expand,' he continued remorse-lessly, 'the tree withers at the roots.'[3] And wither it certainly did, for Sweden's military losses were fast becoming insupport-able: whole villages became depopulated of young men, for a conscription order (as noted on page 193 below) was virtually a sentence of death.

If censorship tended to limit the public expression of discon-tent in Sweden, there was no such constraint in the Empire. All over Germany, tracts calling for peace proliferated, and the call was taken up in a variety of media: prayers, pamphlets, illustrated flysheets, music, medals and plays. The latter were all the more influential, because the best 'peace plays' were written by men who shared the 'pietist' outlook which had begun to rejuvenate Lutheranism. The emotional fervour and moral righteousness of the language in plays such as 'The Victory of Peace' (*Friedens Sieg* by Justus Schöttel, a pastor's son) or 'The Mirror of Peace' (*Friedens Spiegel* by Johan Rist, a Hamburg pastor) was powerful indeed. And it reached a wide audience. Schöttel was a councillor to the dukes of Brunswick, and the first production of *Friedens Sieg* was performed by the duke's children, while Frederick William of Brandenburg watched.[4]

So, by the beginning of 1643, peace was unmistakably in the air breathed by the non-German as well as by the German participants in the war, and before long there were two peace conferences in session. At Frankfurt, representatives of many German princes, including most of the Electors, assembled in January 1643 to resolve the remaining purely German issues, and to determine the best form in which to negotiate with the foreign powers. Plenipotentiaries of the latter were meanwhile converging upon Münster and Osnabrück, the towns specified for negotiations in the Franco-Swedish treaty of 1641, which now became a special 'demilitarized zone'. France, Spain and other Catholic states made their base at Münster; Sweden and her allies negotiated forty-five kilometres away at Osnabrück.

It was Ferdinand III's intention to keep the assemblies separate, since he hoped that his own envoys would be able to conduct talks with the foreign powers in the name of the whole Empire. The Catholic rulers seemed agreeable to this – 'vox caesaris est vox catholicorum', as one of them later noted – but the Protestants were not. Firstly, they were heavily outnumbered in the early days at Frankfurt: two against four Catholics in the Electoral College, four against ten in the Princes' College. Secondly, several leading Protestants were still technically outlaws and thus could not attend the discussions at Frankfurt. The opposition to Ferdinand's binary peace policy was led by Frederick William of Brandenburg from within the assembly, and by Amalia of Hesse-Kassel from without. But they would probably not have had their way without the support of France and Sweden. The views of these two powers were clearly set out by the Swedish plenipotentiary, Johan Adler Salvius, in an open letter to the Protestant princes of April 1643. 'For thirty years', he claimed (incorrectly), 'no Imperial Diet has been held, and in the interim the emperor has managed to usurp everything by right of sovereignty. This is the highroad to absolute rule and the servitude of the territories. The crowns [of Sweden and France] are seeking, as far as they are able, to obstruct this, for their security rests on the liberty of the German territories.'⁵ Gradually the Protestant delegations moved their headquarters to Osnabrück. But still the emperor remained obdurate, refusing to recognize the right of his vassals to vote in the congress meetings. Only on 29 August 1645, a key date in the peace-making process, was the *ius belli ac pacis* conceded to all independent territorial rulers. The deliberations at the conference in Westphalia were now accorded the status of a Diet, so that its resolutions would have the force of Imperial laws. The Frankfurt assembly closed.

In fact the emperor had only been able to prolong the talks at Frankfurt for so long because of a brief stroke of military good fortune: in 1643 Sweden suddenly went to war with Denmark. There were many reasons for this surprising development. Christian IV, his desire for foreign glory unquenched by either advancing years or previous defeats, had long made as much mischief for his northern neighbour as possible: he gave shelter to vengeful political enemies of the Stockholm government; he blockaded Sweden's ally, the port of Hamburg; he harassed and even arrested Swedish shipping in the Baltic. When news leaked out that Christian was secretly negotiating an alliance with the emperor, Sweden decided to strike first. Her best generals, Torstensson and Königsmarck, were instructed to march from the borders of Bohemia (where they had operated since their victory at Breitenfeld in November 1642) towards Denmark. Königsmarck overran the secularized bishoprics of Verden and Bremen, which had enjoyed neutrality since Sweden restored them to Danish control after Nördlingen. Now they were swiftly occupied and placed under a proconsular government, headed by Königsmarck, which paved the way for Swedish annexation after the peace of Westphalia. Meanwhile Torstensson occupied Holstein and in 1644 began the conquest of the Jutland peninsula with the same ease as Tilly and Wallenstein sixteen years before.⁶ In October a major naval engagement at Femmern, in which Christian's forces were defeated, opened the islands to the threat of Swedish invasion; peace talks began the following month. A formal conference, which opened in February 1645, drew up the pro-Swedish peace of Brömsbro on 23 August.

This was far from the outcome that the emperor had anticipated. No sooner had Sweden made clear her intention to invade Denmark than Ferdinand promised to assist Christian IV, and he despatched his field army, under Count Gallas, to pursue Torstensson into Holstein. The Swedes, however, had foreseen this development, and had concluded an alliance with George Rákóczy, successor to Bethlen Gabor as ruler of Transylvania: the prince, with the blessing of the Ottoman sultan, and subsidies from France, promised to invade Habsburg Hungary. This he did in February 1644, seriously compromising Ferdinand III, who was obliged to recall the field army he had sent to aid Denmark. But Torstensson adroitly compelled the Imperialists to retreat through areas so devastated that most of them died of starvation. According to the (admittedly hostile) chronicler Chemnitz, of the 18,000 men who began the retreat, barely 1,000 reached the safety of Bohemia, so that 'it would be hard to find a similar example of an army brought to ruin in such a short time without any major battle'.[7] Gallas, who had also led the disastrous retreat from Burgundy in 1636, was dismissed.

But it needed more than a change of general to stop the Swedes. Early in 1645, with Denmark clearly out of the war for good, the Swedish high command determined to mount an operation that would bring about the immediate collapse of Habsburg resistance. An invasion of Bohemia in full strength, and in conjunction with the Transylvanians, seemed to offer the best chance of this, because it would 'wound the emperor right to the heart'. In addition, the French army of the Rhine was to invade Bavaria, so that Ferdinand III would receive no relief from that quarter. This, however, was easier said than done. The French had not done well in the Rhineland since the death of Bernard of Saxe-Weimar. The need to send support to Catalonia and Portugal, as well as to continue the war along the Netherlands frontier, tended to reduce the supply of men and money to the army of Germany commanded by the viscount of Turenne. At first, the military opportunities offered to Bavaria by this situation were ignored, for Maximilian still hoped to make a separate peace with France (see page 170 above). But when negotiations broke down, the Bavarian army under Franz von Mercy delivered a masterly attack at Tuttlingen (November 1643) which forced Turenne to retreat to the Rhine, abandoning all his army's baggage and equipment. The retreat, carried out in the depths of winter, caused the loss of perhaps two-thirds of Turenne's force of 16,000 (the 'Bernardines' or 'German Brigade', made up of the regiments formerly commanded by Bernard of Saxe-Weimar, was particularly hard hit). Although reinforcements were sent to Alsace in 1644, the French proved unable to break out of the Rhine valley. At Freiburg in August 1644 Mercy again inflicted heavy losses on Turenne (on this occasion the 'German Brigade' was practically annihilated, only three officers and fifty men surviving out of three regiments); and another battle at Mergentheim, in May 1645, confirmed the local superiority of Bavarian over French forces in the area.[8] But the arrival of Swedish reinforcements from the north enabled Turenne to counterattack and, at the battle of Allerheim on 3 August, Mercy was defeated and killed, and his army destroyed as a viable fighting force, by the combined Swedish, French and Hessian host.

The Swedish contingent at Allerheim had already been involved in another great victory five months earlier. The Swedish 'Hauptarmee' had begun its march from Saxony into Bohemia before the spring. Torstensson led a fighting force of only 15,000, and the Imperialists – despite the Transylvanian advance up the Danube – were able to field the same number. But the Swedes had an overwhelming advantage in artillery: sixty field guns against only twenty-six. After some preliminary skirmishing, the two sides met in a prolonged pitched battle at Jankov, south-east of Prague, on 6 March. The result was decisive: the Imperialists lost their artillery, half their men, their field chancery and even their commanders (see Plate 19). Immediately, the emperor and his family fled to Graz.[9] Nor was this an idle precaution, for by the end of the month Torstensson's men had taken Krems, where they created a bridgehead across the Danube (and restored Lutheran worship). The Swedes and Transylvanians now prepared for a siege of Vienna, and the few Lutherans left in the city openly rejoiced and awaited their liberation. But it never came. The emperor was saved by the Turks.

In the spring of 1645, the Ottoman sultan determined to go to war with the Venetian Republic over possession of Crete. He began the campaign in June, and promptly diverted all his military resources to the task: aid for Rákóczy was ended. The prince, thus abandoned and in financial difficulties, lent a favourable ear to Habsburg overtures for peace and – despite a new alliance with France, signed in April – concluded the treaty of Vienna with Ferdinand on 16 December 1645. Religious toleration in Hungary was restored and guaranteed, and extensive territories were ceded anew to Rákóczy. For a state which lacked almost every resource for the conduct of sustained hostilities, Transylvania had done surprisingly well from the Thirty Years' War.

But the defection of Transylvania did not alter the critical importance of the 1645 campaign. That is why it was so hard fought. The battle of Jankov, for example, lasted longer than almost any other engagement in the war precisely because everyone recognized its decisive nature: the emperor hazarded all his economic and military resources, the prestige of his house, and his own reputation as a commander of superior ability. The fact that he lost them all, through defeat, made it almost inevitable that the final peace settlement would be unfavourable to the Habsburgs. After Jankov and Allerheim, there was no longer any Catholic field army able to withstand the Swedes and their allies; and everyone knew it. On 6 September, John George of Saxony reluctantly signed a cease-fire with Sweden at Kötzschenbroda and abandoned the war. Meanwhile, in Westphalia, Oxenstierna noted that 'the enemy begins to talk more politely and pleasantly' and the Imperial representatives at the peace conference offered substantial concessions.[10] The agreement that all princes and towns with a seat in the Imperial Diet should be allowed effective representation at the peace talks came in August 1645; in September, the emperor reluctantly agreed not to seek any advantage in the peace treaty for Catholics living in Protestant territories in the Empire. Shortly afterwards, he issued an amnesty for all his rebellious vassals, to allow them to attend the conference and put forward their own demands in person; and on 29 November 1645, the emperor's confidant and chief negotiator, Count von Trauttmannsdorf, arrived at Münster with broad instructions to make whatever concessions were needed to secure peace.

It was at this point, just as serious discussions about a settlement of the German war began, that representatives from the Dutch Republic chose to arrive in Münster to settle their disagreements with Spain. As early as January 1642, the captain-general of the Republic, Frederick Henry, prince of Orange, had invited the States-General to nominate plenipotentiaries and formulate terms; but delegates and instructions were not finally agreed upon until October 1645. The Dutch embassy left for the peace conference in January 1646.[11] Their presence both completed the jigsaw of political allegiances and complicated the task of making a German peace. It may have been true, as Gustavus Adolphus had once said, that 'all the wars that are on foot in Europe are fused together and have become one war'; but the alliances that bound the various combatants together could not disguise serious divergences of interest. Even the same state (most notably France) might have two policies at the conference: one for Germany, another for the Low Countries. Sometimes different, even contradictory, instructions were issued to the various delegates; sometimes different members of the same delegation acted in contrary ways. The first peace conference of modern times was a law unto itself. (See Plate 18.)

The negotiations were handled by 176 plenipotentiaries (almost half of them lawyers by profession) who acted for 194 European rulers, great and small. Not all of the states represented at the congress sent delegations of their own – only 109 did so – but nevertheless several thousand diplomatic personnel thronged the streets of Münster and Osnabrück between 1643 and 1648. The size of the various embassies ranged from the 200 men, women and children in the French delegation to the lone envoys of the smaller German principalities.

Life at the conference was a curious mixture of scarcity and plenty: on the one hand, the norm for accommodation was often two to a bed (thus, in the Bavarian embassy, the twenty-nine staff had to share only eighteen beds); on the other, food and drink were plentiful (the same Bavarians each appear to have consumed between two and three litres of wine daily, so perhaps they were too befuddled to argue about the beds).[12] But, drunk or sober, the principal activity of the delegates was to communicate and to negotiate, and the outpouring of ink by the diplomats was indeed prodigious. A complex postal network was specially erected to permit the regular exchange of verbose *Denkschriften* and endless letters between the envoys and their principals, so that nothing should be concluded without the full and express consent of every government.[13] Naturally, this caused serious delay in the negotiations, for each letter took between ten and twelve days to travel from Münster to either Paris or Vienna, and between twenty-three and thirty days to reach Madrid. A letter from Osnabrück to Stockholm might take twenty days or more (before the peace of Brömsebro with Denmark, considerably more); and the reply, of course, took just as long. But these delays did not cause any reduction in letter-writing. The correspondence between the delegates of the duke of Württemberg at Osnabrück and their master at Stuttgart was fairly typical: from 1644 until 1649, in theory they wrote to each other only once a week, usually on a Friday, but by the end each side had written almost 400 epistles.[14]

With so many participants and so many conflicting interests, it is hard to see – let alone summarize – the salient trends; nevertheless, it may be argued that negotiations fell into three phases. The first, which was largely procedural, began with the Frankfurt meeting in January 1643 and lasted, with many fits and starts, until November 1645 when Count Trauttmannsdorf arrived in Münster. The second phase of the Congress lasted from this point until the count left again, in June 1647: a period of intense negotiation during which almost every outstanding dispute between the protagonists in both the Dutch and the German conflicts was settled. During the final phase, which lasted until the three peace treaties were signed in 1648, France attempted unsuccessfully to delay the end of hostilities, both in the Netherlands and in Germany, until she had brought Spain to her knees. Throughout the five years, the pace of negotiations, as well as the nature of the concessions, was constantly altered by the fortunes of war. In the cynical phrase of Prior Adami of Murrhart, one of the hard-line Catholics at the conference: 'In winter we negotiate, in summer we fight.'[15] The pathway to peace was narrow and far from straight.

iv 1647–1650: The making of peace

They say that the terrible war is now over. But there is still no sign of a peace. Everywhere there is envy, hatred and greed: that's what the war has taught us . . . We live like animals, eating bark and grass. No one could have imagined that anything like this would happen to us. Many people say that there is no God . . .

This desperate entry in a family Bible, from the Swabian village of Gerstetten, was written on 17 January 1647, after the arrival of yet another band of refugees with news of predatory troops on their heels. 'But we still believe that God has not abandoned us', the entry continued. 'We must all stand together and help each other.'[1] Alas, there were still twenty months of fighting ahead before the peace finally came: a period in which Swabia (like Bavaria, Austria and many other parts of the Empire) was ravaged once more. In fact the fighting in most of Germany continued right up to the moment when the last signatures on the treaties of peace dried on 24 October 1648. Although by then several of the most intransigent figures in the conflict had been removed by death or disgrace – Richelieu and Olivares, Ferdinand II and Gustavus Adolphus, Bernard of Saxe-Weimar and William of Hesse-Kassel – their successors were no less determined to exact the best possible return from the prolonged and prodigal expenditure of blood and treasure. They negotiated as hard as they fought.

Although most of the questions at issue were discussed at the

Peace Congress simultaneously, there was a recognition, among at least the French and Swedish diplomats, that the purely German problems should be resolved first. As Count d'Avaux wrote from Münster in April 1644: 'It would seem that . . . the honour and profit of France will best be served by placing first on the table the items concerning public peace and the liberties of the Empire . . . because if they [the German states] do not yet truly wish for peace, it would be prejudicial and damaging to us if the talks broke down over our own particular demands.' While, on the Swedish side, in December of the same year, the wily Oxenstierna wrote to his son (who was a principal negotiator at Osnabrück): 'So long as "the restitution of the affairs of the Empire to their original state" is our pretext for wanting changes in our favour . . . we must justify all our doings in the light of the same.'[2]

Many of the parameters of 'German liberty' had already been laid down in the peace of Prague and the decisions of the Diet of Regensburg, but the outstanding points were inevitably the thorniest: official toleration for Calvinism, the restitution of secularized church land, the restoration of the Elector Palatine, and a general amnesty. The last, as already noted, was granted in the aftermath of Jankov. The third, although the subject of prolonged haggling, was already envisaged in the emperor's secret instruction to Trauttmannsdorf in October 1645: 'in extreme need, and when there can be no other way', an eighth Electorate was to be created so that both Bavaria and the Palatine might have seats in the Electoral college.[3] But these were matters that could be decided mainly by the emperor alone. It was the other two issues – toleration and restitution – that were truly divisive, for they raised the fundamental questions of who was competent to decide religious issues and whether all territorial rulers possessed the right to ignore Imperial decrees. The Catholic party had often argued that the Augsburg settlement of 1555 had only been a temporary, emergency measure; but everyone realized that the new balance of faith which the Peace Congress established would be permanent. That was why the bargaining was so tough.

Battle was joined in earnest after August 1645, when the first meeting of all the delegations at the Congress took place. Just over a month later the Catholic princes of the Empire held their first separate discussion at Münster, and shortly afterwards the Protestants began to hold regular separate meetings at Osnabrück. Although membership of the two sides was fairly evenly divided (there were seventy-two members of the *Corpus Catholicorum* against seventy-three in the *Corpus Evangelicorum*) the

Catholics seemed initially to hold the advantage. Firstly, the Imperial representatives were clearly on their side; secondly, there was more coherence among the Catholics because several members held more than one vote. The Elector of Cologne topped the list with fifteen, exercised by his chief adviser – and cousin – Bishop Wartenburg of Osnabrück (who also held five proxy votes of his own); Prior Adami of Murrhart represented several Swabian abbeys and forty-one Swabian prelates. It was the same with the Imperial cities: the Augsburg representative, Johann Leuchselring, was empowered to cast the vote of fifteen other towns.[4] Yet this semblance of strength was deceptive. Although the emperor was on the side of the Catholics, not all Catholics were on the side of the emperor. There was a powerful group of anti-Imperialists, led by the Elector of Trier (still smarting from his ten years of Imperial captivity), who favoured concessions to the French, and if necessary to the Protestants, in order to win peace. Ranged against them, within the Catholic camp, were a group of fifteen or so extremists, led by Wartenburg, Adami and Leuchselring – known as 'the triumvirs' – and supported by Spain. These men were determined to make no concessions of substance on religious matters. And, as if this division were not enough to undermine the Catholic cause, differences also occurred between individual voting princes. Thus Maximilian of Bavaria and the duke of Neuburg both claimed the Upper Palatinate, the former as a return for his war costs, the latter because he was the closest Catholic relative to the outlawed Palatine family. The bloc-votes controlled by the main participants, far from being a source of strength, in fact meant that such disunity was paralysing. By the end of 1646 it was already impossible for the Corpus Catholicorum to compose common declarations for the Congress; and, early in 1648, the extremists abandoned Münster, in protest against the 'dove-like' attitude of their colleagues, in order to deliberate separately.

The Corpus Evangelicorum was, on the surface, no more united than the Catholics. To begin with, the party lacked a leader comparable in stature with Maximilian of Bavaria: neither the young Elector Palatine (Charles Louis, son of Frederick V) nor the old Elector of Saxony (still John George) would do; and Frederick William of Brandenburg, by far the most impressive figure among the Protestants, had already made his peace. Perhaps the most active party member was one of the few women at the Congress, Amalia of Hesse-Kassel, widow of William V and regent for their young son. She and a group of lesser princes, including the dukes of Saxe-Weimar and the Calvinist princes of the Rhineland, desired safeguards for Protestantism in predominantly Catholic areas and demanded the total revocation of the Edict of Restitution. Against them were ranged the larger Lutheran states, which desired peace at almost any price. Furthermore, as with the Catholics, there were also disputes among members about territories – the eternal argument between the landgraves of Hesse over Marburg; between Brandenburg and Brunswick over who should have Halberstadt; between Brandenburg and Sweden over who should have Pomerania. But in the end, the Corpus Evangelicorum possessed both the coherence and the will to put aside these 'vanities' (as they were called in an important resolution of March 1646) and vote as a single block whenever issues of confessional importance arose.[5] The Protestants thus managed to hold their own until the fragmentation of the Corpus Catholicorum delivered them the victory. A final agreement on all religious issues – highly favourable to the Protestants – was concluded by the Congress on 24 March 1648. The 'normative date' for all religious matters was now 1 January 1624. Toleration for the private worship of religious minorities was to be allowed wherever this had existed on the 'normative date'; church lands which were in secular hands on the 'normative date' were to remain under Protestant control. Thus the *cuius regio* principle and the *declaratio Ferdinandei* of 1555 were finally abandoned, and the *reservatum ecclesiasticum* was reapplied only to property under Catholic control at the beginning of 1624. Furthermore, any change in these arrangements was to be decided by 'friendly composition' in the Diet between Catholics and Protestants, rather than by simple majority vote.[6]

With the 'items concerning public peace and the liberties of the empire' thus settled first, as the French and Swedish governments had desired (page 180 above), the Congress now had to deal with the demands of the foreign powers. To some extent, these varied according to the fortunes of war, which confused some observers. As the dour Glasgow Presbyterian, Robert Baillie, remarked in 1638: 'For the Swedds, I see not what their eirand is now in Germany, bot to shed Protestant blood.'[7] Yet in fact their targets remained remarkably consistent: they still strove to achieve 'satisfaction' (in the shape of some north German lands); 'security' (in the form of a guarantee that no power in the Empire would ever again pose a threat to Sweden's interests); and an indemnity. The only difference was the scale of these demands. Instead of just Pomerania, the Swedish government now required in addition parts of Mecklenburg and the secularized bishoprics of Bremen and Verden. Instead of the Heilbronn League, the Swedes aimed at 'atomizing' the Empire in order to create a permanent balance of power between the various creeds and princes. Instead of a modest cash indemnity which might be exchanged for Pomerania, the Swedish troops' envoy, Colonel Erskine, in the summer of 1647 put forward a claim for 30 million thalers.

Naturally there was heated opposition at the Peace Congress to all of these demands, even though Sweden backed them up by overwhelming military strength. The question of Pomerania was particularly vexed. The Stockholm government felt it was imperative to keep its Baltic acquisitions and especially Stralsund and Wismar because, as a royal counsellor pointed out in January 1647: 'These two seaports are not only the gateway to Germany, but also the very places where royal fleets may be prepared, and therefore the places whence danger for the crown of Sweden may come.'[8] But Sweden had no legal title to Pomerania: Frederick William of Brandenburg was without question the legitimate successor to the last native duke, who died in 1637 (page 136 above). When in 1643, during Sweden's war with Denmark, the Elector refrained from rendering any assistance to Christian IV, he did so in the hope of gaining Swedish goodwill and concessions. The following year he was rewarded by Swedish evacuation of Frankfurt-on-Oder, but there was no withdrawal from Pomerania. So Frederick William began a diplomatic campaign to persuade the courts of Europe that Pomerania must be restored. In 1646 he moved to Cleves in order to be nearer the peace talks, and it was his sustained diplomacy in and around the conference, more than anything else, that raised Brandenburg from its natural obscurity to the status of a major power. Above all, he enlisted the support of Cardinal Mazarin, who feared that Sweden might become as dominant in north Germany as the emperor had been in 1627–9. France therefore embarked on a policy, which she was long to follow, of building up the power of Brandenburg as a counterweight to Sweden.[9] At last, in February 1647, alarmed by the degree of foreign support for Brandenburg, Sweden resolved to partition Pomerania, keeping only the western part, with its strategic ports, and ceding the east to Frederick William (whose rights over the secularized bishoprics of Halberstadt and Magdeburg and over the duchies of Mark and Cleves were, in addition, confirmed). A settlement with Denmark, which transferred Bremen and Verden to Sweden, was concluded shortly afterwards.

With 'satisfaction' thus achieved on such a heroic scale, 'security' was somewhat less important. It was also more elusive. The Imperial negotiators, led by Count Trauttmannsdorf in 1645–7 and by Dr Isaac Volmar thereafter, proved adept at playing off

France against Sweden, and at mobilizing a residual German patriotism against both. Thus, although Sweden pressed for toleration to be granted to Protestants living in the Habsburg provinces, the Imperial plenipotentiaries allied with France to prevent it. And they also conspired to stop either France or Sweden from gaining a preponderant voice in the Empire. As Count Salvius reported in exasperation to his principals from the Congress late in 1646: 'People are beginning to see the power of Sweden as dangerous to the "balance of power" [*Gleichgewicht*]. Their first rule of politics is that the security of all depends on the equilibrium of the individuals. When one begins to become powerful . . . the others place themselves, through unions or alliances, into the opposite balance in order to maintain the equipoise.' But the idea was scarcely new. As early as 1632 the Papal Curia had advised its diplomats abroad that 'the interest of the Roman church' was better served by a balance of power than by the victory of any individual state. And this was a principle that Sweden herself had invoked in former days often enough: in 1633 Chancellor Oxenstierna claimed to a foreign dignitary that the chief reason for Swedish intervention in Germany was 'to preserve the *aequilibrium* in all Europe'.[10] Now he was being forced to abide by his own rules. It was the beginning of a new order in Europe – of an international balance of power with its fulcrum in Germany – and eventually Sweden was compelled to respect it.

The territorial demands of France were more modest. Mazarin sought recognition of the conquests made in the Rhineland – a handful of bridgeheads on the east bank of the river; jurisdiction over most of Alsace – and the legalization of French control over the three Lorraine bishoprics acquired in 1552. There was considerable reluctance among the emperor's advisers to agree even to this, since Alsace was one of the oldest patrimonial provinces owned by the Habsburg family (a fact of which Ferdinand was constantly reminded by his plenipotentiary at Münster, Isaac Volmar, who had formerly been chancellor of Alsace). But in September 1646, in return for a cash payment of 1.2 million thalers, Alsace was abandoned and a preliminary peace was concluded between France and the emperor.

Yet the war continued for another two years after this agreement. Why? One reason was the policy of Maximilian of Bavaria. In 1646, the Swedish high command determined to concentrate its efforts against Bavaria rather than against Austria for the next campaign. Early in the year, the main army withdrew westwards and, in August, Krems and the other Swedish strongholds in Lower Austria were abandoned. But the Habsburgs found it impossible to counterattack. Although they managed to collect a field army of 40,000 men, which marched as far as Hesse-Kassel, they were no match for the enemy's 'Hauptarmee' of 34,000 veterans under the joint command of Turenne and Karl Gustav Wrangel. Although there was no pitched battle, the Habsburg army was driven back towards Bohemia, leaving Bavaria and the Rhineland to be systematically plundered over the winter of 1646–7. It was scarcely surprising that on 14 March 1647 the desperate Electors of Bavaria and Cologne, with some of their allies, signed a cease-fire at Ulm with the representatives of France, Sweden and Hesse-Kassel. Mainz followed suit in May. It was agreed that the anti-Imperialists would be allowed to occupy three strategic towns in Maximilian's duchy, and that the Catholic Electors would no longer fight on the Imperial side but instead discuss terms for a separate peace. Meanwhile, Wrangel led his forces back into Austria, this time invading the Vorarlberg, taking Bregenz and plundering the surrounding area.

At this point, many observers (like the peasants quoted at the beginning of this section) believed that the war was over. And so it might have been, but for Mazarin's decision to increase his demands. His negotiators at Münster now sought for Louis XIV the status of a prince of the Empire (with a seat in the Diet), a war indemnity, and a solution to the Palatine question that was of no use to Bavaria. Maximilian concluded that 'the French crown does not wish to make a peace that will restore Liberty, but rather to oppress Germany with a new form of Imperialism', and in September 1647 he renewed his former alliance with the emperor. It was a rash move: since the loss of his best men at Allerheim (page 176 above), Maximilian's army was no match for the French. Imperial reinforcements (raised through the efforts of Ernest von Traun, Ferdinand III's able quartermaster-general) were rushed into Bavaria, but to no avail. On 17 May 1648 the last field army to fight for the emperor in the war was cut down at the battle of Zusmarshausen. Maximilian fled to Salzburg.[11] No doubt Mazarin intended to exploit this victory, too, in order to make further gains, but he was hampered by the outbreak of a serious rebellion in France the same month. At first the revolt (known as the Fronde) was confined to Paris, where the civil service went on strike; but the example of disobedience quickly spread to the provinces, depriving the government of all tax-revenue. By mid-August the cardinal was convinced of 'our need to make peace at the earliest opportunity', and he instructed his envoys in Münster to reach a settlement as soon as possible, since

'It is almost a miracle that, amid so many self-made obstacles, we can keep our own affairs going, and even make them prosper; but prudence dictates that we should not place all our trust in this miracle continuing for long.'[12]

Sweden, too, was now anxious for a settlement. By the summer of 1648 there was really only one major point left at issue – the size of the indemnity due to the Swedish army – and in June 1648, after prolonged haggling, the Swedish delegation agreed to accept as a final settlement 5 million thalers (1.8 million in cash, 1.2 million in assignations, and the remaining 2 million within two years). This opened the way to a 'preliminary peace' between Sweden and the emperor, similar to the 1646 agreement with France, and this was signed at Osnabrück on 6 August. The fighting, however, continued and once more the Swedes invaded Bohemia, laying siege to Prague. Lutherans in the area flocked to hear the army chaplains, and the Swedes made a final effort to secure toleration for their co-religionists in Bohemia. But, receiving no support from the French on this point, they failed: although the Protestants of Silesia received guarantees for their faith at the peace of Westphalia, Ferdinand III stood firm on the situation elsewhere. There was to be no restitution of confiscated estates and no toleration for non-Catholics.[13] But the emperor could not withstand French pressure on another issue: in spite of the Fronde, Mazarin was clearly determined to keep on fighting until the Austrian Habsburgs agreed to abandon Spain.

There was no doubt that Philip IV now stood in need of Imperial aid more than ever before. The revolts of Catalonia and Portugal still continued, thanks to French support; in 1647 a major rebellion broke out in the city of Naples which won the backing of an important segment of the aristocracy and the promise of French aid; shortly afterwards there were urban uprisings in Sicily and Andalusia, and the whole of Spain was afflicted by a virulent outbreak of plague. Some in the royal council favoured an immediate agreement with France, but they were outnumbered by those who preferred to settle with the Dutch instead. This party was led by Don Gaspar de Bracamonte, count of Peñaranda, who was Philip IV's chief plenipotentiary at Münster. As soon as the Dutch delegation arrived there, in January 1646, Peñaranda began to offer concessions. He at once indicated Spain's willingness to recognize Dutch sovereignty and independence. Then, in May, he agreed to the permanent closure of the river Scheldt to all traffic, except under Dutch licence; to the cession of extensive lands in North Brabant (the Meierij of 's Hertogenbosch); and to the imposition of Dutch tolls on the ports of Flanders. The only important outstanding point was overseas trade. The Dutch delegates, under pressure from the East and West India Companies, wished to secure total freedom to trade in any part of the Iberian world. This Spain would not concede, and negotiations flagged for a while. But in December 1646 Philip IV consented to recognize all Dutch conquests from the crown of Portugal, in return for an undertaking that the Republic's ships would keep away from Spanish America. A provisional agreement between the negotiators was signed in January 1647, which was ratified, despite Mazarin's efforts at sabotage, in January 1648. The 'Dutch Revolt' was over at last.[14]

Spain was now free to deploy the Army of Flanders solely against France, and some small gains were registered in the early months of 1648. But Mazarin profited from the defeat of Bavaria at Zusmarshausen to transfer to the northern front a large detachment of troops from south Germany. With their aid, on 20 August the French inflicted a crushing defeat at Lens on the Spanish army under the personal command of the emperor's brother, Leopold William, who lost his baggage along with 8,000 men and thirty field guns. It was a poignant moment for Ferdinand III. On the one hand he earnestly desired to send aid to his brother; on the other he had to consider the precarious situation of Bohemia. Already, on 26 July, the 'New Town' suburb of Prague, containing the Hradschin palace, had been captured by the Swedes. The emperor risked losing the entire kingdom unless he swiftly signed the peace. In late September, under relentless military pressure from his enemies and desperate diplomatic urging from his friends, Ferdinand crumbled: he could not afford to fight on simply for the sake of Spain.[15] The links between Spain and Austria, which had so destabilized European politics since the accession of Charles V, were fatally weakened. Since there was no further obstacle to peace, the final instruments to end the war – 128 clauses, including the issues resolved in the preliminary agreements – were signed at Münster on 24 October 1648.

Attention now shifted to implementing the numerous provisions of the treaty, beginning with ecclesiastical matters. In Württemberg, where thirty convents were recatholicized in 1630 following the edict of Restitution, and again after Nördlingen, the Protestants were allowed back over the winter of 1648–9. In April 1649, the Imperial cities which had been ordered to admit parity of religions complied with the treaty: even Augsburg, whose representative (Leuchselring) had been a leading Catholic extremist at Münster, was forced to admit fourteen pastors who swiftly restored a full Protestant church order alongside the

Catholic one.[16] Simultaneously, those whose lands had been forfeited for alliance with Sweden or France (but not for rebellion) were restored. The general amnesty was proclaimed and the Elector Palatine resumed his seat in the Electoral College. Before long the diplomats were packing their bags, exchanging farewell presents (reliquaries proved a favourite gift among the Catholic plenipotentiaries), and writing their last letters. The total cost of their five years of activity was some 3.2 million thalers: about 500,000 each for France and Spain, around 250,000 each for the emperor, Sweden, and the Dutch, an average of 60,000 for each Elector, and so on. These sums were substantial, and were in part paid by the various sovereign territories of the Empire. But it was as nothing, in most cases, compared to the cost of demobilization.[17]

Many of the delegates at Westphalia soon reassembled at Nuremberg, where a new conference opened to supervise paying off the various armies which had fought in the war. The smaller formations were dealt with first. Late in 1648, for example, three months' severance pay was given to the troops raised by Catholic princes (the so-called *Mediatarmee* units, such as the Westphalian army maintained by Elector Ferdinand of Cologne), while the members of the Bavarian Circle became responsible for paying the arrears of the Bavarian army (the archbishopric of Salzburg, for example, was required to pay 240,000 thalers).[18] Next, in January 1649, all Imperialist garrisons were withdrawn from Bavaria. But greater difficulties arose with the main field armies. In August 1649, when the 500 Imperialist troops in Lindau were ordered to march out, a mutiny resulted which lasted two months. The French army, too, was restless. The outbreak of the Fronde interrupted the flow of funds to the troops in Alsace, and even the experienced Erlach could not prevent his men from running amok.

Only the Swedes, occupying the larger part of Germany and in receipt of the first instalment of their 5 million thaler indemnity, seemed relatively unaffected by the delays in demobilization. But their forces still earned pay – almost 1 million thalers a month – and therefore built up further arrears as they waited in their garrisons. In the autumn of 1649 the Swedish commanders threatened to reopen hostilities unless a proper schedule of withdrawal was agreed. But on 26 June 1650, amid firework displays and general rejoicing, the Swedish delegates (led by Prince Charles Gustav) and the Imperialists (led by the indefatigable Ernest von Traun, one of the unsung heroes of the war) signed an agreement for the phased withdrawal, on prearranged days, of all troops from those areas of Germany not ceded to France, Sweden or the emperor (see Plates 20 and 21).

The operation proved protracted. The congress at Nuremberg remained in session until July 1651; a Spanish garrison remained in Frankenthal in the Palatinate until 1653 (when the Emperor offered Philip IV the Imperial city of Besançon in exchange); and the last Swedish troops were not withdrawn to the Baltic until 1654. Nor was the demobilization accomplished without some infringement of the peace of Westphalia, especially by the emperor. Although his troops were withdrawn promptly from Alsace (ceded to France), Upper and Lower Lusatia (given to Saxony) and two Silesian duchies (granted to the Polish crown as security for debts owed by Ferdinand III), some regiments were sent, in clear contravention of clauses III and IV of the Westphalian agreement, to fight for Spain in the South Netherlands and in northern Italy. However, the larger part of the Imperial host, some 25,000 men, was retained in Ferdinand's service. Some entered garrisons in the patrimonial provinces, but the majority went to the Hungarian frontier, which had been dangerously neglected during the last years of the war. The veterans formed, the government observed, 'the core of a good standing army', commanded by experienced generals like Ottavio Piccolomini (who had fought in the war since 1618) and Raimondo Montecuccoli (a field commander since Lützen), and they later proved themselves a match for the French, the Poles, the Turks and any other enemy of their master. The regiments retained in 1648, some of them already with a collective history dating back thirty years, continued to fight for the Habsburgs until the final collapse of the Austro-Hungarian army in 1918.[19] Like Grimmelshausen's 'Mother Courage', many of those who had fought in the war knew no other life and had no wish to leave the ranks: for them, the agreements at Westphalia and Nuremberg were only the transition from one chapter to another, not the end of the tale. But for the rest of mankind, they marked the end of the war. As the poet Johann Vogel of Nuremberg wrote:

> Something you never believed in
> Has come to pass. What?
> Will the camel pass through the Needle's Eye
> Now that peace has returned to Germany?[20]

CHAPTER VI

The war in myth, legend and history

The fifteenth-century Scots poet Gavin Douglas concluded his translation of the *Aeneid*, with an audible sigh of relief, 'Here is endit the lang desparit work.' But history, unlike literature, unfortunately has no obvious conclusion. The significance of the Thirty Years' War has been a bone of contention for both historians and politicians ever since it came to an end, and the debate has been hottest around three topics: one military, one economic, the other political. On the first, there have been, inevitably, the traditional military histories, written from nationalistic points of view, which extol the heroic leaders and indefatigable troops of each army; but, against this, several writers (beginning with eye-witnesses such as Grimmelshausen and Moscherosch) have portrayed the soldiers who fought the war as the most brutal and unprincipled warriors ever seen in Europe, led by officers who were as ineffectual as they were corrupt. The social and economic impact of the war has likewise been evaluated in radically different fashions. Some have argued that the war crippled a booming economy and caused unequalled devastation; others claim that the thirty years of conflict had virtually no adverse economic consequences. Finally, assessments of the political aims and achievements of the statesmen involved in the war show little uniformity. Most non-German analysts confer almost divine powers of foresight and prudence upon such political leaders as Oxenstierna and Richelieu, but dismiss their German allies as incompetent, unprincipled and selfish. German scholars have usually reversed the image. After three hundred years of discussion it is still, regrettably, not possible to offer an open-and-shut verdict on any of these three central issues. However historians now have to hand a great deal more evidence than ever before: a new look at each controversy is therefore justified.

190

i *The universal soldier*

When the peace of Westphalia was signed, the opponents of Ferdinand III – France, Hesse-Kassel and above all Sweden – were maintaining perhaps 140,000 men in the Empire. The Imperialists and their few remaining allies were considerably weaker, although still a force to be reckoned with: perhaps 70,000 men in all. Today, such concentrations of men under arms in Europe would be insignificant; in the seventeenth century, they were unprecedented.

Who were these men who made their living by killing others? Alas, the evidence is exiguous, unsystematic and insufficiently studied to permit broad generalizations.[1] To begin with, we do not know what soldiers looked like, for even the dress worn by the troops who fought the Thirty Years' War is a matter for debate. It would seem, to judge from the art of the period and from the military costumes preserved in various museums, that (at least in the earlier phases of the war) soldiers were often permitted to wear what they wished.[2] But there were efforts in some quarters to standardize dress, and create 'uniforms'. Thus when the duke of Neuburg created a militia in 1605, all men were to be equipped in 'similar military livery'. The city of Nuremberg's guards, raised in 1619, were all to be dressed alike; and the duke of Brunswick-Wolfenbüttel's two new regiments of the same year were all to be clothed in blue. A little later, both Mansfeld and Gustavus Adolphus commanded regiments that were known by colours ('the red' or 'the blue'), but this seems to have referred only to the regimental standards under which they fought. The military colours of the Thirty Years' War, most of them six feet square (with a swallowtail or pointed end for cavalry), excited all the more devotion for being the only common collective symbol possessed by a company or a regiment. Indeed, most contemporary accounts seem to have assessed victory or defeat according to the number of colours won or lost: certainly, in many actions, colours won or lost were the only tangible measure of success or failure.[3]

In his 'Handbook of War', published in 1651, Hans Conrad Lavater of Zürich advised would-be soldiers to wear *sensible* clothes: strong shoes, breeches and stockings, two thick shirts (if not more: Gustavus Adolphus was wearing three at Lützen), a buff coat of leather shielded from the rain by a cloak, and a wide felt hat. The garments should be generously cut, Lavater advised, for added warmth, yet should have no fur and few seams (to deny breeding-grounds to vermin). But, by the time he wrote, the scope for individualism was fast receding. In 1647 the French secretary of state for war, Michel le Tellier, ordered clothes to be made for the army in one of three fittings – half 'normal', a quarter 'large' and a quarter 'small' – but said nothing about the quality or the colour.[4] The Imperial army, however, had already begun to favour the pearl-grey uniforms that were universally adopted in the eighteenth century. Thus, in 1645, when Count Gallas placed an order with Austrian clothiers to supply 600 uniforms for his regiment, he enclosed a sample of the precise material and the colour (pale grey) to be copied. He also sent samples of the powder-horns and cartridge-belts to be manufactured *en masse* by local suppliers.[5] That such artefacts could indeed be mass-produced may be seen from the collection of seventeenth-century arms and armour in the Arsenal at Graz: thousands of weapons and their accoutrements, all standardized to a high degree though made in various workshops, lie ready for immediate use. Eight thousand men could be equipped within a single day. In Sweden, a factory was established at Vira to produce sword-blades for the entire Swedish army according to a single approved design.

But further standardization was beyond the power of most European states at this time. In the first place, not all the troops in an army belonged to the same warlord. Among the Imperialists during the 1640s were Saxon, Bavarian, Westphalian and Spanish units, as well as Austrian regiments. Secondly, even a single formation would include men raised at a wide variety of times and places. In 1644, a Bavarian regiment for which detailed records have survived could boast men from no less than sixteen national groups, of which the largest were Germans (534 soldiers) and Italians (217), with smaller numbers of Poles, Slovenes, Croats, Hungarians, Greeks, Dalmatians, Lorrainers, Burgundians, French, Czechs, Spaniards, Scots and Irish. There were even fourteen Turks.[6] Even if all these men had been issued with the same uniform upon joining the regiment, clothes would soon wear out and require replacement by items either plundered from the civilian population, stripped from the dead, or purchased during rare moments of leisured affluence. Lacking a uniform, troops on the same side were therefore obliged to adopt distinguishing marks. The soldiers of Gustavus Adolphus normally wore a yellow-edged blue band around their hats, and when they joined forces with the Saxons, who had different distinguishing marks, just before the battle of Breitenfeld in 1631, both armies placed a green token (often a leafy branch or a fern plucked from a forest on their line of march) in their hats. Similarly, the soldiers of the Habsburgs – both Spanish and Austrian – could be recognized everywhere by their red tokens (usually a plume or a sash). In May 1632, Wallenstein ordered that they were to wear tokens of no other colour. So although clothing of one particular hue may have predominated for a period, in a given regimental wardrobe, before long the men would become either thread-bare and dust-covered veterans or else the harlequin figures, promiscuously arrayed in rainbow attire, portrayed by the military artists of the period.

One might wonder why any man would freely join such a force; and, indeed, many soldiers were in the ranks against their will. The troops from Sweden and Finland, for example, were recruited by a form of conscription known as the *indelningsverk*, which obliged a specified community to provide a certain number of soldiers. Most of them were peasants: in the voluminous (but as yet little analysed) records of the Swedish and Finnish forces serving Gustavus Adolphus and his daughter, *bönde* (peasant farmer) is by far the commonest entry in the enrolment lists. They came from villages like Bygdeå in northern Sweden, which provided 230 young men for service in Poland and Germany between 1621 and 1639, and saw 215 of them die there, while a further five returned home crippled. Enlistment was thus virtually a sentence of death and its demographic impact was profound. The number of adult males in Bygdeå parish steadily decreased – from 468 in 1621 to 288 in 1639 – and the age of the conscripts gradually fell as more and more teenagers were taken, never to return. The social impact was also high: at first, the 'idle poor' tended to furnish most of the recruits, but after a while it became the turn of the younger sons of more prosperous families, and finally the only sons of even rich peasants were called away to die in Germany. In some smaller settlements, by the end of the 1630s, every available adult male was either on the conscription lists, already in the ranks, or too crippled to serve. Total losses in the Swedish army between 1621 and 1632 have been estimated at 50,000 to 55,000; those between 1633 and the war's end were probably twice as high. Clearly the war was causing depopulation in Sweden and Finland on an unprecedented and – ultimately – unbearable scale.[7]

Several other countries, while reluctant to introduce conscription, resorted to sentencing felons to military service, or to commuting terms of imprisonment in return for enlistment, since there were seldom enough volunteers. The armies of Spain were regularly augmented by released prisoners. Likewise, of the 25,000 or so Scots who fought for the Protestant cause in Germany during the war, a good number were 'masterless men' (i.e. unemployed); others were local troublemakers whom the magistrates allowed to be kidnapped; and not a few were outlaws – in 1629 Colonel Sir James Spens received forty-seven convicted felons (including one woman) from the prisons of London.[8]

Nevertheless, the majority of the men who fought in the Thirty Years' War – even on the Swedish side – were volunteers. In normal times, a disproportionate number of them came from three broad areas: the mountains, the towns, and the war zone itself. The sub-Alpine lands of Germany, Austria and the Swiss cantons had always been rich recruiting areas, and this seems to have remained true throughout the seventeenth century. The primacy of the other two areas – towns and the war zone – is reflected in a pioneering study of some 1,500 veterans recruited into the French army before 1648 who survived to enter the Invalides in Paris in the 1670s and '80s: of those born in France, about half came from the towns (which contained only perhaps 15 per cent of the French population), the other half mainly from villages in the north and north-east, near to the main war theatres. The average age of these men at enlistment was twenty-four and almost a quarter joined up before the age of twenty.[9]

Why did they choose to fight? First among the motives of many volunteers came hardship of one sort or another. Recruiting was always easier in years of high prices, or of political and religious disturbance. Thus in April 1633 Wallenstein was joined by many Protestant recruits from Austria, driven to enlist by the campaign of recatholicization waged by the Emperor Ferdinand.[10] Even when economic recession or religious persecution did not directly threaten, an enlistment bounty paid in cash and a new suit of clothes, plus the promise of pay and plunder to follow, could seem an attractive alternative to a civilian existence in which work and wages were often hard to come by and the risk of being plundered or bankrupted by taxes was high. Although the soldiers' pay was low, it was often *safer* to be inside an army in wartime Germany!

But we must not make the soldiers of the Thirty Years' War into craven economic determinists. Many men explained their reasons for enlisting in some detail, and they seldom mentioned hardship. Instead they stressed the excitement and danger of military endeavour, the chance of winning glory, and the thrill of belonging to an exclusive 'in-group' (which even created a vocabulary of its own).[11] Sir James Turner, a Scot who fought for Denmark and Sweden, wrote that 'a restlesse desire entered my mind to be, if not an actor, at least a spectator of these wars'. Other volunteers, who might be impervious to curiosity, could still be moved by ties of friendship or kinship with their officers: many of the Scots troops brought by James, marquis of Hamilton, to serve Gustavus Adolphus in 1631 bore the same name as their colonel; several members of the Leslie family from Aberdeenshire fought together; and so on. Other men might be induced by their status as tenants-at-will to enlist when their landlord summoned. A fuller range of motives was given by another Scotsman in Swedish service, Robert Monro, who wrote the first regimental history in the English language: he admitted to a desire for travel and adventure, and for military experience under an illustrious leader, but placed above these motives the desire to defend the Protestant faith and the claims and the honour of Elizabeth Stuart, his king's sister and the widow of the 'Winter King' of Bohemia. At more than one point in *Monro his expedition with the worthy Scots regiment called Mackays*, the author stated his belief that the 'cause of Bohemia' was his main reason for fighting, and that high religious motivation explained why so 'few of our Nation are induced to serve these Catholic Potentates'.[12]

This admirable boast of fidelity was a slight exaggeration, however. There were in fact several Scots (and English) who fought in Catholic armies, especially for the French; there were also some, like Captain Sidnam Poyntz (another officer who left an interesting account of his service), who changed sides more than once. Even Sir James Turner later confessed that he 'had swallowed, without chewing, in Germanie, a very dangerous maxime, which military men there too much follow, which was, that soe we serve our master honestlie, it is no matter what master we serve'.[13] This behaviour was particularly common among Lutheran troops, because their political leaders, such as John George of Saxony, stressed (for most of the war) the need for loyalty to the Catholic emperor. Commanders were left to make their own choice between competing religious and political loyalties. General Hans Georg von Arnim, who changed sides more frequently than most during the war, did so for the sake of conscience and not for gain. The number who fought indifferently for any master was probably no larger than in other wars.

The firm allegiance of senior officers like Turner, Monro and Arnim was of more than usual military importance during the Thirty Years' War because of the way in which their armies were organized. From the beginning, the financial weakness of the governments involved in the war was such that they could not afford to raise any troops at all from their current resources. A class of 'military enterprisers' therefore came into existence, advancing cash to recruiting officers on behalf of the government. About 100 individuals operated at any one time during most of the war, increasing to perhaps 300 in the years of maximum hostilities, 1631–4. In the course of the entire conflict, some 1,500 enterprisers are known to have acted in this way, funding the mobilization of a regiment or more for one of the warlords. There were also several successful attempts to raise entire armies in this way, with a 'general contractor' undertaking to recruit a corps of many regiments for an impoverished prince. Although Wallenstein, who raised a whole Imperial army on two occasions (in 1625 and 1631–2), is the most famous example of this extreme form of military devolution, there were others: Count Mansfeld in the service of Frederick V, the marquis of Hamilton in that of Sweden, Duke Bernard of Saxe-Weimar in that of France.

This system of raising armies created several conflicts of allegiance for both junior officers and the rank and file, since the enterprisers rather than the warlords were now the principal source of pay and profit. The choice between following a general (or a colonel) who fed and paid them, and a sovereign who did neither, was not easy. On the whole it is surprising that clear treason was so rare, and that no military enterpriser is known to have raised a force without a valid commission and then offered it for hire (as had often occurred during the Hundred Years' War). But some sailed very close to the wind. The army raised for France in 1635 by Bernard of Saxe-Weimar almost changed sides early in 1639, and even after the death of its creator later that year, the 'Bernardines' or 'German Brigade' (as the regiments were known) continued until the final peace to fight as a semi-autonomous unit within the French army, under the command of its senior officer, the Swiss-born Hans Ludwig von Erlach.

The behaviour of Wallenstein during his first generalship, issuing recruiting patents in his own name, was not of the same order. His reason was purely financial: because the Imperial treasury could not pay wages or purchase equipment, the commander-in-chief was obliged to find men who could, and commission them to do so. The colonels and generals thus provided credit to the government: Wallenstein himself advanced over 6 million thalers to the emperor between 1621 and 1628, and his colonels lent smaller sums to the junior officers of the regiments they had raised. This required considerable financial resources, and it is not surprising to find that several military entrepreneurs were rich: Bernard of Saxe-Weimar, whose inheritance as a younger son was tiny, in 1637 estimated his personal fortune at 450,000 thalers (roughly one-third of it in cash, one-third in letters of exchange and one-third in a Paris bank); the Imperialist commander Henrik Holck, once a poor man, returned to his native Denmark in 1627 rich enough to pay 50,000 thalers in cash for an estate on Funen; the Swedish general Königsmarck, who had formerly served as both a page and a common soldier, died in 1663 with assets worth almost 2 million thalers (183,000 in cash, 1.14 million in letters of credit, 406,000 in lands).[14]

But naturally the credit of even these individuals was not inexhaustible: they could not continue to pay their men indefinitely. Indeed, they could not afford to pay their men very much at all – even Wallenstein's soldiers agreed to serve for wages that were scarcely higher than those of farm hands. The various army commanders therefore evolved a complicated scheme of money-raising, modelled on that perfected by the Dutch and Spanish armies fighting in the Netherlands. The first essential ingredient was a regular (albeit inadequate) input of cash from the state treasury. In a famous letter of January 1626, written at the beginning of his first generalship, Wallenstein informed the Imperial finance minister that he needed 'a couple of million thalers every year to keep this war going'. The money was required to maintain the credit of the military enterprisers, including the general, who had advanced vast sums to the men under their command; it was not paid directly to the troops. This system was bitterly satirized in a famous novel about the war: *The Adventures of Simplicissimus the German*. The author, Hans Jakob Christoph von Grimmelshausen, devoted to the subject an elaborate simile, which compared the army hierarchy on paydays to a flock of birds in a tree.[15] Those on the topmost branches, he claimed,

> were at their best and happiest when a commissary-bird flew overhead and shook a whole panful of gold over the tree . . . for they caught as much of that as they could and let little or nothing at all fall to the lowest branches, so that, of those who sat there, more died of hunger than of the enemy's attacks.

In fact Grimmelshausen's vision was somewhat distorted, because the birds on the lowest branches – the army's rank and file – actually received considerable sustenance by other means. Most important was the provision of free accommodation: for much of the time, soldiers lived in more or less comfortable lodgings, with a bed, service and perhaps food supplied by the householder. This was fortunate, because troops did not long survive in barracks or a military encampment, where they had to supply these items themselves. As Michel le Tellier, then an inspector of the French army in Italy, wrote in 1642: 'two months' pay and lodgings with the peasants in [France] is worth a lot more [to the troops] than three months' pay and a barracks in Turin'.[16] But, after a while, local resources always proved inadequate and had to be supplemented. This was the reason for introducing 'contributions': tax assessments levied directly from each community in the army's vicinity, paid either in cash or in goods needed by the troops (food, clothes, munitions, transport). The exact mechanics of the transfer of goods and services was worked out between the regimental and company clerks on the one hand and the local magistrates on the other. In areas frequently visited by troops, such as Franconia, there was an 'early warning system' among communities along an army's projected line of march, so that the necessary provisions for the troops could be made ready in advance.[17] When prior liaison between military and civilian administrators seemed unlikely to produce sufficient victuals, contractors from areas unaffected by the war might be persuaded to step in. Some generals purchased cattle in bulk from Switzerland, or cloth from England; Wallenstein organized the regular delivery of beer, bread, clothes and other necessaries from his own extensive estates in Bohemia to his army. As le Tellier was later to observe: 'to secure the livelihood of the soldier is to secure victory for the king'. By the end of the war, most military administrators reckoned to supply two-thirds of their troops' wages in kind.

The administrators also needed to arrange bulk supplies of the cumbrous weapons common to mid-seventeenth-century armies. Half the infantry required thirteen-foot pikes, helmets and body-armour; the rest needed five-foot matchlock muskets, with their forked rests, powder flasks, shot and slow match; and all troops, including the cavalry, needed pistols and swords.[18] Although these weapons did not have to be standardized (every soldier was expected to cast bullets from his own lump of lead), nonetheless the task of equipping a field army of 30,000 should not be underestimated. At the siege of Stralsund in 1628, some 760 cannonballs (some of them 50 kg mortar shots) were discharged against the Frankentor alone on the day of the first assault; at the siege of Kronach (in Franconia) in May and June 1632, 1,260 shots were fired against the walls.[19] Nor was the feeding of the multitude achieved with five loaves and two fishes. The daily allowance of 1 kg of bread, ½ kg of meat and 2 litres of beer (which was the notional ration due to every soldier, equerry and officer) required the baking of 30 quintals of bread, the slaughter of 225 bullocks (or the equivalent), and the brewing of 90,000 litres of beer, every day.[20] And then there were the horses: the artillery, the cavalry, the officers, and the baggage wagons all required them, raising the total to perhaps 20,000 beasts with a major field army, consuming some 90 quintals of fodder, or 400 acres of grazing, daily. And the horses themselves often required replacement. At the first battle of Breitenfeld some 4,000 of the 9,000 horses present were killed; at the battle of Lützen General Piccolomini alone had seven horses shot under him. Gustavus Adolphus's massive battle charger, 'Streiff', carried his master to his death at Lützen, and died of wounds shortly afterwards.[21] Organizing such concentrations of military equipment posed serious logistical problems.

Moreover, no early modern army consisted only of combatants and their horses. Many soldiers were accompanied by wives or mistresses; more still had servants or lackeys.[22] When the Spanish Army of Flanders returned to the Netherlands in 1622, after the conquest of the Palatinate, it marched straight to the siege of Bergen-op-Zoom, where three Calvinist pastors in the beleaguered town recorded virtuously that 'such a long tail on such a small body never was seen: . . . such a small army with so many carts, baggage horses, nags, sutlers, lackeys, women, children and a rabble which numbered far more than the army itself'. It may have been true, for although the archives of the Army of Flanders suggest that camp followers in the Low Countries' Wars rarely numbered more than 50 per cent of the total troops, in 1646 two Bavarian regiments consisted of 480 infantrymen accompanied by 74 servants, 314 women and children, 3 sutlers and 160 horses, and 481 cavalry troopers with 236 servants, 9 sutlers, 102 women and children and 912 horses.[23]

This inflation of numbers in fact elevated the problems of military logistics beyond the resources of European governments. It was still possible to maintain – by a combination of direct finance, credit, contractors and contributions – an adequate supply of provisions to either small or stationary bodies of men. Thus the 2,000 English and Scots soldiers who spent the winter of 1627–8 defending Christian IV's new stronghold of Glückstadt, actually received (and signed receipts for) 313,000 kg of bread, 33,500 kg of cheese and 36 barrels of butter, 8 barrels of mutton and 7 of beef, 8 barrels of herring and 9,000 kg of bacon, 37 barrels of salt and 1,674 barrels of beer (most of it a fairly weak concoction known as 'regimental brew'). This constituted a not unreasonable diet.[24] But normal provisioning arrangements often broke down in action, or on the march. With so much to move, it was imperative for armies to keep within easy reach of navigable rivers: only boats and barges could supply war in the seventeenth century. No locality could provide sufficient carts and horses (even though a large four-wheeled wagon could carry up to seven tons of goods). So when the troops moved away from the German river-system, serious difficulties arose. On the night before the first battle of Breitenfeld, for example, the Swedish army slept in the fields in battle order; therefter they fought for seven or eight hours, towards the end in the midst of a dust-storm; yet even after the victory they got neither food nor drink until they reached the abandoned camp of the Imperialists, at Leipzig, the next day.

At other times, the troops moved faster than their supply trains, sometimes covering twenty-five miles in a day – and on one occasion in 1631, to make a surprise attack on Ochsenfurt (north of Würzburg), they marched twenty miles in seven hours at night. It was on occasions such as these, when the troops outstripped their supply train, that plunder, pillage and looting became a major problem. Naturally there was always the temptation of the strong to exploit the weak. There was a saying during the war that 'Every soldier needs three peasants: one to give up his lodgings, one to provide his wife, and one to take his place in Hell.' Looting was normally led by the musketeers in a regiment, who were both more mobile and lower-paid than the pikemen, and sometimes they caused major disorders. Thus, when the Swedish army entered Bavaria in the summer of 1632, according to Colonel Monro:

> The Boores [i.e. peasants] on the march cruelly used our souldiers (*that went aside to plunder*) in cutting off their noses and eares, hands and feete, pulling out their eyes, with sundry other cruelties which they used; being justly repayed by the souldiers, in burning of many Dorpes [i.e. villages] on the march, leaving also the boores dead, where they were found.[25]

But on most occasions, soldiers of Gustavus who oppressed civilians were severely punished – by whipping, extra sentry duty, or public humiliation. At least five men in Monro's regiment were executed by firing squad, and several others were condemned to death by the military provost for the maltreatment of the civilian population: the army could not afford to alienate those who supplied labour, guides, and intelligence of the enemy, as well as food and quarters.

Normally, the only other reasons for military execution were cowardice, mutiny and desertion. Seventeen officers and men were decapitated in 1632, at Wallenstein's command, for alleged cowardice during the battle of Lützen (their sentence being carried out in the same square in Prague where the Bohemian rebel leaders had met their end eleven years before – a coincidence which increased the soldiers' disgrace). Commanders who surrendered places entrusted to them before their superiors considered it was necessary might also be executed, *pour encourager les autres*; so might deserters (as happened to several men from the Cardinal-Infante's army in 1634, who were caught returning to Lombardy before they could become involved in the wars of Germany).[26]

Mutinies were far less common, although the German soldiers had a tradition, when they were either unpaid or mistreated, of electing leaders to negotiate with their warlords, and withholding their services until grievances were redressed. In 1633, the Swedish army – which had marched (according to Monro's exact count) 3,000 miles since their landing at Peencmünde three years before – refused to carry out any duties until their arrears had been paid. In 1635 they repeated the exercise, kidnapping chancellor Oxenstierna for some weeks to improve their bargaining position. In 1638, the French army refused to cross the Rhine into Germany until it received some wages. But these were exceptional moments. The more usual reaction of the troops to low pay or poor conditions was to desert.

The military records of most armies do not, unfortunately, note desertion rates.[27] However, the comparison of the overall wastage rates of French regiments fighting at home, a German regiment (Wallenstein's life guards: the Upper Austrian troops of Count Julius of Hardegg) and those of selected foreign units, reveals a somewhat higher loss among the locally raised troops (see Table 6). This difference is almost certainly explained by desertion, since the losses of foreign soldiers from injuries and death incurred on active service tended to be very high. Thus Mackay's Scots regiment, which defended a crucial section of the walls of Stralsund during the siege of 1628, was on duty under fire for six weeks continuously. Their food was brought to them at their battle stations, and 'we were not suffered to come off our posts for our ordinary recreation, nor yet to sleepe'. Even the colonel's 'cloathes never came off, except it had been to change a suit or linings'. Thanks to this prolonged exposure to danger, of 900 men in the regiment, 500 were killed and 300 more (including Monro) were wounded. Yet the Scots considered themselves lucky, for had Stralsund been taken by assault, they would all

TABLE 6 *Wastage rates in selected regiments* [28]

Date	4 English regiments no.	4 English regiments monthly loss %	Hamilton & Meldrum	Hepburn	Spens	Mackay	total	monthly loss %	3 Swedish regiments no.	3 Swedish regiments monthly loss %	Hardegg's German regiment of guards no.	Hardegg's German regiment of guards monthly loss %	10 French infantry regiments no.	10 French infantry regiments monthly loss %
1627 June	4,913	} 6				2,000		} 13						
Oct.	3,764					900								
1628 Apr.	1,882	} 8												
May	1,630	} 13												
1629 Aug.			2,219											
1630 Jan.						1,000		} 7						
June			600			638	1,900							
1631 Mar.				1,402	830									
May				837	608			} 2						
Sept.				829										
1632 Mar.				1,248		518			2,577	} 9	c.1,400	} 6		
Oct.					416				1,212		866			
Dec.				936	350	300	1,300	} 3	828	} 4				
1634 Feb.											1,156	} 11		
June											654			
Oct.							200							
1635 June											1,101	} 9	5,571	} 20
July											796		4,470	
Oct.											600	} 4		
1636 Jan.														
Aug.														

have been killed, like the garrisons of Magdeburg or Frankfurt-on-Oder in 1631, who were slaughtered in defeat where they stood. After the sack of Frankfurt, where the Imperialist defenders lost 3,000 men and the Swedish army 800, it took six days to bury all the dead and 'in th'end they were cast by heapes in great ditches, above a hundred in every grave'.[29]

Of course, there were many other causes of military losses unconnected with fighting. When Christian IV's headquarters were at Tangermünde on the Elbe, in 1625, 'the stink of the camp got up one's nose' (in the words of a chronicler) and, before long, disease had reduced the Danish forces substantially. The Imperialists quartered in Hesse-Darmstadt during the winter of 1634–5, after their victory at Nördlingen, were forced to sleep ten and twenty to a house; it was therefore not long before illnesses due to overcrowding took their toll.[30] In the Scots Brigade serving in Germany between 1626 and 1633, some 10 per cent of the regiments were sick at any one moment, with epidemics increasing the rate dramatically from time to time. For example, the Scots who garrisoned the lower Oder in 1631 lost 200 men a week from plague, and more still from camp fever (typhus) and the other illnesses common among early modern armies.

But always, for the foreign units at least, the greatest single cause of declining strength was death in action. Losses in battle usually seem to have been heavy, however long the engagement itself lasted, and the foreign troops were always in the front line. If the two sides were evenly matched – as at Lützen in 1632, at Rocroi in 1643, at Freiburg in 1644 or at Jankov in 1645 – the slaughter on the field was terrible. If, on the other hand, the odds were uneven, the defeat of the smaller force would be followed by hot pursuit and perhaps greater slaughter: many fugitive soldiers, and sometimes entire units, might be killed in cold blood either by their adversaries or by the local peasantry. And even if the defeated host managed to keep together, their retreat might turn into a débâcle. Gallas's withdrawal from Burgundy (1636) and Holstein (1642), Baner's from Torgau (1637) and Turenne's after Tuttlingen (1643), all noted above, were major catastrophes on account of the number of troops who died by the wayside.

Carnage was sometimes limited, however, by the practice of ransoming prisoners-of-war. After Jankov (1645) the entire Imperial general staff was offered for ransom by the victors at 120,000 thalers. After other, less catastrophic defeats, ransoms were agreed according to a published tariff: 25,000 thalers for a general, 100 for a colonel and so on down the scale. Sometimes prisoners were simply exchanged, as Torstensson (the Swedish general) was traded for Count Harrach (the Imperial treasurer). It was rare for a commander to be refused the chance of release, but it sometimes happened. Thus Gustav Horn, Oxenstierna's son-in-law, was kept in prison for eight years after his capture at Nördlingen in 1634 (although Maximilian of Bavaria did contemplate, at one point, bartering Horn against all the treasures plundered from Munich during the Swedish occupation; Stockholm, however, was not interested in the deal). But the common soldiers, especially those raised in Germany, were normally neither ransomed nor exchanged: either they were freed, after swearing not to bear arms against the victor for a certain period, or they were encouraged to join the army that had captured them – a development often facilitated in the later phases of the war by the presence in every army of at least a few men who had fought on all sides and might therefore know the captives, and ease their scruples on transferring from one allegiance to another. In 1631, even the Italians captured by Gustavus Adolphus in his Rhineland campaign were welcomed into the Swedish army (though they deserted as soon as they reached the foot-hills of the Alps the following summer).

Soldiers taken prisoner were nevertheless fortunate. Few commanders seem to have had much time for their wounded, except on special occasions – such as at the height of a Swedish attack on the Alte Veste in 1632, when Wallenstein went around his defenders throwing handfuls of coins into the laps of the wounded, to encourage the rest. There seldom seems to have been any provision of medical care for the sick, nor any military hospitals and pensions for the wounded, except in the Swedish and Spanish expeditionary forces; and even there the services provided were far below the level maintained by (for example) the Spanish army in the Netherlands, with its 330-bed military hospital at Mechelen and its home for army pensioners at Hall. The armies of the Thirty Years' War only equalled the Army of Flanders in their chaplaincy service. The troops of the League were normally attended by Jesuit field chaplains, and a full ecclesiastical hierarchy of Lutheran pastors was attached to the Swedish army which invaded in 1630. But, in terms of military administration, despite the semi-permanence of the fighting, the armies of the Thirty Years' War introduced remarkably few innovations. Even Wallenstein's famous contributions system was closely modelled on that of the Spanish army, imposed by Spínola in the Palatinate in 1620, but originally devised in the 1570s.[31]

The one area in which the war gave rise to major changes was tactics and strategy: not for nothing did Napoleon Bonaparte, confined in Egypt in 1798–9, ask his government to send him histories of the Thirty Years' War to read. The starting-point of the new warfare was the military reformation wrought by Maurice of Nassau upon the Dutch army during the 1590s. Inspired by the Roman tactics described by Aelian and Leo VI, Maurice devised new ways of deploying his troops in action. In place of the phalanxes of pikemen, forty and fifty deep, which had fought the battles of the sixteenth century, he drew up his men only ten deep. His formations were smaller, and they achieved their impact more by firepower than by pike charges. No less than half the soldiers in Maurice's army were musketeers. These changes sound simple, but they rendered profound adjustments necessary in military organization. In the first place, reducing the depth of the line inevitably meant extending it, thus exposing more men to the test of hand-to-hand combat; second because the line was thinner, more discipline and more coordination were required from each man. For example, in 1594 the Dutch army perfected the technique of the 'salvo', which involved each rank firing their muskets simultaneously at the enemy, and then retiring to reload while the other nine ranks followed suit, creating a continuous hail of fire. But to perform this manoeuvre in the face of the enemy required considerable fortitude, perfect coordination and great familiarity with all the actions involved. Therefore Maurice reintroduced the drill used in the Roman army. The journal of one of his political advisers, present at a siege during 1595, records the troops being trained almost constantly in exercises, forming and re-forming ranks, drilling and using their weapons. According to an English edition of Aelian's *Tactics* published in 1616:

> The practise of Aelian's precepts hath long lien wrapped up in darkness and buried (as it were) in the ruines of time, untill it was revived and restored to light not long since in the United Provinces of the Low-Countries, which Countries at this day are the schoole of war, whither the most martial spirits of Europe resort to lay downe the apprenticeship of their service in armes.[32]

This treatise was by no means the first to draw attention to the new methods of warfare developed in the Dutch Republic. Maurice's insistence on precision and harmony in war mirrored the general preoccupation of the age with geometrical forms – whether in building, riding, dancing, painting, fencing or fighting. As early as 1603 a French military work devoted an entire chapter to 'The exercises used in the Dutch army', and in 1607 the first pictorial drill manual of western Europe, composed by Maurice's cousin, John of Nassau, was published at The Hague as *The Exercise of Arms* under the name of Jacob de Gheyn, a well-known engraver. Many other works imitated de Gheyn's technique of a numbered sequence of pictures to illustrate the various manoeuvres required to handle military weapons and to organize troops for war. In 1616 Count John opened a military academy at his capital, Siegen, expressly to produce an officer corps for Calvinism. The first director of the *Schola Militaris*, Johann Jacob von Wallhausen, published several manuals of warfare, modelled on the Dutch example, which was the basis of all teaching at Siegen (where training took six months: arms and armour, maps and models for instruction were provided by the school). At the same time, other authors published a range of works explaining the advantages of Dutch-style fortifications, which (characteristically) combined maximum efficiency with minimal cost.[33]

The diffusion of the new warfare did not occur merely in print: Maurice was also asked to supply military instructors to foreign states. Brandenburg requested, and received, two in 1610; others went to the Palatinate, Baden, Württemberg, Hesse, Brunswick, Saxony and Holstein. Even the traditionally minded Swiss, who had first demonstrated the potential of the pike in their struggle against fifteenth-century Burgundy, were forced to take note. In 1628 the Berne militia was reorganized on unashamedly Dutch lines, with smaller companies and greater firepower, by Hans Ludwig von Erlach, the future commander of the 'Bernardines'. However, Maurice's most influential disciple was unquestionably Gustavus Adolphus of Sweden. John of Nassau himself went to Sweden in 1601–2 and gave some advice on how the Swedish army could be improved, but the main influx of Dutch expertise came two decades later. On a tour of Germany in 1620 Gustavus saw many different forms of military organization and fortification, and he read all the major books on the subject. He took Maurice's reforms slightly further, by reducing the depth of his line from ten to six ranks, and by increasing its firepower through the addition of four light field pieces per regiment (the unsuccessful prototypes, which became more famous than the real thing, were 3-pounders made out of light metal reinforced with wood and leather). Gustavus also introduced a new tactical unit, the brigade, made up of four squadrons (or two field regiments) in arrow-shape formation, the fourth squadron in reserve, supported by nine or more field guns. Every man was given rigorous training in his work by the numerous officers and NCOs. An effort was made to keep the troops busy all the time, digging ramparts, scouting, or in drill. The king even gave his troops personal instruction in the new discipline: he would himself show new recruits how to fire a musket standing up, kneeling, and lying down. Units recruited abroad were made to watch demonstrations of the 'Swedish order of discipline' by the veterans, and then had to practise until they were perfect.[34] This included the double salvo, with the musketeers standing but three deep, one rank on their knees, the second crouching, the third upright, in order to 'pour as much lead into your enemies bosom at one time [as possible] . . . and thereby you do them more mischief . . . for one long and continuated crack of thunder is more terrible and dreadful to mortals than ten interrupted and several ones (according to Sir James Turner, who saw the deadly salvo in operation).[35]

The most important difference between the Swedish and Dutch 'military revolutions' lay not in innovations but in application and in scale. Maurice of Nassau rarely fought a battle (and, when he did so, his field army numbered scarcely 10,000 men), because the terrain on which he operated was dominated by a network of fortified cities which made battles largely irrelevant – the towns still had to be besieged. But Gustavus operated in areas which had been spared from war, and even the threat of war, for seventy years and in some cases (such as Bavaria) for even longer. There were therefore far fewer well-defended towns – although, where they existed, they had to be besieged in the 'Dutch manner' – and control of many areas depended upon the ability to win battles. The most favourable publicity that the Dutch system could have found was Gustavus's victory at Breitenfeld. It was the classic confrontation between the traditional battle order, used since the Italian wars, and the new: Tilly's men, standing thirty deep and fifty wide, faced a Swedish army six deep for musketeers and five for pikes, with twice as many field guns. The superiority of firepower was overwhelming. The Swedish artillery could throw a 9 kg iron shot about 1,700 metres every six minutes; Gustavus's musketeers – who made up slightly more than half the total – could fire repeated salvoes of lead shot, each about 20 mm in diameter, with considerable accuracy up to 50 metres (and with about 50 per cent accuracy up to 75 metres). Sharp-shooters, who were armed with special 'long guns' resembling fowling pieces, were accurate at far greater distances (though still nowhere near the 400 metres of modern rifled guns). And these engines of death were manipulated by ever larger concentrations of men. During the decade 1625–35, when the war was at its height, the Empire was fought over by a quarter of a million troops – more than ever before; in the course of the thirty years of conflict, well over a million men must have served in the ranks. Among such unprecedented numbers, there is evidence to support every view on the true nature of the early modern soldier and on the impact of the war he fought.

ii The war and German society

On 11 August 1650, after the last Swedish soldiers had left, a celebration of peace and thanksgiving took place in the Imperial city of Rothenburg ob der Tauber. Accompanied by musicians, the schoolchildren of Rothenburg, many of them wearing wreaths and carrying bouquets, assembled in the city's broad marketplace. Nineteen years earlier their parents and grandparents had knelt in the same square, begging the dreaded General Tilly to spare their city from the fate of Magdeburg. And so he had. For two decades, however, Rothenburg had remained a focus of military activity; the boys and girls who gathered that morning in 1650 had hitherto known only war. But now peace had come, and the children marched solemnly from the marketplace to the great parish church, where they sang hymns of thanksgiving before the city's assembled adults and heard an earnest sermon by Pastor Johann Dümmler before disbanding.[1]

Similar scenes took place in cities and villages all over Germany. Rothenburg itself ruled over a region of 400 square kilometres in south-western Franconia, and sermons of thanksgiving were heard in village churches across the territory. But not everywhere: not, for example, in Linden.

Located in a wooded area north-east of the city, Linden was a small village: in 1618 it had had a total of nine taxable peasant households, plus four landless peasants. Like other subjects of Rothenburg, the inhabitants of Linden had suffered frequent financial exactions since the start of the war, especially after Imperial and Swedish armies began to vie for control of the region in the early 1630s. But the horrors of war really came home to the people of Linden only at the beginning of 1634, when the area lay under Swedish occupation. Late on a January afternoon, twenty

Swedish soldiers rode into the village, demanding food and wine, breaking down doors and searching for valuables. Two of them entered the cottage of Georg Rösch, raped his wife and chased her screaming through the village. But the villagers of Linden roused the neighbouring communities – and from all sides peasants rushed through the woods to Linden, where they seized the soldiers, stripped them of their booty and made off with some of their horses. The next day the soldiers headed to Rothenburg to lay complaints of theft against the villagers, and when the Rothenburg beadle arrived in Linden he arrested four peasants. But soon he acquired a more accurate view of the situation, especially since Rösch's wife was able to identify one of the rapists – a soldier from east Finland. The beadle rode from village to village retrieving the soldiers' horses, saddles and clothes; but the episode was also reported to the Swedish commander, General Horn, who severely reprimanded the responsible officers and reminded them that soldiers were not to molest the peasantry.[2]

By 1641 there were no peasants left to molest in Linden, for the village was uninhabited – and it remained so for the rest of the war. But Linden did not become a permanent ghost village. In the decades following the war, settlers returned, and by 1690 the village had eleven peasant holdings – bringing it, in short, back to its pre-war size.[3]

How typical was Linden? In 1641 Rothenburg officials conducted a house-to-house survey of the villages under their rule, and their report offered a depressing picture of conditions in the region. According to this calculation, the Rothenburg territory, comprising about 100 villages, had included 1,503 taxable peasant households in 1618; but by 1641 there were only 447 – a loss of 70 per cent. About twenty-five settlements – mostly small ones, like Linden – were completely uninhabited in 1641, and a few more were added to the list before the end of the war. But other communities fared better: Oberstetten, a substantial village of seventy-five households, had lost only five of them by 1641: far to the west of the main march route, it was little affected by the tumult of military activity. In 1700 Rothenburg officials counted a total of 1,558 taxable peasant households in their territory – a slight increase over the pre-war total.[4]

Seventeenth-century Germans were scrupulous record-keepers, and the Thirty Years' War did little to change their habits of meticulous documentation. Here and there crucial records were destroyed by negligence or acts of war, but enough documents have survived to provide vast amounts of data about local conditions in central Europe during the war. Stories like that of Linden could be reproduced from almost any part of Germany: everywhere the records describe frequent brutality by soldiers, sporadic resistance by peasants, cautious compliance by townspeople, and desperate efforts by civilian and military officials to maintain minimum standards of justice and prevent a total collapse of law and discipline. Information about the economic and demographic impact of the war also abounds in the tax records, parish registers and other series which German clerks and clerics maintained with such care. Historians can pinpoint hundreds of depopulated villages and reduced cities – along with hundreds of towns and villages which survived the war almost intact.

Despite the wealth of local data, however, it has proved almost impossible to agree on the overall impact of the Thirty Years' War on Germany and the surrounding lands. This is not for want of trying, however; for over a hundred years, historians have debated the economic, social and demographic effects of the war. The debates were first stimulated in the mid-nineteenth century by two literary works. One was Hans Jakob Christoph von Grimmelshausen's *Simplicissimus*. Though written in the 1660s, this early picaresque novel was largely forgotten until the nineteenth century, when its harrowing picture of life during the Thirty Years' War began to attract wide attention. The other influential work was Gustav Freytag's *Bilder aus der deutschen Vergangenheit* (Scenes from the German Past), whose third volume, originally published in 1859, combined carefully documented details with sweeping generalizations about the economic and moral devastation wrought by the war. The impact of these two works was reinforced by the writings of some careless historians whose statements added authority to what has been called the 'myth of the all-destructive fury of the Thirty Years' War'.[5]

Other scholars, however, have taken great pains to rebut this myth, using carefully conducted local research to show that the amount of death and destruction attributed to the war has often been exaggerated. All the evidence is local, or at best regional, since no pan-German censuses or economic surveys were conducted in the seventeenth century. But the gradual cumulation of local data has at least made it possible to advance more reliable suggestions about the impact of the war than were possible a hundred years ago.

This is particularly so with respect to the war's demographic effects. Earlier estimates that the war had destroyed half or two-thirds of the German population are no longer accepted.

More recent estimates are much more conservative, suggesting that the population of the Holy Roman Empire may have declined by about 15 to 20 per cent, from some 20 million before the war to about 16 or 17 million after it. Nor were the population losses necessarily permanent: the post-war decades saw a considerable growth of population, and some experts suggest that the losses were already made good by 1700.[6]

The patterns for different regions, moreover, were extremely varied. The German north-west, which saw little fighting after the first years, experienced almost no population loss, while the war zones of Mecklenburg, Pomerania and Württemberg lost over half of their inhabitants. The population loss was always greater in villages than in cities, whose walls normally protected them from wanton destruction – the sack of Magdeburg in 1631 was such a shock to contemporaries partly because it was an exception to this general rule. In many cases, moreover, what appeared to be a population loss was really a population transfer – while villages emptied, for example, nearby cities often bulged with refugees seeking protection. Thus in 1637, as famine and illness spread across the Saxon countryside, it was reported that over 4,200 persons had sought refuge in Leipzig – temporarily increasing the city's population by over one-third.[7]

There is no doubt, however, that central Europe did experience a generation of substantial demographic decline. The exact causes of the population loss cannot always be determined, but one thing is certain: deaths due to military action represented only a minor element in the total picture. War-related food shortages and outbreaks of epidemic disease were much greater killers. The most spectacular episodes of mortality were due to the bubonic plague, which broke out in many parts of central Europe during the war. The city of Nördlingen in northern Swabia vividly illustrates the lethal impact of the plague. Between 1619 and 1633 there occurred an average of 304 deaths a year among the city's inhabitants, but in the plague year of 1634 the death rate sextupled: a total of 1,549 inhabitants died, along with over 300 refugees then in the city.[8] Yet it would be inaccurate to say that all the plague deaths were due to the war. Many epidemic diseases were spread by the movement of infected soldiers or civilians, but the plague was not among them. For bubonic plague is actually a disease of rats, transmitted to human beings by fleas – and the cycle of infection among rats is influenced by ecological factors that have little to do with the events of human society; the old notion that infected rats and fleas travelled in army baggage is now discounted by demographers. In addition, plague epidemics were of relatively short duration in any one place, and were often followed by a year or two of rapid demographic recovery. In fact the long-term population losses associated with the war were generally due to less spectacular but more persistent diseases spread by human contact – typhus, influenza, dysentery and other illnesses which recurred, year after year, in communities whose inhabitants were already weakened by war-induced malnutrition and stress (see Plate 23).

To establish the demographic impact of the Thirty Years' War is hard enough; to determine the war's economic effects is even harder. There is in fact no shortage of local data, but the information is often difficult to interpret: to use local tithe revenues, toll receipts and tax records to establish national trends of output or overall levels of economic activity is, at best, a chancy business.

Nevertheless, when comparisons are made between, say, 1615 and 1650, almost every section of Germany shows a significant decline in economic activity. There were some exceptions, notably port cities like Hamburg and Bremen, which sustained a brisk maritime trade throughout the war. But most cities and territories experienced a substantial reduction in the output of agricultural products and manufactured goods and in the volume of trade. Furthermore, many once-prosperous families, institutions and governments fell deeply into debt between 1620 and 1650.

Growing indebtedness was a particularly serious problem for Germany's municipal governments. Before the war, many cities had enjoyed comfortable surpluses from taxation and from rural rents. After the war, however, many of the same cities found themselves deeply in debt. The reason is easy to trace. Time and again a city would spare itself from conquest and pillage by agreeing to render financial 'contributions' to the army stationed before its gates. But even grossly escalated taxes usually proved inadequate to cover these payments; and, as a result, the municipal government would have to borrow – from its own citizens, from regional noblemen, or from profiteering soldiers. When the war stopped, the demand for 'contributions' ended, but the cities were left with massive debts. The municipal debt of Nuremberg, for example, quadrupled from 1.8 million gulden in 1618 to 7.4 million at the end of the war.[9] To pay off such loans normally required decades – and meanwhile the cities were burdened, year after year, with massive interest payments to their various creditors.

Developments such as these were obviously caused by the

war. Yet, even so, evidence of economic decline must often be interpreted with caution. After the war, for example, many municipal and territorial governments compiled detailed statements of the sums they or their subjects had been obliged to pay out to soldiers, whether by force or negotiation. But these statements, despite their down-to-the-penny detail, sometimes give a misleading impression of a region's losses. For at least some of the money given to soldiers generally circulated back into the local economy in the form of payments for goods and services. The city of Schwäbisch Hall, for example, reported after the war that it and its citizens had lost a total of 3,644,656 gulden to soldiers during the war. But the total value of all the citizens' real and personal property before the war had been assessed at slightly over 1 million gulden, and they possessed property worth about 750,000 gulden in 1652.[10] If indeed the citizens of Schwäbisch Hall had paid over 3½ million gulden in tribute during the war, much of this must have been pumped right back into the city's economy as soldiers paid local inhabitants for food, lodging and services.[11]

In fact, what appears in local records as a loss of wealth often turns out to have been just a transfer of property. This was particularly the case in rural districts which experienced a massive – but often temporary – collapse of agricultural output. Many peasants were driven off their land when the soldiers appeared. But sometimes, as in Linden, they fought back. And often they relied on a sophisticated warning system to notify them of the soldiers' approach – for with sufficient notice, the peasants could rescue most of their livestock and moveable goods. As one Franconian village official wrote to his prince in 1645: 'None of your subjects are here; they have all gone to Nuremberg, Schwabach and Lichtenau with every bit of their possessions, down to goods worth scarcely a kreuzer.'[12] When the threat passed, the peasants – or their heirs – might return to the land. And even if they did not, their fields would not necessarily remain permanently fallow. For vacated holdings normally reverted to the landlords who, after the war, often consolidated vacant plots into larger and more productive estates. This was particularly common in eastern Germany, where the war accelerated the collapse of an independent peasantry and contributed to the rise of large-scale estate farming.

Facts like these explain why many historians have tried to judge the war's economic impact by looking at the long-term context instead of simply comparing data from before and after the war. Some have claimed, for example, that Germany was already suffering economic decline before 1618 due to its inability to compete with the rising Atlantic economies. Thus, they argue, the visible decay of the German economy during the war years was simply the continuation of a long-term trend. Other historians reply that the German economy remained vigorous right up to 1618: though Germany's role in international trade may have diminished before then, they insist that agricultural and craft production was thriving until the outbreak of war. The debate between what has been called the 'earlier decline' and 'disastrous war' schools of thought has raged for many years.[13] But the 'earlier decline' theory seems to be gaining ground, since German developments are increasingly placed in a pan-European context: it is now recognized that the seventeenth century represented a period of overall economic contraction in Europe after the boom years of the sixteenth century. One recent historian, in fact, has argued that the Thirty Years' War should itself be seen as an economic phenomenon, intimately linked with the cycle of economic expansion and contraction: 'The Thirty Years' War as a social occurrence', Heiner Haan argues, 'resulted from the long-term economic growth of the sixteenth century; it lived off the wealth produced in this expansion, and in the end it destroyed that very wealth.'[14]

It is equally important, of course, to look at economic developments following the war. Here again the dangers of drawing conclusions from the state of things in 1650 are evident. For many regions of central Europe appear to have experienced a rapid economic recovery in the decades following the war: fields were reclaimed, buildings reconstructed, old patterns of production and trade resumed. The evidence of this recovery, however, is sometimes obscured by its short-lived character; for within less than twenty years Germany had been plunged into a new round of expensive wars: beginning in the mid-1660s, the Holy Roman Empire was engaged in a long series of wars against the Turks and the French. These wars had a smaller physical and demographic impact on Germany than the Thirty Years' War, for most of the fighting took place on the frontiers of the Empire. Yet their financial burden was huge. For some communities, in fact, especially in the tightly organized Swabian Circle of the Empire, the financial demands of the French and Turkish wars proved even more burdensome than those of the Thirty Years' War.

What all this suggests is that the short-term economic and demographic catastrophe which made such an impression on contemporaries seems exaggerated when placed in the context of Germany's overall development between about 1550 and 1700. But the perspective of the historian is always different from that of the people who live through the events of their time. The Germans who experienced the Thirty Years' War little knew or cared whether the peaceful half-century before 1618 had been a period of gradual economic decline; nor could they know or care whether the post-war period might bring opportunities for economic renewal or reconstruction. For meanwhile they had to live with the uncertainties and horrors of the longest, most expensive and most brutal war that had yet been fought on German soil. To Georg Rösch's wife, raped by the 'fat soldier' from east Finland and his friend the 'white-haired young soldier', the war was a personal catastrophe.[15] To Dr Johann Morhard of Schwäbisch Hall, who marked his seventy-sixth birthday in 1630 by contributing a pile of family silver to help save his city from Imperial occupation, the war was a nagging drain on his wealth and security.[16] To Hans Heberle, the shoemaker of Neenstetten whose diary recorded thirty separate occasions when he fled with his family to safety in the city of Ulm, the war was an endless source of fear and disruption.[17] Those Germans who survived the war to its end knew that it had been an unprecedented catastrophe for the German people – and they knew, better than their children and better even than some modern-day historians, why the making of peace and the departure of the last Swedish soldiers provided an occasion for hymns of praise and sermons of thanksgiving all over Germany.

iii The war and politics

Until 1939, the Thirty Years' War remained by far the most traumatic period in the history of Germany. The loss of people was proportionally greater than in World War II; the displacement of people and the material devastation caused were almost as great; the cultural and economic dislocation persisted for substantially longer. These social consequences attracted the attention of nineteenth-century men of letters, such as Gustav Freytag; and they were also used by various nationalist political groups who wished to represent the peace of Westphalia, and indeed the entire war, as a monstrous iniquity perpetrated on Germany by foreign powers, especially France. After 1919, parallels were even drawn between the peace of Westphalia and the settlement at Versailles.

That was not, however, the view taken by eighteenth-century Germans, nor by Germany's eighteenth- and nineteenth-century neighbours. Until 1806, the Westphalian settlement was widely regarded as the fundamental constitution of the Empire, and even after that it was sometimes hailed as the principal guarantor of order in central Europe. In 1866, the French leader Alphonse Thiers stated in all seriousness that: 'The highest principle of European politics is that Germany shall be composed of independent states connected only by a slender federative thread. That was the principle proclaimed by all Europe at the Congress of Westphalia'; while in the 1780s, Catherine the Great of Russia criticized the Emperor Joseph II because his policies ran counter to 'the Treaty of Westphalia, which is the very basis and bulwark of the constitution of the Empire'.[1] Perhaps the most extreme eulogy of the beneficial legacy of the Westphalian settlement came in 1761 from the pen of that incurable Romantic, Jean-Jacques Rousseau:

> What really upholds the European state system is the constant interplay of negotiations, which nearly always maintains an overall balance. But this system rests on an even more solid foundation, namely the German Empire, which from its position at the heart of Europe keeps all powers in check and thereby maintains the security of others even more, perhaps, than its own. The Empire wins universal respect for its size and for the number and virtues of its peoples; its constitution, which takes from conquerors the means and the will to conquer, is of benefit to all and makes it a perilous reef to the invader. Despite its imperfections, this Imperial constitution will certainly, while it lasts, maintain the balance in Europe; no prince need fear lest another dethrone him. The peace of Westphalia may well remain the foundation of our political system for ever.[2]

Such rhetoric, especially when also found in the writings of influential German writers such as Leibniz or Schiller, is highly persuasive. But the balance of power created by the Thirty Years' War and preserved by the peace of Westphalia did not of course remain the basis of Europe's political system for ever; nor, indeed, did it solve all of Europe's difficulties. However, it achieved a great deal more than most modern historians have been prepared to concede. C. V. Wedgwood, for example, in her classic study, stated baldly:

> The war solved no problem. Its effects, both immediate and

indirect, were either negative or disastrous . . . It is the outstanding example in European history of meaningless conflict.[3]

This is both untrue and unfair. The war in fact settled the affairs of Germany in such a way that neither religion nor Habsburg Imperialism ever produced another major conflict there. The territorial rulers of the Empire were granted supreme power (*Landeshoheit*, not quite as extensive as sovereignty) in their localities, and collective power, in the Diet and the Circles, to regulate common taxation, defence, laws and public affairs without Imperial intervention.[4] Religious issues were now decided not by majority votes but by the 'amicable composition' of the Protestant and Catholic blocs. The Thirty Years' War also produced a permanent settlement in the lands of the Austrian Habsburgs. There was now little Protestant worship and the Estates (except in Hungary), were largely tamed; moreover there was no restoration of the exiles, so that those granted lands after 1619 were safe at last. The 'Habsburg monarchy', born of disparate units, some held by right of inheritance and others by election, was now a far more powerful entity. Largely purged of dissidents, and cut off from Spain, the compact private territories of the Austrian Habsburgs were still large enough to guarantee them a place among the foremost rulers of Europe, and to perpetuate their hold on the Imperial title until the Empire was abolished in 1806.

These were solid and lasting achievements, which are by no means diminished by the fact that war did not immediately cease in 1648 in all areas. In the east, tension between the emperor and the Turks steadily increased in intensity, and only the war between the sultan and Venice for control of Crete delayed the outbreak of a major conflict in Hungary until 1663. Even within Germany, certain provisions of the peace of Westphalia threatened, or actually caused, new hostilities. Although Sweden and Brandenburg eventually partitioned Pomerania in 1653, creating their own administrations and even marking out their common frontier with boundary stones, Frederick William almost came to blows in the year 1651 with the duke of Neuburg over the partition of Cleves-Jülich. There were minor hostilities – dubbed 'the Düsseldorf cow-war' by contemporaries – before the exact possessions of the two claimants, disputed for almost half a century, were finally fixed.[5] But the position of the French in Alsace and Lorraine was not so swiftly settled. In Alsace, although the Habsburgs' lands and rights had been ceded to France, the ten largest cities in the area (which also became

French) remained members of the Empire with representatives in the Diet. The intricacies of the situation so perplexed the Paris government that in March 1650 a special envoy was sent to the area to investigate. 'You will return', a mystified Mazarin commanded, and 'shed more light than we have at present.' But the ambiguity was not accidental: Isaac Volmar, Imperial plenipotentiary at Westphalia and former chancellor of Alsace, wanted both France and the Empire to retain a grip on the area so that 'the stronger will prevail'. Thanks to this resolve, the hapless province became a battleground whenever Habsburg and Bourbon clashed.[6]

But at least Alsace enjoyed a respite, however brief, in which to recover from the Thirty Years' War. Lorraine was less fortunate. Although French control over the 'three bishoprics' was ratified, the status of the rest of the duchy, conquered by Louis XIII in 1632–3, was intentionally left unresolved until France and Spain should also make peace. To secure an agreement between these two Catholic powers had been one of Ferdinand III's dearest wishes but, as noted above, the emperor was forced to abandon his ally: Spain and France fought on until the peace of the Pyrenees (November 1659). Even after that, hostilities generated by the Thirty Years' War still continued in the Baltic, where Russia, Denmark, Poland and Brandenburg all resented the gains made by Sweden – largely at their expense – in 1648. Only the death in 1660 of the redoubtable Charles X (formerly Prince Charles Gustav, who succeeded Queen Christina in 1654) opened the way to the treaties of Oliva (1660, with Poland), Copenhagen (1661, with Denmark) and Kardis (1661, with Russia), which at last brought peace to northern Europe.

Even these agreements proved short-lived, however. Europe did not enter upon an era of peace in the later seventeenth century, for both Sweden and France – the unquestioned victors of the Thirty Years' War – continued to fight their neighbours for another sixty years. But the struggle against Swedish and French imperialism after 1648 differed, in at least one crucial respect, from the wars of the earlier seventeenth century: there was now no strong religious bond among the various allies. Religion did of course continue to be politically important – for example, it enabled William III to unseat the Catholic James II in 1688 with minimal effort; likewise, fear of Louis XIV's anti-Protestant policies after 1685 certainly helped to unify his northern enemies. But religion no longer dominated international relations as it once had done. Calvinist William's most important ally in the wars against Louis XIV was the Catholic Prince Eugene of Savoy, who served the no less Catholic Austrian Habsburgs; while in the Baltic wars, Lutheran Sweden was eventually laid low by a coalition of Lutheran Denmark, Calvinist Brandenburg, Catholic Poland and Orthodox Russia.

It is hard to date precisely the demise of confessional politics. When a perceptive observer, just after the Westphalian peace congress, noted that 'Reason of state is a wonderful beast, for it chases away all other reasons', he in effect paid tribute to the secularization that had recently taken place in European politics.[7] But when did this process begin? Perhaps the extent of 'foreign intervention' in the conflict offers a clue, for without question those German princes who actually took up arms for and against the emperor were strongly influenced by confessional considerations. The religious sincerity of Frederick V and Anhalt, of Julius Echter and Maximilian, of George of Baden-Durlach and even Christian of Brunswick, is beyond doubt. As long as these men and their German supporters predominated, so too did the issue of religion. But they failed to secure a lasting settlement. As the task of defending the Protestant cause fell into the hands of the Lutherans, less militant and less intransigent than the Calvinists, and as the extent of non-German participation increased, so 'reasons of state' came to the fore. Naturally the balance did not swing entirely away from religion: Maximilian of Bavaria remained invincibly attached to securing a Catholic peace; and although Frederick of the Palatinate died, disillusioned, in 1632, his cousin Charles Gustav of Pfalz-Zweibrücken in 1648 had the satisfaction of leading the Swedish sack of the Imperial Palace in Prague. Yet, despite such evidence of apparent continuity, the place of religious issues relentlessly receded.

The abatement of this major destabilizing influence in European politics was one of the greatest achievements of the Thirty Years' War. Ever since the 1520s, the diplomatic balance of Europe had been constantly rocked by the conflicting tensions of political and confessional allegiance. There were two distinct aspects to this problem. In the first place, the growth of religious divisions destroyed for over a century the internal cohesion of most states. France, for example, was paralysed by a series of civil wars, motivated at least in part by religion, for much of the period between 1559 and 1629. Successive English monarchs, for a century after 1540, were seriously weakened by the failure of all their subjects to conform fully to the religious policy of the sovereign. Except in Spain and Italy, confessional divisions created groups of subjects in every state who refused all compromise or accommodation with their rulers on a whole range of vital issues. The demands framed by these subjects were not negotiable. They were prepared to go to any lengths – even concluding treasonable liaisons with foreign powers – in order to have their way.

It was here that the second political consequence of the Reformation and Counter-Reformation came into play. The diplomatic system created in the century after 1450, first in Renaissance Italy and later elsewhere, permitted the construction of elaborate and sophisticated networks of alliances aimed primarily at preserving the status quo. Larger states found security in weakening their neighbours, rather than in dominating them; threatened states sought to divert their more powerful enemies by creating difficulties for them elsewhere. But the success of the Reformation cut clean across these recently established political affiliations. The traditional amity between England and Castile, for example, was fatally undermined when the Tudor dynasty embraced Protestantism; and the 'auld alliance' between Scotland and France was likewise wrecked by the progress of the Reformation in Scotland after 1560.[8] But these new orientations in international affairs did not discourage diplomatic intercourse; on the contrary, they intensified the creation of alliances, the exchange of ambassadors, and the signature of mutual defence pacts. Periods of relative peace, such as the decade before 1618, saw frenzied attempts to create international alignments which would guarantee support in case of attack; in wartime, governments sought to turn military defeat into political victory by enlisting further allies against their temporarily victorious opponents. As the experienced Spanish diplomat, Count Gondomar, warned his government presciently in 1619:

> The wars of mankind today are not limited to a trial of natural strength, like a bull-fight, nor even to mere battles. Rather they depend on losing or gaining friends and allies, and it is to this end that good statesmen must turn all their attention and energy.[9]

But on what criteria were these 'friends and allies' to be chosen? It was here that the polarization of Europe into separate religious camps between the 1520s and the 1640s proved so unsettling, for confessional and political advantage seldom totally coincided. The foreign policy of France and the Stuart Monarchy, for example, oscillated during the Thirty Years' War so often and so markedly precisely because there was no consensus among the political elite concerning the correct principles upon which foreign policy should be based. Some saw international conspiracies directed against either their state or their church; others did not.

Some perceived the war as a struggle for religious freedom; others refused to consider anything beyond the specific political issues. Richelieu against the *dévots*, Buckingham against advocates of 'the Protestant cause': during the 1620s, in particular, the posture of the French and British governments towards Germany remained the weathercock of faction.

Clearly this tendency towards political inconstancy – which may also be discerned in The Hague, Vienna, Madrid and elsewhere – goes a long way towards answering the question 'Why did the Thirty Years' War last so long?' But there are other explanations. Many eminent historians have found a cause in long-term social and economic factors, such as the economic dislocation caused by overproduction and overpopulation in the early decades of the century, or the worsening climate, or the widespread destruction and depopulation caused by the war itself. There is, indeed, much evidence for this. Almost all of Europe was affected by what has been called 'the General Crisis of the seventeenth century', a combination of economic, social, climatic, political and intellectual changes which made confrontations between governments, and between governments and governed, far more likely.[10] But none of these forces, by themselves, could cause a war to last thirty years. And, in any case, much of the evidence marshalled in their support crumbles under closer scrutiny. As has been skilfully shown by Gerhard Benecke and Christopher Friedrichs, even the seemingly unequivocal post-war records of material destruction may not be entirely trustworthy: the precise estimates of damage sustained are strangely silent on deaths and injuries caused by the war; space is devoted instead to a minute catalogue of every stick of furniture and each brick or garment destroyed or lost. In some cases, the damage claimed far exceeded the total wealth of the community at any time during the century. Like Brecht's 'Mother Courage', the authorities of post-war Germany were ready to sell their sons for profit.[11] Even today, a visitor to the lands of the former Holy Roman Empire meets with numerous surviving edifices which date from the war years or just afterwards, when Germany was allegedly on its knees: the new churches and palace at Neuburg, on the Danube, begun in 1640; the fine wartime buildings and fortifications of Augsburg, Münster, Ulm and Nördlingen; and so on. But for the bombing of 1939–45, there would be far more. The journals left by travellers to Germany after 1648 – such as the Englishmen Edward Brown and Philip Skippon, who both toured the Empire in the early 1660s – contain numerous references to buildings constructed during the war years, yet they seldom, if ever, mention traces of devastation or disaster. Indeed, if their records were the only available source, one would never guess that a major war had taken place! Until the depredations of Louis XIV's armies, Germany made a surprising economic recovery (despite the continuation of 'the General Crisis' elsewhere).[12]

Other explanations of the longevity of the Thirty Years' War have concentrated less on the incompetence of the armies and more on the ineffectiveness of the governments that raised them. Armies once afoot, it is argued, could not be paid, controlled or organized to achieve rapid and decisive victories; so war eternalized itself. Once more, there is much supporting evidence available. Richard Bonney has made manifest, in his admirable study of the interplay between finance and policy in early Bourbon France, that time and again the aims of the French government had to be either altered or abandoned through financial weakness. The entire policy of 'war by diversion' from 1629 to 1635 was rendered necessary principally by the lack of funds to allow total commitment; and in 1647–8 the pace of the peace talks at Westphalia was critically affected by the state of the French treasury.[13] The rhythm of Spanish, Danish and English intervention, as has been stressed in the chapters above, was likewise heavily influenced by financial considerations. Clearly, all these states were engaged in a war that was beyond their means; that is why they fought themselves to a standstill. Yet, surprisingly enough, this experience was not universal. Sweden, the emperor, Bavaria and Hesse-Kassel all managed to maintain large armies in the field until the war's end without provoking internal collapse. It is true that Ferdinand II's financial position in the early 1630s became precarious; but, apart from that brief tremor, from 1625 until 1648 (and of course beyond) the Imperial Court constantly directed the operations of up to 50,000 fighting men. The tax-burden on the Habsburgs' subjects grew inexorably – taxes on property; taxes on produce (especially wine); taxes on luxury goods; taxes on noble status and wealth – but, after the Inner Austrian revolt of 1635, there was no organized resistance resembling that of Normandy against Richelieu, or of Catalonia or Naples against Olivares. Likewise Sweden, from 1630 until 1650, maintained an even larger army (although its pay was partly provided by foreign subsidies, while provisions were mostly extorted from occupied lands rather than from the homeland). Perhaps the most remarkable force was the Hessian army, which in 1648 garrisoned forty-three strongpoints – almost as many as did the French – and yet had virtually no home base, for Hesse-Kassel had been occupied in the 1630s by hostile forces and thereafter was largely devastated.[14] Certainly the Hessians were seldom major actors in the drama, yet they, above all others, demonstrated how far the maxim *bellum se ipse alet* could be put into effect. As long as an almost landless ruler like Amalia of Hesse could maintain 10,000 and more men in arms, despite twenty-five years of continuous hostility on the part of the Holy Roman Emperor, the war in Germany might indeed last for ever.

Nevertheless the Hessians, although they could keep their own flag flying, lacked the strength to win the war themselves. The Swedish army too, for all its great victories, failed to impose unconditional surrender on the emperor: neither Breitenfeld, nor Wittstock, nor Jankov produced the total collapse of the Imperialists. Even the 1648 campaign, in which the Swedish army seemed about to take Prague, would probably not have proved militarily decisive either: Prague had fallen twice before (in 1618 and 1631), yet had been twice recovered; in 1645–6, Vienna had seemed equally doomed and yet survived intact. It took more than the capture of a town or two to bring the Thirty Years' War to an end.

A state of military and political paralysis had, it seems, set in. This was a fact of the utmost significance for, with the military capacity for total victory thus beyond the grasp of any power or group of powers, and with the conflicting considerations of politics and religion so evenly balanced, the quixotic designs and mercurial temperaments of even minor statesmen came to exert a disproportionate influence on the course of events. The prosopography of early seventeenth-century princes and prelates may be neither edifying nor attractive, but it is central to any real understanding of the war's character. Their freedom of action was awesome, and is reflected in the near divine status with which they were credited by their subjects. To quote the funeral address delivered in honour of Landgrave George of Hesse-Darmstadt in 1661:

> Just as the sun in the heavens above is made and fashioned by God, and is a truly wondrous work of the Almighty, so are kings, princes and lords placed and ordered by God in the secular estate. For that reason they may themselves be called gods.[15]

Landgrave George, the last major participant in the war to die, also seems to have been one of the least attractive. A physical coward, vindictive towards his more open and cultivated cousin, Maurice, George's strength of will nevertheless played a crucial role in the war. It was his tireless diplomacy between 1630 and 1635 which, more than anything else, eventually persuaded his father-in-law, John George of Saxony, to make peace with the emperor, thus creating a fatal rift among the supporters of the Protestant cause. No sooner had Gustavus Adolphus landed in Germany than Landgrave George presented the 'Hessische Punkten' to the Regensburg Assembly; when this failed to find favour, he tried – despite Breitenfeld – direct negotiations with the emperor. Almost at once, the irresistible Swedish advance to the Rhine forced him into Gustavus's camp, but George repeatedly tried to escape through a new accommodation with the Imperialists: at Cologne in 1632, at Leitmeritz in 1633, at Pirna in 1634, and finally (and successfully) at Prague in 1635. And what did the landgrave seek from his sustained peace offensive? Unquestionably he wished to restore peace to the Empire by creating a united front of German princes against all their foreign foes. And reinforcing such political considerations was confessional anxiety: he felt deeply that the inroads of Calvinism, which had recently claimed Hesse-Kassel and Brandenburg, had to be stopped. But these lofty public motives by no means excluded private territorial ambition: George also wished to safeguard the gains made from his domestic enemies in the 1620s, and above all to ensure that Hesse-Kassel (Sweden's oldest German ally) never regained her position of pre-eminence. Given the territorial situation of Darmstadt – surrounded by Catholic and Calvinist neighbours and with only 25 per cent of Hesse (as against 50 per cent for Kassel) – absolute loyalty to the emperor and an unshakeable alliance with Electoral Saxony seemed the landgrave's only guarantee for the future.[16]

Such persistent, painstaking opportunism was characteristic of Germany's political elite during the Thirty Years' War. Perhaps too much attention has been focused upon the seeming irrationality of the Palatine leadership after 1618, with Frederick V embracing the destiny offered him by the Bohemian Estates and Christian of Anhalt. Stressing the messianic elements in the Elector's policy is superficially attractive, for messiahs traditionally come to bring not peace, but a sword. Yet Frederick was advised not only by the impetuous Anhalt, but by the experienced Camerarius, Dohna and Rusdorf. The average age of his principal councillors in 1619 was fifty-seven: they were hardly headstrong boys. If they favoured intervention in Bohemia at all, it was as a pre-emptive measure: to prevent the Habsburgs from building up their strength and using it, one day, against the Palatinate. The far from excitable John Donne visited Heidelberg just before Frederick departed for his new kingdom and preached a valedictory sermon on the text 'Now is our salvation nearer than when we believed', with great (and prolonged) emphasis on the word 'now'.[17]

But it needed more than sermons to move other Protestant princes. Christian IV of Denmark's dissolute ways often left him out of pocket and sometimes out of sorts. He gambled heavily (in the course of 1625, the first year of his intervention in Germany, he won 1,007 thalers and lost 1,510); he was promiscuous; and he was regularly drunk for two or three days on end (between two and three weeks of each year in the 1600s were spent totally intoxicated, according to the diaries of his courtiers – see Plate 24). Age did not weaken his powers. 'Such is the life of that king', complained an English envoy at Copenhagen in 1632: 'to drink all day and lye with a whore every night'.[18] John George of Saxony, for his part, found solace in drinking and hunting when faced by the major political and confessional issues of the day. This Teutonic Nimrod claimed to have shot in person over 150,000 animals; his achievements as Bacchus remain, perhaps mercifully, unquantified. Yet the pressures on John George were indeed severe. On the one hand, throughout the 1620s, the emperor deliberately played upon the Lutheran obligation to obey the powers that be, and upon John George's loathing for Calvinism. On the other hand, Saxony's fear and uncertainty about the future of Lutheranism, if the Catholics defeated all their enemies, was exploited by Gustavus Adolphus and the Palatine court-in-exile. No wonder the Elector took to drink; no wonder he partitioned his lands in 1651 among his four sons, thus ensuring that none of them would face the agonizing decisions that had overwhelmed him.

Not all of the great disputes facing John George and his contemporaries were in fact immediately capable of lasting solution. Although one might have expected more results from such a general conflict, fought over so long a period, it is arguable that almost all the tractable problems of the day were actually resolved, leaving only those that were beyond the powers of better men than the bibulous Elector of Saxony. Part of the difficulty in assessing the achievement of the German princes arises from the inevitable temptation to compare their statecraft with that of the foreign leaders. There was obviously nothing indecisive about Zúñiga and Olivares, about Richelieu and Mazarin, about Oxenstierna and Gustavus Adolphus. But the reason for this contrast is obvious: the German war was not being fought on their doorsteps. 'Win or lose', as Oxenstierna once observed, 'it is not our war.' He could afford to take the longer, more detached view of events simply because he was not directly threatened by them. Except perhaps in 1628–9, Sweden was never in danger of invasion from Germany; neither, except in 1636, was France; still less was Spain. The foreign leaders could therefore pursue their goals single-mindedly by every means at their disposal. Oxenstierna could labour for thirteen years to undermine the peace of Prague; Richelieu and Mazarin could continue to fight on, at least in theory, until their enemies – or even the whole of Germany – collapsed from exhaustion. But the princes of the Empire, lacking the power of these foreign rulers and with the war raging all around them, could not.

Weak or strong, thanks to the paralysis of the normal political mechanisms, the personal determination or the prejudices of individuals thus exerted a decisive effect on the course of the Thirty Years' War. Not all were men born to rule: Laurence of Brindisi's stand over the Donauwörth troubles led eventually to the formation of first the Union and then the League; Oñate and Zúñiga between them helped turn the revolt of Bohemia into a major war; Lamormaini relentlessly undermined the Habsburgs' victory by his insistence on the Edict of Restitution. In the final analysis it was these determined figures, and a mere handful of others like them, who made the Thirty Years' War what it was.

Maps

miles
0   100   200

kilometres
0   100   200   300

NORTH SEA

Stralsund 1612–16

Greifswald 1599–1604, 1613–23

Lübeck 1598–1605

Wismar 1595–1600

Stettin 1612–16

Emden 1595–1602

R. Weser

R. Elbe

Lemgo 1609–17

Braunschweig 1601–4, 1613–15

Berlin 1615

9

R. Maas

Xanten 1614

Wesel 1612

5

Höxter 1600–4

8

Antwerp 1609

Paderborn 1601–4

SAXONY

3   4

2

Cologne 1608–10

6

THE ARCHDUKES

Aachen 1598–1614

Wetzlar 1613–14

Hroby

Frankfurt 1612–16

5

R. Moselle

10

4   5

R. Main

6   7

Wörms 1613–15

Schwäbisch Hall 1601–4

13   14

Donauwörth 1607

R. Meuse

11

9

15

12

3

R. Rhine

12

Auhausen 1610

15

R. Danube

MAXIMILIAN

8   8

Lake Constance

10

11

Munich 1619

Lake Geneva

FERDINAND

Graz 1617

Lake Como

Zeng

40

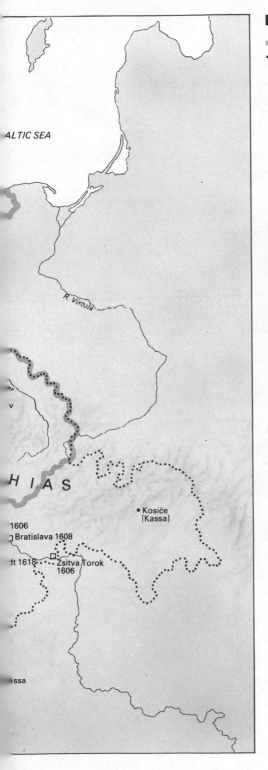

KEY

▬▬▬ Boundary of the Holy Roman Empire

•••••• Boundaries showing Hapsburg Dominions 1616

♟ Members of the Erbverein 1609

♛ Members of the Neuburg Alliance 1605–8

♗ Members of the Catholic League 1612
1   COLOGNE
2   TRIER
3   STRASBOURG
4   MAINZ
5   FULDA
6   WÜRZBURG
7   BAMBERG
8   CONSTANCE
9   ELLWANGEN
10 AUGSBURG
11 BAVARIA
12 EICHSTÄTT

✝ Members of the Protestant Union 1612
1   CLEVES
2   JÜLICH
3   BERG
4   MARK
5   RAVENSBURG
6   HESSE-KASSEL
7   BAYREUTH
8   ANHALT
9   BRANDENBURG
10 LOWER PALATINATE
11 BADEN
12 WÜRTTEMBERG
13 ANSBACH
14 UPPER PALATINATE
15 NEUBURG

⌂ Urban disturbances in Germany 1600–18

□ Treaty locations

• Other Towns

1 Before the war

miles
0   100   200

0   100   200   300
kilometres

SWEDEN

NORTH SEA

D E N M A R K

EAST FRIESLAND

Stralsund 16

Wolgast 1629

Güstrow   POMERANIA

Stade   MECKLENBURG

DUTCH
REPUBLIC

Verden

R. Elbe

BRANDENBURG

Amersfoort

The Hague
1625

's Hertogenbosch
1629

Osnabrück

Minden

Wolfenbüttel   Magdeburg

Breda 1624–5

Stadtlohn 1623   Lutter 1626

Wesel 1629

Hamelin

Dessau Bridge
1626

R. Maas

Göttingen   Goslar   Halberstadt   LUSATIA

Bergen 1622

R. Weser

Fleurus
1622

Jülich 1622

HESSE-MARBURG   HESSE-KASSEL

Mühlhausen
1627

ELECTORAL
SAXONY

Bautzen
1620

SPANISH
NETHERLANDS

Friedberg   Gelnhausen

DUCHY OF
FRIEDLAN

Compiègne
1624

Höchst
1622   HESSE-DARMSTADT

White
Mountain
1620

Mainz 1621

Frankenthal 1622   R. Main

R. Moselle

Mannheim 1622   UPPER
PALATINATE

BOHEMIA

Heidelberg 1622

R. Meuse

LORRAINE

Wiesloch 1622

Wimpfen 1622

LOWER PALATINATE

Záblatí
1619

St Dié

Hagenau

Regensburg
1623, 1630

Peuerbach
1626

Colmar

Ulm 1620

R. Rhine

Memmingen

Augsburg   BAVARIA

Frankham

FRANCHE
COMTÉ

Biberach

Kaufbeuren

Vöcklabru
1626

Lautkirch

ALSACE

Lake
Constance

Kempten

Lake Geneva

Splügen
Pass

GREY
LEAGUE

Stelvio Pass

Lyons 1623

SAVOY

Valtelline

Lake
Como

Mt Cenis

Susa 1629

Milan

Casale
1628–9

Mantua
1629–30

MANTUA

Genoa 1625

KEY

KEY

▨▨▨▨	Boundary of the Holy Roman Empire
●●●●	Lower Saxon Circle
═══	Spanish Road
╱	Economic blockade of Dutch Republic
←	Christian IV's campaign 1625–6
□	Treaty locations
✕	Catholic victory
✕	Catholic defeat
◗	Sieges
■	Major places affected by Edict of Restitution
○	Meetings of the Electoral College
•	Other Towns
▨▨	Areas ceded by Ferdinand II to Bavaria and Saxony 1621
▨▨	Areas affected by 1626 Austrian Revolt
▨▨	Areas ceded by Ferdinand II to Transylvania 1621–9

2 The war 1618–29

SWEDEN

DENMARK

NORTH SEA

Stralsund

Wismar
1638

MECKLENBURG

Hamburg
1638, 1641

Wittstock 1636

Bärwald
1631

R. Weser

R. Elbe

Werben

BRANDENBURG

Tangermünde

Berlin
1631

Frankfurt-on-
Oder 1631

Magdeburg
1631

Torgau

The Downs
1639

Breitenfeld
1631

Leipzig 1631

Pirna 1634

R. Maas

Lützen
1632

ELECTORAL
SAXONY

Leitmeritz 1634

Brussels

Maastricht
1632

Ehrenbreitstein
1632

NASSAU

Koblenz
1634

Frankfurt 1631

Schweinfurt

1635
Prague 1631

SPANISH Jülich

R. Rhine

BOHEMIA

NETHERLANDS

Le Châtelet
1636

La Chapelle
1636

Trier
1635

R. Main

Bamberg

Corbie 1636

Roye
1636

Mainz
1634-7

Hohenlohe

Nuremberg 1632

Compiègne 1635

R. Meuse

Alte Veste 1632

R. Moselle

Philippsburg
1632

Heilbronn
1633

Nördlingen
1634

Regensburg
1630, 1636-7

FRANCE

Paris

Fontainebleau 1631

BADEN WÜRTTEMBERG

Strasbourg

Ulm

Donauwörth

BAVARIA

Rain
1632

Breisach 1638

Rheinfelden 1638

Munich

Dôle 1636

Lake
Constance

TYROL

Lake
Geneva

Valtellina

MILAN

Lake Como

Milan

Cherasco
1631

Mantua
1630

Genoa

▨▨▨   Boundary of the Holy Roman Empire
◄••••   Gustavus's campaigns 1631–2
◄───   Cardinal-Infante's campaign 1634
○   Imperial meetings
✕   Imperial or allied victory
✕   Imperial or allied defeat
▉   Sieges
☐   Treaty locations
•   Other towns

▨▨▨   Heilbronn League

▥▥▥   Area brought under French protection
1632–3

▨▨▨   Area brought under French protection
1633–8

BALTIC SEA

☐ Stuhmsdorf 1635

R. Vistula

R. Oder

ILESIA

R. Danube

3 The war in the 1630s

miles
0   100   200

kilometres
0   100   200   300

NORTH SEA

SWEDEN

D E N M A R K

Brömsebro
1645

POMERAN

FURTHER
POMERANIA

BREMEN-
VERDEN

MECKLENBURG

R. Elbe

BRANDENBURG

R. Oder

WESTPHALIA

The Hague

DUTCH
REPUBLIC

Osnabrück
1643–8

Münster
1643–8

MAGDEBURG
HALBERSTADT

R. Weser

Goslar
1642

Breitenfeld
1642

LUSATIA

CLEVES

Brussels

MARK

Kötzschenbrod
1645

SPANISH
NETHERLANDS

BERG

JÜLICH

COLOGNE

DUCAL
SAXONY

Leipzig
1642

Dresden

ELECTORAL
SAXONY

Lens 1648

Rocroi
1643

LUXEMBURG

PFALZ-
ZWEIBRÜCKEN

Frankfurt
1643–5

LOWER

PALATINATE

R. Main

Nuremberg
1640,
1648–51

Prague
1648

Jankov
1645

UPPER
PALATINATE

BOHEMIA

Kr
16

FRANCE

R. Meuse

METZ

VERDUN

Mergentheim
1645

R. Rhine

Allerheim
1645

Regensburg
1640–1

Linz

LOW
AUST

TOUL

R. Moselle

Freiburg
1644

Zusmarshausen
1648

PFALZ-
NEUBURG

UPPER
AUSTRIA

FRANCHE-
COMT

ALSACE

Tuttlingen
1643

Lake
Constance

Munich

BAVARIA

Einsiedeln
1640

Bregenz
1646

SALZBURG

STYRIA

Lake
Geneva

SWISS
CONFEDERATION

GREY
LEAGUE

TYROL

CARINTHIA

Graz

Valtelline

SAVOY

MILAN

MONTFERRAT

Lake
Como

REPUBLIC OF VENICE

MANTUA

Venice

CARNIOLA

PARMA

Genoa

PAPAL
MODENA STATES

KEY

	Boundary of the Holy Roman Empire
✕	Imperial or allied victory
✕	Imperial or allied defeat
▢	Treaty locations
◼	Sieges
○	Important meetings
●	Other Towns

CHANGES OF TERRITORY AT WESTPHALIA

	to Sweden
	to Brandenburg
	to Transylvania
	to Saxony
	to France
	to Dutch Republic
	to Bavaria
	to Poland

4 The war in the 1640s

Abbreviations

AGRB	Archives Générales du Royaume, Brussels, Belgium
AGS	Archivo General, Simancas, Spain
AMAE	Archives du Ministère des Affaires Étrangères, Paris, France
ARA	Algemene Rijksarchief, The Hague, Netherlands
BGSA	Bayerisches Geheimes Staatsarchiv, Munich, West Germany
BL	British Library, London, England
BNM	Biblioteca Nacional, Madrid, Spain
KrA	Krigsarkivet, Stockholm, Sweden
NLS	National Library of Scotland, Edinburgh, Scotland
PRO, S.P.	Public Record Office, London, England; State Papers Collection
RAC	Rigsarkivet, Copenhagen, Denmark
ZSM	Zentrales Staatsarchiv, Merseburg, German Democratic Republic

Notes

In the following pages, incomplete references concern works which are cited in full in the Bibliographical Essay. See the Index of Authors on pages 304–8 below for the precise location.

Preface

1 See the detailed discussion by K. Repgen, 'Seit wann gibt es den Begriff "Dreissigjähriger Krieg"?', in H. Dollinger *et al.*, eds, *Weltpolitik, Europagedanke, Regionalismus: Festschrift für Heinz Gollwitzer* (Münster, 1982), 59–70. The term was apparently used for the first time on 6 May 1648 by the deputies of the bishopric of Bamberg at the Westphalian Peace Congress (p. 62). Professor Repgen has subsequently discovered some further information. See: 'Noch einmal zum Begriff "Dreissigjähriger Krieg" ', *Zeitschrift für historische Forschung*, IX (1982), 347–52. *Von dem Dreyssigjährigen Teutschen Krieg Kurtze Chronica* (1650) was the third edition of a pamphlet previously issued as *Von dem Dreissig-Jährigen Deutschen Kriege* (1648) and also as *Summarischer Ausszug des dreyssig-Jährigen Deutschen Krigs* (1649). The first edition was also translated into Dutch.

2 Quoted in *The Cambridge Modern History* (Cambridge, 1906), IV, v.

3 Repgen, 'Dreissigjähriger Krieg', 63: quotations from Dr Isaac Volmar and the Salzburg delegation; and L. Weber, *Veit Adam von Gepeckh, Fürstbischof von Freising, 1618 bis 1651* (Munich, 1972), 88–90.

4 K.H. Schleif, *Regierung und Verwaltung des Erzstifts Bremen am Beginn der Neuzeit (1500–1645). Eine Studie zum Wesen der modernen Staatlichkeit* (Hamburg, 1972), 172; H. Jäger, 'Der dreissigjährige Krieg und die deutsche Kulturlandschaft', in H. Haushofer and W.A. Boelcke, eds, *Wege und Forschungen der Agrargeschichte: Festschrift zum 65. Geburtstag von Günther Franz* (Frankfurt, 1967), 131.

5   Lord Acton, 'The Study of History' [Inaugural Lecture, 1895], in
     Acton, *Renaissance to Revolution: the rise of the free state. Lectures on Modern history* (London, 1906; reprinted New York, 1961),
     9 (with a footnote reference to the similar thoughts of Ranke).

6   Dr Paul Dukes of Aberdeen University, who has published an
     English summary of one of Porshnev's books [see *European Studies Review*, IV (1974), 81–8], has pointed out that, after earlier concentration on France before the Fronde, B.F. Porshnev decided to write
     a trilogy comprising a synchronic analysis of the development of
     social, political and international relations throughout Europe
     during the time of the Thirty Years' War, which he considered to be
     the first conflict to embrace the whole continent and, as such, one
     of the principal divisions between medieval and modern times.
     After a series of articles connected with this ambitious project, he
     brought out in 1970 its concluding volume, *France, the English
     Revolution and European Politics at the Middle of the Seventeenth
     Century*. The second part, not yet published although adumbrated
     by a further series of articles, was to consider the turning-point that
     occurred in relations between western and eastern Europe in the
     mid-1630s. The first part of the trilogy, *The Thirty Years' War, the
     Entry of Sweden, and the Moscow State*, came out in 1976 after its
     author's death. It took as its centrepiece the Smolensk War of
     1632–4, which has received little or no mention in English-
     language accounts of the wider conflict. Porshnev argued that,
     even before the outbreak of the Thirty Years' War, the interconnec-
     tions of Europe were greater than has recently been thought,
     placing the conclusion of Muscovy's Time of Troubles in a wider
     context. I am very grateful to Dr Dukes for this information.

7   Historians have traditionally accorded far more attention to the
     first half of the war: Moriz Ritter devoted 596 out of 648 pages on the
     war to the period 1618–35, while Pagès allocated 178 pages out of
     235, Wedgwood 394 pages out of 515, and Polišenský 200 pages out of
     256.

8   This is the title of an excellent brief survey of the war by H.G.
     Koenigsberger, printed in H.R. Trevor-Roper, ed., *The Age of
     Expansion* (London, 1968), chapter 5, and in Koenigsberger, *The
     Habsburgs and Europe 1516–1660* (Ithaca, NY, and London, 1971),
     chapter 3.

Chapter I Europe between war and peace

1   F. Deloffre and J. van den Heuvel, eds, *Voltaire: romans et contes*
     (Paris, 1979), 136–7. Voltaire wrote the piece in 1753–4, just as he
     was completing *Essai sur les Moeurs*. He wrote in some discomfort,
     'entre deux rois' (for he had quarrelled with the rulers of both
     France and Prussia), and 'le cul à terre', in exile in Alsace.

I.i   The Habsburgs and Europe

1   It has been noted that, in the fifty-seven marriages contracted by
    members of the dynasty between c. 1450 and c. 1650, fifty-one
    spouses came from the same seven families, and twenty-four came
    from just three. Philip IV of Spain had only four great-
    grandparents, instead of eight! Perhaps the repeated incest (in
    effect) of the House of Habsburg explains the infertility of so many
    of its members during this period. See P.S. Fichtner, 'Dynastic
    marriage in sixteenth-century Habsburg diplomacy and statecraft:
    an interdisciplinary approach', *American Historical Review*,
    LXXXI (1976), 243–65.
2   Edward Brown, *A brief account of some travels in Hungaria, Servia
    etc* (London, 1673), *passim* (e.g. pages 114–15, 123, 133, 140).
3   Ferdinand's policy is ably described in K.J. Dillon, *King and Estates
    in the Bohemian Lands, 1526–64* (Brussels, 1976).
4   Figures on Protestant strength from G. Mecenseffy, *Geschichte des
    Protestantismus in Österreich* (Graz and Cologne, 1956); G. Rein-
    grabner, *Adel und Reformation. Beiträge zur Geschichte des pro-
    testantischen Adels im Lande unter der Enns während die 16. und
    17. Jahrhunderts* (Vienna, 1976: Forschungen zur Landeskunde von
    Niederösterreich, XXI); and *idem, Protestantismus in Niederöster-
    reich* (Vienna, 1977: Wissenschaftliche Schriftenreihe Niederöster-
    reich, XXVII). For monastic strength and weakness see Evans,
    Making of the Habsburg Monarchy, 4. It should be noted, however,
    that the Protestants only had seventy-eight pastors in Lower Aus-
    tria by 1580 (Chesler, 'Crown, lords and God', 63).
5   Quoted by Schulze, *Landesdefension und Staatsbildung*, 70 n. 119.
    A slightly different version is given by Franzl, *Ferdinand II.*, 17.
    Perhaps the preacher exaggerated: the permanent imposition of
    Türkensteuer in the sixteenth century in fact enabled many other
    princes to gain a measure of financial independence from their
    Estates.
6   Quoted by Schulze, *op. cit.*, 82.
7   Information from A. Posch, 'Aus dem kirchlichen Visitationsbericht
    1617', in Novotny and Sutter, eds, *Innerösterreich, 1564–1619*,
    197–232, at p. 229; and Reingrabner, *Geschichte des Protestantis-
    mus*, 3. There was no printing press at Innsbruck until 1558 and
    none at Graz until 1559, which inhibited the spread of Protestant-
    ism. In Vienna, by contrast, seventeen Lutheran tracts had been
    printed by 1521!
8   See Evans, *Making of the Habsburg Monarchy*, 45.
9   Quoted by Bireley, *Religion and Politics*, 133–4.
10 See Evans, *Rudolf II*, 41–2, and *Habsburg Monarchy*, 39–40, for
    further discussion of these points.
11 Evans, *Habsburg Monarchy*, 18; K. Benda, 'Hungary in turmoil,
    1580–1620', *European Studies Review*, VIII (1978), 281–304, at p.
    295.

12   See Sturmberger, 'Bruderzwist', for details. There had already been a meeting of the Archdukes in 1600, at Schottwein, to discuss Rudolf's alarming incompetence: see K. Vocelka, *Die politische Propaganda Kaiser Rudolfs II (1576–1612)* (Vienna, 1981), 311–16. It has been suggested that the emperor attempted to take his own life in 1600; certainly after that year his behaviour became more erratic (see Evans, *Rudolf II*, 63 – and, on Rudolf's personality in general, all of chapter 2).

13   The treaty was renewed five times between 1615 and 1628. See K. Teply, *Die Kaiserliche Grossbotschaft an Sultan Murad IV. 1628. Des Freiherrn Hans Ludwig von Kuefsteins Fahrt zur hohen Pforte* (Vienna, n.d.). See also Heinisch, 'Habsburg, die Pforte und der Böhmische Aufstand, 1618–20', *passim*.

14   Vocelka, *Politische Propaganda*, 311–12 and 314, quotes and discusses the *Liste von Gravamina*. The original is in Vienna, Haus-, Hof- und Staatsarchiv, *Familienakten*, fasz. 1.

15   There is a rather dull but very thorough biography of this crucial figure by H. Sturmberger, *Georg Erasmus Tschernembl: Religion, Libertät und Widerstand. Ein Beitrag zur Geschichte der Gegenreformation und des Landes ob der Enns* (Linz, 1953). Not much work has been done on Tschernembl since then, but there is an interesting description of his library in *Der oberösterreichische Bauernkrieg 1626*, 137–43. The list of his books, compiled after 1621 by the Jesuits of Linz who secured them, included 1,897 titles (248 of them duplicates): Calvin, Duplessis-Mornay, François Hotman, Luther, Machiavelli and Peter Ramus were all represented. His treatise on resistance was composed *circa* 1600. Tschernembl also possessed a 1612 edition of Mercator's Atlas.

I.ii   *Germany before the war*

1   Maurice of Hesse-Kassel to Louis XIII, 23 March 1615, quoted by A.D. Lublinskaya, *Frantsiya v nachale XVII veka* (Leningrad, 1959), 186. There is, unfortunately, no other edition of this important work: although an English translation was made some years ago by Mr Brian Pearce, it remains unpublished.

2   On Maurice and his world, see E. van den Boogaart, ed., *Johan Maurits van Nassau-Siegen, 1604–1679. A humanist prince in Europe and Brazil* (The Hague, 1979), 17–38. On Maurice's militia see: G. Thies, *Territorialstaat und Landesverteidigung. Das Landesdefensionswerk in Hessen-Kassel unter Landgraf Moritz, 1592–1627* (Darmstadt, 1973: Quellen und Forschungen zur hessischen Geschichte, XXV).

3   Details from J. Petersohn, 'Die Landesdefension in Herzogtum Preussen zu Beginn des 17. Jahrhunderts', *Zeitschrift für Ostforschung*, X (1961), 226–37; G. Oestreich, *Geist und Gestalt des frühmodernen Staates* (Berlin, 1969 – an outstanding collection of essays), 1–79 and 300–55; and R. Naumann, *Das Kursächsiche*

Defensionswerk (1613–1709) (Leipzig, 1917). There were two arsenals at Dresden, capital of Electoral Saxony: one, for the army, in the Albertinum, which has now been dispersed; the second, containing precious items for the Elector and his courtiers, in the Johanneum. The inventory of the latter dated 1606, and running to 1,500 manuscript pages, indicates the size of the collection even then; today it includes some 10,000 items from the early modern period: 1,400 pistols, 1,600 long arms and 2,200 swords and daggers, as well as horse and body armour and all the accoutrements. John George I's principal contribution to the collection during his long reign (1611–56) was, appropriately enough for the Chief Imperial Huntsman, a vast collection of equipment for the chase.

4   P. Charpentrat, 'Les villes, le mécénat princier et l'image de la ville idéale dans l'Allemagne de la fin du XVIe et du XVIIe siècles: l'exemple du Palatinat – Heidelberg et Mannheim', in P. Francastel, ed., *L'urbanisme de Paris et l'Europe 1600–1680* (Paris, 1969), 267–74 and plate 146. See also K. Wolf, 'Von der Einführung der allgemeinen Wehrpflicht in Kurpfalz um 1600', *Zeitschrift für die Geschichte des Oberrheins*, LXXXIX (1936–7), 638–704.

5   None of these masterworks of baroque military architecture now survive: Hanau is virtually a suburb of Frankfurt; Ehrenbreitstein, completely rebuilt in the nineteenth century by the Prussian government, is now the National Monument to the German Army. Philippsburg, whose fortifications have been razed, has even been abandoned by the Rhine – the river now flows a mile to the west. All that remains of the great fortress is a few street names, the moat which defended one bastion, the ceremonial spade used by Bishop Sötern to turn the first sod of his proud citadel (in the town museum), and some pages of Grimmelshausen's novel *Simplicissimus* (for the hero spent some time in the 1630s billeted there)! Only Breisach, because of its superb natural position on a rock outcrop above the Rhine, still retains its seventeenth-century appearance, although most of the defences now visible date from the period of French occupation under Louis XIV and XV.

6   John Taylor, *Three weekes, three daies and three houres observations and travel from London to Hamburgh* (London, 1617), 6. Taylor (1580–1653) wrote this and many other pieces to make fun of the more serious travelogues of Thomas Coryat and others; but he nevertheless undertook his journeys in person. In the same year he went on a sort of sponsored walk from London to the Scottish Highlands (narrated in his *Penniless Pilgrimage*), and in 1619 he walked to Bohemia and back (see *An Englishman's love to Bohemia*).

7   Quoted by H.G.R. Reade, *Sidelights on the Thirty Years' War*, I (London, 1924), 183.

8   Thomas Coryat, *Coryat's Crudities, hastily gobled up in five moneths travells . . . newly digested . . . and now dispersed to the nourishment of the travelling members of this kingdom* (London,

1611), 443–628, cover 'my observations of some parts of High Germany'. John Taylor, on his journey through north-west Germany in 1617, noted the number of wooden crosses along all the roads of Westphalia marking the spots where travellers had been murdered by brigands (see *Three weekes*, 36–7). Fynes Moryson, *An itinerary* (London, 1617), gives less detail on what the traveller saw, but in compensation provides far more information on prices, distances and useful tips for tourists. The facts he gave have been tabulated and confirmed by A. Mączak, *Życie codzienne w podró-żach po Europie w XVI i XVII wieku* (Warsaw, 1978), 81–9; and by W. von Hippel, 'Bevölkerung und Wirtschaft im Zeitalter des dreissigjährigen Krieges. Das Beispiel Württembergs', *Zeitschrift für historische Forschung*, V (1978), 413–48.

9   See Thies, *Territorialstaat*, 18–19; F. Boersma, 'De diplomatieke reis van Daniel van der Meulen en Nicholaes Bruyninck naar het Duitse Leger bij Emmerik, Augustus 1599', *Bijdragen en mededelingen betreffende de Geschiedenis van de Nederlanden*, LXXXIV (1969), 24–66.

10   On the Circles see J.A. Vann, *The Swabian Kreis. Institutional growth in the Holy Roman Empire 1648–1715* (Brussels, 1975); F. Magen, 'Die Reichskreise in der Epoche des dreissigjährigen Krieges', *Zeitschrift für historische Forschung*, IX (1982), 409–60; and R. Endres, 'Zur Geschichte des fränkischen Reichskreises', *Würzburger Diözesangeschichtsblätter*, XXIX (1968), 168–83; on the Knights, see M.J. Le Gates, 'The Knights and the problems of political organization in sixteenth-century Germany', *Central European History*, VII (1974), 99–136; and T.J. Glas-Hochstettler, 'The Imperial Knights in post-Westphalian Mainz: a case study of corporatism in the Old Reich', *ibid.*, XI (1978), 131–49.

11   H. Hiegel, *Le bailliage d'Allemagne de 1600 à 1632. L'administration, la justice, les finances et l'organisation militaire* (Saarguemines, 1961), 148–50: over 200 marker stones, many bearing the arms of Lorraine and each four feet high, were erected between 1605 and 1608; more stones had been erected in 1602–4 by order of Frederick IV of the Palatinate. The tolls on the Elbe in the 1670s are shown in the map of K. Blaschke, 'Elbschiffahrt und Elbzölle im 17. Jahrhundert', *Hansische Geschichtsblätter*, LXXXII (1964), 42–54, at p. 48. On the Rhine tolls, see Coryat, *Coryat's crudities*, 569 ff.

12   There is an excellent description of the composition of the Diet at this time in Bierther, *Der Regensburger Reichstag von 1640/1641*, 48–57. See also the more general surveys of H. Weber, 'Empereur, Electeurs et Diète de 1500 à 1650', *Revue d'histoire diplomatique*, LXXXIX (1975), 281–97; G. Buchda, 'Reichsstände und Landstände in Deutschland im 16. und 17. Jahrhundert', *Standen en Landen*, XXXVI (1965), 193–226; and K.O. Freiherr von Aretin, *Heiliges Römisches Reich 1776–1806. Reichsverfassung und Staatssouveränität*, I (Wiesbaden, 1967), 1–110 (which examine the institutions of the Empire in the seventeenth and eighteenth centuries).

13   W. Schulze has shown in two recent articles that financial embar-
      rassment was far more serious among German rulers than previous-
      ly thought: 'Reichstage und Reichssteuern im späten 16. Jahrhun-
      dert', *Zeitschrift für historische Forschung*, II (1975), 43–58; and
      'Die Erträge der Reichssteuern zwischen 1576 und 1606', *Jahrbuch
      für die Geschichte Mittel- und Ostdeutschlands*, XXVII (1978),
      169–85. See also Petersen, 'From domain state to tax state'.
14   For estimates of Germany's pre-war population see H. Kellenbenz's
      chapter in C.H. Wilson and G. Parker, eds, *Introduction to the
      Sources of European Economic History 1500–1800* (London, 1977),
      especially pages 191–6. There is a masterly discussion of the nature
      of the pre-war crisis in Germany by H. Schilling in P. Clark, ed., *The
      European Crisis of the 1590s* (London, 1984), 135–56. I am most
      grateful to Professor Schilling for allowing me to see his paper in
      advance of publication.
15   E. Klein, *Geschichte der öffentlichen Finanzen in Deutschland
      1500–1870* (Wiesbaden, 1974), 8–26. See also C.P. Clasen's chapter
      in Trevor-Roper, *Age of Expansion*.
16   Maximilian to Duke William, 21 June 1598, quoted by H. Dollinger,
      'Kurfürst Maximilian I. von Bayern und Justus Lipsius. Eine Studie
      zur Staatstheorie eines frühabsolutistischen Fürsten', *Archiv für
      Kulturgeschichte*, XLVI (1964), 227–308.
17   On the Estates of Bavaria see Carsten, *Princes and Parliaments*,
      chap. 5; and K. Bosl, *Die Geschichte der Repräsentation in Bayern.
      Landständische Bewegung, Landständische Verfassung, Landes-
      ausschuss und altständische Gesellschaft* (Munich, 1974).
18   On the Augsburg settlement, see H. Tüchle, 'The peace of Augs-
      burg: New Order or lull in the fighting?' in H.J. Cohn, ed., *Govern-
      ment in Reformation Europe 1520–1560* (London, 1971), 145–65; T.
      Klein, 'Minorities in central Europe in the sixteenth and early
      seventeenth centuries', in A.C. Hepburn, ed., *Minorities in History*
      (London, 1979: Historical Studies, XII), 31–50; Holborn, *A History
      of Modern Germany*, 243–6 and chapters 10 and 11; and Bireley,
      Religion and Politics, 25–6. I am grateful to Fr Bireley for discus-
      sions which cleared up some of my misconceptions about the
      Peace.
19   On the war of Cologne see M. Lossen, *Der Kölnische Krieg* (2 vols,
      Munich, 1897); G. von Lojewski, *Bayerns Weg nach Köln. Ge-
      schichte der bayerischen Bistumspolitik in der zweiten Hälfte des
      16. Jahrhunderts* (Bonn, 1962: Bonner Historische Forschungen,
      XXI); and D. Albrecht, 'Das konfessionelle Zeitalter', in M. Spind-
      ler, ed., *Handbuch der bayerischen Geschichte*, II (Munich, 1969),
      358–61.
20   Most of the exceptions concerned Imperial Free Cities, several of
      which until 1593 claimed the *ius reformandi* and Protestantized
      their church order: see K. von Greyerz, *The Late City Reformation
      in Germany. The case of Colmar 1522–1628* (Wiesbaden, 1980), and
      H. Schilling, 'Burgerkämpfe in Aachen zu Beginn des 17. Jahrhun-

derts. Konflikte im Rahmen der alteuropäischen Stadtgesellschaft oder im Umkreis der frühbürgerlichen Revolution', *Zeitschrift für historische Forschung*, I (1974), 175–231. Colmar (1575) and Aachen (1581) apart, Essen (1563), Hagenau (1565) and Aalen (1575) also adopted the Reformation after the Augsburg settlement.

21   [Andreas Erstenberger], *De Autonomia, das ist, von Freystellung mehrerlay Religion und Glauben* (written c. 1580; printed Munich, 1586). See the learned discussion of this work and of its significance in M. Heckel, '*Autonomia* und *Pacis Compositio*: Der Augsburger Religionsfriede in der Deutung der Gegenreformation', *Zeitschrift der Savigny-Stiftung für Rechtsgeschichte. Kanonistische Abteilung*, XLV (1959), 141–248.

22   References from Heiss, 'Konfession, Politik und Erziehung'; E. Schubert, 'Gegenreformation in Franken', *Jahrbuch für fränkische Landesforschung*, XXVIII (1968), 275–307; and J. Meier, 'Die katholische Erneuerung des Würzburger Landskapitels Karlstadt im Spiegel der Landskapitelsversammlungen und Pfarreivisitationen, 1579–1624', *Würzburger Diözesangeschichtsblätter*, XXXIII (1971), 51–125. Bishop Julius's efforts to end clerical concubinage were not immediately successful because, as he told his chapter in 1581, 'the peasants of their own free will come themselves to the young priests and present their daughters, and a dowry too' (page 80). Not surprisingly, twenty-six of the twenty-nine priests affected by the episcopal visitation of 1579 had a concubine, as did 50 per cent of those visited in 1588. Not until 1619 had the practice entirely disappeared. See also the admirable collection of essays, F. Merzbacher, ed., *Julius Echter und seine Zeit* (Würzburg, 1973).

23   J. Köhler, *Das Ringen um die tridentische Erneuerung im Bistum Breslau: vom Abschluss des Konzils bis zur Schlacht am Weissen Berg, 1564–1620* (Vienna and Cologne, 1973), 155–6. Between 1564 and 1620, sixty-four young men from the 'German college' came to the diocese of Wrocław (Breslau) in Silesia.

24   The Calvinization of the Palatinate is covered by O. Chadwick, 'The making of a Reforming Prince: Frederick III Elector Palatine', in R.B. Knox, ed., *Reformation, Conformity and Dissent. Essays in honour of Dr. Geoffrey Nuttall* (London, 1977), 44–69; and B. Vogler, *Le clergé protestant rhénan au siècle de la Réforme 1555–1619* (Strasbourg, 1967). The polemics between the Lutherans and Calvinists in Hesse and elsewhere are discussed by H. Gross, *Empire and Sovereignty: a history of the Public Law Literature in the Holy Roman Empire 1599–1804* (2nd edn, Chicago, 1975), 105ff.

25   On the brief but tempestuous reign of Christian I, father of John George, see T. Klein, *Der Kampf um die zweite Reformation in Kursachsen, 1586–91* (Cologne and Graz, 1962). For the religious change in Brandenburg, the importance of which is often overlooked, see E. Faden, *Berlin im dreissigjährigen Krieg* (Berlin, 1927), 136ff.; and O. Hintze, 'Calvinism and Raison d'État in early

seventeenth-century Brandenburg', in F. Gilbert, ed., *The Historical Essays of Otto Hintze* (Oxford, 1975), 88–154. On the 'second Reformation' in the north-west, and for a perceptive general survey of the phenomenon, see Schilling, *Konfessionskonflikt und Staatsbildung*.

26 See Neveux, *Vie spirituelle*, 8–12.

27 On urban disturbances, see C.R. Friedrichs, 'Subjects or citizens? Urban conflict in early modern Germany', in M.U. Chrisman and O. Grundler, eds, *Social Groups and Religious Ideas in the Sixteenth Century* (Kalamazoo, 1978: Studies in Medieval Culture, XIII), chap. 6; and *idem*, 'German town revolts and the 17th-century crisis', *Renaissance and Modern Studies*, XXVII (1983).

28 The best account of the troubles at Donauwörth is by A. de Carmignano, 'La part de S. Laurent de Brindes dans le Ban de Donauwörth, 1607', *Revue d'histoire ecclésiastique*, LVIII (1963), 460–86. But see also F. Stieve, *Der Ursprung des dreissigjährigen Krieges. I. Der Kampf um Donauwörth* (Munich, 1875), and R. Breitling, 'Der Streit um Donauwörth 1605/1611. Eine Ergänzung', *Zeitschrift für bayerische Landesgeschichte*, II (1929), 275–98.

29 Quoted by Kossol, *Die Reichspolitik des Pfalzgrafen Philipp Ludwig*, 167.

I.iii *The Union, the League and the politics of Europe*

1 Schubert, *Camerarius*, 46, 52.

2 van Deursen, *Honni Soit*, 45–6.

3 The dispute over the Cleves-Jülich succession arose from the fact that only John William's four sisters had left heirs and it was not clear whether the duchies could be inherited undivided through the female line. Brandenburg was married to the only daughter of the eldest sister; Neuburg was married to the second sister and argued that their son Wolfgang William had a stronger claim than a daughter. By 1593 Neuburg was prepared to accept a partition, but Brandenburg was not. See Kossol, *Neuburg*, and Hans Schmidt, 'Pfalz-Neuburgs Sprung zum Niederrhein. Wolfgang Wilhelm von Pfalz-Neuburg und der Jülich-Klevische Erbfolgestreit', in Glaser, ed., *Um Glauben und Reich*, II/i, 77–89.

4 As nearest agnate, Neuburg could expect under the terms of the Golden Bull to be appointed administrator of the Palatinate during the minority of Frederick V if, as was widely expected, Frederick IV died in the immediate future. His fervent Lutheranism, however, made him an unpalatable candidate and, in December 1602, Frederick IV revised his will to nominate Neuburg's Calvinist brother Duke John of Pfalz-Zweibrücken instead. When Zweibrücken died in 1604 the will was further revised to transfer the nomination to his son John II, who was ultimately appointed on the death of Frederick IV in October 1610. Neuburg resented his exclusion bitterly.

5   PRO, S.P. 81/9/6, James I to Frederick IV, 8/18 June 1603 (i.e. 8 June Old Style, 18 June New Style).

6   Anhalt's descendants were still demanding repayment as late as 1818! See Bonney, *The King's Debts*, 273.

7   *Briefe und Akten*, II, 55–6: Protocol, Rothenburg Assembly, 7–14 August 1608.

8   Quoted by Kossol, *Neuburg*, 218–19.

9   Quoted by Herold, *Ansbach*, 134.

10   E. Sawyer, ed., *Memorials of Affairs of State during the Reigns of Queen Elizabeth and King James I* (London, 1725), III, 83: Winwood to the earl of Salisbury, 2/12 November 1609.

11   Kessel, *Spanien und die geistlichen Kurstaaten*, 59, 66. On the bishops' motives, see Baumgart's chapter in Merzbacher, *Echter*.

12   The refusal of the princes to permit the cities an equal vote to theirs also caused the leagues of the counts of the Wetterau and Franconia to reject invitations to join the Union. See F. Magen, *Reichsgräfliche Politik in Franken. Zur Reichspolitik der Grafen von Hohenlohe am Vorabend und zu Beginn des dreissigjährigen Krieges* (Schwäbisch Hall, 1975: Forschungen aus Württembergisch Franken, X), 114–15, 119.

13   van Deursen, *Honni Soit*, 60.

14   Sawyer, *Memorials*, III, 78: 7/17 October 1609. Sir Henry Wotton thought similarly to Winwood: see 'A few humble remembrances upon the proposition of my employment to some of the German princes on my return' (? June 1609), Historical Manuscripts Commission, *Calendar of the Manuscripts of the Marquess of Salisbury*, XXI (London, 1970), 75–7.

15   Discussed in further detail in Adams, 'Protestant Cause', 168–9.

16   See *ibid.*, 183–221 *passim*. For the impact of these events in the United Provinces, and on Maurice of Nassau in particular, see van Deursen, *Honni Soit*, 76, 91–101. Christian IV remained neutral at this time through lack of money after the War of Kalmar. Professor E.L. Petersen has kindly drawn my attention to a letter of the king, written early in 1614, in which he lamented that 'ich fuhr meine Persohn [bin] mit gelde itzo nicht versehen . . . dan ich mit allerhandt wmkosten ihn vergangendem Kriige seindt gewessen' (RAC, Tyske kancelli, udenlandske afdeling II. Brandenburg A.I.8: letters to the Electress of Brandenburg, 12 February – 18 April 1614). See also J. Skovgaard, ed., *Kong Christian den Fjerdes egenhaendige Breve*, VIII (Copenhagen, 1947), nos 22, 24–5. Without money of his own, the king had to heed the cautious 'advice' of his council on foreign affairs.

17   In 1612 Nuremberg complained that the princes were dealing with Union affairs at weddings, hunting parties and private meetings: see Herold, *Ansbach*, 152.

18   BGSA, Kasten Schwarz 16688, f. 150, 'PAD' to William Trumbull, 22 July 1614.

19   Schubert, *Camerarius*, 50–1; Herold, *Ansbach*, 171, 184.

20 For the politics of Aachen see Schilling, 'Burgerkämpfe in Aachen'.
21 Albrecht, *Auswärtige Politik*, 34; Altmann, *Reichspolitik*, 24.
22 Altmann, *op. cit.*, 13.
23 *Ibid.*, 76, 84, 113–14.
24 For Dutch policy in the crisis, see A. Th. van Deursen, *De Val van Wezel* (Kampen, 1967).
25 BGSA, Kasten Schwarz 16734, f. 141, Frederick to Winwood, 19 January 1615.
26 For the activities of the cities at the Heilbronn Assembly, see J. Müller, 'Reichsstädtische Politik in den letzten Zeiten der Union', *Mitteilungen des Instituts für Oesterreichischen Geschichtsforschung*, XXXIII (1912), 484–5.
27 Herold, *Ansbach*, 206, 209, 217; Schubert, *Camerarius*, 50–1.
28 Herold, *Ansbach*, 229.
29 BL, Additional MS. 34324, f. 119, Diary of Sir Julius Caesar: notes on privy council meeting on 29 September/9 October 1620. See also NLS, Advocates Library MS. 33.1.12, art. 35, Zweibrücken to James I, 19 March 1612.
30 For the Palatine approaches to Maximilian, see Schubert, *Camerarius*, 82, and Albrecht, *Auswärtige Politik*, 35–6. Maximilian's private memorandum on the subject is printed in Altmann, *Reichspolitik*, 480–5. (But see also pp. 199–226 where Altmann discusses the implications of this document.) For Frederick's attempt to gain the support of James I for the scheme and the still mysterious meeting held between him, Bouillon and the English ambassador in France (Sir Thomas Edmondes) at Sedan in July 1617, see BL, Stowe MS. 176, f. 144, Frederick to Edmondes, 21 August 1617; A. Ballesteros y Beretta, ed., *Correspondencia Oficial de Don Diego Sarmiento de Acuña, Conde de Gondomar* (Madrid, 1936: Documentos Inéditos para la Historia de España, 1), 150–1: Gondomar to Archduke Albert, 16 December 1617; and S.R. Gardiner, ed., *Letters and Documents illustrating the Relations between England and Germany . . . 1618–1620*, I (London, 1865: Camden Society, XC), 27–8: *consulta* by Gondomar, 19 January 1619.
31 Altmann, *Reichspolitik*, 199.
32 BGSA, Kasten Schwarz 16688, f. 171, James I to Frederick, 12/22 March 1616.

I.iv The gathering storm

1 Quotations from Sturmberger, 'Die Anfänge des Bruderzwistes in Habsburg', 164; and Franzl, *Ferdinand II*, 116.
2 Quoted in Novotny and Sutter, *Innerösterreich*, 110. Later on, when the Jesuits could boast among their number the confessors of both Maximilian of Bavaria (Adam Contzen) and Ferdinand (William Lamormaini), the General of the Order wrote more than ten times as often to Vienna as to Munich, so frequently was Lamormaini's advice taken by his august charge.

3   See Mecenseffy, *Geschichte des Protestantismus in Oesterreich*, 136; and Reingrabner, *Adel und Reformation*, 17–18.

4   See J. Köhler, 'Franz Kardinal von Dietrichstein, Bischof von Olmütz (1599–1636) und die Prämonstratensen in Mähren', *Archiv für Kirchengeschichte von Böhmen-Mähren-Schlesien*, V (1977), 256–70.

5   Quotations from A. Tenenti, *Piracy and the Decline of Venice, 1580–1615* (Eng. edn, London, 1967), vi, 12, 15. There is no adequate study of the uzkok war, but much information can be gleaned from the following: P. Geyl, *Christofforo Suriano. Resident van de Serenissime Republiek van Venetië in den Haag, 1616–1623* (The Hague, 1913); S. Gigante, 'Venezia e gli Uscocchi', *Fiume: revista semestrale della società di studi fiumani in Fiume*, IX (1931), 3–87; and H. Valentinitsch, 'Ferdinand II, die innerösterreichischen Länder, und der Gradiskanerkrieg (1615–18)', in P. Urban and B. Sutter, eds, *Johannes Kepler 1571–1971. Gedenkschrift der Universität Graz* (Graz, 1975), 497–539. See also p. 303 below.

6   On the first Mantuan succession war see A. Bombín Pérez, *La cuestión de Monferrato 1613–1617* (Vitoria, 1976: note, however, that the maps of Spain's Imperial communications included at the back of the book are largely incorrect. The correct itineraries are shown on Map 2 in the present volume.) On the culture of the Gonzaga dukes, see the excellent catalogue of the exhibition displayed in 1981 at the Victoria and Albert Museum: D. Chambers and J. Martineau, eds, *Splendours of the Gonzaga* (London, 1981), especially pages 203–47. There was almost war in Italy in 1610 also, again provoked by the ambitious and fickle duke of Savoy, Charles Emmanuel: see A. Bombín Pérez, 'La Política anti-española de Carlos Manuel I de Saboya, 1607–10', *Cuadernos de investigación histórica*, II (1978), 153–73.

7   Totals from AGS, Contaduría Mayor de Cuentas 2a época, 706 and 2059. The Oñate treaty was signed on 20 March 1617 and ratified in July.

8   Franzl, *Ferdinand II*, 169. Heinrich Schütz composed a setting (now lost) of *Apollo and the nine muses* for this occasion. It was practically his first commission as Chapel Director to the Elector of Saxony.

9   There is a fine sonnet by Wordsworth on the Fuentes Fort, and also a description in his wife's journals (1821–2). See: W. Knight, ed., *The Poetical Works of William Wordsworth*, VI (London, 1896), 328–32. See also A. Giussani, *Il forte di Fuentes. Episode e documenti di una lotta secolare per il dominio della Valtellina* (Como, 1905). On the Valtelline crisis of 1618–20, see *The Cambridge Modern History*, IV, chapter 2: 'The Valtelline'; and A. Rotondò, 'Esuli italiani in Valtellina nel '500', *Rivista storica italiana*, LXXXVIII (1976), 756–91.

10 AGS, Guerra Antigua, 808, unfol., *consulta* of 26 December 1616. In fact the Dutch troops went to help Venice, so hostilities were

averted; but the decision illustrates the government's belligerent mood. For an admirable account of developments during the Truce, see Israel, *The Dutch Republic and the Hispanic World*, chaps 1–2, and Brightwell, 'The Spanish system and the Twelve Years' Truce'.

11 Quoted in *The New Cambridge Modern History*, IV (Cambridge, 1970), 280.

12 Quoted by Polišenský, *Thirty Years' War*, 94.

13 See J.V. Polišenský and F. Snider, *War and Society in Europe, 1618–48* (Cambridge, 1978), 202–16.

14 Details from R. Schreiber, *Das Spenderbuch für den Bau der protestantischen Salvatorkirche in Prag, 1610–1615* (Salzburg, 1956).

15 Quoted by J.K. Zeman, 'Responses to Calvin and Calvinism among the Czech brethren (1540–1605)', *American Society for Reformation Research Occasional Papers*, I (1977) 41–52, at page 45.

16 Details from J. Polišenský, 'Die Universität Jena und der Aufstand der Böhmischen Stände in den Jahren 1618–1620', *Wissenschaftliche Zeitschrift der Friedrich-Schiller-Universität Jena*, VII (1957–8), 441–7; and A. Ernstberger, *Die Universität Nürnberg-Altdorf während des dreissigjährigen Krieges in ihrem Bestande bedroht* (Munich, 1966: Bayerische Akademie der Wissenschaften, philosophische-historische Klasse, Jahrgang 1966, part II).

17 And the hatred was well-founded. In 1547 the Ernestine branch was deprived by Charles V of the Electoral title, and most of their lands, in favour of the Albertine branch. The dukes of Saxe-Weimar were descended from the former Electoral family and never forgave either their cousins or the Habsburgs.

18 See R.J.W. Evans, 'Learned societies in Germany in the seventeenth century', *European Studies Review*, VII (1977), 129–51; and M. Bircher and F. van Ingen, eds, *Sprachgesellschaften, Sozietäten, Dichtergruppen* (Hamburg, 1978: Wolfenbütteler Arbeiten zur Barockforschung, VII). The latter note that, of the twenty-three learned societies founded in Germany during the seventeenth century, seven were established in or before 1620 and thirteen in or before 1649 (page 54). Ironically, so many foreigners belonged to the *Fruchtbringende Gesellschaft* that most of its transactions had to be carried out in French!

Chapter II The indecisive war

1 The importance of faction in the formation of government policy during the 1620s has been argued most convincingly by Simon Adams: see 'The Protestant cause' and 'Spain or the Netherlands: the dilemmas of early Stuart foreign policy'. I have learnt a great deal from both works, and also from frequent discussions with Dr Adams, about these complex matters.

II.i   The war for Bohemia

1   AGS, Estado 2503 f. 7, Oñate *parecer* of 30 May 1618; BNM, MS. 18434, unfol., Oñate to the king, 10 January 1619.
2   AGS, Estado 1867, f. 256, Philip III apostil on a consulta of 11 January 1619.
3   Figures from Kessel, *Spanien und die geistlichen Kurstaaten*, 53 n. 171.
4   Details from R.R. Heinisch, *Salzburg im dreissigjährigen Krieg* (Vienna, 1968), 10–11. Salzburg, however, never became a full member of the League – much to Maximilian's chagrin.
5   See Reade, *Sidelights on the Thirty Years' War*, I, 182–3. Savoy's aid had its price, however: the duke asked for the Union's support in his bid to be elected king of Bohemia and, if possible, Holy Roman Emperor, too.
6   Quotation from Toegel, 'Příčiny saského vpádu do Čech', 560 n. 16.
7   M. Lee, ed., *Dudley Carleton to John Chamberlain, 1603–1624* (New Brunswick, 1972), 270–1: letter of 18 September 1619.
8   The treaty is discussed by Geyl, *Christofforo Suriano*, 188–9; and A. van der Essen, 'L'alliance défensive hollando-venétienne de 1619 et l'Espagne', in *Miscellanea historica in honorem Leonis van der Essen* (Louvain, 1947), 819–29.
9   AGS, Estado 2504 f. 110, Pedro de San Juan to Oñate, 21 August 1619. The Palatine vote was originally cast for Maximilian of Bavaria, but the Union leaders demanded unanimity in the final election, so in the end the Palatine vote also went to Ferdinand.
10   Quotations from P. Brightwell, 'The Spanish system and the Twelve Years' Truce', *English Historical Review*, LXXXIX (1974), 289; and AGS, Estado 1897, f. 375, paper of 10 December 1619.
11   Straub, *Pax et Imperium*, 161, quotes the forecast of the Spanish Council of State that there would be 'eternal war'. See other predictions quoted in G. Parker, *Europe in Crisis 1598–1648* (London, 1979), 163.
12   Lord Digby quoted by Zaller, 'Interest of State', 166.
13   S.R. Gardiner, *Letters and Documents Illustrating the Relations between England and Germany*, II (London, 1868: Camden Society, XCVIII), 7: Carleton to Naunton, 13 September 1619; Smit and Roelevink, eds, *Resolutiën der Staten-Generaal*, n.r. IV, resolutions 332, 585, 759, 1548, 1554, 1779, 3911, 4119, 4178, 4486 and 4535.
14   Quotations from Magen, *Reichsgräfliche Politik in Franken*, 190.
15   Chancellor Lobkovic to Angoulême, quoted by Pagès, *Thirty Years' War*, 71.

II.ii Europe and the Palatine war

1   Conway, English envoy in Prague, quoted by Reade, *Sidelights on the Thirty Years' War*, I, 388. Many in England were incredulous;

others downcast. Cf. Mr Aylesbury to Sir Henry Martin, 28 November 1620: 'The news of the overthrow in Bohemia is confirmed, but is too bad to repeat' (O. Ogle and W. Bliss, eds, *Calendar of the Clarendon State Papers preserved in the Bodleian Library*, I [Oxford, 1872], 19).

2   See the observations of Schubert, *Camerarius*, 96, 194–5. Ferdinand II also employed precedents from the war of the Schmalkaldic League to justify both the publication of the Ban against Frederick in January 1621 without summoning a Diet, and the transfer of the Palatine electorate to Bavaria: Albrecht, *Auswärtige Politik*, 49.

3   When Ansbach died in 1625, Christian of Denmark commented savagely 'he should have died seven years ago'. (Quoted by Herold, *Ansbach*, 257–8.)

4   Ten Raa and de Bas, *Het Staatsche Leger*, III, 227–30, 243–4. ARA, Eerste Afdeling, Staten-Generaal, Lias Duitsland 6065 (1622), n.f., Elizabeth, queen of Bohemia, to the States-General, 22 March 1622. See also the comments of Schubert, *Camerarius*, 219–22, and Israel, *The Dutch Republic*, 99, 154–7, assessing the policies of Maurice of Nassau.

5   Magen, *Reichsgräfliche Politik*, 228–9; Wertheim, *Braunschweig*, II, 210; Schubert, *Camerarius*, 146. For the Segeberg conference, see Christiansen, *Christians IV*, 43–57, and PRO, S.P. 75/5/235–7, 243–4, Sir Robert Anstruther to Sir George Calvert, 10/20 March, 31 March/ 10 April 1621. James I provided the security for Christian IV's loan to Frederick: at the time of his death in 1625 both the principal and the interest (18,000 thalers annually) remained outstanding.

6   PRO, S.P. 14/164/11, Bishop Carleton to his brother, ? May 1624; W. Notestein, F.H. Relf and H. Simpson, eds, *The Commons Debates for 1621*, V (New Haven, 1935), 203–4. See also, in general, White, 'Suspension of arms'; Straub, *Pax et Imperium*, chap. 5; and M.S. Junkelmann, 'Feldherr Maximilians: Johann Tserclaes, Graf von Tilly', in Glaser, ed., *Um Glauben und Reich*, II/i, 379–80 (plus copious notes).

7   PRO, S.P. 81/24/42, James to Frederick, 22 April/2 May 1622.

8   See PRO, S.P. 81/26/179–80, Frederick to Elizabeth, 14 August 1622.

9   For French policy toward the Valtelline question, see the two articles by Pithon: 'Les Débuts Difficiles du Ministère de Richelieu' and 'La Suisse, Théâtre de la Guerre Froide'. Spanish policy can be traced in the correspondence and *consultas* of the *consejo de estado* in AGS, Estado K 1492, ff. 20–80; see especially f. 55 for the concern over the military situation in August 1622; ff. 67, 70, 72, 73 for the decision to accept the papal garrisons; and ff. 76, 78 for Olivares's attitude toward the crisis.

10   Digby to Calvert, 12 August 1621, in *State Papers collected by Edward earl of Clarendon*, I (Oxford, 1767), appendix p. xvii.

11   The German edition, *Prodromus*, was published at Emden on 22 March 1622; the Latin version appeared at Amsterdam. Both were the work of the Palatine minister, Ludwig Camerarius. Its 173 pages

of document-and-commentary proved sensational – not least because seventeenth-century governments so rarely published official documents – and it was reprinted several times. See Schubert, *Camerarius*, 108–43; and Nolden, *Reichspolitik Kaiser Ferdinands*, 91–7.

12 Quoted by Kessel, *Spanien und die geistlichen Kurstaaten*, 90.

13 It was argued that in 1329, by the treaty of Pavia, the Palatine and Bavarian branches of the Wittelsbach family had agreed that the Electorate should alternate between them, even though the arrangement had never actually operated. But Maximilian's defence betrayed the underlying weakness of the Catholic case, for the reason why the 1329 pact was stillborn lay in the terms of a far more important later document: the Golden Bull of 1356, which vested the Wittelsbach Electorate in the Palatine branch for ever. The treaty of Pavia also detached the Upper Palatinate from Bavaria. See K.F. Krieger, 'Bayerische-Pfälzische Unionsbestrebungen vom Hausvertrag von Pavia (1329) bis zur Wittelsbachischen Hausunion vom Jahre 1724', *Zeitschrift für historische Forschung* IV (1977), 385–413.

14 There is a fine account of the 'Spanish Match' in R. Lockyer, *Buckingham. The life and political career of George Villiers, First Duke of Buckingham 1592–1628* (London, 1981), chapter 5; and of the consequences of its failure in chapter 6.

15 Gustavus Adolphus's propaganda campaign is discussed in S. Arnoldsson, *Krigspropagand i Sverige före Trettioåriga Kriget* (Gothenburg, 1941). We are very grateful to Professor E.L. Petersen for this reference. For Oxenstierna's dominance in the Swedish council see N. Ågren, 'Rise and decline of an aristocracy: the Swedish social and political elite in the seventeenth century', *Scandinavian Journal of History*, I (1976), 55–80. Of seventy-two councillors appointed between 1602 and 1647, no less than fifty-four belonged to a group related to the chancellor and his closest allies.

16 For the war in Poland, see Roberts, *Swedish Imperial Experience*, 33–5, which relies (as does the present account) on A. Norberg, *Polen i svensk politik 1617–1626* (Stockholm, 1974) – described, rightly, by Roberts (p. 33) as perhaps 'the most significant contribution to the debate on the king's foreign policy to appear for forty years'.

17 Camerarius to Baron Rusdorf, 24 December 1623, quoted by Schubert, 'Die pfälzische Exilregierung', 672.

18 Schubert, *Camerarius*, 252–4, 257.

19 For the negotiations leading to the 'French match' see Adams, 'Foreign policy', 157–8. Details of France's resumption of influence on the Rhine, and beyond, are given in Kessel, *Spanien und die geistlichen Kurstaaten*, part III; and Weber, *Frankreich, Kurtrier, passim*.

20 For the complicated terms of the treaty, see Bonney, *King's Debts*, 122.

21 D.L.M. Avenel, ed., *Lettres, Instructions diplomatiques et Papiers d'Etat du Cardinal de Richelieu*, I (Paris, 1853), 85, Richelieu to Sieur Eschieli [= Father Joseph], ? May 1625. On the dilemmas of Richelieu's foreign policy, see also the comments of Pithon, 'Débuts Difficiles', 316–18, and Albrecht, *Auswärtige Politik*, 124, 127, 144.

II.iii The Danish intermezzo

1 See, on this question, Petersen, 'Defence, war and finance'.

2 On the government of Bremen-Verden, and Christian's relations to Hamburg, respectively, see Schleif, *Regierung und Verwaltung des Erzstifts Bremen am Beginn der Neuzeit*, and H.–D. Loose, *Hamburg und Christian IV. von Dänemark während des dreissig-jährigen Krieges* (Hamburg, 1963), chapters I–III.

3 Christiansen, *Die Stellung König Christians IV*, 33; E. Ladewig Petersen, *Christian IV.s pengeudlån til danske adelige. Kongelig foretagervirksomhed og adelig gældsstiftelse 1596–1625* [Christian IV's loans to the Danish nobility. Royal Enterprise and noble indebtedness, 1596–1625] (Copenhagen, 1974), 46–58, 102f., 116–18, 169–71.

4 See BL, MS. Stowe 176 f. 258, Anstruther to Sir Thomas Edmondes, 10 August 1624; PRO, S.P. 84/120/169. Anstruther to Sir Dudley Carleton, 3 November 1624; and S.P. 75/6/30, Abstract of negotiations with Denmark and Sweden, January–February 1625. (References kindly communicated by Dr Simon Adams.)

5 BL, MS. Harley 1584, ff. 29–30, Instructions for Buckingham concerning Denmark, 17/27 October 1625. In the end, the duke managed to persuade the allies to integrate Mansfeld's diminished forces into the Danish army. (My thanks again to Dr Adams.)

6 The text of the 'Hague Convention' is to be found in L. Laursen, ed., *Danmark-Norges Traktater 1523–1750* (Traités du Danemark et de la Norvège, 1523–1750), III (Copenhagen, 1916), no. 38; cf. the introduction, pp. 620–37.

7 See, on the battle, the interesting reconstruction by K.J.V. Jespersen, 'Slaget ved Lutter am Barenberg, 1626', *Krigshistorisk tidsskrift*, IX (1973), 80–9.

8 Petersen, 'Defence, war and finance', based upon a study of the royal war ledgers in *Rigsarkivet*, Copenhagen.

9 S. Heiberg, 'De ti tønder guld: Rigsråd, kongemagt og statsfinanser i 1630'erne' [The ten barrels of gold: State council, monarchy and public finance in the 1630s], *Historisk tidsskrift* [Dansk]., LXXVI (1976), 39ff.

10 *Ibid.*, 49–57; on the social and economic consequences of the postwar period, see E. Ladewig Petersen, *Fra rangssamfund til standssamfund, 1550—1700: Dansk socialhistorie*, III (Copenhagen, 1980), 317–413. See also pp. 302–3 below.

Chapter III The Habsburgs victorious

III.ii The practice of absolutism I

1   The most up-to-date survey of the question is A. Klima, 'Inflation in Bohemia in the early stage of the seventeenth century', in M. Flinn, ed., *Seventh International Economic History Conference* (Edinburgh, 1978), 374–86. Figures on the composition of the Bohemian nobility are taken from Polišenský and Snider, *War and Society in Europe 1618–1648*, 202–16, and F. Snider, 'The restructuring of the Bohemian nobility in the seventeenth century'. There were, naturally, exceptions to this bleak picture – such as the lands owned by Wallenstein (*Terra felix* as his domain was known). Hence Bohemia's grain exports to Saxony, which had averaged 1,800 tons annually in 1597–1621, still averaged 1,300 tons in 1629–43. (See V. Sadova, 'Eksport czeskiego zboza do Niemieć . . . w okresie przed Biala Gora', *Roczniki dziejów spolecznych i Gospodarczych*, XXII (1960), 37–47.)

2   Friedrichs, *Nördlingen*, 27 n. 45.

3   There is a sound if somewhat dated account of the background to the currency fluctuations of the early 1620s by W.A. Shaw, 'The monetary movements of 1600–21 in Holland and Germany', *Transactions of the Royal Historical Society*, new series IX (1895), 189–213. See also Friedrichs, *Nördlingen*, 27–8, and F. Redlich, 'Die deutsche Inflation des frühen 17. Jahrhunderts in der zeitgenössischen Literatur: die Kipper und Wipper', in H. Kellenbenz, ed., *Forschungen zur internationalen Sozial- und Wirtschaftsgeschichte* VI (Cologne and Vienna, 1972). It is notable that of forty or so publications condemning the inflation, all of them composed by Lutherans, thirteen were popular tracts, eleven were written by churchmen, but sixteen were produced by jurists (who condemned the coining of cheap money from the standpoint of constitutional law).

4   W. Gegenfurtner, 'Jesuiten in der Oberpfalz. Ihr Wirkung und ihr Beitrag zur Rekatholisierung in den oberpfälzischen Landen, 1621–50', *Beiträge zur Geschichte Bistums Regensburg*, XI (1977), 71–220, at p. 170. See also P. Schertl, 'Die Amberger Jesuiten im ersten Dezennium ihres Wirkens (1621–32)', *Verhandlungen des historischen Vereins für Oberpfalz und Regensburg*, CII (1962), 101–94, and CIII (1963), 257–350.

5   Details from Evans, *Habsburg Monarchy*, 123, and 425–6.

6   See F. Menk, 'Restitution vor dem Restitutionsedikt. Kurtrier, Nassau und das Reich, 1626–9', *Jahrbuch für westdeutsche Landesgeschichte*, V (1979), 103–30 – a most important article.

7   See Egler, *Spanier in der linksrheinischen Pfalz*, 134 and map on p. 149; and Kessel, *Spanien und die geistlichen Kurstaaten*, 269ff.

8   On the finances of the League, demonstrating that only Bavaria's contributions were paid promptly or in full, see F. Stieve, 'Das

"Contobuch" der deutschen Liga', *Deutsche Zeitschrift für Geschichtswissenschaft*, 1st series X (1893), 97–106. Tilly's army cost around 5 million thalers a year and Bavaria paid three times as much to the war-chest in 1619–27 as all the other League members put together. The bishops of Würzburg, for example, may have been mighty warriors in the Lord, but of the 1.4 million thalers they owed in contributions to the Catholic League, 1620–31, less than 500,000 were paid. (See R. Weber, *Würzburg und Bamberg im dreissigjährigen Krieg: die Regierungszeit des Bischofs Franz von Hatzfeldt, 1631—42* [Würzburg, 1979].)

9　*Der oberösterreichische Bauernkrieg*, 8–11; H. Tüchle, ed., *Acta SC de Propaganda Fide, Germaniam Spectantia. Die Protokolle der Propagandakongregation zu deutschen Angelegenheiten 1622–1649* (Paderborn, 1962), 488.

10　Tüchle, *Acta*, 181 (resolution of 4 February 1628).

11　Father Hyacinth to Dr Jocher in May 1624, quoted by W. Goetz, 'Pater Hyazinth', *Historische Zeitschrift*, CIX (1912), 101–28, at p. 122.

12　Lamormaini quoted by Bireley, *Religion and Politics*, 21.

III.iii The practice of absolutism II

1　See Gross, *Empire and Sovereignty*, passim; and the useful review article of H. Dreitzel, 'Das deutsche Staatsdenken in der frühen Neuzeit', *Neue politische Literatur*, XVI (1971), 17 12. Most helpful of all, however, is the thesis of Nolden, *Die Reichspolitik Kaiser Ferdinands II*.

2　Onno Klopp, 'Das Restitutions-Edikt im nordwestlichen Deutschland', *Forschungen zur deutschen Geschichte*, I (1862), 75–132, especially pp. 86–90, which is still the best essay on the subject. John George's patience began to fray when the emperor forced the Protestant canons of Magdeburg to accept his teenage son Leopold William as Administrator, despite the fact that they had already declared their support for John George's son August. (See Ritter, *Deutsche Geschichte*, II, 422–3.)

3　Quoted from Mann, *Wallenstein* [German edn], 369.

4　Kessel, *Spanien und die geistlichen Kurstaaten*, 197n. On the 'Almirantazgo' system and the blockade see Alcalá-Zamora, *España, Flandes y el mar del Norte*, part 2, and Israel, *The Dutch Republic and the Hispanic World*, 204–23. The Elector of Cologne and his fellow prelates clearly suspected that Spain was endeavouring to build up a power-base in the Empire from which to subvert German liberties. They sent envoys to Brussels, and they directed a constant barrage of criticism towards the courts of Vienna and Madrid in an effort to persuade Spain to withdraw her forces. But these spiritual rulers could not afford to protest too loudly: if ever the armies of Frederick V or his allies returned, as they had done in 1622 and 1623, the rich corridor of ecclesiastical territories in the Rhine and Main area would be a prime target. Even as they petitioned for the evacuation of the Palatinate, they felt obliged to plead for guarantees that troops would be sent back from the Netherlands to defend them in case of Protestant attack. Despite their deep desire to remain neutral in the struggle between the Habsburgs and their enemies, the Rhineland prelates were caught in Spain's net for as long as France lacked the power to intervene effectively abroad. The most they could do was refuse to aid Spain's campaigns against the Dutch, in the hope that the war there would prevent the Habsburgs from exploiting their advantage. As the exasperated Elector of Cologne wrote in June 1626: 'The Netherlands *must* remain divided, with one side controlling just as little territory as the other'. (Kessel, *op. cit.*, 190n.)

5   For further details, see K. Beck, *Der hessische Bruderzwist zwischen Hessen-Kassel und Hessen-Darmstadt in den Verhandlungen zum westfälischen Frieden von 1644 bis 1648* (Frankfurt, 1978); Thies, *Territorialstaat, passim*; and Keim, 'Landgraf Wilhelm V von Hessen-Kassel'. Maurice abdicated in 1627, in a vain attempt to thwart the sequestration order. Many items belonging to him are displayed in the Landgräfliche Kunstkammer preserved in the Town Museum of Kassel.

6   The ducal palace of Güstrow, extended by Wallenstein, still stands. Besides the antlers of countless giant stags, lavishly mounted and accompanied by helpful notes on the kill by the dukes who shot them, the palace boasts a large collection of hunting weapons and even a dining hall decorated with stags in bas relief bearing real antlers. It was a baroque fantasy which that German Nimrod, John George of Saxony, might have envied.

7   The best account still seems to be that of Gindely, *Waldstein während seines ersten Generalats*, who shows how Wallenstein's actions polarized the various Catholic and Lutheran factions of Germany in reaction to his brutally destructive military methods. It is worth also re-examining the debate of the 1880s between Hallwich and Gindely about Wallenstein's economic motives and methods, which seems to be as fresh now as it was then, despite all the biographical and archival work on Wallenstein undertaken in the last decade by Golo Mann, H. Diwald, J. Kollmann, P. Suvanto, J. Polišenský and others: compare Anton Gindely, *Zur Beurtheilung des kaiserlichen Generals im dreissigjährigen Krieg, Albrechts von Waldstein* (Prague, 1887), with the same author's *Zweite Antwort an Dr. Hallwich* (Vienna, 1887). Despite the attempt of M. Ritter, 'Das Kontributionssystem Wallensteins', *Historische Zeitschrift*, LV (1903), 193–249, to show that Wallenstein kept good military discipline, the fact remains that the cost of his army was too great to be borne by anyone in the long term. As yet, the last word remains with F.H. Schubert, 'Wallenstein und der Staat des 17. Jahrhunderts', *Geschichte in Wissenschaft und Unterricht*, XVI (1965), 597–611 [reprinted in Rudolf, ed., *Der dreissigjährige Krieg*, 185–207], who saw him as a financier and

military mercantilist, far too impatient to be able to influence at a stroke Imperial foreign policy with its laboriously entangled confessionalism and bureaucracy.

8 Hans Schulz, ed., *Der dreissigjährige Krieg*, I (Leipzig, 1917), document 21: Wallenstein to Ferdinand, 6 July 1626. An earlier plea along similar lines is contained in a letter of Wallenstein to Ferdinand, from Stötterlingenburg, 25 October 1625, in J. Kollmann, ed., *Documenta Bohemica Bellum Tricennale illustrantia*, IV, *1625–30* (Prague, 1974), document 88.

9 On Bishop Franz Wilhelm, see Klopp, 'Das Restitutionsedikt' (note 2 above); also T. Tupetz, *Der Streit um die Geistlichen Güter und das Restitutionsedikt 1629* (Vienna, 1883). J.H. Gebauer, *Kurbrandenburg und das Restitutionsedikt von 1629* (Halle, 1899) shows how politically unwise extreme Catholics were prepared to be. Above all, see H. Günter, *Das Restitutionsedikt von 1629 und die katholische Restauration Altwirtembergs* (Stuttgart, 1901).

10 Bireley, *Religion and Politics*, 51, quoting Ferdinand's Instructions to his representative (Stralendorf) at Mühlhausen, 4 October 1627. Clearly, the emperor was under some pressure on this point.

11 The Edict is printed in M.C. Lundorp, ed., *Acta publica*, III (Frankfurt, 1668), 1048–54. Over 100 copies still survive of the various editions – a surprisingly large number. For details on how it was published, see H. Urban, 'Druck und Drucke des Restitutionsedikts von 1629', *Archiv für Geschichte des Buchwesens*, XIV (1974), cols 609–54 – the *Radix omnium malorum* copy is reproduced at col. 635. Further discussion of the Edict's preparation and significance may be found in Bireley, *op. cit.*, 52–9 and 74–94.

12 'Quicquid concessum non reperitur, prohibitum censeri debet': see *Pacis compositio inter principes et ordines catholicos atque Augustanae confessionis adhaerentes* (Dillingen, 1629), Bk VI, chap. 37, paras 4–7. On Laymann and the 'Dillingen book', sponsored by Bishop Knöringen of Augsburg and distributed with the blessing of the Imperial Privy Council, see Heckel, 'Autonomia und Pacis Compositio', and R. Bireley, 'The origins of the "Pacis Compositio" (1629): a text of Paul Laymann S.J.', *Archivum historicum societatis Iesu*, XLII (1973), 106–27.

13 There is a splendid account of the siege in *Monro his expedition*, part I, 62–80 ('Trailesound' = Stralsund). For a modern, more comprehensive account of the city and its history, see: H. Langer, *Stralsund 1600–1630: eine Hansestadt in der Krise und im europäischen Konflikt* (Weimar, 1970).

14 Schulz, *Der dreissigjährige Krieg*, document 33.

15 Kollmann, ed., *Documenta Bohemica*, IV, 414–46. Although the figures represent only paper-strength, they indicate the scale of the problem. The cost was, of course, awesome. The archbishopric of Magdeburg reckoned its expenditure on contributions by September 1627 at 687,000 thalers; the duchy of Pomerania claimed to have paid 1.7 million by July 1628; and so on.

16 See Klopp, *op. cit.*, 815, 853. The *Kurfürstentag* at Mühlhausen, a Free City in Thuringia, was used by Elector John George as a stage for self-advertisement. He commissioned his court composer, Heinrich Schütz, to write the work *Da pacem* for the occasion. It included an anthem for two choirs, one singing outside the assembly point as each Elector arrived, the other within, intoning the Latin collect for peace. See R. Petzoldt, *Heinrich Schütz and his times in pictures* (Kassel and London, 1972).

17 *Die Politik Maximilians I. von Bayern*, 4.ii, 1628 – Juni 1629, 348.

18 See the excellent account of these campaigns in Israel, *The Dutch Republic*, 162–81.

III.iv Spain and the war

1 Olivares to count of Gondomar, quoted in Brown and Elliott, *A Palace for a King*, 190.

2 AGS, Estado 2331 f. 126, Olivares in the Council of State, 10 November 1630.

3 A Junta of the Council of State, meeting on 2 June 1625, recommended that the proposed alliance should not be based on religious affiliation – an argument with which Olivares concurred, on the grounds that Saxony's participation was indispensable (AGS, Estado 2327 ff. 371 and 372).

4 Straub, *Pax et Imperium*, 285n: opinion from December 1627. The Spanish government tried to avoid declaring war on Denmark even as late as June 1626, 'because we find ourselves with so many inescapable enemies, it does not seem right to seek more deliberately'. Olivares believed that the Habsburgs should learn to live with the Lutherans. (Günter, *Die Habsburger-Liga*, 14 n. 53: Olivares's opinion dated 20 June 1626.) On the suspicions in Paris, see Lutz, *Kardinal Giovanni Francesco Guidi di Bagno*, book II.

5 C. Seco Serrano, *Cartas de Sor María de Jesús de Ágreda y de Felipe IV*, I (Madrid, 1958: Biblioteca de Autores Españoles, CVIII), 28: letter of Philip IV, Zaragoza, 20 July 1645 (thus written over two years after the fall of Olivares); Q. Aldea Vaquero, *España, el Papado y el Imperio durante la Guerra de los Treinta Años. II Instrucciones a los nuncios apostólicos en España (1624–32)* (Comillas, 1958), 32: Urban VIII's instructions to nuncios, 1 May 1632.

6 In this he may well have been correct. See the analysis of the political views of Ferdinand's leading advisers in Bireley, *Religion and Politics*, chapter 1. Certainly Eggenberg went to Spain in 1598–9 and 1605 and collected Spanish objets d'art and books – his library included *Don Quixote* and a complete edition of Lope's plays (extensively annotated by Eggenberg). The prince's splendid castle, built just outside Graz in the early seventeenth century, could almost pass as Spanish.

7 AGS, Estado 2331 f. 126, Olivares in the Council of State, 10 November 1630.

8   However, by insisting on his right to invest the new duke of
      Mantua, the emperor at least made one gain from the war: he
      established for all time his rights of suzerainty over the states of
      northern Italy. Never again would they be challenged. But this
      development, which smoothed the path to eventual direct rule by
      Austria between the Alps and the Po, lay far in the future. For the
      moment, Habsburg humiliation was as visible in Vienna as it was
      in Madrid. See K.O. von Aretin, 'Die Lehensordnungen in Italien
      im 16. und 17. Jahrhundert und ihre Auswirkungen auf die euro-
      päische Politik', in H. Weber, ed., *Politische Ordnungen und
      soziale Kräfte im Alten Reich* (Wiesbaden 1980: Veröffent-
      lichungen des Instituts für europäische Geschichte Mainz.
      Abteilung Universalgeschichte. Beiheft VIII), 53–84 – especially
      pp. 57–9 and 77.

Chapter IV Total war

1   See the interesting study of Gross, *Empire and Sovereignty*, on the
      'Public Law' debate. See also O. Brunner, 'Souveränitätsproblem
      und Sozialstruktur in den deutschen Reichsstädten der frühen
      Neuzeit', *Vierteljahrschrift für Sozial und Wirtschaftsgeschichte*, L
      (1963), 329–60, especially pp. 347–51. There is a clear parallel here
      with the 'Ancient Constitution' debate in early Stuart England: in
      both countries, the language of law dominated the vocabulary of
      politics.
2   Figures from P. Hohenemser, ed., *Flugschriftensammlung Gustav
      Freytag* (Frankfurt, 1925), nos 4771–5794. Admirable collections of
      popular literature about the war may be found in D. Alexander and
      W.L. Strauss, *The German Single-Leaf Woodcut 1600–1700. A
      pictorial catalogue* (New York, 1978); E.A. Beller, *Caricatures of
      the 'Winter King' of Bohemia* (Oxford, 1928); *idem, Propaganda in
      Germany during the Thirty Years' War* (Princeton, 1940); M.
      Bohatcová, *Irrgarten des Schicksals: Einblattdrucke vom Anfang
      des dreissigjährigen Krieges* (Prague, 1966); and W.A. Coupe, *The
      German Illustrated Broadsheet of the Seventeenth Century* (2 vols,
      Baden-Baden, 1966–7).
3   P. Rassow, *Die geschichtliche Einheit des Abendlandes* (Cologne
      and Graz, 1960), 306.

IV.i On the edge of the abyss

1   Bireley, *Religion and Politics*, 125: the account was by Kaspar
      Schoppe (Scioppius), an anti-Jesuit Catholic polemicist. It would
      seem that the Protestants did not expect any concessions on the
      Edict of Restitution. And yet the emperor gained surprisingly little
      from maintaining it: although thirty-seven Imperial cities suffered
      from strictly illegal attempts to implement the Edict, in only seven

was a clear change of political regime effected.

2   On papal diplomacy during the later 1620s, see Lutz, *Kardinal Giovanni Francesco Guidi di Bagno*, book II; Aldea, *España, el Papado y el Imperio*; and *idem*, 'La neutralidad de Urban VIII'. On the French campaigns in Italy, see J. Humbert, *Les Français en Savoie sous Louis XIII* (Paris, 1960).

3   Quoted by O'Connell, 'A cause célèbre in the history of treaty-making', 84.

4   'The Catholic Electors to the Bishop of Bamberg, Regensburg, 18 December 1630', in M.C. Lundorp, *Der Römischen Kayserlichen Majestät und Dess Heiligen Römischen Reichs . . . Acta Publica*, IV (Frankfurt-am-Main, 1668), 103.

5   See Matthias Hoë von Hoënegg, *Homiliae über den 83 Psalm, so zu Leipzig in dem Convent der Evangelischen und Protestierenden Chur-Fürsten und Ständen, den 10. Februarij, Anno 1631 Erkläret, und auff jnständiges anhalten und begehren in Truck gegeben* (n.p., 1631).

6   Bergius's influence in Brandenburg church politics is discussed in Bodo Nischan, 'John Bergius: Irenicism and the beginning of official religious toleration in Brandenburg-Prussia', *Church History*, LI (1982), 389–404; and *idem*, 'Calvinism, the Thirty Years' War, and the beginning of Absolutism in Brandenburg: the political thought of John Bergius', *Central European History*, XV (1982), 203–23. His Leipzig sermons were published under the title *Brüderliche Eynträchtigkeit Auss dem Hundert Drey und Dreyssigsten Psalm Bey der Protestirenden Evangelischen Chur-Fürsten und Stände Zusammenkunfft zu Leipzig Anno 1631 . . . in Drey Predigten erkläret* (Frankfurt-an-der-Oder, 1635).

7   See Johannes Bergius, *Abermaliger Abdruck der Relation der Privat-Conferentz, welche bey währendem Convent der Protestirenden Evangelischen Chur-Fürsten vnd den Ständen zu Leipzig im Jahr 1631. Monats Martii zwischen den anwesenden beyderseits Evangelischen, so wol Lutherischen als Reformirten Theologen gehalten worden* (Berlin, 1644). The protocol is also found in Wolfgang Gericke, *Glaubenszeugnisse und Konfessionspolitik der Brandenburgischen Herrscher bis zur Preussischen Union, 1540 bis 1815* (Bielefeld, 1977), 143–56.

8   ZSM, Rep. 21. 127 p. I, pp. 27–9. Minutes of the Leipzig Conference. See also Bodo Nischan, 'Brandenburg's Reformed Räte and the Leipzig Manifesto'.

9   The Leipzig Manifesto is found in Lundorp, *Acta Publica*, IV, pp. 144–6; and J.P. Abelin, *Theatrum Europaeum*, II (Frankfurt-am-Main, 1646), 309–11.

10 See Aldea, *España, el Papado y el Imperio*, 34: Urban VIII's instructions to nuncios going to Spain, 1 May 1632. Maximilian's fears were not unfounded: by the so-called 'Cottington treaty', concluded after the peace of Madrid (which put an end to the Anglo-Spanish conflict in 1631), Spain did make a vague commitment to

'do right' in the Palatinate. See Simon Adams, 'Spain or the Netherlands: the dilemmas of early Stuart Foreign Policy', 100.

11 See Bireley, *Maximilian von Bayern, Adam Contzen*, 168f. On papal promotion of a Franco-Bavarian peace see Aldea, 'Neutralidad', 174f. Some historians have neglected the papacy's role in all this because of the silence of certain sources; however Bagno's correspondence (now among the Barberini Manuscripts of the Vatican archives) affords ample proof. In fact Bagno devoted more space to the Franco-Bavarian negotiations, in his dispatches to Rome between 1628 and 1631, than to any other item. He tried to keep his involvement secret – in a letter to the Bavarian councillor Jocher he noted, 'This matter must be kept most secret, because it might seriously affect my dealings with Spain if it were known that I am involved in creating a close union between France and Bavaria' – but the truth emerged when Bagno's Paris apartment was burgled by a Spanish spy (Bireley, *Religion and Politics*, 160).

12 The text of the treaty of Fontainebleau is given by Albrecht, *Auswärtige Politik*, 378–9.

IV.ii The intervention of Sweden

1 An English version of the *Kriegsmanifest* is printed in G. Symcox, ed., *War, Diplomacy and Imperialism 1618–1763* (London, 1974), 102–13.

2 Quotations from D. Böttcher, 'Propaganda und öffentliche Meinung im protestantischen Deutschland, 1628–36', *Archiv für Reformationsgeschichte*, XLIV (1952), 181–203, at pp. 191–4 (reprinted in Rudolf, *Dreissigjährige Krieg*, 325–67); and Roberts, *Essays in Swedish history*, 84. The exact nature of Sweden's war aims in 1630–1 remains murky, since the available evidence is all open to objection. Thus it might be argued that the Manifesto was moderate in tone because that is the essence of such documents. And Oxenstierna in 1636 might have become more cautious following Sweden's defeat at Nördlingen; or he might have been merely repeating the cautious policies that he (rather than his more impulsive king) had sought to follow in 1630. See further discussion of Sweden's war aims at pp. 156–61 and 182–4 above.

3 The cost to Sweden of the Prussian campaigns, 1626–9, has been estimated at 5 million thalers: Petersen, 'Defence, war and finance', 35.

4 Quoted in K.R. Böhme, 'Das Amt Memel in schwedischer Sequestratur (Nov. 1629 – Jul. 1635)', *Zeitschrift für Ostforschung*, XVIII (1969), 655–703, at p. 657. On the tolls see E. Wendt, *Det Svenska Licentväsendet i Preussen, 1627–35* (Uppsala, 1933), 89, 98, 107, 184–202. There is a good discussion of the peace talks in J.K. Fedorowicz, *England's Baltic Trade in the Early Seventeenth Century. A study in Anglo-Polish commercial diplomacy* (Cambridge, 1980), 189–206.

5   There has been much exaggeration of the Russian subsidy: over the entire period 1629–33, Sweden only gained 160,000 thalers from this source. See the figures and the discussion of L. Ekholm, 'Rysk spannmål och svenska krigsfinanser, 1629–33', *Scandia*, XL (1974), 57–103, partially reprinted in Ekholm, *Svensk krigsfinansiering*.

6   Events were to show that Richelieu had no means of forcing his ally to comply with these restrictive terms. The treaty is published in *Sverges Traktater*, V, 438–40, and discussed in detail in Roberts, *Gustavus Adolphus*, II, 466–9. An English translation of the main clauses is provided in Roberts, *Sweden as a Great Power*, 136–8.

7   Böhme, *art. cit.*, 701; Ekholm, *Svensk krigsfinansiering, passim*. See also the larger, earlier study of K.R. Böhme, *Die schwedische Besetzung des Weichseldeltas 1626–36* (Würzburg, 1963: Beihefte zum Jahrbuch der Albertus-Universität Königsberg, XXII).

8   Newspapers, pamphlets and broadsheets describing the sack, which ranged from exoneration (published in Munich) to accusations of criminal brutality (according to Leipzig) are described and analysed by W. Lahne, *Magdeburgs Zerstörung in der Zeitgenössischen Publizistik* (Magdeburg, 1931; a tricentennial commemoration). See also N. Henningsen, ed., *Die Zerstörung Magdeburgs 1631. Eine Darstellung der historischen Begebenheiten nach Otto von Guerickes Handschrift und nach urkundlichen Quellen* (Cologne, 1911). Wedgwood gives an excellent English account of the sack: *Thirty Years' War*, 286–91.

9   The story is well told in A. Wang, 'Information und Deutung in illustrierten Flugblättern des Dreissigjährigen Krieges. Zum Gebrauchscharakter einiger Blätter des Themas *Sächsich Confect* aus den Jahren 1631 und 1632', *Euphorion: Zeitschrift für Literaturgeschichte*, LXX (1976), 97–116.

10   There are excellent accounts of the battle in *Sveriges Krig*, IV, and Roberts, *Gustavus Adolphus*, II, 535–8. Several of Tilly's banners, which once hung in the Riddarholm Church, are today displayed in the 'State Trophy Collection' of the Army Historical Museum (Stockholm). The tactical innovations of the Swedish army are discussed at pp. 206–7 above.

11   Oluf Hansson's map of 'Mark Brandenburg', which was the best one available to Gustavus in 1631, only covered Germany as far as Frankfurt-on-Oder, Magdeburg and Dessau. (KrA, Krigskådeplatserna 1630–48, 4: Stortformat 2:51.)

12   Stritmatter, *Der Stadt Basel während des dreissigjährigen Krieges*, 66, notes that in 1633 Basle alone contained 5,256 refugees, accompanied by 1,776 cattle. On Sweden's reorganization of Franconia and the Rhineland, see Deinert, *Die Schwedische Epoche*; Müller, *Der schwedische Staat*; and Weber, *Würzburg und Bamberg*. For further details on the Frankfurt convention, see Bireley, *Religion and Politics*, chap. 8 (especially pp. 159 and 167–8).

13   E. Sticht, *Markgraf Christian von Brandenburg-Kulmbach und der dreissigjährige Krieg in Ostfranken 1618–35* (Kulmbach, 1965: see

p. 154 for details on the peasants' revolt and its repression).

14   K. Beck, 'Die Neutralitätspolitik Landgraf Georgs II. von Hessen-Darmstadt. Versuch und Möglichkeiten einer Politik aus christlichen Grundsätzen', *Hessisches Jahrbuch für Landesgeschichte*, XXII (1972), 162–228.

15   *The continuation of our forraine avisoes*, no. XX (28 April 1632), 6. War reporting began during the German conflict and the war was itself a major stimulus to the growth of the newspaper.

16   Opinion of a Bavarian war commissar or war councillor, December 1631, quoted by S. Riezler, *Geschichte Bayerns*, V (Munich, 1890), 395–6. Tilly's tomb in a special chapel by the shrine at Altötting (near Bavaria's border with Austria) is a masterpiece of Post-Tridentine Baroque art. His skull gazes grimly out of a window in the stone sarcophagus, while his figure may be observed in the pietà behind the altar: Tilly kneels incongruously in battle dress to the left of the Cross.

17   On Maximilian in exile, see Heinisch, *Salzburg im dreissigjährigen Kriege*, 141ff.; on Bavaria under Swedish occupation, see: G. Rystad, 'Die Schweden in Bayern wahrend des dreissigjährigen Krieges', in Glaser, ed., *Wittelsbach und Bayern*, II/1, 424–35. See also the eyewitness account of devastation in H. Hörger, 'Die Kriegsjahre 1632 bis 1634 im Tagebuch des P. Maurus Friesenegger, nachmaligen Abtes von Andechs (1640–55)', *Zeitschrift für bayerische Landesgeschichte*, XXXIV (1971), 866–76.

18   The conspirators' identities were revealed to an English agent in Brussels, the painter Balthasar Gerbier, and he sold the names to the Spanish government in November 1633: all were arrested. Further details in A. Waddington, *La République des Provinces-Unies, la France et les Pays-Bas espagnols de 1630 à 1650*, I (Paris, 1895), 147–80; P. Janssens, 'L'échec des tentatives de soulèvement dans les Pays-Bas méridionaux sous Philippe IV (1621–65)', *Revue d'histoire diplomatique*, XCII (1978), 110–29; and Israel, *The Dutch Republic*, 181–90. Pappenheim's assault on the Dutch camp at Maastricht, at the behest of the Elector of Cologne, marked a serious breach in the neutrality observed by the Empire during much of the Dutch Revolt: see P.J.H. Ubachs, 'Neutraliteit, theorie en praktiek tijdens de Tachtigjarige Oorlog', *Tijdschrift voor Geschiedenis*, XCVI (1983), 165–78.

19   AGS, Estado 3336 f. 138, duke of Feria to Philip IV, 12 April 1631. In fact an army of some 12,000 men did cross from Lombardy to the Low Countries later in the year, but they were recruited in Spain and Naples. The most famous account of the plague of 1631 appears in Alessandro Manzoni's novel *The Betrothed* (*I promessi sposi*, first published in 1825–6). For more recent assessments see Sella, *Crisis and Continuity*, 52; and C.M. Cipolla, *Cristofano and the Plague. A study in the history of public health in the age of Galileo* (London, 1973), chap. 1. There is also a useful collection of documents available: *La guerra e la peste nella Milano dei 'Promessi*

Sposi'. *Documenti inediti tratti dagli archivi Spagnoli* (Madrid, 1975: Istituto Italiano di Cultura, Madrid; Collana 'Documenti e Ricerche', IV). Chapter 7 concerns the plague, chapters 3–5 the war.

20   Barberini, papal secretary of state, to Rocci, nuncio in Germany, 27 December 1631, quoted by Repgen, *Die römische Kurie und der Westfälische Friede*, 290, n. 347. This was a fairly threadbare excuse: although the volcanic activity of Vesuvius over the winter of 1631–2 killed thousands and wiped out forty communities, few were papal subjects, and the disaster did not interrupt Pope Urban VIII's lavish spending on his three nephews, which totalled 30 million thalers by the end of his pontificate. On Barberini nepotism, see J. Grisar, 'Päpstliche Finanzen, Nepotismus und Kirchenrecht unter Urban VIII', *Xenia Piana: Miscellanea historiae pontificiae*, VII (Rome, 1943), 205–366; compare the money sent to Germany before 1630 in Albrecht, 'Zur Finanzierung des dreissigjährigen Krieges'.

21   Questenburg, Aulic councillor, to Wallenstein, 23 April 1631, quoted by Suvanto, *Wallenstein und seine Anhänger*, 72.

22   Lukas Behaim, quoted by Ernstberger, 'Die Universität Nürnberg-Altdorf', 10.

23   Goodrick, ed., *The Relation of Sydnam Poyntz*, 73; Elster, *Die Piccolomini-Regimenten*, 40.

24   Examples taken from M.E. Seaton, *Literary Relations of England and Scandinavia in the Seventeenth Century* (Oxford, 1935), 79, 83. See also M.A. Breslow, *A Mirror for England: English Puritan views of foreign nations, 1618–1648* (Harvard, 1970: Harvard Historical Studies, LXXXIV), 134–7.

IV.iii Oxenstierna versus Wallenstein

1   AGRB, Secrétairerie d'État et de Guerre, 207 ff. 293–4, Infanta Isabella to Philip IV, 24 October 1633; *ibid.*, ff. 330–2, same to same, 12 November 1633; and AGS, Estado 3341 f. 88, Cardinal-Infante to the king, 23 February 1634. By the time the last letter was written, Feria was dead and his army decimated. There are some details on his last campaign in K. Beyerle, *Konstanz im dreissigjährigen Kriege. Schicksale bis zur Aufhebung der Belagerung durch die Schweden, 1628–33* (Heidelberg, 1900: Neujahrsblätter der badischen historischen Kommission, N.F. III). On Lorraine during the war, see J. Florange, 'La guerre de trente ans en Lorraine', *Annuaire de la Société d'Histoire et d'Archéologie de Lorraine*, XLVI (1935), 55–123, and Gaber, *La Lorraine meurtrie*. French aggression in this period is discussed more fully in Section IV.iv.

2   See Altmann, *Landgraf Wilhelm V*, part I. The battle of Hessisch-Oldendorf was viewed by Sweden as a major success: see its place of honour on the Triumphal Arch erected by the Regency Council for the coronation of Queen Christina in 1650 (S. Karling, 'L'arc de

triomphe de la Reine Christine à Stockholm', in M. von Platen, ed., *Queen Christina of Sweden. Documents and Studies* (Stockholm, 1966), 159–86, at pp. 170–1).

3   Details from Roberts, 'Oxenstierna in Germany, 1633–1636', 63–71.

4   See B.F. Porshnev, 'Les rapports de l'Europe occidentale et l'Europe orientale à l'époque de la guerre de trente ans', *Rapports du XIe Congrès des Sciences Historiques*, IV (Stockholm, 1960), 136–63.

5   The Gustavsburg is illustrated in Munthe, *Kongliga Fortifikationens Historia*, I, plates 31–2; and described by Müller, *Schwedische Staat*, 145ff.

6   Quoted by M. Roberts, *Sweden as a Great Power 1611–1697* (London, 1968), 146–7. See, in general, R. Nordlund, 'Krig genom ombud. Det svenska krigsfinanserna och Heilbronn förbundet 1633', in Landberg *et al.*, *Det kontinentala krigets ekonomi*, 271–451. Rather like the Protestant Union of 1608–21, the Heilbronn League included too many small states for stability.

7   Quoted in Suvanto, *Wallenstein*, 181.

8   Further details available in Suvanto, *Oxenstierna*, 146–66.

9   Piccolomini to Aldringen, quoted by Mann, *Wallenstein*, 801. On Piccolomini's role in Wallenstein's fall, and for an excellent account of the affair in general, see Barker, *Army, Aristocracy, Monarchy*, 79–97 (part of an extended essay on the Tuscan commander).

10   Suvanto, *Wallenstein*, 158–9, reconstitutes the text of the Göllersdorf agreement with great ingenuity. His argument is reinforced, from other sources, by Lutz, 'Wallenstein, Ferdinand II. und der Wiener Hof'.

11   See the interesting details reproduced from a contemporary pamphlet by A. Hollaender, 'Some English documents on the end of Wallenstein', *Bulletin of the John Rylands Library*, XL (1958), 358–90. Of course, Oxenstierna too was 'a subject become a soveraigne', but few seem to have resented that.

12   How serious was Wallenstein about his 'peace initiative'? Duke Franz-Albrecht of Saxe-Lauenburg, one of the general's closest associates, who was captured three days after his master's death, had no doubt about the matter: 'den praetext der friedens nur vorwendete' he told his captors. And the balance of modern opinion inclines to the view that peace was indeed only a 'pretext' – a bargaining counter that Wallenstein was prepared to exchange for an appanage in the Empire like Bernard of Saxe-Weimar's duchy of Franconia, or like his own duchy of Mecklenburg. On the other hand, it would not have been entirely ridiculous for Wallenstein to dream of becoming king of his native Bohemia. His remote relative, George of Poděbrad, had been elected in 1458; Frederick of the Palatine had been elected in 1619 (and, conveniently, had died in 1632); and, in between, the kingdom had elected rulers from the Jagiellonian and Habsburg dynasties. The young Wallenstein had spent some time in northern Italy, mostly at Padua: he cannot have

been unaware of the state-building activities of condottieri such as Francesco Sforza, Sigismondo Malatesta and Cesare Borgia. No doubt in Padua itself he admired Donatello's flattering statue of the city's chief mercenary captain, Gattamellata. In the age of Oliver Cromwell, one cannot ignore the political careers open to success-ful soldiers. (See the sensitive analysis of F.H. Schubert, 'Wallen-stein und der Staat des 17. Jahrhunderts', *Geschichte in Wissen-schaft und Unterricht*, XVI [1965], 597–611; reprinted in Rudolf, *Dreissigjährige Krieg*, 185–207.)

13   Mutio Vitelleschi, Superior-General of the Jesuit Order, to Lamor-maini, 1 April 1634, quoted by Bireley, *Religion and Politics*, 203. Wedgwood, *Thirty Years' War*, 346–60, provides a fine set-piece, reconstructing Wallenstein's end through meticulous use of the printed sources.

14   See G. Rystad, *Kriegsnachrichten und Propaganda während des dreissigjährigen Krieges: die Schlacht bei Nördlingen in den gleichzeitigen gedruckten Kriegsberichten* (Lund, 1960). There are illustrations of the battle in Angela and Geoffrey Parker, *European Soldiers 1550–1650* (Cambridge, 1977), 46–55. On the battlefield itself, the traces of the gun emplacements thrown up on the Altbuch the night before the battle are still clearly visible, and there is a small memorial column: the site is, like Lützen, well worth a visit.

15   Quotations from Roberts, 'Oxenstierna in Germany', 86, 98 n. 15.

16   William V quoted by Altmann, *Landgraf Wilhelm V*, 84.

17   See the admirable summary of the terms in *Theologische Realen-zyklopädie*, IX (Berlin, 1981), 180 (by K. Repgen). Four of the nine 'Nebenrezesse' have never been published: see Bierther, 'Zur Edi-tion' (page 295 below).

18   Quoted by Repgen, *Römische Kurie*, 337 n. 124, 333 n. 116 and 335–6.

IV.iv France's 'war by diversion'

1   A. Leman, *Urbain VIII et la rivalité de la France et de la maison d'Autriche de 1631 à 1635* (Lille and Paris, 1920), 492.

2   *Acta Pacis Westphalicae*, I, 18–20: Louis XIII to Richelieu, 4 August 1634. The royal views were classified 'top secret': 'âme qui vive ne les a veues', the document states.

3   Leman, *Urbain VIII et la rivalité*, 382.

4   A.J. du Plessis, Cardinal de Richelieu, *Mémoires*, ed. J.F. Michaud and J.J.F. Poujoulat, 2nd ser., VIII (Paris, 1838), 437: 'une longue guerre dans ses entrailles . . .'.

5   *Acta Pacis Westphalicae*, I, 47. (Feb./March 1637).

6   Richelieu, *Mémoires*, 620: 'parce que Sa Majesté n'ayant point de guerre declarée contre l'Empereur . . .'.

7   Montglat gives figures for the relative size of the armies and losses: Montglat, *Mémoires*, ed. J.F. Michaud and J.J.F. Poujoulat, 3rd

ser., V (Paris, 1838), 27, 30. For the finance minister's estimates of the total size of the French army: Bonney, *The King's Debts*, 173 n. 3.

8   *Acta Pacis Westphalicae*, I, 47.
9   Richelieu used the term 'Finnish' (*finnois*) but this was a play on the word for 'cunning' (*finaud*). See Avenel, ed., *Lettres, instructions diplomatiques*, IV, 735.
10   Montglat, *Mémoires*, 41–2.
11   Bonney, *The King's Debts*, 306–7. Conversions based on J.J. McCusker, *Money and Exchange in Europe and America, 1600–1715* (Chapel Hill, N.C., 1978).
12   Montglat, *Mémoires*, 38.
13   Avenel, *Lettres . . . de Richelieu*, V. 965.
14   AMAE, Mémoires et Documents: France, vol. 820 f. 131: Bullion and Bouthillier to Richelieu, 22 February 1636.
15   See, for example, Montglat's comment that the elder Condé, 'quoique grand politique, n'entendoit point la guerre . . .'. (Montglat, *Mémoires*, 41).
16   Livet, *L'intendance d'Alsace sous Louis XIV*, 68, 78–9.
17   AMAE, Mémoires et Documents: France, vol. 834 f. 11v. Bullion to Richelieu, 1639, following the death of Bernard of Saxe-Weimar, who, in Bullion's view, had 'dans l'esprit les fantazie[s]'.

Chapter V Countdown to peace

1   KrA, *Historiska planscher*, 1648, 24 folio: 'Amore pacis: geographische Carten von gantz Teutschland', reproduced here as Plate 17. The manuscript original is in Kungliga Bibliotheket, Stockholm, Kartavd. Y50. An inferior version of the map, but with its commentary in full, was republished in J.G. von Meiern, *Acta pacis Westphalicae publica*, VI (Hannover, 1736; reprinted Osnabrück, 1969), 'Beylage'. The location of the garrisons is revealing. The Swedish army had nineteen garrisons in Alsace, Franconia and Swabia; twenty-nine in the Bohemian lands; twenty-four in Saxony, Brandenburg and Magdeburg; nineteen in Westphalia and the Palatinate; and no less than twenty-seven in Pomerania. The French were all in the south-west; the Hessians all in the north-west. Only the Swedes were everywhere. Imperial bases in 1648 are shown on the map included in the thesis of Hoyos, 'Ernest von Traun'.

V.i The Swedish dilemma

Note: All dates in the correspondence cited in the notes to this section are in OLD STYLE: for New Style, add ten days.
1   Oxenstierna to the Council of State, 4 February 1633, A[xel] O[xen-

stiernas] S[*krifter och*] B[*revvexling*], 1st series, VIII, 162; cf. *ibid.*, XII, 324–5 (Memorandum for Johan Oxenstierna, 28 August 1634).

2 Oxenstierna to Baner, 28 October 1634: *AOSB*, 1st series XII, 633.

3 Oxenstierna to the Council of State, 7 January 1635: *AOSB*, 1st series, XIII, 27.

4 *Svenska riksrådets protokoll* (Handlingar rörande Skandinaviens Historia, 3rd series), VII, 423, 427 (22 January 1639); and VIII, 315 (14 November 1640), where this dictum is quoted.

5 *Svenska riksrådets protokoll*, IV, 253 (4 December 1634); VI, 185 (25 April 1636).

6 *Ibid.*, VI, 504 (30 July 1636).

7 See the new study of the French subsidies paid to Sweden, and how they were employed, by Lorenz: 'Schweden und die französichen Hilfsgelder' (pages 298–9 below).

8 In the debate in the Council of State on 21 November 1640 Oxenstierna told them: 'I may now say, what I have never said here openly before – and what perhaps many think that I do not believe – that there can well come a time when we could retire from the German war and let it go at any price, not retaining a foot of land. I should indeed be prepared to be persuaded easily to that, and had long since advised you to it, if the contempt which some of those out there have for us had not been so great, and if it could have been done with reputation and safety'. And a little later in the same debate: '[Pomerania] is not so important as gaining and retaining the Princes' affection and restoring them to their former condition': *Svenska riksrådets protokoll*, VIII, 330, 333.

9 *Ibid.*, VIII, 571–3 (16 April 1641). It should be noted that Oxenstierna's views reflected the general sense of the meeting.

V.ii *The deadlock broken*

1 Haan, *Kurfürstentag*, 163–4: 'votum' of George William at the eighteenth session.

2 Springell, *Connoisseur*, 105–10, gives an admirable account of this bizarre episode. The book-trade as a whole was 'down' in 1637: only 408 new works were published in Germany that year, compared with 1757 titles in 1618 (see R. Engelsing, *Analphabetentum und Lektüre. Zur Sozialgeschichte des Lesens in Deutschland zwischen feudaler und industrieller Gesellschaft* [Stuttgart, 1973], 42).

3 The revolt was led by Martin Aichinger (or Laimbauer), who claimed to be the Messiah and to be proof against bullets. He was captured after the defeat of his peasant army at Frankenburg in May 1636. The banners of his troops survive in the Linz Museum. See F. Wilflingseder, 'Martin Laimbauer und die Unruhen im Machlandviertel, 1632–6', *Mitteilungen des oberösterreichischen Landesarchivs*, VI (1959), 136–208.

4 Sir Thomas Roe, in January 1639, quoted by E.A. Beller, 'The mission of Sir Thomas Roe to the conference at Hamburg, 1638–40',

English Historical Review, XLI (1926), 61–77, at p. 74; cannibalism reported in Kuczynski, *Geschichte des Alltags des deutschen Volkes*, I, 87–8, and in Wedgwood, *Thirty Years' War*, 410–12.

5   Details from A. Ernstberger, 'Plünderung des Leipziger Messege-leites Nürnberger und Augsburger Kaufleute am 26. Januar 1638 bei Neustadt an der Heid', *Jahrbuch für fränkische Landesforschung*, XXII (1962), 101–20. Nuremberg had also suffered severe disloca-tion and destruction during the siege of 1632: see page 130 above.

6   Weber, *Würzburg und Bamberg im dreissigjährigen Krieg*, 171; Müller, *Der schwedische Staat in Mainz*, 140, 237–8.

7   F. Herrmann, ed., *Aus tiefer Not: hessische Briefe und Berichte aus der Zeit des dreissigjährigen Krieges* (Friedberg, 1916), 115: *Denk-schrift* of 19 December 1634. H. Börst *et al.*, 'Die evangelischen Geistlichen in und aus der Grafschaft Nassau-Saarbrücken', *Zeit-schrift für die Geschichte der Saargegend*, XXIII–XXIV (1975–6), 39–93, at pp. 39f.

8   See von Hippel, 'Bevölkerung und Wirtschaft'. In fact, the duchy's economy was especially vulnerable, for it had never produced enough foodstuffs to achieve self-sufficiency: instead, fine wine from the vineyards around Stuttgart was exported to buy grain. The war destroyed both the production and the trade. Many of the peasants died; many more took refuge abroad, above all in Switzer-land. (See Stritmatter, *Die Stadt Basel*, 75. The 7,561 refugees in Basel in 1638 almost outnumbered the native residents.)

9   Data taken from F. Mager, *Geschichte des Bauerntums und der Bodenkultur im Lande Mecklenburg* (Berlin, 1955), 137–40; W. Zahn, *Die Altmark im dreissigjährigen Krieg* (Halle, 1904: Schrif-ten des Vereins für Reformationsgeschichte, XXI/3), 58–60; F. Schröer, *Das Havelland im dreissigjährigen Krieg. Ein Beitrag zur Geschichte der Mark Brandenburg* (Cologne and Graz, 1966: Mit-teldeutsche Forschungen, XXXVII), 118–20, 127–31; and Faden, *Berlin im dreissigjährigen Krieg*, 232.

10   See E. Sparmann, *Dresden während des dreissigjährigen Krieges* (Dresden, 1914), 15–19; and G. Lammert, *Geschichte der Seuchen, Hungers- und Kriegsnoth zur Zeit des dreissigjährigen Krieges* (1890; reprinted Wiesbaden, 1971), 87, 233. Not all the demo-graphic losses were due to the troops, of course: between 1631 and 1634 few parts of Germany escaped the ravages of plague. At Amberg, capital of the Upper Palatinate, for example, eighteen Jesuit Fathers in the newly opened college died of the plague in the year 1634. (See Gegenfurtner, 'Jesuiten in Oberpfalz', 170.)

11   For an indication of the prevailing burden of tax see Weber, *Veit Adam von Gepeckh, Fürstbischof von Freising*, 129–32. One hun-dred and twenty *Römermonate* were imposed on the Bavarian Circle at the peace of Prague in 1635, 120 at the Electoral Meeting of 1636, 75 at the Circle Assembly of 1638, 120 at the Imperial Diet of 1641: 435 *Römermonate* in all, in just six years! Cf. the level of pre-war taxation, noted on page 17 above.

12 P. Antony and H. Christmann, eds, *Johann Valentin Andreä: ein schwäbischer Pfarrer im dreissigjährigen Krieg* (Hildesheim, 1970: Schwäbische Lebensläufe, V), 128.

13 Springell, *Connoisseur*, 113 n. 96.

14 See A. Leman, 'Urbain VIII et les origines du Congrès de Cologne de 1636', *Revue d'histoire ecclésiastique*, XIX (1923), 370–83; and Beller, 'The mission of Sir Thomas Roe'. The Anglo-Danish treaty of Hamburg, which was directed primarily against the Dutch, formed part of the campaign conducted (since 1637) by the Danish government to define more precisely and restrictively its territorial rights over the seas around it. It has been suggested that Denmark's policies may have been prompted by the publication of John Selden's *Mare clausum* in 1635–6. (See S. Dalgård, 'Østersø, Vestersø, Nordsø. Dominium maris Baltici et maris septentrionalis 1638', *Historisk Tidsskrift* [*Dansk*], 11th series, V [1956–9], 295–320. I am grateful to Professor E.L. Petersen for this reference.) Charles I was also hostile to Sweden at this point because the Stockholm government was supplying arms to his Scottish rebels – many of them veterans from Gustavus's army.

15 Further details in R. Leffers, *Die Neutralitätspolitik des Pfalzgrafen Wolfgang Wilhelm als Herzog von Jülich-Berg in der Zeit von 1636–1643* (Neustadt, 1971: Bergische Forschungen, VIII). There was a parallel attempt by Frederick William of Brandenburg, the Elector's heir, to arrange a truce in Cleves in 1637, but it also failed (see Opgenoorth, *Friedrich Wilhelm: der grosse Kurfürst*, chapter 3). In 1639, the Lower Saxon Circle also tried to secure neutrality, with more success (see Magen, 'Die Reichskreise', 451–2). The secret peace talks of Bavaria with France, at Einsiedeln in January 1640, are noted on page 170 above.

16 The Regensburg settlement thus superseded the peace of Prague, which had only suspended the Edict; but it was modified in its turn by the peace of Westphalia, which fixed the 'normative date' at 1624 (far less favourable to the Catholics than 1627).

17 On Brandenburg's neutrality, and its consequences, see Opgenoorth, *op. cit.*, and Schröer, *Das Havelland*. See also Kretzschmar, *Gustavus Adolfs Pläne und Ziele*, for the early stages of Brunswick's alliance with Sweden, and M. Reimann, *Der Goslarer Frieden von 1642* (Hildesheim, 1979: Quellen und Darstellung zur Geschichte Niedersachsens, XC), for the end.

18 The Swedish campaigns of these years, so often overlooked, are admirably described (with the aid of helpful plans) in Tingsten, *Johan Baner och Lennart Torstensson*. I am grateful to Professor Michael Roberts for assistance in assessing the importance of Baner's operations.

19 See K. Schweinesbein, *Die Frankreichpolitik Kurfürst Maximilians I. von Bayern, 1639–1645* (Munich, 1967), chapters 3–4. The papacy was unable to play an active role in this peace initiative, because in 1642 Urban VIII opened hostilities against the duke of Parma. Within two years, Urban squandered some 6 million thalers on 'the

war of Castro' and in July 1644, broken in spirit, he died. (See the figures in Grisar, 'Päpstliche Finanzen', 208.)

V.iii The defeat of the Habsburgs

1 AGS, *Contaduría Mayor de Cuentas*, 3a época 949, gives the level of Spanish spending in Germany in 1635–43. 3.5 million florins of 60 kreuzers were received by the 'Treasury General of Germany' in 1635–40, but only 1.8 million in 1640–3. A thaler was worth 90 kreuzers at this time.

2 'It seems to me that we have no choice but to look for a general peace, or at least a settlement in one or two of the wars in which the House of Austria is at present engaged.' Oñate to Olivares in 1640, quoted by Stradling, *Europe and the Decline of Spain*, 104.

3 Roberts, *The Swedish Imperial Experience*, 25.

4 L. Stein, 'Religion and patriotism in German peace dramas during the Thirty Years' War', *Central European History*, IV (1971), 131–48. Perhaps the author's link between Lutheran pietism and German patriotism in this period is overdrawn, but the material he presents is both important and unusual.

5 'Vox Caesaris', a phrase used by the Elector of Mainz's councillor in 1646, quoted by Wolff, *Corpus evangelicorum*, 179; Salvius's letter of April 1643 quoted by Dickmann, *Der Westfälische Frieden*, 115. On the Frankfurt 'Deputationstag' in general, see Dickmann, chaps 3 and 5, and R. von Kietzell, 'Der Frankfurter Deputationstag von 1642–1645. Eine Untersuchung der staatsrechtlichen Bedeutung dieser Reichsversammlung', *Nassauische Annalen*, LXXXIII (1972), 99–119.

6 See Böhme, *Bremische-Verdische Staatsfinanzen*, 13–165, and H. Eichberg, *Militär und Technik. Schwedenfestungen des 17. Jahrhunderts in den Herzogtümern Bremen und Verden* (Düsseldorf, 1976: Geschichte und Gesellschaft. Bochumer historische Studien, VII).

7 B.P. von Chemnitz, *Königlichen schwedischer in Teutschland geführten Kriegs vierter Teil* (Stockholm, 1859), 168. Chemnitz, who wrote his account in the 1650s, was a noted anti-Imperialist.

8 On the campaigns of 1643–5 in the south-west, see H.H. Schaufler, *Die Schlacht bei Freiburg-im-Breisgau 1644* (Freiburg, 1979). The battle of Freiburg was described by a Bavarian commander, Johann Werth, as the worst he had ever seen: 'In the twenty-two years I have been involved in the carnage of war,' he claimed, 'there has never been such a bloody encounter.' (Quoted *ibid.*, 7.)

9 The emperor was in Prague, and he left the city on 7 March, the day after the battle: see P. Broucek, *Der schwedische Feldzug nach Niederösterreich 1645/46* (Vienna, 1967: Militärhistorische Schriftenreihe, VII), 11. On the 1645 campaign in general, see also Ruppert, *Kaiserliche Politik*, chap. 3, part II, and Chesler, 'Crown, lords and God', 209–10.

10 Quotation from C.T. Odhner, *Die Politik Schwedens im Westphäl-ischen Friedenscongress und die Gründung der schwedischen Herr-schaft in Deutschland* (Gotha, 1877; reprinted Hannover, 1973), 97n. The agreement at Kötzschenbroda was in fact only a truce for six months, but in April 1646, at Eilenburg, it was prolonged to the war's end. Saxony was made to pay contributions to the Swedish army and to allow Swedish garrisons in Leipzig and Torgau; but three of the Saxon regiments in the Imperial army were permitted to remain there, provided they did not fight against Sweden.

11 On the Dutch–Spanish negotiations, see the classic account of J.J. Poelhekke, *De vrede van Munster* (The Hague, 1948). An English survey is conveniently provided by Israel, *The Dutch Republic and the Hispanic World*, 347–74.

12 Details from F. Bosbach, *Die Kosten des Westfälischen Friedens-kongresses. Eine strukturgeschichtliche Untersuchung* (Münster, 1984: Schriftenreihe der Vereinigung zur Erforschung der neueren Geschichte, XIII), 14, 16, 33, 57, 110, 168, 196, 211 and 224ff. I am most grateful to Dr Bosbach for letting me read and quote from his most interesting work in advance of publication.

13 The delegates' attention to procedural detail has often been ridi-culed by historians, but the experience of the abortive peace of Regensburg in 1630 and the treaty of Wismar in 1638 (pages 114 and 159 above), when an agreement signed by plenipotentiaries was later repudiated by their government, remained fresh in men's minds. No one wanted a repetition at Westphalia. See O'Connell, 'A cause célèbre in the history of treaty-making'.

14 Bosbach, *Kosten*, I, 167–8; Philippe, *Württemberg*, 1.

15 Quoted in Heckel, 'Zur Historiographie des Westfälischen Friedens', 324.

V.iv The making of peace

1 Quoted in Kuczynski, *Geschichte des Alltags des deutschen Volkes*, 117. For the 1646–7 campaign see P. Broucek, *Die Eroberung von Bregenz am 4. Jänner 1647* (Vienna, 1971: Militärhistorische Schrif-tenreihe, XVIII).

2 D'Avaux quoted by Philippe, *Württemberg und der Westfälische Friede*, 54; Oxenstierna quoted by G. Schmid, 'Konfessionspolitik und Staatsräson bei den Verhandlungen des Westfälischen Friedenskongresses über die Gravamina Ecclesiastica', *Archiv für Reformationsgeschichte*, LIV (1953), 203–23, at page 206.

3 Imperial instructions quoted by Ruppert, *Die kaiserliche Politik*, 134.

4 Bosbach, *Kosten*, I, 15–16; Ruppert, *Kaiserliche Politik*, 251.

5 Schmid, 'Konfessionspolitik', 209. This most interesting article is based on documents from the archives of ducal Saxony, whose

delegates were among the Protestant hard-liners.

6　The originality of this compromise, enshrined in Article V paragraph 52 of the 'Instrumentum Pacis Osnabrugense', and known as 'Itio in Partes', has not always been appreciated: an age which normally revered the majority principle sanctioned an alternative method for reaching decisions on certain key issues. Admittedly, the principle of parity between two unequal groups had been accepted a century before by the Swiss Confederation; the Holy Roman Empire, however, was so much larger, and therefore the formula of 'Itio in Partes' was correspondingly more difficult to operate. But operate it did. Constitutional lawyers in the eighteenth century saw the arrangement as the masterwork of the peace-makers – 'the foremost bulwark of Freedom and Equality, built with so much blood' – because confessional dualism strengthened and protected the political balance established in Germany between emperor and princes. (See C.G. Hoffman, *Gründliche Vorstellung deren in dem Heiliger Romische Reiche . . . Religions-Beschwerden* [1722], quoted by Heckel, 'Itio in Partes'; see all of Heckel's penetrating analysis at pp. 291–308 of his article entitled 'Itio in Partes'.) The achievement of the Congress is further considered on pp. 215–18 above.

7　Quoted by Seaton, *Literary relations of England and Scandinavia*, 81. Note also the sentiments of Sir Edward Peyton, *The Divine Catastrophe, or the rise, reign and ruine of the house of Stuarts* (London, 1652): 'God raised Gustavus Adolphus to turn the scales to the United princes' side; yet, in conclusion, the Swedes have sought more their own interest than God's.'

8　Sten Bielke to the council, 9 February 1647, quoted by Odhner, *Die Politik Schwedens*, 4n.

9　This important aspect of French policy in Germany during the 1640s is played down by Dickmann, *Der Westfälische Frieden*. Most other, less monumental German studies of this phase of the war also tend to belittle the role of Mazarin. See the helpful comments of D. McKay and H.M. Scott, *The Rise of the Great Powers, 1648–1815* (London, 1983), 4–5.

10　Quotations from Odhner, *op. cit.*, 163n; Aldea, *España, el Papado y el Imperio*, 78–80; and Müller, *Der schwedische Staat in Mainz*, 19 n. 66.

11　See Heinisch, *Salzburg im dreissigjährigen Krieg*, 195–6; on the last Imperial campaign of the war see Hoyos, 'Ernst von Traun', part II. On the policy of Cologne at this time see J.F. Foerster, *Kurfürst Ferdinand von Köln. Die Politik seiner Stifter in den Jahren 1634–1650* (Münster, 1976: Schriftenreihe der Vereinigung zur Erforschung der neueren Geschichte, VI).

12　A. Chéruel, ed., *Lettres du Cardinal de Mazarin*, III (Paris, 1883), 173–81: Mazarin to Servien, 14 August 1648.

13　Chesler, 'Crown, lords and God', 209–10; Evans, *Habsburg Monarchy*, 76. Uncertainty concerning the fate of the New Order in

Bohemia continued almost until the end of the war. As late as 1645, Countess Cernin (one of the *arrivistes*) could write: 'The dice are still on the board, and who knows who will reap the profit from what we possess?' (Quoted by O. Odložilík, 'The nobility of Bohemia, 1620–1740', *East European Quarterly*, VII (1973), 15–30, at p. 19.) See also the discussion in R.J.W. Evans, 'The significance of the White Mountain for the culture of the Czech lands', *Bulletin of the Institute of Historical Research*, XLIV (1971), 34–54, at p. 44 (a most important article).

14 The fighting overseas, particularly in Asia, continued for some time longer, however. Israel, *Dutch Republic*, 336, notes that 'the very last battle of the Eighty Years' War was fought on Ternate on 18 July 1649, more than a year after the ratification of the treaty of Münster, but before official publication of the news in parts of the East'.

15 Odhner, *Die Politik Schwedens*, 238, reports the Swedish plenipotentiaries' complaint, as late as January 1648, that 'the cause of Spain' was 'the emperor's guiding star in the German negotiations'. Ruppert, *Die kaiserliche Politik*, 350–8, describes the emperor's anguish at having to make peace without Spain.

16 Philippe, *Württemberg*, *passim*; and *Welt im Umbruch. Augsburg zwischen Renaissance und Barock*, I (Augsburg, 1980), 409ff. In 1645 Augsburg, whose population before the war had numbered 33,000, contained only 21,000 people: 14,000 Lutherans, 6,000 Catholics and 1,000 soldiers.

17 See details in Bosbach, *Kosten des Friedenskongresses*, 224ff. The author makes the point that, for some territories, the cost of the conference could equal, and even exceed, the 'satisfaction of the soldiery'. Thus Brandenburg had to find 134,522 thalers for the diplomats and 162,692 for the Swedish army, while the Imperial City of Bremen had to pay 88,413 for the former against only 28,480 for the latter, But for most areas, the proportions were reversed.

18 Heinisch, *Salzburg im dreissigjährigen Krieg*, 196ff. All Archbishop Lodron and his vassals obtained in return for their money was freedom from quartering. The rest of the Empire was equally heavily burdened: see G. Buchstab, 'Die Freie Reichsstadt Köln und die schwedische Armeesatisfaktion', in Repgen, ed., *Forschungen und Quellen*, 149–62.

19 On the Swedish demobilization, see the admirable vintage study of T. Lorentzen, *Die schwedische Armee im Dreissigjährigen Kriege und ihre Abdankung* (Leipzig, 1894), chaps 6,7. More recent data is presented in G. Buchstab, *Reichsstädte, Städtekurie und westfälischer Friedenskongress* (Münster, 1976: Schriftenreihe der Vereinigung zur Erforschung der neueren Geschichte, V), 170–7. On the Imperialists' demobilization, see part III of Hoyos, 'Ernst von Traun' (which has been printed in *Der dreissigjährige Krieg*, 169–232); and Elster, *Die Piccolomini Regimenter*, 104ff.

20 Quoted in Glaser, ed., *Wittelsbach und Bayern*, II/2, 483. Pages

483–90 of this magnificent catalogue describe and illustrate items made to celebrate the outbreak of peace.

Chapter VI The war in myth, legend and history

VI.i The universal soldier

1   There are, of course, exceptions: most notably, the Krigsarkiv in Stockholm. Furthermore, important military archives may turn up in unlikely places. For example, the detailed records of Wallenstein's lifeguards (the foot regiment of Count Julius of Hardegg) are today preserved in the Niederösterreichische Landesarchiv, Vienna, Herrschaft Stetteldorf, Kartons 1–6. See the admirable article based on them: F. Hausmann, 'Das Regiment hochdeutscher Knechte des Grafen Julius von Hardegg, seine Geschichte, Fahnen und Uniform', in *Der dreissigjährige Krieg*, 79–167. This is the only modern history known to me of a regiment which fought in the war. The Piccolomini papers, formerly preserved in the castle of Náchod and now in the State Archive, Zámrsk, enabled Otto Elster to prepare in 1903 a short but interesting study of the regiments raised by Ottavio Piccolomini between 1629 and 1650 (see Elster, *Die Piccolomini Regimenter*). A more systematic use of these records would be worthwhile.

2   On uniforms, see Hausmann, *art. cit.*, 129–35. Reconstituted military costumes of the period are displayed in several museums of Europe, especially in the 'Thirty Years' War Room' of both the Heeresgeschichtliches Museum in Vienna and the Armémuseum in Stockholm.

3   There is a fine collection of Thirty Years' War colours captured from Imperial and League forces in the Statens Trofé Samlung (a part of the Armémuseum) in Stockholm. The collection includes some 4,000 objects, almost all from the period 1610–1720, of which forty-five, including the Thirty Years' War pennants, are displayed.

4   H.C. Lavater, *Kriegsbüchlein. Das ist grundtliche Anleitung zum Kriegswesen* (Zürich, 1651; 2nd edn, 1667), 63; André, *Michel le Tellier*, 339.

5   Gallas's order and samples are presently on display in a case in the Heeresgeschichtliches Museum in Vienna. Pearl-grey was adopted as the colour of all uniforms in the Austrian army in 1708.

6   Redlich, *Military Enterpriser*, I, 456.

7   Information from J. Lindegren, *Utskrivning och utsugning. Produktion och reproduktion i Bygdeå 1620–1640* (Uppsala, 1980: Studia Historica Upsaliensia, CXVII), 256–7, and from further details kindly supplied to me by Dr Lindegren in January 1980. Denmark also introduced conscription in 1627, but only for de-

fence: see Petersen, 'Defence, war and finance', 33.

8 G. Parker, *The Army of Flanders and the Spanish Road 1567–1659* (Cambridge, 1972), 46–7, on Spanish jail recruiting; *Calendar of State Papers Domestic 1628–9*, 395, 568 on the English parallel.

9 R. Chaboche, 'Les soldats français de la guerre de Trente Ans: une tentative d'approche', *Revue d'histoire moderne et contemporaine*, XX (1973), 10–24.

10 H. Jessen, *Der Dreissigjährige Krieg in Augenzeugenberichten* (2nd edn, Munich, 1964), 335.

11 A nine-page 'Sprachbüchlein' of military terms, many of them bizarre and improbable, was included in H.M. Moscherosch, *Wunderliche und warhafftige Gesichte Philanders von Sittewald* (2 vols, Strasbourg, 1640–2), 'sechsters Gesichte: Soldaten Leben'. See also the sources noted in Langer, *The Thirty Years' War*, 100.

12 Monro, *Expedition*, II, 62–3, 75; Dukes, 'The Leslie family'; H.L. Rubinstein, *Captain Luckless. James, first duke of Hamilton 1600–1649* (Edinburgh, 1973), 26–37; and I. Grimble, *Chief of Mackay* (London, 1965), 81–105.

13 Turner, *Memoirs of his own life and times*, 14. It is notable, for example, that five of Wallenstein's murderers were, like Turner, subjects of Charles I: Lesley, Devereux, Geraldine, Gordon and Butler.

14 Redlich, *Military Enterpriser*, I, 420–6; K.R. Böhme, *Bremische-Verdische Staatsfinanzen 1645–76* (Uppsala, 1976), 34. The palaces of generals, such as Wrangel (at Skökloster, north of Stockholm) or Wallenstein (in Prague, Mnichovo Hradiště and Jičín), testify even today to the wealth that could be gained through war. The newly rich generals brought with them a style of expenditure that few had seen before in northern Europe: Marshal de la Gardie boasted circa 1650 that he had introduced luxury into Sweden single-handed.

15 Grimmelshausen, *Simplicissimus*, book I, chapter XVI, quoted by Redlich, *Military Enterpriser*, I, 370–1.

16 André, *Michel le Tellier*, 64.

17 The 'Selbstschutzsysteme' is described by I. Bog, *Die bäuerliche Wirtschaft im Zeitalter des Dreissigjährigen Krieges. Die Bewegungsvorgänge in der Kriegswirtschaft nach den Quellen des Klosterverwalteramtes Heilsbronn* (Coburg, 1952), 142–54; and G. Benecke, 'Labour relations and peasant society in North-West Germany, c. 1600', *History*, LVIII (1973), 350–9.

18 A display cabinet in the 'Thirty Years' War Room' of the Heeresgeschichtliches Museum in Vienna contains the short, thick broadsword of Tilly, c. 1610, next to the long, thin rapier of Ferdinand III, c. 1635. Both are typical of the styles current in their day.

19 Monro, *Expedition*, I, 68–75; M. Pusch, *Der Dreissigjährige Krieg 1618–1648* (Munich, 1978), 112–13.

20 See M. van Crevelt, *Supplying War: logistics from Wallenstein to Patton* (Cambridge, 1977), 34ff., and Kroener, *Les Routes et les Étapes, passim*. Naturally rations due were not always provided.

See the complaint of a miserable Imperial soldier at the siege of Münster in 1634, lamenting to his wife that he only received 1 lb of bread every four days: Kuczynski, *Geschichte des Alltags des deutschen Volkes*, 100–2.

21 'Streiff' – called after Colonel Johan Streiff von Lauenstein, who sold it to the king in 1631 for 1,000 thalers – was injured at Lützen and died, probably of wounds, a few months later. The beast was promptly flayed and its hide sent to Stockholm, where it was fitted over a wooden frame and set up in the Royal Palace. It is still there, in the Livrustkammaren, bearing the saddle and harness given to Gustavus by his wife at New Year, 1630.

22 Chaboche, 'Les soldats français', notes that only 46 per cent of the Thirty Years' War veterans who later entered the Invalides were, or had been, married.

23 C.A. Campan, ed., *Bergues sur le Soom assiégée* (1622: 2nd edn, Brussels, 1867), 247; Redlich, *Military Enterpriser*, I, 521–2.

24 Figures from Fallon, 'Scottish mercenaries'.

25 Monro, *Expedition*, II, 122.

26 AGRB, Secrétairerie d'État et de Guerre, 34, f. 5v: Order of Cardinal-Infante, 8 July 1634 to pay 50 escudos reward to the peasants who caught nine deserters as they fled through the Valtelline. Examples of executions for cowardice are noted on pp. 131 and 152 above.

27 The exception, once again, is the 'Rullor' of the Swedish army, preserved in the Krigsarkiv, Stockholm, which detail desertions and other causes of wastage. But there is, to my knowledge, as yet no systematic study of this source.

28 Sources: *Sveriges Krig*, IV, 124, 387–8, 453; V, 138, 548–9; VI, 423, 483; Fallon, 'Scottish mercenaries', 246ff.; Hausmann, 'Das Regiment', 166; Kroener, 'Truppenstärken', 197. Data is also available on the loss of English troops in Danish service: 5,013 in November 1626, but 2,472 by February 1627. The force was increased to 4,913 men by June, falling to 4,707 in August, 4,412 in September and 3,764 in October. In May 1628 there were only 1,400 English and 230 Scots left. The average monthly loss was thus 4 per cent. See E.A. Beller, 'The military expedition of Sir Charles Morgan to Germany, 1627–9', *English Historical Review*, XLIII (1928), 528–39.

29 Monro, *Expedition*, I, 62, 67, 79–80; II, 35.

30 W. Zahn, *Die Altmark im Dreissigjährigen Krieg*, 16. Tangermünde, which is today one of the most beautifully preserved seventeenth-century towns in central Europe, had to be entirely rebuilt after the war. A general's headquarters on fourteen occasions, and plundered seven times, its 623 occupied houses of pre-war days had been reduced by 1645 to 228 and its birth-rate had been halved. On Darmstadt see Herrmann, ed., *Aus tiefer Not*, 123.

31 On Jesuit chaplains during the Thirty Years' War, see Duhr, *Geschichte der Jesuiten*, II.2, chap. 6 (based on the campaign journals kept by several chaplains); cf. Parker, *Army of Flanders*, 170–2. On contributions, see *ibid.*, 142–3; and F. Redlich, 'Contributions in

the Thirty Years' War', *Economic History Review*, XII (1959–60), 247–54.

32 L. Mulder, ed., *Journaal van Anthonis Duyck, advocaat-fiskaal van den Raad van State 1591–1602* (The Hague and Arnhem, 1862), 636; John Bingham quoted along with many other works, by W. Hahlweg, *Die Heeresreform der Oranier und die Antike* (Berlin, 1941), 176. This volume should not be confused with Hahlweg's later edition of John of Nassau's *Kriegsbuch*, of similar title: Hahlweg, *Die Heeresreform der Oranier: das 'Kriegsbuch' des Grafen Johann von Nassau-Siegen* (Wiesbaden, 1973: Veröffentlichungen der historischen Kommission für Nassau, XX).

33 On Maurice of Nassau and his cousin, see E. Kist's introduction to Jacques de Gheyn, *The Exercise of Arms* (New York, 1971); on the 'school of war' at Siegen, see L. Plathner, *Graf Johann von Nassau und die erste Kriegsschule. Ein Beitrag zur Kenntnis des Kriegswesens um die Wende des 16. Jahrhunderts* (Berlin, 1913). It was certainly an exclusive school: only twenty students had attended when the Academy closed its doors in 1623! Actually Siegen was not quite first: court-based schools of war had been established at Tübingen, Kassel and Sedan in the late sixteenth century. For the diffusion of Dutch techniques see F. Walker, *Niederländische Einflüsse auf das eidgenössische Staatsdenken im späten 16. und frühen 17. Jahrhundert: Neue Aspekte der Zürcher und Berner Geschichte im Zeitalter des werdenden Absolutismus* (Zurich, 1979), chap. 1.

34 von Frauenholz, *Heerwesen*, I, 41; *Sveriges Krig*, VIII, 99–100 (quoting a French pamphlet of 1634).

35 Turner, *Pallas Armata*, 237. The 'double salvo' was certainly used at Breitenfeld in 1631: see *The Swedish Intelligencer*, I (London, 1632), 124.

VI.ii The war and German society

1 K. Holstein, *Rothenburger Stadtgeschichte* (Rothenburg ob der Tauber, 1969), 96–7.

2 Schmidt, 'Der dreissigjährige Krieg', IV (1956), 71–2; VI (1958), 23.

3 H. Woltering, *Die Reichsstadt Rothenburg ob der Tauber und ihre Herrschaft über die Landwehr*, I (Rothenburg, 1965), 32 (map).

4 Schmidt, 'Dreissigjähriger Krieg', VI (1958), 15–16, 22–4; Woltering, *Reichsstadt Rothenburg*, 38.

5 R. Ergang, *The Myth of the All-Destructive Fury of the Thirty Years' War* (Pocono Pines, Pa., 1956).

6 Franz, *Der dreissigjährige Krieg und das deutsche Volk*, provides fundamental data. Franz avoids giving overall population estimates for Germany or the Empire, and most other authors follow suit. But the conservative figures provided by C. McEvedy and R. Jones, *Atlas of World Population History* (London, 1978), 67–72, correctly reflect the most recent trend of thought on the subject.

7   Lammert, *Geschichte der Seuchen*, 233.
8   Friedrichs, *Nördlingen*, 47–9, 306–11.
9   W. Schwemmer, *Die Schulden der Reichsstadt Nürnberg und ihre Übernahme durch den bayerischen Staat* (Nürnberg, 1967), 8.
10   Buchstab, *Reichsstädte, Städtekurie und Westfälischer Friedenskongress*, 210–11; G. Wunder, *Die Bürger von Hall: Sozialgeschichte einer Reichsstadt, 1216–1802* (Sigmaringen, 1980), 188–9, 269–70.
11   For some parallel data from north-west Germany, see Benecke, 'The problem of death and destruction in the Thirty Years' War', 239–53.
12   Bog, *Die bäuerliche Wirtschaft*, 126.
13   See Rabb, 'The effects of the Thirty Years' war', 40–51.
14   Haan, 'Prosperität und Dreissigjähriger Krieg', 117.
15   Schmidt, 'Dreissigjähriger Krieg', IV (1956), 72.
16   J. Morhard, *Haller Haus-Chronik* (Schwäbisch Hall, 1962), 136.
17   G. Zillhardt, ed., *Der Dreissigjährige Krieg in zeitgenössischer Darstellung: Hans Heberles 'Zeytregister' (1618–1672)* (Ulm, 1975), passim.

VI.iii The war and politics

1   Quoted in M. Walker, *German Home Towns, Community, state and general estate 1648—1871* (Ithaca and London, 1971), 14, 15.
2   J.-J. Rousseau, 'Extrait du projet de paix perpétuelle de Monsieur l'Abbé de St Pierre' (1761), in *Oeuvres complètes de Jean-Jacques Rousseau*, III (Paris, Editions de la Pléiade, 1964), 572.
3   Wedgwood, *Thirty Years' War*, 526.
4   See, for further detail, Vann, *The Swabian Kreis*.
5   Details in Opgenoorth, *Friedrich Wilhelm: der grosse Kurfürst*, chap. 4.
6   Quotation and analysis taken from Livet, *L'intendance d'Alsace*, 123ff.
7   Schmid, 'Konfessionspolitik', 222–3: von Thumshirn, representing Saxe-Altenburg, on 28 November 1648.
8   See J. Vicens Vives, 'La politique européenne du royaume d'Aragon-Catalogne sous Jean II (1458–79)', *Annales du Midi*, LXV (1953), 405–15; and J. Wormald, *Court, Kirk and Community. Scotland 1470–1625* (London, 1981), 100–2.
9   *Documentos inéditos para la historia de España*, II (Madrid, 1943), 140: Gondomar to the king, 28 March 1619.
10   See G. Parker and L.M. Smith, eds, *The General Crisis of the Seventeenth Century* (London, 1978), chaps 1, 2 and 8. For detailed evidence about the climate in Germany during the war years see: W. Lenke, *Klimadaten von 1621–1650 nach Beobachtungen des Landgrafen Hermann von Hessen* (Offenbach, 1960: Berichte des deutschen Wetterdienstes, nr. LXIII, vol. 9). The landgrave, although he lacked both barometer and thermometer, left a record of continuous observations, at Kassel and (after 1640) at Fulda,

four times every day from 1635 until 1650 (except for one missing year: 1645). His data provide clear evidence of a cooler, wetter climate than today, especially in the 1640s. In 1648 there were 157 days of rain, snow or other precipitation; in 1649 there were 147 days, and in 1650, 179.

11 See G. Benecke, *Society and Politics in Germany 1500–1750* (London, 1974), 234–9, and pp. 212–14 above.

12 P. Skippon, 'An account of a journey through the Low Countries, Germany, Italy and France', in A. Churchill, ed., *A collection of voyages and travels*, VI (London, 1732), 418–84. See also Friedrichs, *Nördlingen*, chaps 2, 4, 5. Admittedly, the overall standard of living did not regain its pre-war level in most areas until after 1700, but that was largely due to Louis XIV.

13 Bonney, *The King's Debts*, 126–7, 200, 202–5.

14 See Beck, *Der hessische Bruderzwist*, for a succinct, recent account of the later stages of the war from the Hessian point of view. As for the Habsburg lands, war was not without deleterious economic effects, but they were less serious than might have been expected. See, for one area, R. Sandgruber, 'Zur Wirtschaftsentwicklung Niederösterreichs im 16. und 17. Jahrhundert', *Unsere Heimat*, XLV (1974), 210–21.

15 Quoted by L.W. Forster, *The Temper of Seventeenth-Century German Literature* (London, 1952), 9. See the similar eulogies of political theorists and preachers in England quoted by J.N. Figgis, *The Theory of the Divine Right of Kings* (London, 1894), chaps 7, 8 and 9.

16 George's peace policy is sensitively discussed by Frohnweiler, 'Die Friedenspolitik Landgraf Georgs II.', especially pp. 163–70.

17 G.R. Potter and E. Simpson, eds, *Sermons of John Donne*, II (Berkeley and Los Angeles, 1955), 250–68. Dr Donne began: 'There is not a more comprehensive, a more embracing word in all Religion, than the first word of this text: NOW.' The preoccupation with Time, and in particular with immediacy, was common to most writers of the day. It is reflected in the popularity of lyric poetry, sonnets and epigrams (all of which aimed at holding fast a momentary emotion, thought or act taken from the stream of Time), and in the epithalamia written to stress the uniqueness of almost every event, however trivial.

18 Details in E.L. Petersen, 'Conspicuous consumption: the Danish nobility of the seventeenth century', *Kwartalnik historij Kultury materialnej*, I (1982), 64–5.

Bibliographical Essay

A General works

Several thousand books and articles have been written on the subject of the Thirty Years' War – most of them bearing the same title as this volume. The best available in this category, in alphabetical order, are: H. Langer, *The Thirty Years' War* (Leipzig, 1978; Eng. edn, Poole, 1980); G. Livet, *La guerre de Trente ans* (Paris, 1963); G. Pagès, *The Thirty Years' War* (Paris, 1939, Eng. edn, London, 1970); J.V. Polišenský, *The Thirty Years' War* (London, 1971); and C.V. Wedgwood, *The Thirty Years' War* (London, 1938; frequently reprinted). There are also items with slightly different titles, such as G. Benecke, *Germany in the Thirty Years' War* (London, 1978); S.H. Steinberg, *The 'Thirty Years' War' and the Conflict for European Hegemony, 1600—1660* (London, 1967); D. Maland, *Europe at War, 1600–1650* (London, 1980); and T.K. Rabb, ed., *The Thirty Years' War. Problems of motive, extent and effect* (Lexington, 1964). See also a new item on p. 302 below.

All of these works have their strengths but, as noted above in the Preface, none is entirely adequate. Langer's excellent book is really a cultural history of Germany during the war; Pagès, Polišenský and Wedgwood each deal with one aspect of the conflict at the expense of the rest. Benecke presents an invaluable English translation of many key documents, but not a general history of the war; Steinberg's interpretation is overstated and marred by numerous factual errors; Maland relies exclusively on secondary works; Rabb presents, rather breathlessly, the views of twenty-one different authors in less than 100 pages. The best brief overview is unquestionably Livet's, but there are limits to what can be crammed into 125 duodecimo pages. None of these more modern surveys thus match the superb vintage study of Moriz Ritter, *Deutsche Geschichte im Zeitalter der Gegenreformation und des dreissigjährigen Krieges, 1555–1648* (3 vols, Stuttgart, 1889; reprinted Darmstadt, 1974). Volume I covers 1555–86; volume II deals with 1586–1618 in two parts, divided by the Donauwörth Incident of 1607 and the conflict between Rudolf II and his brother; volume III covers the years 1618–35 in detail. Nowhere else are the international repercussions of each separate event in the Empire so thoroughly and lucidly presented: for the war to 1635, and for developments leading up to the conflict, Ritter remains fundamental and indispensable.

It is not possible to recommend any other general work with the same confidence. Even the solid chapters of the *Cambridge Modern History*, volume IV, first published in 1906, are uneven: although some (such as that on the Valtelline question) are still outstanding, others are definitely out-of-date. But what can be put in their place? It depends, of course, on the amount of time at the reader's disposal. The *apparatus criticus* that follows is therefore designed to do two things: to indicate and evaluate all the sources on which the text of this book is based; and to draw attention to the score or so most useful works among them (indicated with *). An index of scholars whose works are cited, whether in this bibliography or in the notes, appears on pages 304ff below.

B Antecedents

According to a leading German historian, writing in 1950, interest in Germany between 1555 and 1618 had declined to such a point that it was close to extinction. This is still true. For English readers who cannot cope with the first two volumes of Ritter's *Deutsche Geschichte* (above), there are only three brief outlines available: one by G.D. Ramsay in the *New Cambridge Modern History* (in two parts – vol. III, chap. 10, and vol. IV, chap. 10); the second, by *C.P. Clasen in H. Trevor-Roper, ed., *The Age of Expansion. Europe and the world 1559–1660* (London, 1968), chap. 4; the third, in slightly more detail, by Hajo Holborn, *A History of Modern Germany: the Reformation* (London, 1965), chaps 10 and 11.

One of the major gaps in almost every history of the war – including even Ritter – is a consideration of developments in the Austrian lands. Scholars should therefore be particularly grateful for the important new study of *R.J.W. Evans, *The Making of the Habsburg Monarchy 1550–1700: an interpretation* (Oxford, 1979), equipped with a comprehensive bibliography in many languages. Attention should also be paid to the following studies: H. Sturmberger, 'Die Anfänge des Bruderzwistes in Habsburg', *Mitteilungen des Oberösterreichischen Landesarchivs*, V (1957), 143–88, which gives an admirable account of Rudolf's dealings with his brothers; an earlier work by Dr Evans, *Rudolf II and His World. A study in intellectual history 1576–1612* (Oxford, 1973); and the new volume of essays *Rudolf II and His Court* (Delft, 1982: Leids Kunsthistorisch Jaarboek, I). Similar studies of Ferdinand II would be welcome, but none exist. The fullest view of his policies remains the contemporary chronicle of one of his privy councillors, first published in the 1640s and given its final form in twelve imposing folio volumes (plus two supplements) by the Elector of Saxony's printer in the 1720s: *Frantz Christoph Khevenhillers Annales Ferdinandeorum*. A companion work by the same author, *Conterfet Kupfferstich* (2 vols, Leipzig, 1721–2), provides illustrated biographical sketches. F. Hurter, *Geschichte Kaiser Ferdinands II. und seiner Eltern* (11 vols, Schaffhausen, 1850–67), is tendentious but remains essential. On a smaller scale, one may consult J. Franzl, *Ferdinand II. Kaiser im Zwiespalt der Zeit* (Graz, 1978); H. Sturmberger, *Kaiser Ferdinand II und das Problem des Absolutismus* (Munich, 1957); and G. Franz, 'Glaube und Recht im politischen Denken Kaiser Ferdinands II.', *Archiv für Reformationsgeschichte*, XLIX (1958), 258–69. See also F. Stieve in *Allgemeine deutsche Biographie*, VI (1877), 644–64. For the emperor's skilful manipulation of public opinion, especially in Lutheran Germany, see K. Nolden, *Die Reichspolitik Kaiser Ferdinands II. in der Publizistik bis zum Lübecker Frieden 1629* (Cologne, 1958). There is also much of value on decision-making at the emperor's court in the important new study of *R. Bireley, *Religion and Politics in the Age of the Counter-Reformation. Emperor Ferdinand II, William Lamormaini, S.J., and the formation of Imperial policy* (Chapel Hill, N.C., 1981). On Ferdinand's homeland there is an excellent collection of essays: A. Novotny and B. Sutter, eds, *Innerösterreich 1564–1619* (Graz, 1967); and a fine monograph by W. Schulze, *Landesdefension und Staatsbildung: Studien zum Kriegswesen des innerösterreichischen Territorialstaates (1564–1619)* (Vienna, 1973).

The only problems facing the Empire in these years which have attracted broad surveys, covering the entire period, have been religion, the economy and (perhaps surprisingly) representative institutions. On the general state of Protestantism in Germany at this time, see J.B. Neveux, *Vie spirituelle et vie sociale entre Rhin et Baltique au XVIIe siècle* (Paris, 1967); H. Schilling, *Konfessionskonflikt und Staatsbildung. Eine Fallstudie über das Verhältnis von religiösem und sozialem Wandel in der Frühneuzeit am Beispiel der Grafschaft Lippe* (Gütersloh, 1981: Quellen und Forschungen zur Reformationsgeschichte, XLVIII); B. Vogler, 'La politique scolaire entre Rhin et Moselle, l'exemple du duché de Deux-Ponts 1555–1619', *Francia*, III (1975), 236–320, and IV (1976), 287–364; and *idem, Le monde germanique et helvétique à l'époque des Réformes, 1517–1618*, II (Paris, 1981). On the Formula of Concord, see the quatercentenary articles edited by L.W. Spitz in *Sixteenth-century Journal*, VIII no. 4 (1977). On the economy, the best surveys are by H. Kellenbenz in H. Aubin and W. Zorn, eds, *Handbuch der deutschen Wirtschafts- und Sozialgeschichte*, I (Stuttgart, 1971), 386–494; and, from a 'socialist' point of view, by J. Kuczynski, *Geschichte des Alltags des deutschen Volkes. I: 1600–50* (East Berlin, 1981). See also I. Bog, 'Wachstumsprobleme der oberdeutschen Wirtschaft 1540–1618', in F. Lütge, ed., *Wirtschaftliche und soziale Probleme der gewerblichen Entwicklung im 15.–16. und 19. Jahrhundert* (Stuttgart, 1968), 44–89; and R. Endres, 'Zur wirtschaftlichen und sozialen Lage in Franken vor dem dreissigjährigen Krieg', *Jahrbuch für fränkische Landesforschung*, XXVIII (1968), 5–52.

Among studies of representative assemblies, the most celebrated (at least among English readers) is F.L. Carsten, *Princes and Parliaments in Germany from the Fifteenth to the Eighteenth Century* (Oxford, 1959).

However, although it contains a mass of fascinating data and a wealth of bold and clear generalizations, Carsten's work has been criticized by German historians as too Anglocentric: the author, it is argued, over-stresses the resemblance between German assemblies and the English Parliament. See, for example, P. Herde, 'Deutsche Landstände und englisches Parliament', *Historisches Jahrbuch*, LXXX (1966), 286–97. A very different view of south German representative assemblies, stressing their truly democratic structure (so unlike the English model), is offered by P. Blickle, *Landschaften im alten Reich. Die staatlichen Funktionen des gemeinen Mannes in Oberdeutschland* (Munich, 1973). For further literature on the Imperial Diet and the Circles, see notes 10 and 12 on page 242 above. On the Estates of the Austrian lands, two long articles are of crucial importance: on the origins, see M. Mitterauer, 'Ständegliederung und Ländertypen', in E. Bruckmüller *et al.*, eds, *Herrschaftsstruktur und Ständebildung II. Beiträge zur Typologie der österreichischen Länder aus ihren mittelalterlichen Grundlagen* (Munich, 1973), 115–203; on the Protestant schools, founded by the Estates and the symbol of their independence, see G. Heiss, 'Konfession, Politik und Erziehung. Die Landschaftsschulen in der nieder- und innerösterreichischen Ländern vor dem dreissigjährigen Krieg', in G. Klingenstein *et al.*, eds, *Bildung, Politik und Gesellschaft* (Vienna, 1978), 13–63.

The political groups outside the Habsburg lands which took an interest in Bohemian developments before 1618 have also attracted their share of scholarly attention. The archives of both the League and the Union are presently located in the various sections of the Bayerisches Hauptstaatsarchiv in Munich, which contain the pre-war archives of the Rhine Palatinate as well as of the duchy of Bavaria. For the period 1599–1613 most of the contents of these archives, together with much subsidiary documentation from other sources, were printed in the series *Briefe und Akten zur Geschichte des Dreissigjährigen Krieges*, edited by Moriz Ritter *et al.*, vols I–XII (Munich, 1870–1978).

The best study of Palatine policy in English is the brief outline by C.P. Clasen, *The Palatinate in European History 1559–1660* (London, 1963). There is far more available in German: above all V. Press, *Calvinismus und Territorialstaat: Regierung und Zentralbehörden der Kurpfalz 1559–1619* (Stuttgart, 1970: Kieler historische Studien, VII); *idem*, 'Die Grundlagen der kurpfälzischen Herrschaft in der Oberpfalz 1499–1621', *Verhandlungen des historischen Vereins für Oberpfalz und Regensburg*, CXVII (1977), 31–67; and F.H. Schubert, *Ludwig Camerarius, 1573–1651: Eine Biographie* (Kallmünz, 1955: Münchener historische Studien: Abteilung Neuere Geschichte, I). Anhalt lacks a modern biography, but his connexions with the central European Protestants are briefly outlined in A.A. van Schelven, 'Der Generalstab des politischen Calvinismus in Zentraleuropa zu Beginn des dreissigjährigen Krieges', *Archiv für Reformationsgeschichte*, XXXVI (1939), 117–41. There is no recent study of the Union, but several of its members have been the subject of valuable monographs. See, in particular, H.G. Herold, *Markgraf Joachim-Ernst von Brandenburg-Ansbach als Reichs-*

fürst (Göttingen, 1973: Schriftenreihe der Historischen Kommission bei der bayerischen Akademie der Wissenschaften, X); E. Kossol, *Die Reichspolitik des Pfalzgrafen Philipp Ludwig von Neuburg (1547–1614)* (Göttingen, 1976: Schriftenreihe der Historischen Kommission bei der bayerischen Akademie der Wissenschaften, XIV); and E.L. Sticht, *Markgraf Christian von Brandenburg-Kulmbach und das Oberland der Markgrafschaft im dreissigjährigen Krieg (1618–1635)* (Neuhaus-an-der-Eger, 1964).

There are two excellent studies of Bavaria and the League: F. Neuer-Landfried, *Die Katholische Liga: Gründung, Neugründung und Organisation eines Sonderbundes, 1608–1620* (Kallmünz, 1968: Münchener historische Studien, Abteilung bayerische Geschichte, IX), and H. Altmann, *Die Reichspolitik Maximilians von Bayern, 1613–1618* (Munich, 1978: Briefe und Akten zur Geschichte des dreissigjährigen Krieges, neue Folge, XII). Other volumes in this series bear the collective title *Die Politik Maximilians I. von Bayern und seiner Verbündeten 1618–1651.* Volume I (in two parts, published Munich, 1966–70) covers the period 1618–22. Volume II covers 1623–35 in 10 parts, not all of them yet available: parts 1–3 (published Leipzig, 1907, 1918 and 1942) and 4–5 (published Munich, 1948 and 1964) take the story to 1630. Part 8 (for 1633–4) appeared in 1981, part 9 (for 1634–5) in 1986. Volume III, covering 1635–48, will probably never be published, since all relevant material is to appear in the Bavarian sub-section of the *Acta Pacis Westphalicae* (page 298 below).

Paradoxically there is no entirely adequate biography of the League's Director – although the material concerning him is voluminous and is best approached through A. Kraus, 'Kurfürst Maximilian I von Bayern. Das neue Bild eines grossen Fürsten', *Historisches Jahrbuch*, XCVII/XCVIII (1978), 505–26 – which reviews all literature since 1963. Beyond this, on Maximilian before the war, see H. Dollinger's full-length work: *Studien zur Finanzreform Maximilians I. von Bayern in den Jahren 1598–1618. Ein Beitrag zur Geschichte des Frühabsolutismus* (Göttingen, 1968: Schriftenreihe der historischen Kommission bei der bayerischen Akademie der Wissenschaften, VIII). Also recommended are H. Dotterweich, *Der junge Maximilian. Jugend und Erziehung des bayerischen Herzogs und späteren Kurfürsten Maximilian I. von 1573 bis 1593* (Munich, 1962: a charming study based on ducal household papers and the young duke's exercise books) and K. Pfister, *Kurfürst Maximilian von Bayern und sein Jahrhundert* (Munich, 1948: insufficiently rigorous but full of interesting anecdotes). Perhaps the best, and certainly the most up-to-date portrait, is presented in the catalogue of a huge exhibition mounted in 1980 in the Munich *Residenz*: H. Glaser, ed., *Wittelsbach und Bayern. II. Um Glauben und Reich: Kurfürst Maximilian I. 1. Beiträge zur bayerischen Geschichte und Kunst 1573–1657* and *2. Katalog der Ausstellung* (Munich and Zürich, 1980). Further studies on the theme of Maximilian and the arts appeared in H. Glaser, ed., *Quellen und Studien zur Kunstpolitik der Wittelsbacher vom 16. bis zum 18. Jahrhundert* (Munich and Zürich, 1980).

For the policy towards events in the Empire pursued by other European powers at this time, see, for England: S.L. Adams, 'The Protestant Cause: Relations with the west European Calvinist communities as a political issue in England, 1585–1630' (Oxford University D. Phil. thesis, 1973), and J.V. Polišenský, *Anglie a Bílá Hora* (Prague, 1949); for France: R. Mousnier, *The Assassination of Henry IV* (English edn, London, 1973), and J.M. Hayden, 'Continuity in the France of Henry IV and Louis XIII. French foreign policy, 1598–1615',*Journal of Modern History*, XLV (1973), 1–23; for the United Provinces: J. den Tex, *Oldenbarnevelt* (English edn, 2 vols, Cambridge, 1973), and A. Th. van Deursen, *Honni Soit qui Mal y Pense? De Republiek tussen de Mogendheden (1610–1612)* (Amsterdam, 1965: Mededelingen der Koninklijke Nederlandse Akademie van Wetenschappen, Afdeling Letterkunde, N.S., XXVIII/i). For Spain, see: P. Brightwell, 'Spain and Bohemia: the decision to intervene, 1619', *European Studies Review*, XII (1982), 117–41; *idem*, 'Spain, Bohemia and Europe, 1619–21', *loc. cit.*, 371–99; and Straub's monograph noted immediately below.

C The 1620s

There is an excellent brief survey of the Bohemian revolt by H. Sturmberger, *Aufstand in Böhmen. Der Beginn des dreissigjährigen Krieges* (Munich and Vienna, 1959); but A. Gindely, *Geschichte des dreissigjährigen Krieges* (4 vols, Prague, 1869–80) still remains indispensable for the 'Bohemian phase' of the war. On Ferdinand's reaction to the crisis, apart from the works of Franzl and Bireley (above), much further information is to be found in P. Broucek, 'Feldmarschall Bucquoy als Armeekommandant, 1618 bis 1620', in *Der dreissigjährige Krieg: Beiträge zu seiner Geschichte* (Vienna, 1976: Schriften des Heeresgeschichtlichen Museums, VII), 25–57; and H. Kretschmer, *Sturmpetition und Blockade Wiens im Jahre 1619* (Vienna, 1978: Militärhistorische Schriftenreihe, XXXVIII). Dieter Albrecht has dealt with both papal and Bavarian policy towards the revolt in magisterial manner. See his three studies: 'Zur Finanzierung des dreissigjährigen Krieges', *Zeitschrift für bayerische Landesgeschichte*, XIX (1956), 534–67; *Die deutsche Politik Papst Gregors XV* (Munich, 1956: Schriftenreihe zur bayerischen Landesgeschichte, LIII); and *Die auswärtige Politik Maximilians von Bayern, 1618–1635* (Göttingen, 1962: Schriftenreihe der historischen Kommission bei der Bayerischen Akademie der Wissenschaften, VI).

On Spanish policy, see P. Brightwell, 'The Spanish origins of the Thirty Years' war', *European Studies Review*, IX (1979), 409–31 (and two further articles noted immediately above); and the important study of E. Straub, *Pax et imperium. Spaniens Kampf um seine Friedensordnung in Europa zwischen 1617 und 1635* (Paderborn, 1980: Rechts- und staatswissenschaftliche Veröffentlichungen der Görres-Gesellschaft, Neue Folge XXXI). Note, however, that there are some curious gaps in Straub's list of authorities, and that his entire interpretation has been attacked for neglecting the role of Bavaria and Austria (see the review by H. Altmann in *Zeitschrift für bayerische Landesgeschichte*, XLV [1982], 723–7). One of the works not cited by Straub is the study of J. Alcalá-Zamora y Queipo de Llano, *España, Flandes y el Mar del Norte (1618–1639). La última ofensiva europea de los Austrias madrileños* (Barcelona, 1975), which largely supersedes the relevant chapters of B. Chudoba, *Spain and the Empire 1519–1643* (Chicago, 1952), and considerable parts of R. Ródenas Vilar, *La política europea de España durante la Guerra de Treinta Años, 1624–1630* (Madrid, 1967). Alcalá-Zamora has, however, been criticized (along with the present writer and most others in the field) by *J.I. Israel, *The Dutch Republic and the Hispanic World 1606–1661* (Oxford, 1982), for defective coverage of the war in the Low Countries. Israel, on the other hand, fails much of the time to integrate events in the Low Countries with those in Germany. No one, it seems, is perfect.

There is much of value on the 'Baltic design', in A.E. Sokol, *Das habsburgische Admiralitätswerk des 16. und 17. Jahrhunderts* (Vienna, 1976: Biblos-Schriften, LXXXIX); and a useful collection of Spanish documents, together with a long introduction, concerning the negotiations between the two branches of the House of Austria during the period is provided by H. Günter, *Die Habsburger-Liga 1625–1635. Briefe und Akten aus dem General-Archiv zu Simancas* (Berlin, 1908; reprinted 1965). The most recent overview of all this is provided in the balanced and impressively documented article of M.E.H.N. Mout, ' "Holendische propositiones". Een Habsburgs plan tot vernietigung van handel, visserij en scheepvaart der Republiek (ca 1625)', *Tijdschrift voor Geschiedenis*, XCV (1982), 345–62. On the court of Spain, where so many crucial decisions were taken, see Jonathan Brown and J.H. Elliott, *A Palace for a King. The Buen Retiro and the Court of Philip IV* (London and New Haven, 1980). Elliott is currently preparing a political biography of the count-duke of Olivares and has just published an essay in comparative history: *Richelieu and Olivares* (Cambridge, 1984). The German policy of the government in Brussels, which did not always see eye-to-eye with Madrid, is examined by J. Kessel, *Spanien und die geistlichen Kurstaaten am Rhein während der Regierungszeit der Infantin Isabella (1621–1633)* (Frankfurt-am-Main, 1979).

Of Ferdinand's principal opponent, the Elector Palatine Frederick V, there is no adequate study – though much may be gleaned from Schubert's *Camerarius* and Press, *Calvinismus und Territorialstaat* (page 284 above). See also J.G. Weiss, 'Die Vorgeschichte des böhmischen Abenteuers Friedrichs V. von der Pfalz', *Zeitschrift für die Geschichte des Oberrheins*, N.F. LIII (1940), 383–492; and F.H. Schubert, 'Die pfälzische Exilregierung im dreissigjährigen Krieg: ein Beitrag zur Geschichte des politischen Protestantismus', *Zeitschrift für die Geschichte des Oberrheins*, CII (1954), 575–680.

The best account of the 1621 and 1622 campaigns in the west is found in H. Wertheim, *Der Tolle Halberstädter: Herzog Christian von Braunschweig im Pfälzischen Krieg, 1621–1622* (Berlin, 1929). For the

1623 campaign, see W. Brünick, *Der Graf von Mansfeld in Ostfriesland (1623–1624)* (Aurich, 1957: Abhandlungen und Vorträge zur Geschichte Ostfrieslands, XXIV), which also provides the most convincing portrait of Mansfeld. On the occupation of the Rhine Palatinate, see A. Egler, *Die Spanier in der Linkrheinischen Pfalz, 1620–32. Invasion, Verwaltung, Rekatholisierung* (Mainz, 1971: Quellen und Abhandlungen zur mittelrheinischen Kirchengeschichte, XIII); and W. Dautermann, *Alzey im dreissigjährigen Krieg. Eine Studie über die Wirkung des dreissigjährigen Krieges in einer pfälzischen Stadt* (Berlin, 1937: Historische Studien, CCCXVIII). Finally, on the Upper Palatinate, see K.–O. Ambronn and A. Fuchs, eds, *Die Oberpfalz wird bayerisch: die Jahre 1621 bis 1628 im Amberg und der Oberpfalz* (Ausstellungskatalog: Amberg, 1978); and J. Staber, 'Die Eroberung der Oberpfalz im Jahre 1621. Nach dem Tagebuch des Johann Christoph von Preysing', *Verhandlungen des historischen Vereins für Oberpfalz und Regensburg*, CIV (1964), 165–221.

For Danish intervention, H. Gamrath and E. Ladewig Petersen, *Gyldendal's danmarkshistorie, II, 2: 1559–1648* (Copenhagen, 1980), give a narrative account and a full critical bibliography, including all the literature in Danish, to which readers are referred. The prelude to that intervention – and its relation to the Danish-Swedish context – has most recently been described by L. Tandrup, *Mod triumf eller tragedie. En politisk-diplomatisk studie i forløbet af den dansk-svenske magtkamp fra Kalmarkrigen til Kejserkrigen*, (2 vols, Århus, 1979). Cf. the reviews by S. Heiberg and K.J.V. Jespersen in *Fortid og Nutid*, XXVIII (1980), 636–43 and *Historisk tidsskrift [Dansk]*, LXXXI (1981), 242–53, respectively. Tandrup's work largely supersedes T. Christiansen, *Die Stellung König Christians IV. von Dänemark zu den Kriegsereignissen im deutschen Reich und zu den Plänen einer evangelischen Allianz 1618–1625* (Kiel, 1937). The still unrivalled study (in the Rankean tradition) of Christian IV's post-war foreign relations until 1645 is J.A. Fridericia, *Danmarks ydre politiske Historie fra Freden i Lübeck til Freden i Kjøbenhavn*, (2 vols, Copenhagen, 1876–81; reprinted 1972). On public finance, see E. Ladewig Petersen, 'From Domain state to Tax state', *Scandinavian Economic History Review*, XXIII (1975), 116–48, and * 'Defence, war and finance: Christian IV and the Council of the Realm 1596–1629', *Scandinavian Journal of History*, VII (1982), 277–313.

The role of Transylvania, and behind her of the Turks, during the early phases of the Thirty Years' War is often neglected; yet material for study is not lacking. See D. Angyal, 'Gabriel Bethlen', *Revue historique*, LIII (1928), 19–80; J.V. Polišenský, 'Bohemia, the Turk and the Christian Commonwealth, 1462–1620', *Byzantinoslavica* XIV (1953), 82–108; R.R. Heinisch, 'Habsburg, die Pforte und der Böhmische Aufstand (1618–20)', *Südostforschungen*, XXXIII (1974), 125–65, and XXXIV (1975), 79–124; and H. Valentinitsch, 'Die Steiermark, Ungarn und die Osmanen, 1606–1662', *Zeitschrift des Historischen Vereines für Steiermark*, LXV (1974), 93–128.

For English foreign policy in the 1620s, see S.L. Adams, 'The Protestant cause' (page 286 above), and his articles: 'Foreign Policy and the

Parliaments of 1621 and 1624', in K. Sharpe, ed., *Faction and Parliament: Essays on Early Stuart History* (Oxford, 1978), 139–71; and 'Spain or the Netherlands? The dilemmas of early Stuart foreign policy' in H. Tomlinson, ed., *Before the Civil War* (London, 1984), 79–101. See also E. Weiss, *Die Unterstützung Friedrichs V. von der Pfalz durch Jakob I, und Karl I von England im dreissigjährigen Krieg (1618–32)* (Stuttgart, 1966: Veröffentlichungen der Kommission für geschichtliche Landeskunde in Baden-Württemberg, series B, XXXVII); and R. Zaller, ' "Interest of state": James I and the Palatinate', *Albion*, VI (1974), 144–75. James I's attempts to mediate in the Palatinate are discussed in detail in A.W. White, 'Suspension of Arms: Anglo-Spanish Mediation in the Thirty Years' War, 1621–1625' (Tulane University PhD thesis, 1978). Dutch foreign policy during the Thirty Years' War lacks a modern study, but details of military assistance to the German Protestants can be found in: F.J.G. ten Raa and F. de Bas, *Het Staatsche Leger, 1573–1795. III (1609–1625)*, (Breda, 1915); J.V. Polišenský, *Nizozemská politika a Bílá Hora* (Prague, 1958); J.H. Hora Siccama, *Schets van de diplomatieke betrekkingen tusschen Nederland en Brandenburg 1596–1678* (Utrecht, 1867), chaps 1–2; and J.G. Smit and J. Roelevink, eds, *Resolutiën der Staten-Generaal*, nieuwe reeks IV–V (The Hague, 1981–3).

Of the other interventionist states, the policies of France are the best covered. See V.L. Tapié, *La politique de la France et le début de la guerre de trente ans* (Paris, 1934); R. Pithon, 'Les débuts difficiles du Ministère de Richelieu et la crise de la Valtelline (1621–1627)', *Revue d'Histoire Diplomatique*, LXXIV (1960), 298–322; and 'La Suisse, théâtre de la Guerre Froide entre la France et l'Espagne pendant la crise de la Valtelline (1621–1626)', *Schweizerische Zeitschrift für Geschichte*, XIII (1963), 33–53. There seems to be no entirely satisfactory study of Richelieu's foreign policy: the best consideration of the man in English – W.F. Church, *Richelieu and Reason of State* (Princeton, 1972) – has little to say on foreign affairs after 1627. Perhaps the most illuminating introduction is part II of J. Wollenberg, *Richelieu: Staatsräson und Kircheninteresse. Zur Legitimation der Politik des Kardinalpremier* (Bielefeld, 1977). Many fine insights into French foreign policy throughout the war are to be found in *R.J. Bonney, *The King's Debts. Politics and Finance in France 1589–1661* (Oxford, 1981). For some other powers interested in the struggle during the 1620s, see: R. Kleinman, 'Charles Emanuel I of Savoy and the Bohemian election of 1619', *European Studies Review*, V (1975), 3–29; J. Krebs, *Die Politik der evangelischen Union im Jahre 1618* (Breslau, 1890–1); and M. Roberts, *Gustavus Adolphus. A History of Sweden 1611–32*, I (London, 1953), chaps 4–5.

Yet the fact remains that the principal victor of the 1620s was not a foreign prince but the emperor, thanks to the crushing military defeats inflicted by the Catholic generals on one adversary after another. Tilly, strangely, lacks a modern biography, though the relevant (illustrated) section in Glaser, ed., *Wittelsbach und Bayern* II/1, 377–99, goes some way towards bridging the gap. The serious student is forced to rely on the work of Tilly's great apologist, O. Klopp, *Tilly im dreissigjährigen Krieg* (2 vols, Stuttgart, 1861; revised edn, Paderborn, 1891–6). The other central figure in the story, Albrecht von Waldstein, or Wallenstein, has suffered no such neglect: there are perhaps 4,000 works concerning him in various languages. For English readers, the best available biography is Golo Mann, *Wallenstein, His Life Narrated* (London, 1976: the original German edition – Frankfurt, 1971 – includes notes and a detailed bibliography). Also useful is H. Diwald, *Wallenstein: eine Biographie* (Munich, 1969), although its outlook is more Germanic than Mann's and it has not attracted the same controversy (see, for example, the 'for and against' review articles of Mann's biography in the journals *Merkur*, XXVI (1972), 282–96, and *Neue Rundschau*, LXXXIII (1972), 343–9). Most non-German historians seem agreed, however, that neither of these modern studies differs greatly from earlier interpretations. Indeed, in many cases, they are less informative than such classic works as A. Gindely, *Waldstein während seines ersten Generalats* (2 vols, Prague, 1886), or the more recent A. Ernstberger, *Wallenstein als Volkswirt im Herzogtum Friedland* (Reichenberg, 1929), and *idem, Hans de Witte, Finanzmann Wallensteins* (Wiesbaden, 1954: Vierteljahrschrift für Sozial- und Wirtschaftsgeschichte, Beiheft XXXVIII). There is no escape, for the diligent Wallenstein scholar, from the need to consult the massive documentary collections noted on page 294 below. There is nothing adequate on Eggenberg, but H. von Zwiedineck-Südenhorst, *Hans Ulrich Fürst von Eggenberg* (Vienna, 1880), and W.E. Heydendorff, *Die Fürsten und Freiherren zu Eggenberg und ihre Vorfahren* (Graz, 1965), provide some information.

A good deal of material has been published concerning the internal history of the Habsburg Monarchy after the White Mountain. There is, of course, the invaluable study of Evans, *The Habsburg Monarchy* (page 282 above), after which perhaps the best starting-point is A. Coreth, *Pietas Austriaca. Ursprung und Entwicklung barocker Frömmigkeit in Österreich* (Munich, 1959). For the central institutions of the Monarchy see: T. Fellner and H. Kretschmayr, *Die österreichische Zentralverwaltung*, I (2 vols, Vienna, 1907); L. Gross, *Die Geschichte der deutschen Reichshofkanzlei von 1559 bis 1806* (Vienna, 1933); and H.F. Schwarz, *The Imperial Privy Council in the Seventeenth Century* (Cambridge, Mass., 1943). Political and military events in the separate Habsburg territories must still be approached largely through old-fashioned source and narrative works. For Bohemia, T.B. Bílek, *Dějiny konfiskací v Čechách po r. 1618* (2 vols, Prague, 1882–3), gives every detail of changes in landholding; but his figures have been revised by F.L. Snider, 'The restructuring of the Bohemian nobility in the seventeenth century' (University of California at Berkeley PhD thesis, 1972). A. Gindely, *Geschichte der Gegenreformation in Böhmen* (ed. T. Tupetz, Leipzig, 1894), is authoritative but incomplete; E. Denis, *La Bohême depuis la Montagne Blanche* (Paris, 1903), whose Czech translation (by J. Vančura) contains many additions and corrections, is the classic splenetic liberal. Perhaps the best modern treatment is to be found in K. Bosl, ed., *Handbuch der Geschichte der böhmischen Länder*, II (Stuttgart, 1974). The new constitution is printed in H. Jireček, ed., *Constitutiones regni Bohemiae anno 1627 reformatae* (Prague, etc.,

1888). I. Kollmann, ed., *Acta Sacrae Congregationis de Propaganda Fide res gestas Bohemicas illustrantia* (2 vols, Prague, 1923–54), covers the early days of planned Counter-Reformation; J.V. Polišenský, M. Toegel *et al.*, eds, *Documenta Bohemica Bellum Tricennale illustrantia* (7 vols, Prague, 1971–7), contains much hitherto unknown material. For Hungary, the writings of Pázmány are fundamental and they were printed complete in 13 volumes (Budapest, 1894–1905), followed by his correspondence, ed. J. Hanuy (2 vols, Budapest, 1910–11). The latest view of the cardinal-primate is F. Bitskey, *Humanista erudíció és barokk világkép, Pázmány Péter prédikációi* (Budapest, 1979). László Nagy recounts military events in *Bethlen Gábor a független Magyarországért* (Budapest, 1969), and *Magyar hadsereg és hadmüvészet a harmincéves háborúban* (Budapest, 1972); and a new synthetic view is expected shortly in Zs. P. Pach, ed., *Magyarország története*, III (1526–1686). There is nothing satisfactory on Esterházy. For Austria, J. Loserth, ed., *Akten und Korrespondenzen zur Geschichte der Gegenreformation in Innerösterreich unter Karl II und Ferdinand II* (2 vols in 3, Vienna, 1898–1907), documents the fate of Styrian Protestants. That of their co-religionists elsewhere in the Empire is covered, from a Catholic perspective, in B. Duhr, *Geschichte der Jesuiten in den Ländern deutscher Zunge*: volumes II.1 and II.2 (Freiburg, 1913) cover the first half of the seventeenth century.

For the implementation of Habsburg absolutism in Upper Austria, see above all H. Sturmberger, *Adam Graf Herberstorff. Herrschaft und Freiheit im Konfessionellen Zeitalter* (Munich, 1976). There are also two volumes commemorating the 350th anniversary of the 1626 revolt which range far more widely than their titles suggest: *Der oberösterreichische Bauernkrieg 1626: Ausstellung des Landes Oberösterreich im Linzer Schloss und im Schloss zu Scharnstein* (Linz, 1976); and G. Heilingsetzer, *Der oberösterreichische Bauernkrieg 1626* (Vienna, 1976: Militärhistorische Schriftenreihe, vol. XXXII). The impact of Habsburg absolutism on Upper Austrian peasant society is covered by H. Rebel, *Peasant Classes. The bureaucratization of property and family relations under early Habsburg absolutism, 1511–1636* (Princeton, 1983), chap. 8. On the revolt and submission of Lower Austria, see the excellent dissertation of R.D. Chesler, 'Crown, lords and God: the establishment of secular authority and the pacification of Lower Austria, 1618–48' (Princeton University PhD thesis, 1979).

Finally, Ferdinand III remains a Cinderella of scholarship. Consult M. Koch, *Geschichte des deutschen Reiches unter der Regierung Ferdinands III* (2 vols, Vienna, 1865–6), for his German policies, and F. Stieve in *Allgemeine deutsche Biographie*, VI (1877), 664–71, for a brief interpretation.

D 1630–1635

On the disastrous war of Mantua, which was to prove the turning-point in Habsburg fortunes, the standard study is still R. Quazza, *La guerra per la successione di Mantova e del Monferrato* (2 vols, Mantua, 1926).

There is also a useful collection of Spanish material in *Colección de documentos inéditos para la historia de España*, LIV, and in M. Fernández Álvarez, *Don Gonzalo Fernández de Córdoba y la guerra de sucesión de Mantua y del Monferrato 1627–9* (Madrid, 1955, with a long introduction). Papal attitudes over Mantua are examined (independently) by Q. Aldea, 'La neutralidad de Urbano VIII en los años decisivos de la Guerra de treinta años (1628–32)', *Hispania Sacra*, XXI (1968), 155–78, and by G. Lutz, *Kardinal Giovanni Francesco Guidi di Bagno. Politik und Religion im Zeitalter Richelieus und Urbans VIII* (Tübingen, 1971: Bibliothek des deutschen historischen Instituts in Rom, XXXIV). For a survey of the economic consequences of the war, see D. Sella, *Crisis and Continuity. The economy of Spanish Lombardy in the seventeenth century* (Cambridge, Mass., 1979).

The events at Regensburg in the summer of 1630 can best be followed through the works written or edited by Dieter Albrecht: *Die auswärtige Politik Maximilians* (page 286 above); *Briefe und Akten zur Geschichte des dreissigjährigen Krieges, neue Folge: die Politik Maximilians I von Bayern und seiner Verbündeten 1618–51*, II, part 5 (Munich, 1964), document 170 (315 pages of sources concerning the Electoral Meeting); *Richelieu, Gustav Adolf und das Reich* (Munich and Vienna, 1959); and 'Der Regensburger Kurfürstentag 1630 und die Entlassung Wallensteins', in D. Albrecht, ed., *Regensburg. Stadt der Reichstage* (Regensburg, 1980), 51–71. See also the vintage study of O. Heyne, *Der Kurfürstentag zu Regensburg von 1630* (Berlin, 1866). For a more modern perspective, see R. Bireley, SJ, *Maximilian von Bayern, Adam Contzen S.J., und die Gegenreformation in Deutschland 1624–35* (Göttingen 1975: Schriftenreihe der Historischen Kommission bei der bayerischen Akademie der Wissenschaften, XIII), and *idem*, *Religion and Politics in the Age of the Counter-Revolution*, chap. 6. On the politics of the Protestant Electors after Regensburg, see B. Nischan, 'Reformed Irenicism and the Leipzig colloquy of 1631', *Central European History*, IX (1976), 3–26, and 'Brandenburg's Reformed Räte and the Leipzig Manifesto of 1631', *Journal of Religious History*, X (1979), 365–80.

The writings of Michael Roberts form the indispensable starting-point – and, for English readers, often the finishing-point too – for all study of Swedish intervention in the war. First comes his major biography of Sweden's king, the second volume of which deals with the war in Germany: *M. Roberts, Gustavus Adolphus: a history of Sweden 1611–1632* (2 vols, London, 1953–8; one-volume abridgement, *Gustavus Adolphus and the Rise of Sweden*, London, 1973). Further themes are developed in M. Roberts, *Essays in Swedish History* (London, 1967), especially chapter 6 ('The political objectives of Gustavus Adolphus in Germany, 1630–32'); and many translated documents are printed with a helpful commentary in the same author's *Sweden as a Great Power 1611–1697: government, society, foreign policy* (London, 1968). Many points are re-examined, and several new ones explored, in Roberts's most recent survey: *The Swedish Imperial Experience 1560–1718* (Cambridge, 1979).

There is very little else on the subject in English, but naturally readers of Swedish have a far greater choice. On the war itself, pride of place must go to the definitive study produced by the Swedish Army's General Staff: *Sveriges Krig 1611–1632* (8 vols, Stockholm, 1936–9, of which vols 3–6 deal with the war in Germany 1629–1632). With its maps, tables and diagrams, and with a text based on sources drawn from archives all over Europe, it is unlikely that this work will ever be superseded. For a useful illustrated study of Sweden's fortifications, see L.W. Munthe, *Kongliga Fortifikationens Historia* I (Stockholm, 1902, taking the story to 1641), and II (Stockholm, 1904, covering 1641–76). In recent years, the attention of Swedish military historians has focused on the economy of the Empire at war. See, for example: H. Landberg, L. Ekholm, R. Nordlund and S.A. Nilsson, *Det konintentala krigets ekonomi. Studier i krigsfinansiering under Svensk Stormaktstid* (Stockholm, 1971); S.A. Lundkvist, 'Svensk Krigsfinansiering 1630–5', *Historisk Tidsskrift [Svensk]*, LXXXVI (1966), 377–421; L. Ekholm, *Svensk krigsfinansiering* (Uppsala, 1974: Studia historia Upsaliensia, LVI); R. Nordlund, 'Kontribution eller satisfaktion. Pommern och de Svenska krigsfinanserna, 1633', *Historisk Tidsskrift [Svensk]*, XCIV (1974), 321–402, and *idem*, *Krig på avveckling. Sverige och tyska kriget 1633* (Uppsala, 1974).

On the policies of Sweden in the Empire, two vintage studies by Johannes Kretzschmar remain fundamental: 'Die Allianz-Verhandlungen Gustav Adolfs mit Kurbrandenburg in Mai und Juni 1631', *Forschungen zur brandenburgischen und preussischen Geschichte*, XVII (1904), 341–82; and *Gustav Adolfs Pläne und Ziele in Deutschland und die Herzöge zu Braunschweig und Lüneburg* (Hannover and Leipzig, 1904). On Sweden's relations with Hesse, see W. Keim, 'Landgraf Wilhelm V von Hessen-Kassel vom Regierungsantritt 1627 bis zum Abschluss des Bündnisses mit Gustav Adolf 1631', *Hessisches Jahrbuch für Landesgeschichte*, XII (1962), 130–210, and XIII (1963), 141–222. There is nothing similar on the shot-gun marriage imposed by Sweden upon Electoral Saxony, although the reasons why John George was persuaded to invade Bohemia in 1631 are discussed in M. Toegel, 'Příčiny saského vpádu do Čech v roce 1631', *Československý časopis historický*, XXI (1973), 553–81 (with German summary). A new German biography of the king gives some attention to these matters: G. Barudio, *Gustav Adolf der Grosse. Eine politische Biographie* (Frankfurt, 1982). Swedish policy in Germany after the king's death is splendidly surveyed by *M. Roberts, 'Oxenstierna in Germany, 1633–1636', *Scandia*, XLVIII (1982), 61–105; while *S. Goetze, *Die Politik des schwedischen Reichskanzlers Axel Oxenstierna gegenüber Kaiser und Reich* (Kiel, 1971), offers a significant advance on the traditional viewpoint exemplified by J. Kretzschmar, *Der Heilbronner Bund 1632–5* (3 vols, Lübeck, 1922), or A. Kuesel, *Der Heilbronner Convent. Ein Beitrag zur Geschichte des dreissigjährigen Krieges* (Halle, 1878) – although both these older works nevertheless contain much material unavailable elsewhere. Finally, for Sweden's administration of her conquests, see: C. Deinert, *Die schwedische Epoche in Franken von 1631–5* (Würzburg, 1966); and H.D. Müller, *Der schwedische Staat in Mainz 1631–1636. Einnahmen,*

Verwaltung, Absichten, Restitution (Mainz, 1979: Beiträge zur Geschichte der Stadt Mainz, XXIV). See also the sources noted on page 296
below.

What all these admirable and meticulously detailed works omit is
the charisma of the principal actors: neither Gustavus nor Oxenstierna
emerges from the printed page as the larger-than-life figure perceived by
contemporaries. For the king, at least, this popular appeal may be
grasped through the flattering reports of his deeds in every Protestant
newspaper and pamphlet of the period 1630–2, and even more in the
'Gustaviana' – the innumerable artefacts fashioned in the likeness of the
king. Statuettes, ceremonial tankards, medallions, portraits and even
stained-glass windows were all employed as propaganda. There are
examples in most of the museums and galleries of Protestant Europe.

The situation concerning Sweden's principal antagonist in these
years, Wallenstein, is far less satisfactory. The recent biographies of
Mann and Diwald (page 290 above) are inadequate on his second
generalship: they certainly do not replace the massive documentary
collections and studies produced two and three generations ago. The
major ones, in alphabetical order are as follows: A. Gaedeke, *Wallensteins Verhandlungen mit den Schweden und Sachsen 1631–4. Mit
Akten und Urkunden aus dem Königlich Sächsischen Hauptstaatsarchiv zu Dresden* (Frankfurt, 1885); H. Hallwich: *Wallensteins Ende,
Ungedruckte Briefe und Akten* (2 vols, Leipzig, 1879); idem, *Fünf
Bücher Geschichte Wallensteins* (3 vols, Leipzig, 1910); and idem, *Briefe
und Akten zur Geschichte Wallensteins 1630–34* (4 vols, Vienna, 1912:
Fontes Rerum Austriacarum, section II, vols LXIII–LXVI); K.G. Helbig,
*Der Kaiser Ferdinand und der Herzog von Friedland während des Win-
ters 1633–4* (Dresden, 1852); G. Irmer, *Die Verhandlungen Schwedens
und seiner Verbündeten mit Wallenstein und dem Kaiser 1631–4* (3 vols,
Leipzig, 1888–9); J. Pekař, *Wallenstein 1630–1634. Tragödie einer Ver-
schwörung* (2 vols, Berlin, 1937; original Czech edn, 1895. On Pekař's
book, see the informative review by W. Goetz, 'Wallenstein und Kurfürst Maximilian von Bayern', *Zeitschrift für bayerische Landesgeschichte*, XI [1938], 106–20); and Heinrich Ritter von Srbik, *Wallensteins
Ende*, (2nd edn, Salzburg, 1952). These vast compilations of documents-
and-commentary illuminate, better than any later work the exceeding-
ly complicated negotiations in which the general was engaged; they
therefore explain much of the 'mystery' of Wallenstein and the greater
part of the 'Wallenstein problem'. Also recommended are three further
studies by H. Hallwich – *Heinrich Matthias Thurn als Zeuge im Prozess
Wallensteins* (Leipzig, 1883); *Gestalten am Wallensteins Lager. I.
Johann Merode and II. Johann Aldringer* (Leipzig, 1884–5) – and a
collection of important letters from Moravian archives: P. von
Chlumecky, ed., *Die Regesten der Archive im Markgrafthume Mähren.
I . . . Briefen Kaiser Ferdinands des Zweiten, Albrechts von Waldstein,
und Romboalds Grafen Collalto* (2 parts with separate pagination bound
as one volume, Brünn, 1856).

The only major breakthrough in recent years has been made by the
Finnish scholar *P. Suvanto: *Wallenstein und seine Anhänger am*

Wiener Hof zur Zeit des Zweiten Generalats 1631–4 (Helsinki, 1963) and
**Die deutsche Politik Oxenstiernas und Wallensteins* (Helsinki, 1979:
Studia historica, IX). Some of the more controversial deductions in the
first study were supported (albeit amid criticisms), from other
documentary sources, by G. Lutz, 'Wallenstein, Ferdinand II. und der
Wiener Hof. Bemerkungen zu einem erneuten Beitrag zur alten
Wallensteinfrage', *Quellen und Forschungen aus italienischen
Archiven und Bibliotheken*, XLVIII (1968), 207–43. Yet more sources are
discussed in note 7 on page 256 above.

Two other powers were deeply involved in this phase of the war –
Spain and Hesse-Kassel. On the former, see A. van der Essen, *Le
Cardinal-Infant et la politique européenne de l'Espagne, 1609–1641*, I
(Louvain, 1944); *idem*, 'Le rôle du Cardinal-Infant dans la politique
espagnole du XVIIe siècle', *Revista de la Universidad de Madrid*, III
(1954), 357–83; and R.A. Stradling, *Europe and the Decline of Spain. A
study of the Spanish system 1580–1720* (London, 1981), chaps 2 and 3.
The war in Hesse is covered by R. Altmann, *Landgraf Wilhelm V von
Hessen-Kassel im Kampf gegen Kaiser und Katholizismus* (Marburg,
1938), and L. van Tongerloo, 'Beziehungen zwischen Hessen-Kassel und
den Vereinigten Niederlanden während des dreissigjährigen Krieges',
Hessisches Jahrbuch für Landesgeschichte, XIV (1964), 199–270.

Hesse-Darmstadt's crucial role in bringing about the peace of Prague between the emperor and most of his Lutheran vassals is subjected to
penetrating analysis by K.H. Frohnweiler, 'Die Friedenspolitik Landgraf
Georgs II. von Hessen-Darmstadt in den Jahren 1630–5', *Archiv für
hessische Geschichte und Altertumskunde*, N.F. XXIX (1964), 1–185. On
the negotiations leading up to the peace of Prague see Bireley, *Religion
and Politics*, chap. 11; and *K. Repgen, *Die römische Kurie und der
westfälische Friede. I.i Papst, Kaiser und Reich 1521–1644* (Tübingen,
1962), 329–88; and the early sections of *F. Dickmann, *Der Westfälische
Frieden* (4th edn, Münster, 1977). The text of the peace is discussed at
length by K. Bierther, 'Zur Edition von Quellen zum Prager Frieden vom
30. Mai 1635' in K. Repgen, ed., *Forschungen und Quellen zur Geschichte des Dreissigjährigen Krieges* (Münster, 1981: Schriftenreihe der
Vereinigung zur Erforschung der neueren Geschichte, XII), 1–31. Its
military consequences are ably analysed by H. Haan 'Kaiser Ferdinand
II. und das Problem des Reichsabsolutismus. Die Prager Heeresreform
von 1635', in H.U. Rudolf, ed., *Der Dreissigjährige Krieg. Perspektiven
und Strukturen* (Darmstadt, 1977), 208–64.

E   1635–1641

Both of the major assemblies held during this period to resolve the
divisions in Germany have been the subject of meticulous study: H.
Haan, *Der Regensburger Kurfürstentag von 1636/1637* (Münster, 1967:
Schriftenreihe der Vereinigung zur Erforschung der neueren Geschichte,
III), and K. Bierther, *Der Regensburger Reichstag von 1640/1641* (Kallmünz, 1971). In connexion with the Electoral Meeting of 1636, there is a
fine study of the English embassy led by Thomas, earl of Arundel, which

reproduces William Crowne's 'True Relation' and many of Wenceslas Hollar's engravings: F.C. Springell, *Connoisseur and Diplomat: the earl of Arundel's embassy to Germany in 1636* (London, 1963).

Oxenstierna's correspondence remains the most important single source for this period and, since 1888, much of it has been printed in two series by the Royal Swedish Academy of Letters, History and Antiquities: *Axel Oxenstiernas skrifter och brevvexling*, 1st series (containing the chancellor's outgoing correspondence to 1636), 15 volumes; and 2nd series (containing incoming correspondence arranged by writers rather than by date), 12 volumes. Both series are still in the course of publication. The attitude of the Regents and the Council of State to the war is documented in *Svenska riksrådets protokoll (Handlingar rörande Skandinaviens Historia*, 3rd series, III–VIII, Stockholm, 1885–8), which print the Council minutes; and in *Handlingar rörande Skandinaviens Historia*, 1st series, XXIV–XXX and XXXII–XXXVIII (Stockholm, 1842–57), which print letters and instructions from the Regents and the Council to Oxenstierna. Sweden's treaties with foreign powers, and relevant documents connected with them, are printed in Carl Hallendorff, ed., *Sverges Traktater med främmande magter jemte andra hit hörande handlingar, V. 2 (1632–1645)* (Stockholm, 1909). On Franco-Swedish relations, see Erik Falk, *Sverige och Frankrike 1632–4* (Stockholm, 1911); Sverker Arnoldsson, *Svensk-fransk krigs- och fredspolitik i Tyskland 1634–6* (Göteborg, 1937); Sune Lundgren, *Johan Adler Salvius. Problem kring freden, krigsekonomien och maktkampen* (Lund, 1945); L. Tingsten, *Huvuddragen av Sveriges Politik och Krigföring i Tyskland efter Gustav II Adolfs död till och med sommaren 1635* (Stockholm, 1930); *idem, Fäldmarskalkarna Johan Baner och Lennart Torstensson såsom härförare* (Stockholm, 1932); and B. Steckzén, *Johan Baner* (Stockholm, 1939).

The general study of Pagès, *The Thirty Years' War*, is specially strong on French matters, and certain important aspects are given fuller treatment in the same author's 'Autour du "grand orage". Richelieu et Marillac. Deux politiques', *Revue Historique*, CLXXIX (1937), 63–97. Although primarily a review of Richelieu's relations with his domestic critics, this study contains fundamental observations on the importance of the acquisition of Pinerolo. See also the two general works on the period by R.J. Bonney: *Political Change in France under Richelieu and Mazarin 1624–1661* (Oxford, 1978), and *The King's Debts* (page 289 above). *D.P. O'Connell, 'A cause célèbre in the history of treaty making. The refusal to ratify the peace treaty of Regensburg in 1630', *British Yearbook of International Law*, XLII (1967), 71–90, is an important analysis of a crucial incident in the development of the French struggle with the emperor, to be read in conjunction with Pagès's comments on the domestic situation. On French policy in Alsace, the reader should turn first to G. Livet, *L'intendance d'Alsace sous Louis XIV, 1648–1715* (Strasbourg and Paris, 1956): difficult to read, and centred outside the period, book I nevertheless contains an excellent account of the contradictions of French 'protection'. It is not entirely superseded by two more recent studies: W.H. Stein, *Protection royale.*

Eine Untersuchung zu den Protektionsverhältnissen im Elsass zur Zeit Richelieus. 1622–1643 (Münster, 1978: Schriftenreihe der Vereinigung zur Erforschung der neueren Geschichte, IX); and R. Oberlé, *La République de Mulhouse pendant la guerre de trente ans* (Paris, 1965). Swiss interest in the area is brought out by R. Stritmatter, *Die Stadt Basel während des dreissigjährigen Krieges. Politik, Wirtschaft, Finanzen* (Bern, Frankfurt and Las Vegas, 1977). On Habsburg policy in Alsace, see the thorough survey of W.E. Heydendorff, 'Vorderösterreich im dreissigjährigen Krieg. Der Verlust der Vorlande am Rhein und die Versuche zu deren Rückgewinnung', *Mitteilungen des österreichischen Staatsarchivs*, XII (1959), 74–142 and XIII (1960), 107–94.

French policy on the Lower Rhine has also been extensively studied. See, above all, H. Weber, *Frankreich, Kurtrier, der Rhein und das Reich, 1623–35* (Bonn, 1969), which is conveniently summarized in the same author's article, * 'Richelieu et le Rhin', *Revue Historique*, CCXXXIX (1968), 265–80. The useful article of R. Pillorget, 'Louis XIV and the electorate of Trier, 1652–76', in R.M. Hatton, ed., *Louis XIV and Europe* (London, 1976), 115–32, also contains comments on the 1640s. For the devastation caused in Burgundy by the war after 1635, see the classic study of G. Roupnel, *La ville et la campagne au 17e siècle. Étude sur les populations du pays dijonnais* (2nd edn, Paris, 1955); for that of Lorraine, see S. Gaber, *La Lorraine meurtrie: les malheurs de la Guerre de Trente Ans* (Nancy, 1979).

F 1642–1650

The outstanding work on the peace which brought the war to an end is Dickmann, *Der Westfälische Frieden*. A useful appreciation of this book, which pays tribute to its definitive nature while making certain criticisms, is provided by M. Heckel, 'Zur Historiographie des Westfälischen Friedens. Die Bedeutung des Werkes von Fritz Dickmann für die deutsche Verfassungs- und Kirchenrechtsgeschichte', *Zeitschrift der Savigny-Stiftung für Rechtsgeschichte. Kanonistische Abteilung*, LVII (1971), 322–35. The simultaneous negotiations in Münster concerning peace between Spain and the Dutch Republic are ably analysed by J.J. Poelhekke, *De vrede van Munster* (The Hague, 1948), and Israel, *The Dutch Republic and the Hispanic World*, chap. 6.

The works of Konrad Repgen of Bonn, and of his pupils, are steadily expanding our understanding of the labyrinthine diplomatic activity that took place in the last five years of the war. Particularly useful are Repgen's study of papal policy towards a settlement (even though it ends in 1644) – see page 295 above – and his article 'Über den Zusammenhang von Verhandlungtechnik und Vertragsbegriffen. Die kaiserlichen Elsass-Angebote vom 28. März und 14. April 1646 an Frankreich', in A. Besch, ed., *Die Stadt in der europäischen Geschichte. Festschrift Edith Ennen* (Bonn, 1972), 638–66. The works of Repgen's students, published in the series *Schriftenreihe der Vereinigung zur Erforschung der neueren Geschichte*, are also outstanding. Special mention must be made of *F. Wolff, *Corpus Evangelicorum und Corpus Catholicorum auf* *dem Westfälischen Friedenskongress. Die Einfügung der konfessionellen Ständeverbindungen in die Reichsverfassung* (Münster, 1966: vol. II in the series); W. Becker, *Der Kurfürstenrat. Grundzüge seiner Entwicklung in der Reichsverfassung und seiner Stellung auf dem Westfälischen Friedenskongress* (Münster, 1973: vol V); R. Philippe, *Württemberg und der Westfälische Friede* (Münster, 1976: vol. VIII); and *K. Ruppert, *Die kaiserliche Politik auf dem Westfälischen Friedenskongress (1643–8)* (Münster, 1979: vol. X). Repgen is also the general editor of the series *Acta Pacis Westphalicae*, in process of publication. There are three series: 'Instructions' (1 volume published, 2 more to come); 'Correspondence' (6 volumes published, 18 more envisaged); and 'Protocols, negotiations, diaries and varia' (4 volumes published and 14 or more further volumes either in preparation or announced).

It might seem to some that this is enough on the subject; but the conference that lasted five years, and involved the representatives of 194 different states, has left more documentary debris than almost any other comparable phenomenon. Historians have accordingly been attracted to the subject like flies. On Poland and the peace, see J. Leszczynski, *Wladislaw IV a Slask w latach 1644–8* (Wroclaw, 1969); on Brandenburg see E. Opgenoorth, *Friedrich Wilhelm: der grosse Kurfürst von Brandenburg. Eine politische Biographie*, I (Göttingen, 1971), chaps 3–4; and on the religious settlement brought about at Westphalia, see M. Heckel, 'Itio in partes. Zur Religionsverfassung des Heiligen Römischen Reiches deutscher Nation', *Zeitschrift der Savigny-Stiftung für Rechtsgeschichte. Kanonistische Abteilung*, LXIV (1978), 180–308. There is a useful English abridgment of the terms of the peace in G. Symcox, ed., *War, Diplomacy and Imperialism, 1618–1763* (London, 1974), 39–62.

Remarkably little has been written about the final campaigns of the war. A few actions have been described; a few commanders have become the subject of a biography; but there is no better general assessment of the fighting itself than Ruppert's study noted above. Only Sweden's war effort has been properly surveyed, albeit solely from a financial viewpoint. See K.R. Böhme, 'Geld für die schwedische Armee nach 1640', *Scandia*, XXXIII (1967), 54–95; and G. Lorenz, 'Schweden und die französischen Hilfsgelder von 1638 bis 1649', in K. Repgen, ed., *Forschungen und Quellen zur Geschichte des Dreissigjährigen Krieges* (Münster, 1981: Schriftenreihe der Vereinigung zur Erforschung der neueren Geschichte, XII), 98–148. On the demobilization of the Imperial army, see the admirable (largely unpublished) dissertation of P. Hoyos, *Ernst von Traun, Generalkriegskommissär, und die Abdankung der kaiserlichen Armee nach dem 30-jährigen Krieg* (Vienna, 1970). Part III, on the demobilization itself, has been published in *Der dreissigjährige Krieg* (page 301 below), 169–232.

G   Armies and destruction

The interested student of military history will find rewarding material in the art of the period, particularly in the work of painters such as Vranckx and Snaeyers, and of engravers like Callot, Richter and Franck.

A fine selection is reproduced in Langer, *The Thirty Years' War*. There are also 'wargames' for most of the great battles, produced by the Avalon-Hill Company of Maryland and SPI of New York. A feature film entitled *The Last Valley*, with screenplay by John Prebble, vividly depicts the everyday life of the armies that fought the war; and a curious book of illustrations – E. Wagner, *European Weapons and Warfare 1618–1648* (London, 1979) – reconstructs military scenes in a lively style.

All these visual sources help our understanding of the period because they convey an immediacy that mere words lack. Nevertheless, there are some excellent printed works about everyday life during the war, commencing with the literature of the period itself. In Germany, leading writers such as Opitz, Moscherosch and Grimmelshausen covered wartime existence in poems and prose. But to what extent can we take these works of literature at their face value? Hans (or Johann) Jakob Christoph von Grimmelshausen, for example, was born about 1621, and had received, before his capture, a few years of Lutheran education at the local school. He spent the next five years with the Imperial, the Hessian, and once again the Imperial army. In 1640 he became a regimental clerk and after the war continued to serve his colonel as a secretary until 1660, when he set up as a publican. From then until his death in 1676 he supplemented his income from the sale of drink by writing books about his war experiences. The first, published in 1668, was entitled *The Adventures of Simplicissimus the German*, and it had gone through five editions by 1672. By 1700, there were a further thirty works in print either based on it or on one of its characters, of which two were written by Grimmelshausen himself: *The Vagabond Courage* and *Springinsfeld* (both published in 1670). Between them, Grimmelshausen's books have influenced decisively all historical study of the soldiers who fought the war, and their world.

This is unfortunate, because it has been shown that Grimmelshausen much preferred literary effect to realism. Thus the vivid account in *Simplicissimus* of the battle of Wittstock in 1636, which the author claims to have seen for himself, is plagiarized – in parts word-for-word – from the 1629 German edition of Sir Philip Sidney's *Arcadia*. In the early pages of *The Vagabond Courage*, which describe the events of 1620–1, Grimmelshausen repeats verbatim the erroneous account of events contained in another popular contemporary work, Wassenberg's *Teutscher Florus*. No reliance can thus be placed on these descriptions. Perhaps one should not be surprised by this: after all, Grimmelshausen was a novelist and not a historian. But the consequences for historical accuracy are significant. The creative writer is, often, necessarily more concerned with the dynamic than with the static elements of a war: his interest lies in the battles, marches and massacres; he can afford to remain indifferent to the financial, logistical and command structures that underlay them. But Grimmelshausen is not indifferent, he is hostile: commanders and sutlers are portrayed as the real enemy. Even the promiscuous Courage consorts with no one above the rank of captain, and her principal adversaries are the Major and the Colonel. So Grimmelshausen's characters smell unmistakably of the campfire, not of headquarters, as they are shown brawling, gambling or darning socks while they wait for action; and although the events in the war described in *Simplicissimus* may be imaginary, the actors are not. There is nothing to match Grimmelshausen's picture of life in the ranks until the journals written by the British privates of the Peninsular War. See C. Hohoff, ed., *Johann Jacob Christoph von Grimmelshausen in Selbstzeugnissen und Bilddokumenten* (Reinbeck-bei-Hamburg, 1978); and H. Geulen, ' "Arkadische" Simpliciana. Zu einer Quelle Grimmelshausens und ihrer strukturellen Bedeutung für seinen Roman', *Euphorion: Zeitschrift für Literaturgeschichte*, LXIII (1969), 426–37.

In Britain, too, several contemporaries – most of them participants – wrote about their experiences. Four accounts are of special value: Sydnam Poyntz, 'Relation [1624–36]', ed. A.T.S. Goodrick in *Camden Society Publications*, 3rd series XIV (1908); Sir James Turner, *Pallas Armata. Military essayes of the ancient Graecian, Roman and modern art of war* (London, 1683), 157–372; *idem, Memoirs of his own life and times* (Edinburgh, 1829); and R. Monro, *Monro his expedition with the worthy Scots regiment call'd Mackays* (London, 1637). Very little is known about these three authors (though Monro reappeared, thinly disguised, in Daniel Defoe's *Memoirs of a Cavalier* and as Sir Walter Scott's 'Dugald Dalgetty'). Poyntz's career is narrated in Goodrick's edition of his work; the later military efforts of Turner and Monro are assessed and described in D. Stevenson, *Scottish Covenanters and Irish Confederates. Scottish-Irish relations in the mid-seventeenth century* (Belfast, 1981), 80–3 and 312–13. Among more recent works on the soldiers who fought in the war, Langer, *The Thirty Years' War*, 61–102, is an excellent starting-point, to be followed by the important and more detailed study of *F. Redlich, *The German Military Enterpriser and His Workforce, 13th to 17th Centuries* (2 vols, Wiesbaden, 1964–5: Vierteljahrschrift für Sozial- und Wirtschaftsgeschichte, Beihefte XLVII–XLVIII).

On the general conduct of war during this period, the forthcoming volumes in the Fontana series *War and Society*, by J.R. Hale (1450–1618) and M. Anderson (1618–1770), seem likely to prove the standard works. But until they are published, readers must rely either on H.W. Koch, *The Rise of Modern Warfare 1618–1815* (London, 1981) and other general works; or on three articles which set the military changes of the period in a broader perspective: M. Roberts, 'The Military Revolution 1560–1660' in Roberts, ed., *Essays in Swedish History* (London, 1967), 195–225; G. Parker, 'The Military Revolution 1560–1660 – a myth?' in Parker, *Spain and the Netherlands 1559–1659: ten studies* (London, 1979), 86–103; and H. Eichberg, 'Geometrie als barocke Verhaltensnorm. Fortifikation und Exerzitien', *Zeitschrift für historische Forschung*, IV (1977), 17–50. None of these entirely replace the older general study of E. von Frauenholz, *Das Heerwesen in der Zeit des Dreissigjährigen Krieges* (2 vols, Munich, 1938–9 – volume III, parts 1–2 of the author's *Entwicklungsgeschichte des deutschen Heerwesens*).

Finally, there are numerous histories of the troops fighting for a particular warlord. For the Imperialists see: J.C. Allmayer-Beck and E.

Lessing, *Die Kaiserliche Kriegsvölker von Maximilian I bis Prinz Eugen 1479–1718* (Munich, 1978 – handsomely illustrated); O. Elster, *Die Piccolomini-Regimenter während des dreissigjährigen Krieges, besonders das Kürassier-Regiment Alt-Piccolomini* (Vienna, 1903); *Der Dreissigjährige Krieg. Beiträge zu seiner Geschichte* (Vienna, 1976: Schriften des Heeresgeschichtlichen Museums in Wien, VII); T.M. Barker, *The Military Intellectual and Battle: Raimondo Montecuccoli and the Thirty Years' War* (Albany, N.Y., 1975); and the four opening essays of *idem, Army, Aristocracy, Monarchy: essays on war, society and government in Austria 1618–1780* (New York, 1982). There is no adequate modern study of the Bavarian army during the war, but see R. Baumann, *Das Söldnerwesen im 16. Jahrhundert im bayerischen und süddeutschen Beispiel. Eine gesellschaftsgeschichtliche Untersuchung* (Munich, 1978). For the anti-Imperialists, see: J.W. Wijn, *Het Krijgswezen in den tijd van Prins Maurits* (Utrecht, 1934); J.A. Fallon, 'Scottish mercenaries in the service of Denmark and Sweden, 1626–32' (University of Glasgow PhD thesis, 1972); P. Dukes, 'The Leslie family in the Swedish period (1630–5) of the Thirty Years' War', *European Studies Review*, XII (1982), 401–24; L. André, *Michel le Tellier et l'organisation de l'armée monarchique* (Paris, 1906); B. Kroener, *Les Routes et les Étapes. Die Versorgung der französischen Armeen in Nordostfrankreich (1635–61). Ein Beitrag zur Verwaltungsgeschichte des Ancien Régime* (2 vols, Münster, 1980: Schriftenreihe der Vereinigung zur Erforschung der neueren Geschichte, XI); *idem*, 'Die Entwicklung der Truppenstärken in den französischen Armeen zwischen 1635 und 1661', in K. Repgen, ed., *Forschungen und Quellen zur Geschichte des Dreissigjährigen Krieges* (Münster, 1981: Schriftenreihe der Vereinigung zur Erforschung der neueren Geschichte, XII), 149–220; and [Swedish Army General Staff, ed.,] *Sveriges Krig, 1611–1632* (page 293 above).

On the destruction caused by the troops, there is an excellent summary of the voluminous but often contradictory material published before circa 1960 in T.K. Rabb, 'The effects of the Thirty Years' War on the German economy', *Journal of Modern History*, XXXIV (1962), 40–51. An important survey of conditions on the eve of the war was provided by F. Lütge, 'Die wirtschaftliche Lage Deutschlands vor Ausbruch des dreissigjährigen Krieges', *Jahrbücher für Nationalökonomie und Statistik*, CLXX (1958), 43–99. Among more recent studies, the interested reader may turn with profit to the following: G. Benecke, 'The problem of death and destruction during the Thirty Years' War: new evidence from the Middle Weser Front', *European Studies Review*, II (1972), 239–253; *G. Franz, *Der Dreissigjährige Krieg und das deutsche Volk* (4th edn, Stuttgart, 1979); C.R. Friedrichs, *Urban Society in an Age of War: Nördlingen, 1580–1720* (Princeton, N.J., 1979); H. Haan, 'Prosperität und Dreissigjähriger Krieg', *Geschichte und Gesellschaft*, VII (1981), 91–118; and H. Kamen, 'The economic and social consequences of the Thirty Years' War', *Past and Present*, XXXIX (1968), 44–61.

There is an inexhaustible fund of local studies on the destruction caused by the war, of which some are very good and some are appalling.

Extensive references will be found in the volume by Franz cited above. An unusually rich fund of data for one German region is provided by H. Schmidt, 'Der dreissigjährige Krieg: wie er sich auf das Rothenburger Land und seine Leute auswirkte', *Fränkischer Feierabend*, vols I–IX, published as monthly supplements to the *Fränkischer Anzeiger* (Rothenburg ob der Tauber, 1953–61). For other sources on the destruction up to 1635, see notes 2–12 to Section V.ii above.

Addenda

While this book was being printed, a number of new works on the war were published. Firstly, Peter Limm, *The Thirty Years' War* (London, 1984), a volume in the series 'Seminar Studies in History', offers a useful brief interpretation, and a selection of key documents (all translated into English). Secondly, pp. 253–351 of that excellent journal, *Zeitschrift für historische Forschung*, X (1983), are devoted to German political developments between 1555 and 1618, with the title: 'Möglichkeiten der Reichspolitik zwischen Augsburger Religionsfrieden und Ausbruch des dreissigjährigen Kriegs'. The articles by K. Vocelka (on Matthias and Rudolf, 1606–12) and K. Schlaich (on the majority principle in the Diet between 1495 and 1613) are particularly useful.

For the 1620s, a new article examines the intervention of England at a crucial juncture: T. Cogswell, 'Foreign Policy and Parliament: the Case of La Rochelle, 1625–6', *English Historical Review*, XCIX (1984), 241–67. The frosty meeting between the kings of Denmark and Sweden at Ulfsbäck in 1629 (page 79 above) is the subject of K.J.V. Jespersen, 'Kongemødet i Ulfsbäck praestegard februar 1629', *Historie*, N.S. XIV (1982), 420–39. And the intervention of Christian IV is set in a broader context by E. Ladewig Petersen, 'War, Finance and the Growth of Absolutism: some Aspects of the European Integration of seventeenth-century Denmark', in G. Rystad, ed., *Europe and Scandinavia. Aspects of the Process of Integration in the seventeenth century* (Lund, 1983), 33–49. Finally, J.I. Israel, 'Central European Jewry during the Thirty Years' War', *Central European History*, XVI (1983), 3–30, shows that Jewish communities could and did prosper under the French, the Swedes and the Imperialists. And M.E. Mallett and J.R. Hale, *The Military Organization of a Renaissance State. Venice c. 1400 to 1617* (Cambridge, 1984) give the best available account in English of the Uzkok war: see pp. 242–7, 327–9 and 482–4.

Works noted since 1984

The past two years have yielded an interesting crop of new works. Pride of place must go to two new general studies of the war, both in German but on very different scales. G. Schormann, *Der dreissigjährige Krieg* (Göttingen, 1985), offers a terse, helpful summary of events in just 150 pages; G. Barudio, (*Der teutsche Krieg 1618–1648* (Frankfurt, 1985), by contrast, takes some 700 pages to cover the ground. Both provide, first and foremost, a narrative of the war; and both tend to concentrate on the German side of events (although Barudio has worked extensively on the Scandinavian sources).

Recent studies of Germany itself before, during and after the war, include the excellent monograph of James A. Vann, *The Making of a State: Württemberg 1593–1793* (Ithaca and London, 1984); R.P. Hsia, *Society and Religion in Münster 1535–1618* (New Haven and London, 1984); J. Whaley, *Religious Toleration and Social Change in Hamburg 1529–1819* (Cambridge, 1985); D.W. Sabean, *Power in the Blood: Popular culture and village discourse in early modern Germany* (Cambridge, 1984), chapter 2; and R.J.W. Evans, 'Culture and anarchy in the Empire, 1540–1680', *Central European History*, XVIII (1985), 14–30. On France, see J. Bergin, *Cardinal Richelieu: Power and the pursuit of wealth* (New Haven and London, 1985); on England, T. Cogswell, 'Prelude to Ré: the Anglo-French struggle over La Rochelle, 1624–7', *History*, LXXI (1986), 1–21; and on Spain, R.A. Stradling, 'Olivares and the origins of the Franco-Spanish war, 1627–1635', *English Historical Review*, CI (1986). 68–94. The last item makes it clear that Spain was prepared to declare war on France at any time from September 1634 onwards, and regarded a breach as inevitable after January 1635. In the end, of course, it was France which declared war; but recent research shows that the Paris government, too, under pressure from its Dutch allies, regarded full hostilities with Spain as inevitable from June 1634 onwards. In both cases, the monarch led the 'hawks' who favoured an early breach, while both chief ministers pleaded for moderation; but the parallel assumptions at both courts that war was just around the corner clearly made a declaration more likely, because the threshold of expectations was perceptibly lowered. Further discussion of this and many other points will be found in the biography of the count-duke of Olivares by J.H. Elliott, published by Yale University Press in 1986; and in the proceedings of a conference on the Thirty Years' War held in Munich in August 1984, edited by Konrad Repgen and to be published by Oldenbourg Verlag of Munich with the title: *Krieg und Politik 1618–1648: europäische Studien und Perspektiven*.

The military side of the war has also attracted further attention. Richelieu's army and war aims in the first three years after the breach with Spain have been exhaustively studied by D.W. Parrott, 'The Administration of the French Army during the Ministry of Cardinal Richelieu' (Oxford University PhD thesis, 1985); while the general behaviour of troops at this time has been perceptively analysed by B. Kroener, 'Soldat oder Soldateska? Programmatischer Aufriss einer Sozialgeschichte militärischen Unterschichten in der ersten Hälft des 17. Jahrhunderts', in M. Messerschmidt *et al.*, eds, *Militärgeschichte. Probleme, Thesen, Wege* (Frankfurt, 1982), 100–23. On the final stages of the war, however, there is still nothing to replace two items edited by the General Staff of the Swedish army, and inadvertently omitted from the bibliography above: Förvarsstabens krigshistoriska avdelning, *Slaget vid Jankow 1645–1945* (Stockholm, 1948) and idem, *Från Femern och Jankow till Westfaliska Freden. En minnesskrift år 1948* (Stockholm, 1948).

Index of authors

General index

absolutism in early modern Europe, 84–7, 219–20

Acton, Lord, 19th-cent. historian: views of, xv

Adami von Murrhart, Adam, b. 1610, Rhineland; educated by Jesuits; entered Benedictine order 1628; prior of Murrhart (Württemberg) from 1639; represented secularized Swabian abbeys at Westphalian peace congress; d. 1663: views of, 179; at Westphalian peace conference, 181

Adler Salvius, see Salvius

Aelian, Greek military writer of 2nd cent. AD: writings of, 205

'Alais, Grace of' (28 June 1629), issued by Louis XIII of France to end Huguenot revolts, 114

Albert of Austria, b. 1559, son of Emperor Maximilian II; Archduke; Cardinal 1577; first viceroy of Portugal for Philip II 1583–93; principal adviser to Philip II 1593–6; governed Netherlands for Philip II 1596–8; sovereign ruler, with Isabella, of South Netherlands 1598–1621: claim to succeed as emperor, 33–4; death of (15 July 1621), 64; Netherlands government of, 2, 4; see also Archdukes

Aldringen, Johan von, b. 1588, Thionville (Luxemburg); entered Imperial (1618) and Bavarian (from 1623) armies; fought in Mantua (1630–1); commander of Bavarian army after Tilly's death 1632–4: leads Bavarian army, 140; killed (1634), 140

Algiers (North African state): foreign policy of, 4; Spanish attack on, projected (1618), 50

Allerheim (or Alerheim, Swabian village): Bavarians and Imperialists routed by French and Hessians in battle at (3 Aug. 1645), 176, 177

Almirantazgo (Admiralty created in Spain to control commerce, 1625), 95–6

Alsace (German territory, part of Further Austria): defences of, 13; and France, 146, 151–2, 170, 184, 217–18; government of, 86, 184; literature on, 297; and Spain, 40–4, 132; warfare in, 65, 152, 153, 163, 168, 175

Altdorf, university of (near Nuremberg): and Bohemian Revolt, 45

Alte Veste (fortress near Nuremberg): Wallenstein fortifies and withstands Swedish siege of (1632), 130, 204

Altmark (town in Prussia): Swedish–Polish truce signed at (1629), 102, 122, 141, 158

Amalia of Solms, b. 1602, Hanau; married William V of Hesse-Kassel 1619; regent after his death 1637–50; d. 1651: army of, see army of Hesse-Kassel; family connexions of, 53; during Thirty Years' War, 167, 168, 185, 222–3; at Westphalian peace congress, 173, 181

Amberg (capital of Upper Palatinate): Catholics in, 90, 269 n. 10; culture in, 45

America, European colonies in, 43, 171, 187

Amersfoort (Dutch town): captured by Spaniards (1629), 102

Amsterdam (Dutch city): economic power of, 123

Andreä, Johann Valentin, b. 1586; Utopian writer and Lutheran pastor; from 1620 superintendent in Calw; court preacher to duke of Württemberg